Law, Language and the Courtroom

This book explores the language of judges. It is concerned with understanding how language works in judicial contexts. Using a range of disciplinary and methodological perspectives, it looks in detail at the ways in which judicial discourse is argued, constructed, interpreted and perceived. Focusing on four central themes – constructing judicial discourse and judicial identities, judicial argumentation and evaluative language, judicial interpretation, and clarity in judicial discourse – the book's ultimate goal is to provide a comprehensive and in-depth analysis of current critical issues of the role of language in judicial settings. Contributors include legal linguists, lawyers, legal scholars, legal practitioners, legal translators and anthropologists, who explore patterns of linguistic organisation and use in judicial institutions and analyse language as an instrument for understanding both the judicial decision-making process and its outcome.

The book will be an invaluable resource for scholars in legal linguistics and those specialising in judicial argumentation and reasoning, and forensic linguists interested in the use of language in judicial settings.

Stanisław Goźdź-Roszkowski is Associate Professor and Head of the Department of Specialised Languages and Intercultural Communication, University of Lodz (Poland), where he has been teaching various seminars in specialised communication and legal discourse analysis. His research focuses on functional and corpus-based approaches to the study of judicial discourse in US and Polish courts. He has published widely in the area of variation in legal language, legal phraseology and communicating evaluative meanings in judicial opinions. He is now involved in researching legal argumentation in the justification of judicial decisions.

Gianluca Pontrandolfo holds a PhD in translation and interpreting studies. He is currently Senior Research Fellow at the University of Trieste (Italy) in the Department of Legal, Language, Interpreting and Translation Studies (IUSLIT), where he lectures on specialised translation from Spanish into Italian. His research interests include corpus linguistics, legal phraseology, legal translation training, Languages for Special Purposes, genre analysis and corpus-assisted critical discourse studies. He has published widely in the area of legal and judicial discourse from a contrastive corpus-based perspective.

Law, Language and Communication

Series Editors
Anne Wagner, *Université du Littoral Côte d'Opale*, France and
Vijay Kumar Bhatia, formerly of *City University of Hong Kong*

This series encourages innovative and integrated perspectives within and across the boundaries of law, language and communication, with particular emphasis on issues of communication in specialized socio-legal and professional contexts. It seeks to bring together a range of diverse yet cumulative research traditions in order to identify and encourage interdisciplinary research.

The series welcomes proposals – both edited collections as well as single-authored monographs – emphasizing critical approaches to law, language and communication, identifying and discussing issues, proposing solutions to problems, offering analyses in areas such as legal construction, interpretation, translation and de-codification.

Phraseology in Legal and Institutional Settings
A Corpus-based Interdisciplinary Perspective
Edited by Stanisław Goźdź-Roszkowski and Gianluca Pontrandolfo

Fiction and the Languages of Law
Understanding Contemporary Legal Discourse
Karen Petroski

Law and Imagination in Troubled Times
A Legal and Literary Discourse
Edited by Richard Mullender, Matteo Nicolini, Thomas D.C. Bennett and Emilia Mickiewicz

Social Media in Legal Practice
Edited by Vijay Bhatia and Girolamo Tessuto

Law, Language and the Courtroom
Legal Linguistics and the Discourse of Judges
Edited by Stanisław Goźdź-Roszkowski and Gianluca Pontrandolfo

For more information about this series, please visit: www.routledge.com/Law-Language-and-Communication/book-series/LAWLANGCOMM

Law, Language and the Courtroom

Legal Linguistics and the Discourse of Judges

Edited by Stanisław Goźdź-Roszkowski and Gianluca Pontrandolfo

Routledge
Taylor & Francis Group
LONDON AND NEW YORK

First published 2022
by Routledge
2 Park Square, Milton Park, Abingdon, Oxon OX14 4RN

and by Routledge
605 Third Avenue, New York, NY 10158

Routledge is an imprint of the Taylor & Francis Group, an informa business

British Library Cataloguing-in-Publication Data
A catalogue record for this book is available from the British Library

Library of Congress Cataloging-in-Publication Data
A catalog record for this book has been requested

ISBN: 978-0-367-72185-5 (hbk)
ISBN: 978-0-367-72188-6 (pbk)
ISBN: 978-1-003-15377-1 (ebk)

DOI: 10.4324/9781003153771

Typeset in Galliard
by Apex CoVantage, LLC

Contents

List of contributors viii
Foreword x
Editors' introduction xvi

PART I
Constructing judicial discourse and judicial identities 1

1 **The judicial English Eurolect: a genre profiling of CJEU judgments** 3
ŁUCJA BIEL, DARIUSZ KOŹBIAŁ AND DARIUSZ MÜLLER

2 **Evidentiality in US Supreme Court opinions: focus on passive structures with *say* and *tell*** 26
MAGDALENA SZCZYRBAK

3 **Standardisation in the judicial discourse: the case of the evolution of the French *Arrêts de la Cour de Cassation* and the use of forms in European procedural law** 39
MARGARETE FLÖTER-DURR AND PAULINA NOWAK-KORCZ

4 **The consensus case law of the European Court of Human Rights in light of the Court's legitimacy over time: a corpus-linguistic perspective** 51
ANNE LISE KJÆR

5 **Spider Woman beats Hulk: Baroness Hale and the prorogation of Parliament** 69
RUTH BREEZE

PART II
Judicial argumentation and evaluative language 83

6 Making a corpus-linguistic U-turn in multilingual adjudication 85
MARTINA BAJČIĆ

7 Evaluative language and strategic manoeuvring in the justification of judicial decisions: the case of teleological-evaluative argumentation 98
STANISŁAW GOŹDŹ-ROSZKOWSKI

8 "Without proof of negligence or a causative connection": on causal argumentation in the discourse of the Supreme Court of Ireland's judgments on data protection 112
DAVIDE MAZZI

9 A corpus-based comparative analysis of the evaluative lexicon found in judicial decisions on immigration 126
MARÍA JOSÉ MARÍN PÉREZ

PART III
Judicial interpretation 145

10 Pedagogies of context: language ideology and expression rights at the European Court of Human Rights 147
JESSICA GREENBERG

11 Free speech, artistic expression and blasphemy laws within the ECHR margin of appreciation 160
JOANNA KULESZA

12 The US Supreme Court's language of racism 173
KATHRYN M. STANCHI

13 Do the words of the American Constitution still matter? The question of "the meaning of meaning" in current judicial argumentation 185
ANNA TOMZA-TULEJSKA AND J. PATRICK HIGGINS

14 How interdisciplinarity could improve the scientific value of legal studies of international judicial decisions 198
MAREK JAN WASIŃSKI

PART IV
Clarity in judicial discourse 215

15 Conveying the right message: principles and problems of multilingual communication at the European Court of Human Rights 217
JAMES BRANNAN

16 Concision and clarity in Italian court proceedings 231
ANTONIO MURA AND JACQUELINE VISCONTI

Index 243

Contributors

Martina Bajčić, University of Rijeka, martina.bajcic@pravri.hr

https://orcid.org/0000-0003-0654-6779

Łucja Biel, University of Warsaw, l.biel@uw.edu.pl

https://orcid.org/0000-0002-3671-3112

James Brannan, Senior Translator, European Court of Human Rights, james.brannan@echr.coe.int

Ruth Breeze, University of Navarra, rbreeze@unav.es

https://orcid.org/0000-0002-8132-225X

Margarete Flöter-Durr, University of Strasbourg, info@mg-traductions.eu

https://orcid.org/0000-0003-4667-9277

Stanisław Goźdź-Roszkowski, University of Lodz, stanislaw.gozdz@uni.lodz.pl

https://orcid.org/0000-0002-4323-8647

Jessica Greenberg, University of Illinois, jrgreenb@illinois.edu

J. Patrick Higgins, University of Lodz, pat.higgins2014@gmail.com

https://orcid.org/0000-0003-4405-2614

Anne Lise Kjær, University of Copenhagen, anne.lise.kjer@jur.ku.dk

Dariusz Koźbiał, University of Warsaw, d.kozbial@uw.edu.pl

https://orcid.org/0000-0003-4395-3138

Joanna Kulesza, University of Lodz, joanna_kulesza@wpia.uni.lodz.pl

https://orcid.org/0000-0003-0390-6062

María José Marín Pérez, University of Murcia, mariajose.marin1@um.es

https://orcid.org/0000-0003-0177-4860

Davide Mazzi, University of Modena and Reggio Emilia, davide.mazzi@unimore.it

Dariusz Müller, University of Warsaw, d.muller@uw.edu.pl

https://orcid.org/0000-0002-7138-6284

Antonio Mura, Prosecutor General at the Rome Court of Appeal, antonio.mura@giustizia.it

Paulina Nowak-Korcz, University of Lodz, paulina.nowak-korcz@uni.lodz.pl

https://orcid.org/0000-0002-7857-7171

Gianluca Pontrandolfo, University of Trieste, gpontrandolfo@units.it

https://orcid.org/0000-0002-9128-0321

Kathryn M. Stanchi, William S. Boyd School of Law, University of Nevada, kathryn.stanchi@unlv.edu

Dieter Stein, Heinrich-Heine-University Düsseldorf, stein@hhu.de

Magdalena Szczyrbak, Jagiellonian University, Kraków, magdalena.szczyrbak@uj.edu.pl

https://orcid.org/0000-0002-0182-0938

Anna Tomza-Tulejska, University of Lodz, atomza@wpia.uni.lodz.pl

https://orcid.org/0000-0002-3300-5997

Jacqueline Visconti, University of Genoa/Honorary Research Fellow at Birmingham University, j.visconti@unige.it

Marek Jan Wasiński, University of Lodz, mwasinski@wpia.uni.lodz.pl

https://orcid.org/0000-0003-0109-9164

Foreword

This book is another significant contribution to the field of legal linguistics as covered by the activities of the International Language and Law Association (ILLA) with the aim of presenting scientific, language-based approaches to the domain of law. It adds to the already existing body of published work produced in the context of ILLA general and specialised/focus conferences.

From a philosophical perspective, there are roughly two ways of understanding how law exists: the first view sees law in a legal-positive way through linguistic "fiat" acts, involving speech acts of a much-discussed kind. The other view is "performative" in character as it sees law in existence, and in continuous development, through acts of adjudication. Both perspectives on how law can come into existence involve the use of language in constitutive ways.

Development and interpretation of law are at a first go easier to conceptualise in a performative view of law: just as language changes permanently through use in ever new situations – unless you adhere to some form of unrealistic "structural" static Procrustean idea of language – so each act of adjudication is different, and consequently law changes permanently.

This dynamic aspect of law is therefore less of a problem for a performative view than for a legal-positivist view of law. Naturally, legal interpretation and the bounds of vagueness of statutes – intended or unintended – offer natural spaces for gravitational shifting in shaping legal norms. Evolution of law also takes place in peri-legal processes like arbitration.

But a very specific playground for shifting currents to carve out new more entrenched directions and pathways is the court, and in particular the specific situation of transnational European justice systems, such as the European courts. The topics of the present volume represent a variety of issues and processes related to how law is made by performing it in the courts.

The topics treated in this volume present a rich fabric of recurrent motives and themes, some of which I will take up in this foreword, not necessarily in the order in which they appear in the volume, but by relevance to theoretical and methodological issues that have come to the fore in recent developments in the field of legal linguistics. This procedure seems also justified by the fact that most chapters are woven into this fabric through several links, and I will take the liberty to single out and give prominence to individual such links.

The present volume is more concerned with how law "is made" through the process of applying the law, even though it may appear to be locked in by statutes. The European courts present a very specific challenge, as they have to navigate the space between general principles – like freedom of speech – guarded by the transnational court on the one hand and the national legislations. Typically, the European situations in courts involve a structural dialectic between national law on the one side and transnational, European law on the other. The situation is often characterised by divergences in legal attitudes between national, cultural-based norms and the postulates of general principles like freedom of speech. The standard way to handle the necessary positioning and compromise between both different national states and individual national states versus the European Court of Human Rights (ECtHR), and therefore key concepts in law making in the European situation, are the notions of the "consensus" and the "margin of interpretation", which figure prominently in a couple of chapters.

Contrary to a common expectation that a key concept like consensus would be standardised in its conceptual meaning and word form, it is the case that there is a range of competing lexemes that are candidates for referential identity with consensus, such as "trend", "tendencies" or "virtual consensus". While the European legal world encourages us to treat these competing terms as synonyms, Kjær (Chapter 4) turns up substantial evidence from massive linguistic electronic corpus analyses that tells against such an assumption of reference identity – or at best, meaning identity. It will be interesting to see if the legal world will listen to the linguistic analysis and eventually offer a solution to what must appear a challenge to the doctrinal side. While the linguistic fact of variation is based on divergences in legal doctrine, there is also variation in the interpretation of transnational or universal legal concepts tied to linguistic issues.

Just as in the case of consensus, variation and standardisation (Flöter-Durr and Nowak-Korcz, Chapter 3) are an issue in both legal and linguistic perspectives. On a hierarchically higher level of expressions (as in prepositional phrases like *attendu que*), the so-called *formules* (staying with the French term) are in the nature of genre markers for judicial genres and have a discourse-structuring function. Their standardisation has been a major concern in efforts towards clarity and standardisation in the French system – and on a higher level, on the European level of judicial language – and might well become part of a drift towards a Eurolect, such as discussed by Biel, Koźbiał and Müller (Chapter 1). The *formules* also include so-called legal standards, which are even a larger legal issue as they are a major built-in source of vagueness and are therefore by their very relative nature recalcitrant to standardisation.

Moving to the content of reasoning itself, this core process of courts is happening in language and is in very specific ways tied to beliefs and ideologies about language in situations where the same use of language is at issue in cases where charges are brought against uses of language for offensive or hurtful language, as in the case discussed by Greenberg (Chapter 10). The author demonstrates how the charge itself (the famous *Handyside* case, involving a charge of offensive speech corrupting youths through its explicit depiction of drugs, sex and other sensitive issues) hinges on a conception of what the "text" is, whether a text pure as a string of morphemes with language meanings or the product of comprehensional construction contextualised by national local cultural presuppositions. Greenberg shows how the ECtHR carves out a "margin of appreciation" by manoeuvring between the absoluteness of the legal principle and the national (in this case English) moral presuppositions, again in a metadiscursive way involving specific ideas of what "language" and "text" are. The ECtHR aims to strike a sensible compromise between national conditions and a more abstract principle of free speech that is definitional for a liberal democracy, but within limits – which are again nationally defined. Where the consensus (cf. above) is to be found depends on the way language ideologies about the nature of the text are located.

Another instantiation of this important theme of the specific linguistic situation in Europe – exemplifying paradigmatically how culture, language and law are inextricably tied up with each other in the issue of the "translation" of international rights, such as the freedom of speech, into national adjudication – is presented by Kulesza (Chapter 11), on the example of Polish blasphemy laws. She shows how national legal practices use a "margin of appreciation" approach to navigate a compromise between the more universal right and national cultural exigencies. A linguistically intriguing differentiation between "insulting" and "offending" exemplifies how intimately interwoven linguistic and legal issues are.

Moving from judicial activities in making law to citizens receiving the law as handed down by the court, Breeze's contribution (Chapter 5) shows how the people for whom the law is made at the receiving end can be beguiled into a kind of meaning making of judgments on their part that borders on demagoguery by the media and parties with vested interests behind them. Breeze's chapter is an illuminating exercise in how a post-Brexit public can be induced to contextualise and interpret a ruling by a female British High Court judge (Baroness Hale's ruling declaring Johnson's dissolution of Parliament unlawful) in populist, even Trumpian and misogynistic terms, and in the process instrumentalising the female judge's brooch. While in this particular case populist ideologies are instrumentalised in framing reactions to a judgment, Stanchi (Chapter 12) identifies another deep layer of cultural presuppositions, this time racism, on the other side: in the rulings of the Supreme Court. Racism is identified not only in what is said, as is commonly done, but the chapter is remarkable in identifying a kind of "weak rhetoric" which is manifested by *not* calling decisions racist or by not explicitly calling decisions racist where this would be expected.

Law is not a solipsistic institution that exists for itself, but it is a normative system that regulates the lives of the individuals to the extent that these individuals are social beings and citizens. One group of chapters addresses an issue that is central to this raison d'être of the law, to the extent that it is formulated and executed in language: it is, among other things, the medium through which law is accessed by the citizens as social and political beings. The complaint is that language, in this function as transmission belt – or, in fact, the "translator" – between the normative system and its execution in law in action and in relating to citizens, has long been recognised both in the linguistic and the legal community, be it in the popular complaints about the complexity of the language of statutes or rulings, or in discussions relating to jury instructions or more serious linguistic concerns, such as represented in the chapter by Mura and Visconti (Chapter 16). The authors point out that, beyond the "default" issue of linguistic obstacles to the accessibility to the law, there are added and exacerbating factors contributing to the urgency to introduce reform: there are both local historical and stylistic traditions of legal language in Italy and the internationalisation of law in Europe (and, one may add, in the world). Concrete steps to accommodate language and the law to the comprehensibility needs of the citizens are becoming ever more imperative. Mura and Visconti describe not only the formulation of the need but the factual concrete steps that have been and are being taken – a welcome change from proclamation to enforcement.

What essentially makes a citizen a citizen is political participation and access to the law. The latter is challenged in Europe in a specific way. In addition to the usual or default challenge by the way what is perceived (variously) as the obscurity and the complexity of legal language, there is the challenge of being conducted in several languages, giving rise to issues of translation and the concomitant legal issue of constancy of especially legal meanings. The contribution by Brannan (Chapter 15) gives a concrete overview of the types of text that are produced in the context of the ECtHR and that are implicated in this discussion of both the stylistic complexity of the texts produced and the issues arising from the coexistence of different language versions.

While most chapters have a European focus, there is a group of chapters that deal with American issues but that take up issues that also surface in principle in the European context. Tomza-Tulejska and Higgins (Chapter 13) address the issue of "legal interpretation", where the American Constitution is the classical text and object of interpretation, as (as the authors see it) the language of the Constitution is linguistically deficient as it contains too many expressions that were left vague due to the linguistic situation at the time of drafting. The authors discuss the main conflicting schools of interpretation and suggest a theory of "judicial behaviour" as a guiding principle.

There is, finally, a group of chapters that deal with important meta-issues that are at the bottom of interpretative activities. While deficiencies in language are seen by Tomza-Tulejska and Higgins as something that gave rise to interpretive schools as a kind of remedy, invoking the analysis of language and the linguistic base of the law and seeing inherent linguistic indeterminacy as an aspect of normative indeterminacy is seen by Wasiński (Chapter 14) as a move towards a more scientific character of normative work and adjudication as the hitherto unscientific aspect of the world of law, and narrowing the gap between the norm-executing, practical side of the world of the law and the scientific character of disciplines – among them linguistics – that are applied to "explaining" legal norms.

As a major methodological development, the chapters in this volume manifest a clear trend towards the increasing use of electronic tools: computers and corpora. While most chapters more or less make use of these tools, there is a group of chapters whose merit is achieved by these tools in a prominent way. This new development comes in two shapes: at the "top" is the use in adjudication, legal interpretation and legal translation, and at the "bottom" is the use of corpus data by the linguist to investigate interpretable quantitative language data to access a variety of inherent features of the legal discourse. As an example of the latter approach, Mazzi (Chapter 8) identifies as a result of automatic corpus analysis clustering of n-grams into bundles which are then linked in a qualitative interpretive step to types of causative argumentation in judgments. In a similar vein, Marín Pérez (Chapter 9) takes as a logical point of departure the results of a corpus search, carried out like the other chapters in this group with considerable statistical sophistication, of expressions, together with their first- and second-order collocates, of affective stance in English and Spanish court judgments. Several interesting results are turned up which point to interesting differences between the Spanish and English corpus, such as the importance of the *odio* (hate) in the Spanish corpus, or the lower degree of evaluative judgments in the Spanish corpus compared to the British corpus, arguably due to the nature of common law as judges' law. These chapters make an important contribution to identify ideologies in jurisdiction that might not become transparent or at least might not so well be documentable without this type of data.

It is methodologically characteristic of the latter group of chapters, those that start at the "bottom" end, to logically employ a bottom-up procedure in two ways. These chapters either predefine what kind of expression is evaluative or let the computer define via cluster analysis that could be interpreted as evaluative. This is based on an a priori concept of what "evaluation" is semantically.

The other group of chapters do employ electronic corpus analysis, but they pursue a top-down concept in that there is a logically preceding concept of the superstructural, functional structure of the genre at hand, and there is an interpretive procedure that identifies lexical structures that perform functions that define given superstructural slots. The approach is in principle primarily a close reading and qualitative one. In the case analysis presented by Goźdź-Roszkowski (Chapter 7), the focus is on which lexical structures carry evaluative meanings in the structural genre slot "argumentation", one of the four canonical structural slots of the genre. These evaluative structures are pivotal in that they mark the reasons picked – among other legal-interpretational options – and which move the judicial decision in a particular interpretive reason, in this case a teleologically informed judicial interpretive direction.

As these expressions are more of an open set and not a priori fixed, they receive their "meaning" only within the genre frame. Such an integrational, top-down procedure must appear intuitively much more satisfying than operating with the (unlikely) assumption that certain expressions will once and forever and in all genre and usage contexts have the same function.

Representative for the effect of the new technical medial affordances at the "top" end is also the chapter by Bajčić (Chapter 6), who argues for the creation of parallel corpora of EU legislation in order to help fulfil an important legal postulate that national adjudication has to apply in conformity with all other language versions of a law.

In one of the chapters that deal with the American situation, Szczyrbak (Chapter 2) deals with a very specific variety of the intersection between law and language, one that captures an element of linguistic development, not legal or doctrinal. The opinions formulated by judges (in this case the US Supreme Court) are based on arguments and evidence. These must be understood as "authenticated" by referring to the sources. It is not the arguments themselves but the way they are presented as authenticated that is the subject of this chapter. Focusing on passive structures, Szczyrbak demonstrates that there has been considerable and hitherto unaccounted for development in the grammatical way to express evidentiality in the case of passive structures involving "tell" and "says" since 1790.

Another chapter that deals with linguistic development in the legal domain is concerned with a varietal development within EU law. Biel, Koźbiał and Müller (Chapter 1) substantiate empirically, on the basis of a large electronic corpus study, the pre-existing impression that there seems to be developing a kind of "Eurolect", in the sense that the law domain evolves a domain-specific variety that is distinct from common law legal style and that is also internally differentiated by types of legal written genres. This development is just as interesting from the varieties-linguistic view, as it is based not on lexical markers but on syntactic and discourse-structural ones. Biel et al. discuss the possible internal sources of this development, such as the specific language regimen with its particular translation directions and therefore lines of linguistic influences in these areas of grammar. What is significant is the very fact that the bottom line is the development of a variety as an identity-building element.

This volume offers an impressive panorama of how language is deeply and critically involved in all facets of making law in the context of courts and their modes of operation on all levels of analysis. There is a wide range of methodologies in demonstrating how the analysis of language can provide access to the workings and determinants of the judicial process in an equally wide range of types of cases and legal issues. I am confident that this volume, with all its results and valences for further directions of research, will represent another standard-setting milestone in the further development of legal linguistics.

Dieter Stein
Heinrich-Heine-University Düsseldorf

Editors' introduction

The genesis of this book was an international conference, *Spotlights on Courts: Judges and Their Discourse from a Multidisciplinary Perspective*, planned to be held at the University of Łódź in September 2020 but then postponed (online) to March 2021 due to the COVID-19 pandemic. Organised under the auspices of the International Law and Language Association (ILLA), it brought together law, linguistics and anthropology scholars interested in the various relationships between law and language. The meeting drove home the simple truth that it is essential to foster intellectual cross-fertilisation if we want to broaden our understanding of complex and multifarious phenomena such as judicial discourse. The importance of judicial decision-making and its surrounding discourse is often taken for granted. However, recent outbreaks of the rule of law crisis in Europe and the contemporary challenges posed by populism and disinformation for people's perceptions of European democratic institutions, including courts and the justice system, have highlighted the need for a closer examination of how judges justify their decisions and how their output is discursively constructed, interpreted and perceived by other legal, institutional and social actors as well as the public.

It comes as a surprise to realise how few monographs or edited volumes have delved into the intricacies of the language of judges seen from a multitude of perspectives. Our aim, therefore, has been to look closely into the different phases of constructing and interpreting judicial discourse and also into its manifold faces. Released 25 years after Lawrence Solan's milestone *The Language of Judges*, this book has been envisaged to fill the void by offering a distinctly unified volume integrating quantitative and qualitative approaches and making use of a plethora of analytical methods. It is an attempt to open, update and extend various avenues of research that have been made possible thanks to fruitful collaboration between linguists and lawyers within the framework of the burgeoning field of legal linguistics. It is precisely from the legal linguistics perspective that we examine different forms of discourse from EU, common law and civil law jurisdictions with the final (and basic) aim of understanding how language works in judicial contexts.

In an attempt to scrutinise as many dimensions of the phenomenon as possible, we use a wide range of disciplinary and methodological perspectives to look in detail at the ways judicial discourse is argued, constructed, interpreted and perceived. This is why the contributions in this book explore patterns of linguistic organisation and use in judicial institutions and analyse language as an instrument for understanding both the judicial decision-making process and its outcome. Its ultimate goal is to provide a comprehensive and in-depth overview of current critical issues of the crucial role of language in judicial settings and to map out current developments in the research into judicial discourse against the complex background of the rapidly changing world of law.

We believe that the methodological strengths of this book lie in the already mentioned cross-fertilisation made possible by the different backgrounds of the contributors (legal linguists, lawyers, legal scholars, legal practitioners, legal translators and anthropologists). That they come from different geographical areas of the world (Poland, France, Denmark, Spain, Croatia, Italy and the United States) is an additional strength of the volume.

With a view to offering a comprehensive and up-to-date analysis of judicial discourse from different research perspectives, we have arranged the contributions around four major themes reflecting what we believe are the most central issues in the field: constructing judicial discourse and judicial identities (Part I), judicial argumentation and evaluative language (Part II), judicial interpretation (Part III) and clarity in judicial discourse (Part IV).

Contributions to the volume

Part I focuses on the linguistic construal of judicial discourse and on the views on judges and courts.

In Chapter 1, Łucja Biel, Dariusz Koźbiał and Dariusz Müller profile the judicial variety of the English Eurolect. To better understand the genre profile of judgments issued by the Court of Justice of the European Union (CJEU), the authors sketch it against (1) UK Supreme Court (UKSC) judgments to track its hybridisation and (2) EU legal acts to identify its similarities and differences to this fundamental legal genre. They use large comparable corpora of texts published in 2010–2019. Compared to regulations, judgments use more argumentative patterns, interpersonal and textual metadiscourse, and more verbs, determiners, adverbs and subordinators. Their findings confirm the existence of the judicial English Eurolect, pointing to distinct CJEU and UKSC judicial styles. In particular, CJEU judgments more actively use features which foreground impartiality, power and distance: more rigid macrostructure, depersonalised authorial presence, stronger modals, distant determiners, organisational markers (inference, addition, apposition as opposed to more confrontational contrast/concession markers), numerals and framing with complex prepositions. They are also less lexically rich and use fewer verbs, which reduces their dynamicity. Our data also demonstrate the considerable internal variation of CJEU judgments, with General Court (GC) judgments being more convergent to UKSC judgments in terms of length and selected key genre markers.

In Chapter 2, Magdalena Szczyrbak looks at passive structures with *say* and *tell* in US Supreme Court opinions and explores their diachronic developments (1790s–present) and examines their evidential and discourse-organising uses. The analysis focuses on *it is said (that)* and the present-tense variants of the *BE said to* and *BE told (that)* constructions, and it reveals that the structures report information which is attributable to named sources, found in the co-text, and also ensure cohesion and mark progression in the text. The data also demonstrate that *it is said (that)* came out of fashion in the second half of the 20th century, whereas *we are told (that)* became more frequent in the second decade of the 20th century. The least variability was noted in the case of the *BE said to* construction. Taken together, the trends seem to indicate a move away from impersonal discourse towards a more direct style.

In Chapter 3, Margarete Flöter-Durr and Paulina Nowak-Korcz explore standardisation in judicial discourse by taking as example the French *arrêts de la Cour de Cassation* and the use of forms in European procedural law. Standardisation in judicial discourse can be analysed on two levels, linguistic and legal, with regard to concepts pertaining both to positive law and to procedural law. In fact, these two levels are not distinct but entwined, since law as a discursive phenomenon is part of the language. The approach on such a twofold level reflects the two dimensions of standardisation: "the speciality, which is systematically linked to a discipline of reference, on the one hand, and, on the other hand, the linguistic and discursive dimension which can be assessed by analysing texts." The authors demonstrate that standardisation is a pervasive phenomenon both linguistically and legally. Linguistically, the major difficulty regarding the standard lies in the variety of formulations being used. While the standard may take the form of a noun, it may also come in the form of adjectives, adverbs or adnominal phrases.

In Chapter 4, Anne Lise Kjær investigates the consensus case law of the European Court of Human Rights (ECtHR) from a corpus-linguistic perspective. Consensus is applied by the Court when it is in need of interpreting the European Convention on Human Rights (ECHR) dynamically in light of the present-day conditions in the Member States. The Court has used various different phrases over time to denote the concept of consensus (e.g. *consensus, trend, common ground common denominator, a uniform or common approach, a common standard*). In legal research, it is maintained that the variations in terminology do not affect the legal meaning of the concept, and especially, that *consensus* and *trend* are synonymous. Based on an empirical corpus-based study of Grand Chamber judgments, the author shows that the practical meaning of the terms is not identical. *Consensus* and *trend* are not used interchangeably by the Court, and the use of *consensus* increases more over time than *trend*. In a sociolegal perspective, the results reflect the legitimacy crisis that the Court is experiencing in the present time. It is under attack from national governments that have taken over the role of lawmaking that should rightly be the task of national parliaments. This has caused the Court to show "self-restraint" by preferring a consensual rather than an evolutive interpretation of the Convention.

In Chapter 5, Ruth Breeze examines the digital media representations of the 2019 UK Supreme Court's ruling that declared Prime Minister Boris Johnson's suspension of Parliament to be unlawful. Using framing analysis supported by corpus-assisted discourse analysis, it explores how this ruling, and presiding Supreme Court Judge Baroness Hale, were woven into public debates concerning Brexit and democracy. Digital comments on the events were subsumed into populist anti-establishment frames, and the judges themselves were discredited through symbolic representations as "conspiratorial", "unpatriotic", and "treacherous", with particular misogynist undertones evoked through references to witchcraft and the supernatural used in the context of Baroness Hale herself.

Part II covers judicial argumentation and evaluation from the viewpoint of the strategies adopted by judges in the judicial decision-making process. The chapters in this part highlight the key role played by axiological values used by judges in their decisions.

In Chapter 6, Martina Bajčić explores the role corpus linguistics can play in judicial interpretation. Despite initial scepticism of legal scholars towards the application of linguistics to jurisprudence, tools and methodologies of linguistic disciplines are today convincingly applied to judicial interpretation. In fact, some countries have witnessed a corpus-linguistic turn in jurisprudence, as judges endorse the use of corpus linguistics in construing the meaning of statutory instruments. Shifting the focus to the potential usage of parallel corpora in judicial decision-making, this chapter hypothesises whether parallel corpora can facilitate the multilingual interpretation of EU law, deriving arguments from analysed case law. It is maintained that parallel corpora of EU legislation could by employed to compare different language versions and in order to comply with the principle of consistent interpretation, putting the spotlight on the national courts of EU Member States.

In Chapter 7, Stanisław Goźdź-Roszkowski integrates the linguistic study of evaluation into the model of strategic manoeuvring embraced within the pragma-dialectic approach in order to shed light on discursive practices adopted by judges in the justifications of their decisions. The concept of critical discussion was adopted to reconstruct the different stages of the Supreme Court of Poland's justification and to determine how evaluative language contributes to the realisation of each move in the argumentational discourse. The analysis is grounded in the argumentative reality of cassation proceedings heard before the Supreme Court. The study reveals that the use of evaluative language is motivated institutionally when the Supreme Court reiterates and attributes to the Attorney-General the negative assessment of the Appeals Court's decision in order to signal a difference of opinion and to establish the compliance of the cassation appeal with the formal requirements of the cassation procedure. Evaluative lexis appears salient in the argumentation stage where it expresses a positive assessment of the Court of Appeal's argumentation in light of the attacks by the Attorney-General. The results show that the Supreme Court in its justification manoeuvres strategically to resolve both the difference of opinion and to determine the argumentative role of a contested legal rule. The latter was achieved by using teleological-evaluative argumentation as a counterargument to reject an interpretation proposed by the Attorney-General.

In Chapter 8, Davide Mazzi investigates the discourse and use of causal argumentation in a corpus of the Supreme Court of Ireland's judgments on data protection. The research consisted of two main stages. The first was a preliminary quantitative study of recurrent phraseology in order to identify its most common usage patterns in context. The second stage lay in a qualitative study of the judgments, where the usage patterns established earlier on were observed to be most frequent. This allowed to detect and reconstruct textual sequences embedding causal argumentation. While phraseology was observed to shed light on the subject matter covered by the corpus as well as the interpretive and argumentative dimensions inherent in the Court's discourse, the argumentative analysis provided evidence of the flexibility of causal argumentation as a reasoning tool that ties in with valid legal norms at two main levels. The first is the combination of causality with more literal approaches to legal text. The second level is represented by more schematic or teleological approaches to norms, as was the case with the necessity to embrace principles or uphold values underlying domestic statutes, international law or the Constitution of Ireland.

In Chapter 9, María José Marín Pérez compares two sets of Spanish and British judicial decisions which revolve around the topic of immigration. The lexical networks of some of the terms falling under the category *affect*, as defined by systemic linguistics, were obtained. Using the statistical data associated to their constituents as a point of departure, the scrutiny of these vocabulary items led to the identification of fundamental topics. Such topics illustrate the key concerns and the legal trouble that surround the process of seeking asylum or migrating to a European country in both the Spanish and the British legal systems. Reuniting families, the depiction of the living conditions of vulnerable migrants or escaping criminal organisations, which children and women are prey to, stand among the most frequent scenarios which migrants are involved in, as portrayed in both legal corpora.

Part III focuses on the semantics and interpretation of judicial decisions seen from the perspective of legal scholars. In sharp contrast with the previous two parts, mainly characterised by a strong empirical (corpus-based) basis, the chapters in this part are more theoretically oriented, showing the importance of qualitative analyses in judicial linguistics.

In Chapter 10, Jessica Greenberg investigates how judicial language ideologies (beliefs about the social significance and power of language) shape the way courts regulate speech and freedom of expression. The author analyses key cases at the ECtHR, arguing that analysis of expression rights needs to account for beliefs about speech as a set of social relations and textual and interpretative practices. In analysing speech as a social and ideological process rather than a matter of content, we can better understand how judges determine the limits of legal management of speech and the balance between margin of appreciation and individual rights.

In Chapter 11, Joanna Kulesza highlights the diversity in applying the ECtHR margin of appreciation doctrine. The author discusses the evolution of the Court's jurisprudence based on Article 10 of the ECHR in the context of recent case law. The author reviews key decisions and attempts to reconstruct notions crucial to national judicial discourses among Council of Europe countries, making references to current national and regional events. The ECtHR "margin of appreciation" doctrine is set against local perceptions of morality, public decency and third-party interests. Spanning from Das Liebeskonzil through the case of *Sinkova v. Ukraine* up to recent Polish case law dealing with public statements by celebrities and controversial religious art, the author attempts to identify and define linguistic concepts crucial to drawing a legal line for free speech in Europe.

In Chapter 12, Kathryn M. Stanchi explores the US Supreme Court's use of the words "racism", "racist" and "white supremacy", treating these expressions as cultural keywords, which are words that are socially prominent but which change meaning over time. The chapter's thesis is that the Supreme Court exerts powerful influence over the cultural meaning of these keywords. The author explores several patterns in the Supreme Court's use of the keywords. First, the Supreme Court never once uses the words in a majority opinion to acknowledge the racism of a prior Supreme Court decision, even when overturning a plainly racist decision. Second, the use of the words in separate decisions to criticise the Court is infrequent and has decreased in frequency. Third, the use of the words to deny or minimise the harms of racism has increased in frequency. Thus, the language of the Court has contributed to the distortion of the definitions of racism and white supremacy. This distortion makes it more difficult for advocates to pursue racial justice, particularly through the federal courts.

In Chapter 13, Anna Tomza-Tulejska and J. Patrick Higgins discuss the current positions of American scientists on the role of the meaning of words within judicial argumentation, thus answering the question posed in the title of the chapter: whether the problem of the meaning of the meaning of the words used in the Constitution is still relevant in the newest branch of American jurisprudence, judicial science. The current theories of American law propose several leading ways to argue judicial decisions, the most popular being textualism, originalism, intentionalism and judicial activism. Their common feature is a foundation in the philosophy of language, which considers the meaning of words. Each of them perceives the role of the meaning of the words, used by the Founding Fathers in creating the Constitution, in a different way, as demonstrated in the chapter.

In Chapter 14, Marek Jan Wasiński reflects upon the mainstream, normative approach to analysing decisions of international courts. The author presents a critique of the strand of this academic practice that is sometimes denounced for producing allegedly unscientific outputs aimed pragmatically at organising case law, explaining judgments or merely opining on the technical correctness of interpretation made by an adjudicating body. It is posited that the intrinsic limits of the normative jurisprudence have prompted some normative scholars to borrow from the non-mainstream toolbox, thus avoiding the accusation of subjectivism and unscientific practice.

Part IV draws inspiration from a highly topical issue in courtroom discourse, the importance of clarity and plain language, seen from two different but complementary perspectives: European and national.

In Chapter 15, James Brannan looks at the way in which the ECtHR disseminates its case law and considers how its language and style are not necessarily barriers to effective reception or implementation. The Court conveys its message in various forms, mainly through the texts of its judgments and decisions, with emphasis on "key" cases, but also through case law notes, press releases and other material. Efforts have been made over the years to broaden its readership especially in view of the language barrier, which is the result of having just two official languages (French and English) and limited resources for translation. Strasbourg judgments may also be criticised as "foreign", unidiomatic or convoluted in style, and not sufficiently accessible to the general public. The chapter answers the following question: how is the Court's "production" perceived by the wider audience (lawyers and laypersons), and does it convey its message effectively across 47 European States?

In Chapter 16, Antonio Mura and Jacqueline Visconti report on the main achievements of an Italian project on clarity and concision in court proceedings carried out by a group of leading experts appointed by the Italian Minister of Justice in February 2018. The overall result was the perception that, besides introducing specific reforms in the legislation, what was necessary was to achieve a global culture of clarity in judicial writing, one that would motivate both judges and counsels to distance themselves from stereotypical legalese habits. Avenues for further research are highlighted, such as an enlargement of the scope of the investigation to other judicial systems, in particular to the one that lies farthest from the Italian (continental) legal culture: common law.

We believe that this book can be of use not only for experienced scholars who study judicial discourse but also for legal practitioners (judges, advocates, etc.), legal translators and students who consider pursuing research in the area. It is our hope that the work of all the authors in this collection will help and inspire these scholars, practitioners and students along their study, professional practice and research paths.

Stanisław Goźdź-Roszkowski and Gianluca Pontrandolfo

Part I

Constructing judicial discourse and judicial identities

1 The judicial English Eurolect

A genre profiling of CJEU judgments

Łucja Biel, Dariusz Koźbiał and Dariusz Müller

Eurolects are "Europeanised" hybrid varieties of national languages which have evolved to serve the linguistic needs of the European Union (EU) functioning as a supranational organisation. These are 24 "mirror" realisations in the official EU languages, mediated through various stakeholders, including translators and revisers. As a result, they are linguistically constrained and different from the corresponding national legal varieties of EU languages (Biel 2020, pp. 315–316). While most of the existing and recently growing studies on Eurolects focus on legal acts (cf. Biel 2014; Mori 2018), their judicial variety has rarely been studied until now (cf. Koźbiał 2020).[1] This niche is filled by the present chapter, which examines the judicial English Eurolect. Although EU judgments are originally drafted in French, our interest lies in the English-language versions (translations) due to the increasing rôle of English both in EU institutions and across Europe. To profile the judicial Eurolect, we contrast EU judgments with (1) a corpus of UK Supreme Court (UKSC) judgments and (2) a corpus of EU legal acts. This study design is motivated by the fact that legal acts and judgments belong to the same legal genre chain. As observed by Robertson (2015, p. 39), these genres capture two crucial phases – when law is created and when it is interpreted and applied by courts – and hence form the nexus of the strongest EU-related factors. Yet, although these genres may be expected to share certain features common to all Eurolects, they have different contexts of production, communicative purposes and discourse communities. These differences are likely to result in the legislative and judicial genres having distinct habitual sets of linguistic conventions. Their comparison will allow us to understand how EU judgments differ from the related genre of EU legal acts, while the comparison to UK judgments will shed more light on the hybridisation of judgments in the EU context.

1 The Court of Justice of the European Union and its judicial style

The Court of Justice of the European Union (CJEU) is the judicial institution of the EU perceived as its constitutional and administrative court (Kuijper 2018,

1 See Koźbiał (2020) on the judicial variety of the Polish Eurolect.

DOI: 10.4324/9781003153771-2

pp. 81–82). It is the "supreme authority" on EU law and its judicial decisions are one of the sources of EU law (Woods et al. 2017, pp. 46, 89). Functionally, it deals with two main categories of cases: (1) references for a preliminary ruling from national courts to interpret or assess the validity of EU law and (2) direct actions against Member States and the EU institutions, which include actions for failure to fulfil the obligations of a Member State, for annulment of EU legal acts, for failure to act and for damages (Albors-Llorens 2017, pp. 263–267). These two types of cases require the Court to adopt fundamentally different roles, adjudication in direct actions and interpretation in preliminary rulings:

> In direct actions, the Court adjudicates on the dispute between the parties, whereas in preliminary rulings it simply gives advice on a specific point of EU law, leaving the final resolution of the dispute to the national court.
>
> (Albors-Llorens 2017, p. 265)

Thematically, the CJEU decides mainly on economic matters (e.g. taxation, internal market, competition, intellectual property, state aid, agriculture, customs) and increasingly more on other matters, such as judicial cooperation, the environment and social policy (Bobek 2015, p. 159).

The CJEU is composed of the General Court (GC) and the Court of Justice (CJ). Acting as an administrative court, the GC hears at first instance actions for damages and civil service cases as well as direct actions not involving disputes between the Member States and the major EU institutions, whereas the CJ, acting more as a constitutional court, examines all preliminary rulings, other types of direct actions and appeals against the GC decisions on points of law (cf. TFEU[2] and Kuijper 2018, pp. 81–82). For example, according to the CJEU's 2019 Annual Report,[3] 90% of new cases brought before the GC in 2019 were direct actions, while in the case of the CJ, 66% of new cases were preliminary rulings, 27% appeals and only 4% direct actions.

CJEU judgments are "a collective enterprise" of judges, Advocates General and référendaires (Bobek 2015, p. 168). The GC currently has two judges from each Member State, whereas the CJ has only one judge from each Member State and 11 Advocates General. The Court sits mostly in the multinational and multilingual chambers of three and five judges (Woods et al. 2017, p. 46). Although under the CJEU Rules of Procedure any of the EU's official languages may be chosen as the language of the case, judgments are deliberated on and drafted in the CJEU's only working language: French, or, more specifically, hybrid "Court French" (Wright 2016, p. 3). De facto original judgments are translated into the EU's official languages by native lawyer-linguists (Derlén 2015, p. 58).

2 Consolidated version of the Treaty on the Functioning of the European Union, OJ C 326/01, October 26, 2012, pp. 47–390.

3 https://curia.europa.eu/jcms/upload/docs/application/pdf/2020-05/ra_pan_2019_interieur_en_final.pdf

In contrast to legal acts, the only authentic (de jure original) judgment is the one translated into the language of the case (Derlén 2015, p. 58).

The internal arrangements of the CJEU are derived from continental models where there is no system of binding precedent, at least "in the English sense" (Woods et al. 2017, p. 48). Originally influenced by the French drafting style, the CJEU has over the years developed its own judicial style, one more of a "civilian" nature (Bobek 2015, p. 169; Wright 2016). Despite some differences between the CJ and the GC, with the former having "somewhat enunciative/proclaiming style" and the latter a "more argumentative style" (Kuijper 2018, p. 85), there are common features. They include abstract deductive reasoning, a rather succinct and depersonalised drafting style (compared to the common law tradition), macrostructural and microstructural formulaicity, and extensive cluster citations from previous rulings (Bobek 2015, pp. 169–170). The lack of dissenting or concurring opinions results in a less clear and "enigmatic" "consensus language" (Kuijper 2018, p. 85). Furthermore, from the common law perspective, CJEU judgments may look "terse, cryptic, with little indication of the reasoning" (Woods et al. 2017, p. 48), but this may well be a purposeful audience design: the overwhelming majority of CJEU's "judicial clients" are continental judges who are accustomed to a civilian drafting style (Bobek 2015, p. 171).

2 EU English: the legislative and the judicial Eurolects

EU English has cemented its status as the EU's lingua franca in the last two decades. Except for the CJEU, English is the procedural language of the EU institutions: it is the principal drafting language of legal acts and the main source language of numerous institutional documents. EU English is regarded as a neutral metalanguage (Šarčević 2010, pp. 34–35), quite frequently moulded by non-native speakers to meet the EU's institutional, political and legal needs (cf. Biel et al. 2018). This, accompanied by the filtering through other EU working languages, results in the hybridity of EU English. Additionally, EU English is projected to strengthen its role in the post-Brexit EU and accelerate linguistic nativisation through further hybridisation (Modiano 2017, pp. 319–321).

Corpus studies into the hybridity of EU English legislation did indeed report differences with the British English variety at many levels: lexical (EU-specific terminology, borrowings, acronyms, Latinisms), morphological (international prefixes, e.g. *inter-*, *non-*), grammatical (e.g. *shall* as a deontic modal), phraseological (*here-* and *there-* compound prepositions, more complex prepositions with referencing (*in accordance with*, *pursuant to*) and particularisation (*as regards*) functions (cf. Biel 2015; Sandrelli 2018).

The status of EU English is obviously less prominent in the CJEU, where the working language is French. Because judgments are (1) based on pleadings translated from the language of the case into French (Wright 2016, p. 6), (2) deliberated and drafted in French by mainly non-native judges and their référendaires (McAuliffe 2012, pp. 203, 207) and (3) later translated, the judicial English Eurolect may show features of translationese (a translator-mediated constrained form of language). Compared to EU legal acts and judgments from other jurisdictions, EU judgments are under-researched. First attempts to describe English language versions of CJEU judgments focused on selected distinctive lexico-grammatical patterns used in argumentation, such as reporting verbs, in particular the verb *to hold* (Mazzi 2007), concessions (Szczyrbak 2014), and paragraph-initial metadiscursive signalling devices (McAuliffe and Trklja 2019). Some studies point to the hybridity of CJEU English judgments compared to UK judgments: increased formulaicity in terms of words in bundles (Trklja 2018) and marked preference for certain complex prepositions (e.g. *in accordance with*, *relating to*; Koźbiał 2018). Yet, to the best of our knowledge, no global analysis of the judicial English Eurolect has been conducted to date, and we intend to fill this gap.

3 Corpus design

The study applies comparable corpus methods, supplemented with a qualitative analysis of selected over- and under-represented lexico-grammatical patterns. It was conducted on four large English-language corpora with the same ten-year timeframe of 2010–2019 (calendar years, not judicial years). The CJEU focus corpus includes two sub-corpora: CJ judgments and GC judgments. Two reference corpora are the corpus of UKSC judgments and the corpus of EU regulations. The files were downloaded in 2020, uploaded to Sketch Engine (Kilgarriff et al. 2014), part-of-speech tagged and lemmatised. Table 1.1 shows the corpus design.

The CJEU corpus contains judgments downloaded automatically[4] from Curia,[5] with the search criteria limited to English-language judgments given in cases closed. It covers both CJEU courts to account for the different types of cases they hear.

Table 1.1 Corpus design

	# of texts	Tokens	Average text length	Lexicon size: words	Lexicon size: lemma_lc
Focus corpus: CJEU judgments					
CJEU_CJ	3671	25,110,814	6840	100,711	67,904
CJEU_GC	1184	17,655,295	14,911	72,451	45,381
Reference corpora					
UKSC	669	9,989,448	14,931	73,603	45,156
EU_Reg	1080	12,490,190	11,564	160,324	88,179

4 xml2: Parse XML, R 3.5.0, https://cran.r-project.org/web/packages/xml2/
5 https://curia.europa.eu

The UKSC corpus comprises judgments issued by the UKSC which were downloaded manually from its website.[6] Doubled judgments dealing with multiple appeals were removed. The UKSC is the highest court of appeal for civil and criminal cases from England, Wales, Northern Ireland and, in certain cases, Scotland, hearing cases of general public and constitutional importance (Slapper and Kelly 2017, p. 243). Only 6% of the cases in the UKSC corpus deal with criminal cases, the remaining ones being civil cases. The English common law system applies the doctrine of a binding precedent (*stare decisis*), and the UKSC judgments are binding on lower-ranking courts (Slapper and Kelly 2017, pp. 137, 142).

The EU_Reg corpus includes regulations downloaded automatically from the EUR-Lex[7] directory of legal acts. The search was limited to basic acts in force, excluding delegated, implementing and amending acts. We chose regulations as the most prototypical type of EU secondary legislation: binding in their entirety and directly applicable in the Member States. Regulations were downloaded in full, including non-normative preambles, with citations and recitals.

4 Analysis of the judicial Eurolect: the genre profile of CJEU judgments

4.1 Text length and lexical richness

Although the EU judicial drafting style has been described as "succinct" compared to the common law style (see Section 1), the average text length (Table 1.1) does not fully confirm this observation. While CJ judgments are indeed 2 times shorter (6840 words) than UKSC ones (14,931), the length of GC judgments (14,911) is nearly identical to that of UKSC judgments.

Another feature of CJEU judgments is their substantially lower lexicon size compared to the UKSC corpus (Table 1.1). This is clearly visible in the GC corpus, the lexicon size of which is similar to the UKSC corpus despite having twice as many tokens. This means that the CJEU judgments are less lexically rich, idiosyncratic and varied. These features, known as levelling out (Baker 1996, p. 184), are hypothesised to be typical of translations. Yet, these processes might be at play in the case of French originals as well, due to increased standardisation in international institutions and possibly a higher thematic diversification of cases at the national level.

4.2 Macrostructure of CJEU judgments

Table 1.2 shows the macrostructure of CJEU and UKSC judgments, their rhetorical moves and steps, depending on the procedure.

6 www.supremecourt.uk/
7 https://eur-lex.europa.eu

Table 1.2 Macrostructure of CJEU and UKSC judgments (abbreviations of direct actions: actions for annulment – A; actions for damages – D; actions for failure to act – F; actions for failure to fulfil obligations – O; italics mark optional steps)

	CJEU judgments				UKSC judgments
	Direct actions	**Appeals**	**Preliminary rulings**		
Move 1	Identifying the case			**Move 1**	Identifying the case
Move 2	Identifying the scope of the proceedings			**Move 2**	Establishing facts of the case
Move 3	Retrieving relevant EU or (inter)national law (A, F, O) OR Stating the background to the dispute (D)	Retrieving relevant EU or (inter)national law		Step 1	*Relevant legal provisions and binding precedents*
Step 1	*International law (O)*	–	*International law*		
Step 2	EU law (A, F, O)				
Step 3	*National law (O)*	–	*National law*		
Move 4	Stating the background to the dispute (A, F, O), procedure and parties' demands (A, D, F, O)	Stating the background to the dispute, the judgment under appeal, and parties' demands	Stating the background to the dispute and the questions referred	Step 2	*Legal questions*

Step 1	Background to the dispute (A, F, O)			Step 3	*Background to the dispute*
Step 2	Procedure and forms of order sought (A, F) OR Pre-litigation procedure (O)	Pre-litigation procedure	Question(s) referred for a preliminary ruling		
Step 3	Forms of order sought (O)		–		
Move 5	Arguing the case		Considering the question(s) referred	**Move 3**	Arguing the case
Step 1	Arguments of the parties (A, F, O)		–	Step 1	Arguments
Step 2	Findings of the Court (A, F, O)		–	Step 2	Ratio decidendi
Move 6	Settling costs			**Move 4**	Pronouncing judgment
Move 7	Pronouncing judgment				
Move 8	Signatures			Step 1	Judgment
				Step 2	*Concurring/ dissenting opinions*

CJEU judgments exhibit a clear, sequential and standardised template-like macrostructure. They are divided into numbered paragraphs (except for moves 1, 7 and 8), where move-step transitions are usually visually signalled with bold section headings. CJEU judgments first identify the case and the scope of proceedings, then retrieve relevant legal provisions and state the background to the dispute (informative moves 1–4). The argumentative move (5) argues the case or considers the questions referred. The final moves (6–8) are performative: they settle costs and pronounce the judgment (cf. Szczyrbak 2014, p. 127; Koźbiał 2020). The largest variation is observable at moves 3, 4 and 5.

The macrostructure of UKSC judgments is also sequential but far less rigid due to an increased idiosyncratic variation. Similarly, UKSC judgments are divided into numbered paragraphs, but the move-step transitions are not signalled with standardised headings. UKSC judgments typically start with informative moves which identify the case and establish the facts of the case; the following moves argue the case and pronounce the judgment (cf. Bhatia 1993, pp. 230–244). The judgment may be accompanied by dissenting or concurring opinion(s). Although the UKSC judgments have fewer and less pronounced moves and steps with optional elements, the key moves – identifying the case, arguing the case, and pronouncing the judgment – are shared and are functionally similar.

4.3 *Keyword analysis: genre features*

The keyword analysis identified a range of genre features related to the microstructure. For want of space, our discussion is limited to selected functional categories:

- key terms and n-grams;
- parts of speech and grammatical categories;
- impersonal argumentative patterns;
- authorial presence;
- modal, reporting and performative verbs;
- proximity and distance;
- markers of evaluation and stance;
- textual metadiscourse;
- framing.

Tables in the subsequent part provide normalised frequencies (NF) per million words (pmw) for selected patterns. The full data set, including raw frequencies and %DIFF values, is available in RepOD at https://doi.org/10.18150/JOQPG1, Biel et al. 2021.

4.4 *Key terms and lexical bundles*

Most frequent terms and lexical bundles reveal the key concepts behind the texts. As shown in Table 1.3, simple terms are functionally similar across the corpora,

Table 1.3 Top 10 single-word terms (items shared in judgments are in bold)

CJEU_CJ	NF	CJEU_GC	NF	UKSC	NF	EU_Reg	NF
article	7639	*commission*	7717	**court**	4725	**article**	7207
court	6063	*applicant*	6221	*case*	4052	*regulation*	4691
directive	4133	*decision*	5278	*section*	2824	*member*	3345
paragraph	3659	**article**	4483	*lord*	2662	*union*	2633
member	3533	**paragraph**	4437	*para*	2508	*commission*	2361
regulation	3101	*regulation*	3103	**act**	2493	*ec*	2119
state	3092	*case*	2921	*law*	2386	*authority*	2070
law	2766	**court**	2692	*appeal*	2234	*accordance*	1998
judgment	2711	*eu*	1973	**right**	1920	*state*	1994
case	2479	*infringement*	1792	*article*	1889	*product*	1890

Table 1.4 Top 10 nested 4-grams

CJEU_CJ	CJEU_GC	UKSC	EU_Reg
in the main proceedings	*of the contested decision*	*the Court of Appeal* *the Secretary of State*	*the European Parliament and*
for a preliminary ruling	*in the present case*	*Secretary of State for*	*referred to in article*
at issue in the	*the board of appeal*	*the House of Lords*	*of the European Parliament*
within the meaning of	*in the light of*	*for the purposes of*	*in accordance with article*
issue in the main	*on the basis of*	*in relation to the*	*European Parliament and of*
the judgment under appeal	*in so far as*	*in the case of*	*Parliament and of the*
on the basis of	*in the context of*	*in the present case*	*and of the Council*
for the purposes of	*and the case-law cited*	*v Secretary of State*	*in accordance with the*
in the light of	*in the contested decision*	*of the court of*	*of the European Union*
must be interpreted as	*the fact that the*		*of the Council of*

attesting to the common conceptual basis, and include editing units (*article, paragraph/para*), names of documents (*directive, judgment, (legal) act*), institutions, participants (*court, commission, member states, applicant*), procedural elements (*proceedings, case*). Differences are more visible when terms refer to the subject matter: *appeal* (UKSC), and *product* (EU_Reg).

Table 1.4 presents the top 10 nested 4-grams. These multi-word patterns show less similarity across the corpora. Only judgments share a few top n-grams: *on the basis of, in the light of* (CJ, GC), *for the purposes of* (CJ, UKSC) and *in the present case* (GC, UKSC). Most top 4-grams are prepositional phrases or parts of larger noun phrases (*request/reference for a preliminary ruling; annulment/adoption of the contested decision*). Functionally, they are referential bundles (*the Board of Appeal, the judgment under appeal*) and text-oriented bundles (*in the light/context of, for the purposes of*). Table 1.4 has only one stance bundle (*must be interpreted as*, CJ).

4.5 Parts of speech and selected grammatical categories

Using the Sketch Engine's Modified TreeTagger POS tagset with some adjustments, we analysed key parts of speech and grammatical categories (Table 1.5).

All judgments have a similar frequency of nouns, simple prepositions, conjunctions and adjectives, which are significantly more frequent in regulations (e.g. the *or* conjunction is 2–3 times more frequent); and determiners, which are less common in regulations. Additionally, judgments use more past tense verbs, adverbs, *wh-* and *that* subordinators and fewer gerunds compared to regulations; yet, these categories are more similar in the GC and the UKSC compared to the CJ. On the other hand, CJEU judgments have a similar distribution of verbs, modals, past participles and personal pronouns, all of which are markedly more common in the UKSC. The judicial and legislative Eurolects use fewer verbs but more phrasal verbs (particle tag) and substantially more numerals than UKSC judgments.

Table 1.5 Key parts of speech and grammatical categories (figures in bold indicate strong over-representation)

	CJEU_CJ	CJEU_GC	UKSC	EU_Reg
nouns	277,456	268,545	256,012	**318,439**
verbs	109,468	114,338	**135,490**	88,209
verb, past tense	11,314	19,925	**26,245**	4953
verb, gerund/present participle	15,812	13,243	12,134	**17,688**
verb, past participle	29,908	30,618	**32,886**	27,523
modal	9497	9296	**13,378**	**13,604**
adjectives	55,195	55,204	57,393	**66,179**
adverbs	24,404	**32,429**	**35,844**	15,166
personal pronouns	13,928	18,188	**29,817**	6614
prepositions, subordinating conjunctions	**147,123**	141,912	135,526	116,026
coordinating conjunctions	24,807	23,111	25,758	**35,303**
particles	2492	2161	1745	**2409**
that & wh-subordinators	20,197	22,353	**26,732**	9066
wh-subordinators	9182	6780	**12,194**	5876
that as subordinator	11,015	**15,573**	**14,538**	3190
determiners	115,432	**120,495**	114,899	84,591
numerals	**52,503**	**52,527**	29,909	**54,772**

4.6 Impersonal argumentative patterns

Compared to regulations, one of the distinctive features of judgments is the pervasive use of impersonal argumentative patterns (Table 1.6), parts of which can be easily identified in keywords and n-grams (e.g. *it* over-represented in GC and UKSC judgments; existential *there* and hedges *seem, appear* over-represented in UKSC judgments).

Table 1.6 Frequent argumentative patterns

	CJEU_CJ	CJEU_GC	UKSC	EU_Reg
it	6327	**9371**	**9634**	1823
it **[modal]** ***be*** **[verb-passive]** CJ/GC: *it must/should be ~ noted, recalled, held, borne in mind, observed, pointed out*, etc. UKSC: *it would/may be ~ said, noted, seen* Reg: *it shall/should be ~ prohibited*	**874**	**1518**	232	106
*it * be noted*	**258**	**399**	13	3
it **[verb|modal+*be*] [adjective]** *~ it is/was | would/must be apparent, necessary, clear, true, common, important, possible, appropriate*, etc.	1076	**1437**	**1496**	332
*it * apparent from/that*	**341**	**451**	38	1
*it * necessary*	165	227	126	90
it follows *from/that*	**398**	**452**	31	1
there EX	543	814	**2382**	251
there **[verb|modal+*be*] [determiner/noun]** *~ is/are/was/were (a/no/any/ nothing) doubt, reason, question, evidence, grounds, need, suggestion, question*, etc.	415	620	**1567**	171
seem patterns *it/this/that seems | would/does not seem* (UKSC: *to me*) *that* | infinitive (*to be, to have been*) | adjective (*necessary, clear, likely, reasonable*)	21	35	**331**	3
appear [*to, that*, adj] patterns *it*/noun *appears | does not appear that* | infinitive (*to be, have, suggest*) | adjective (*necessary, appropriate, possible, clear*)	78	72	**291**	18

There is a relatively high similarity among CJEU judgments in how they use the aforementioned patterns both in terms of preferences, variant forms and collocates. CJEU judgments more frequently use the pattern *It [modal] be [verb-passive]* (mainly with strong modals *must* and *should*) and *it follows from/that*. UKSC judgments more frequently use *there [verb] [determiner/noun]* and hedging *seem/appear* patterns. The *it [verb] [adjective]* pattern has a similarly high distribution in the GC and UKSC judgments, yet the most frequent realisation of this pattern in CJEU judgments is *it is apparent from/that* (with a range of variants, e.g. *it is/was/becomes (not/also/furthermore/clearly/therefore) apparent from/that*), nearly 10 times more frequent than in UKSC judgments.

4.7 Authorial presence

One of the most striking differences in the CJEU and UKSC keywords is the use of first-person pronouns, which signal judges' authorial presence through self-references (Table 1.7).

The UKSC judgments show a very strong over-representation of the first-person pronouns *I* and *we*, whereby judges express their stance, judgment and concurring and dissenting opinions: *in my/our view, in my opinion, I agree (with), I (do not) think, I/we consider that, we are concerned with*. Self-references are occasionally depersonalised (e.g. *the Court is divided; the Court is being asked to*). The UKSC judgments also frequently refer to honorifics and titles: *Mr., Lord, Lady, Sir*. The high distribution of personal pronouns combined with the more vivid, metaphorical and emotional language of UKSC judgments contribute to their dialogicity and more personal nature.

By sharp contrast, CJEU judgments are highly depersonalised and of a clearly signalled collegiate nature, resembling in this regard more the French than the UK drafting style. By using the third-person collective self-reference *the Court* *(e.g. *the Court should, rules, held, considers*), the judges never become visible, neither through the first-person pronoun (which appears only in direct quotes from other documents, mostly witness testimonies) nor by dissenting or concurring opinions. This de-individualisation was aptly captured by Bobek: "judicial individuality is suppressed. . . . No individual judicial faces emerge from the

Table 1.7 Authorial presence: self-references

	CJEU_CJ	CJEU_GC	UKSC	EU_Reg
I	3	50	2360	1
we	2	34	558	1
Court's proper name: *CJ, GC, SC* or *COURT*	666	568	141	n/a
*the/this Court**	1679	1443	281	n/a

Note: *the/this Court** is an approximation; it includes some references to other courts.

collegiate court, at least in the judicial capacity" (2015, p. 166). Judges become a unanimous and anonymous voice of the institution, which creates the impression of objective impersonal authority behind the judgment. In this respect, CJEU judgments are similar to regulations, devoid of first-person pronouns.

4.8 Modal, reporting and performative verbs

Another salient keyword category comprises the verb group, under-represented in the Eurolect. As for modal and semi-modal verbs, judgments tend to use them to express epistemic modality in reported speech and citations, while regulations use them to express deontic modality (obligation and permission) in normative parts. As shown in Table 1.8, each corpus has its own preferred modals: the CJEU – *must*; the UKSC – *would* and regulations – *shall*.

There are marked differences in the use of modals between CJEU and UKSC judgments. CJEU judgments have ca. 30% fewer modals, frequently use a strong modal *must* and use fewer conditional forms. The CJ and the GC have a relatively similar distribution of modals, but the GC has more *could, would* and *should* since they often rely on reported speech, while the CJ has more *shall* and *may*, as they cite relevant legal provisions more extensively than the GC.

Must, one of the top CJEU keywords, triggered in translation by a wide range of French patterns, is strongly over-represented in CJEU judgments compared to both UKSC and regulations. It is used in highly repetitive argumentative patterns, mainly to signal logical necessity: *must be interpreted* (CJ: 491 pmw), *the plea (in law), complaint* or *argument must (*/therefore/also/ accordingly) be rejected* (GC: 406 pmw), *must * be held*. This strong modal, often combined with the agentless passive voice, signals an impersonal authority behind the argumentation, making it more objective and hence less contestable. The UKSC judgments have much more varied and less frequent patterns with *must: must be taken, the court must*, etc. They more frequently use a weaker modal *should* and semi-modals (periphrastic modals) *be to* and *have to* (e.g. *is to be found in*).

Table 1.8 Modal auxiliary verbs and semi-modals

	CJEU_CJ	CJEU_GC	UKSC	EU_Reg
must	**2584**	**2709**	1178	324
have to	178	256	**524**	69
be to	845	684	**1041**	268
shall	1739	328	476	**8182**
should	1080	1481	1784	**2062**
may	1576	974	1635	**1830**
can	1058	1237	**1671**	538
could	412	802	**1196**	128
might	98	193	**648**	52
would	674	1142	**3464**	210

Finally, CJEU judgments have markedly fewer conditional forms of modals, such as *would, could, might*, which are over 2–3 times more frequent in UKSC judgments. They express logical possibility and prediction and appear in reported speech. They may be combined with *if* hypothetical structures, twice as frequent in UKSC judgments (2530 pmw) as in CJEU judgments (1223; 937) and regulations (1164). Conditional modals also function as hedging devices, toning down the strength of the utterance. Interestingly, this is clearly visible in the operative part, where CJEU judgments use the standardised formula in the present simple tense accompanied by the solemn performative *hereby* (absent in the French versions; added in translations):

On those grounds, the Court hereby rules [preliminary rulings]
On those grounds, the Court hereby: 1. Declares 2. Dismisses 3. Orders [direct actions],

whereas the UKSC operative parts are far more varied and personalised, quite frequently hedged with a conditional modal:

For these reasons I would dismiss the appeal.
Accordingly, albeit without enthusiasm, I would allow the appeal.
We therefore dismiss the appeals.

The above examples show the most frequent performative verbs in the Pronouncing the Judgment move *dismisses, annuls, orders, declares* and *rules* in CJEU judgments and *dismiss* and *allow* in UKSC judgments.

Another prominent group of verbs can be broadly referred to as reporting verbs, as they report on actions and attitudes, including self-references. They mainly appear in third-person singular (*contends, submits, claims, considers, disputes*) and the third-person past tense forms (*held, stated, considered, found, observed, submitted*; Table 1.9), with quite a lot of forms (in brackets) shared among the top 10 verbs in CJEU and UKSC judgments. Present tense forms occasionally appear in the third-person plural (e.g. *the applicants submit*) and

Table 1.9 Top reporting verbs: past forms

CJEU_CJ		CJEU_GC		UKSC		EU_Reg	
held	270	*stated*	285	*said*	543	*issued*	8
stated	122	*considered*	179	**held**	238	*claimed*	5
failed	106	*found*	164	*considered*	127	*submitted*	5
found	83	**held**	133	*agreed*	115	*accepted*	5
decided	76	*failed*	129	*observed*	114	*decided*	4

in the first person in UKSC only (e.g. *I/we consider*, *accept*). UKSC keywords include more conversational *said* and *says* forms.

4.9 Proximity and distance

The concluding formulas show an interesting difference in the use of proximal and distant determiners (e.g. *on those grounds* (CJEU), *for these reasons* (UKSC); Table 1.10). UKSC judgments have a similar distribution of both types of determiners. CJEU judgments have a strong preference for the distant determiners *that* and *those*, which are seven to eight times more frequent than their proximal determiners *this* and *these* (and twice as frequent as distant determiners in the UKSC). This creates an impression of detachment and distance. The over-representation is partly due to phrases: *in that regard* (the UKSC prefers *in this regard*), *(see) to that effect, that directive, in those circumstances, on those grounds.* It may be a side effect of translation, as the French simple determiners *ce(t), cette, ces* do not correspond to the English set of proximal and distant determiners. In other words, *à cet égard* can be translated both as *in this* regard and *in that regard*, depending on the context. Curiously, it is the latter set of markers that is triggered in translation rather than the former. The preference for distant determiners is not observed in the regulations.

Other distancing devices due to their immediate associations with formal register and legalese are compound prepositions with *here** (*hereby, hereinafter*) and *there** (*thereof, thereby, thereto, therein*). They are strongly over-represented in the Eurolect, in particular in CJ judgments and regulations.

Table 1.10 Proximity and distance markers

	CJEU_CJ	CJEU_GC	UKSC	EU_Reg
1. Proximal determiners				
this	1331	944	**4504**	**3576**
these	270	155	**1131**	304
Total	*1601*	*1099*	*5635*	*3880*
2. Distant determiners				
that	**8458**	**6682**	4504	1492
those	**2994**	**2647**	1226	1207
Total	*11,452*	*9329*	*5730*	2699
3. Compound prepositions				
*here** compounds	**172**	75	22	75
hereby	**152**	70	10	31
*there** compounds	**528**	**262**	161	**559**
thereof	**329**	111	21	**366**

4.10 Markers of evaluation and epistemic stance: adverbials and adjectives

Another key feature of judgments is the ubiquitous use of markers of evaluation and epistemic stance, which is communicated with a range of devices: adverbials (in particular *-ly* adverbials), adjectives, nouns, conjunctions (e.g. a CJEU keyword: ***in so far as***), determiners and boosters (***every, never, often***, which are UKSC keywords), and the modal verbs discussed above. Table 1.11 shows the most frequent evaluation and stance adverbials, with *clearly* and ***likely*** being shared in all the corpora. These adverbials are much more frequent in judgments, in particular in the UKSC and GC judgments. The most common adverbials are quite similar in judgments, and they are predominantly high-level epistemic markers (*clearly, actually, expressly, in fact, indeed, necessarily, merely, reasonably, simply*) or hedge the content with a small (*in essence, in principle, essentially, generally*, more prominent in CJ judgments) or larger (*likely*) margin of doubt. UKSC keywords include the more conversational ***indeed, simply*** and ***of course***. Adjectives, which are under-represented in judgments, are surprisingly similar across the corpora, with as many as five top adjectives shared.

Table 1.11 Top evaluation and stance adverbials (excluding organisational markers) and adjectives

CJEU_CJ	NF	CJEU_GC	NF	UKSC	NF	EU_Reg	NF
Adverbials							
in essence	254	*in essence*	255	***indeed***	274	*duly*	75
in principle	151	***merely***	228	*simply*	222	***likely***	73
actually	128	***indeed***	170	***clearly***	200	***clearly***	64
merely	117	***clearly***	150	*reasonably*	177	*principally*	31
expressly	113	***in fact***	136	*properly*	174	*generally*	28
likely	101	***likely***	129	*generally*	173	*properly*	26
essentially	93	*expressly*	128	***merely***	145	*actually*	25
in fact	92	*actually*	127	***in fact***	136	*reasonably*	21
indeed	86	*necessarily*	122	*necessarily*	133	*substantially*	20
clearly	88	*correctly*	109	***likely***	129	*notably*	18
Adjectives							
necessary	751	*contested*	3201	***relevant***	902	***relevant***	1093
appropriate	423	***relevant***	696	***necessary***	602	***appropriate***	766
relevant	400	***necessary***	660	*clear*	534	***necessary***	702
contested	384	*apparent*	486	*reasonable*	454	***possible***	331
apparent	369	***sufficient***	405	***appropriate***	377	*significant*	185
possible	318	*clear*	397	***possible***	336	***sufficient***	134
clear	305	***possible***	368	***sufficient***	234	*essential*	113
sufficient	218	***appropriate***	347	*great*	228	*potential*	100
essential	143	*alleged*	242	*significant*	222	*adequate*	93
unfair	130	*manifest*	202	*correct*	221	*serious*	88

4.11 Textual metadiscourse

Compared to legal acts, judgments are characterised by the pervasive use of markers that organise discourse, ensure cohesion and guide readers through the text. They include linking adverbials, which link ideas between sentences, and conjunctions, which link ideas between clauses. The most frequent metadiscursive devices in judgments can be divided into the following functional groups: (1) inference, (2) addition, (3) apposition, (4) contrast and concession and (5) cause (Table 1.12).

Table 1.12 Organisational markers

	CJEU_CJ	CJEU_GC	UKSC	EU_Reg
Inference				
therefore	677	**1222**	638	255
thus	413	**564**	316	52
consequently	**309**	**419**	24	23
accordingly	246	**351**	171	83
*then**	93	111	**511**	70
Addition				
first	326	**551**	161	0
moreover	258	**539**	72	31
furthermore	**197**	**377**	58	57
secondly; second	329	589	173	2
in addition	158	**302**	37	76
finally	87	143	77	14
next	70	**131**	66	2
in the first place	62	**133**	34	0
lastly	57	**149**	3	0
further	59	92	**183**	117
And	1	1	**105**	1
Apposition				
such as	**817**	310	366	316
in particular, particularly	862	875	417	617
namely	206	**341**	183	38
that is to say, that is, i.e., ie	117	161	153	76
for example, for instance, e.g., eg	51	72	**322**	214
Contrast and concession				
however	601	717	**830**	195
but	554	655	**2738**	400
But	0	1	**915**	2
while	188	177	**277**	113
although	180	276	**472**	20
even if	129	203	200	20
nevertheless	102	104	111	20
though	89	117	134	9
on the other hand	85	97	88	8

Table 1.12 (Continued)

	CJEU_CJ	CJEU_GC	UKSC	EU_Reg
otherwise	84	46	**287**	147
even though	83	**112**	66	5
still	69	96	**154**	34
Cause				
because	149	212	**795**	44

The GC corpus has significantly more inference markers (over 50% more than the CJ and the UKSC) and addition markers (two times more than the CJ and three times more than the UKSC). CJEU judgments, in particular the CJ, have 25%–45% more apposition markers, which clarify, exemplify or reformulate the item preceding it. Compared to the CJEU corpus, UKSC judgments have twice as many contrast/concession markers, often used in argumentation to introduce a counterclaim (cf. Szczyrbak 2014), and four times more occurrences of the cause marker *because*. Thus, CJEU judgments more clearly and frequently sequence arguments, while UKSC judgments more actively shift arguments and introduce counterclaims. Significantly more frequent markers in the CJEU are ***consequently, first, second, moreover, furthermore*** and ***namely***, while the UKSC-preferred markers are ***then*** (both inference and addition), ***further, for example, however, otherwise, although*** and ***but***, in particular the conversational sentence-initial *But* and *And* (virtually non-existent in CJEU judgments).

4.12 Latinisms

The next feature of judgments is the use of Latinisms, which shows a relative similarity across the judicial corpora (Table 1.13). CJEU judgments have a similar

Table 1.13 Top Latinisms

CJEU_CJ	NF	CJEU_GC	NF	UKSC	NF	EU_Reg	NF
inter alia	418	***inter alia***	247	***per***	212	***ex***	405
per	76	***per***	83	*in re*	133	***per***	223
via	30	***via***	31	***ex***	95	*eg, e.g.*	116
res judicata	21	*a fortiori*	28	*ie, i.e.*	93	*etc., etc*	96
mutatis mutandis	15	*indicia*	25	*eg, e.g.*	62	***via***	93
de facto	13	***de facto***	21	***inter alia***	39	*quantum satis*	72
a fortiori	13	***ex***	**21**	*prima facie*	37	*ie, i.e.*	70
in rem	12	*prima facie*	14	***de facto***	32	***inter alia***	60
ratione temporis	11	*ad hoc*	13	*etc., etc*	30	*de minimis*	32
ex	**10**	*res judicata*	12	*ex parte*	15	*mutatis mutandis*	18
				via	15		

number of Latinisms to UKSC judgments in terms of types; but 10%–20% fewer Latinisms in terms of total distribution. Regulations have fewer types but these have a higher distribution compared to judgments (from ca. 700 pmw in the GC to 1300 in regulations). Top Latinisms are either discourse organisers used for clarification and exemplification (*inter alia, etc., e.g., i.e.*) or prepositions (*per, via, ex*). In this group, *inter alia* is strongly over-represented in CJEU judgments. Lower-ranking Latinisms refer to legal concepts or maxims, capitalising on shared pan-European knowledge of Latin among legal professionals, especially continental ones.

4.13 Framing: complex and marginal prepositions

This group focuses on complex and marginal prepositions which frame the content and argumentation. They have a similar distribution in the Eurolect, where they are strongly over-represented (50%–70%) compared to UKSC judgments. Table 1.14 shows the most frequent complex prepositions, with two shared prepositions (*in order to, in accordance with*), while Table 1.15 groups them functionally.

Although they are multifunctional, top prepositions are used mainly to frame discourse with inter- and intratextual references, legal authority and conflict avoidance/resolution, purpose, particularisation and anchoring. CJEU judgments use two to three times more prepositions in each of these categories. A majority of complex prepositions in Table 1.15 are strongly over-represented in CJEU judgments compared to UKSC, in particular *as regards, relating to, concerning, according to, in accordance with* and *in order to.*

Table 1.14 Top complex and marginal prepositions in each corpus

CJEU_CJ	CJEU_GC	UKSC	EU_Reg
in accordance with	*according to*	*as to*	***in accordance with***
in respect of	***relating to***	*in relation to*	*including*
relating to	*as regards*	*subject to*	*excluding*
according to	*concerning*	***in respect of***	***in order to***
in order to	***in order to***	*for the purpose(s) of*	*pursuant to*
for the purpose(s) of	***in accordance with***	***in order to***	*subject to*
concerning	*in the light of*	***in accordance with***	*for the purpose(s) of*
within the meaning of	*on the basis of*	***relating to***	*other than*
as regards	*in the context of*	*out of*	*concerning*
subject to	***in respect of***	*in the case of*	*on the basis of*

Table 1.15 Top complex prepositions according to functions

	CJEU_CJ	CJEU_GC	UKSC	EU_Reg
Inter- and intratextual references				
in accordance with	882	536	252	**1995**
according to	**709**	**871**	125	207
within the meaning of	**586**	292	107	103
on the basis of	**475**	**481**	112	312
pursuant to	384	353	118	**598**
subject to	**555**	230	404	**467**
*in the light of**	**441**	**508**	177	36
Particularisation and anchoring				
in respect of	**746**	418	399	229
relating to	**712**	**833**	214	283
concerning	**599**	**679**	77	383
as regards	**572**	**829**	46	151
as to	390	378	**762**	136
in relation to	246	306	**582**	185
in the context of	236	**427**	146	67
in the case of	161	119	202	**233**
Purpose				
in order to	**691**	**671**	278	**709**
for the purpose(s) of	**641**	409	359	425

5 Conclusions

This study is the first comprehensive attempt to profile the judicial variety of the English Eurolect. It contributes to the growing body of research on Eurolects by confirming the existence of the judicial English Eurolect with its unique hybrid style and providing descriptive corpus data on its hybridisation.

The study has identified the following distinctive genre features shared by CJEU and UKSC judgments: a macrostructure with a relatively similar organisation of informative, argumentative and performative moves and a similar conceptual background formed by top single-word terms and adjectives from functionally similar categories. At the microstructural level, the most salient features of judgments include argumentative patterns, interpersonal metadiscourse (authorial presence markers, epistemic modality, evaluation and stance markers), textual metadiscourse, reporting and performative verbs, Latinisms and framing with complex prepositions. More specifically, compared to regulations, judgments use more verbs, in particular past tense verbs, personal pronouns, determiners, adverbs, simple prepositions and subordinators, as well as fewer nouns, coordinating conjunctions, adjectives and gerunds.

However, the corpus data reveal marked differences between CJEU and UKSC judgments on many levels, pointing to their distinct styles. First, CJEU judgments have a much more rigid, template-like macrostructure with clearly signalled move-step transitions. The structural rigidness accompanied by extensive "cluster citations" "enhances the sensation of 'inevitability' as to the results reached" by the CJEU (Bobek 2015, p. 170), in particular when combined with other microstructural features which foreground impartiality and power. These features include (1) a depersonalised and collegiate authorial presence (*the Court*) with third-person verbs, as compared to the ubiquitous personal pronouns *I* and *we* in UKSC judgments; (2) an over-representation of the strong modal *must* together with a much lower use of other modals, in particular weaker conditional hedging modals (*would, might*); (3) the frequent use of depersonalised argumentative patterns (*it [modal] be [verb], it * apparent, it follows*, and a rare use of hedging verbs *seem* and *appear*); (4) a strong preference for distant determiners (*that, those*), which create an impression of detachment and distance; (5) the formal performative *hereby*; (6) the frequent use of evaluation and stance adverbials, which mainly communicate high-level epistemicity or hedge the content; (7) the more active use of textual metadiscursive devices, which sequence or exemplify arguments (inference, addition, apposition) and a significantly lower use of more confrontational contrast/concession devices and cause markers; (8) significantly more complex and marginal prepositions framing content with inter- and intra-references, purpose and particularisation/anchoring, which (when combined with (9), significantly more numerals) imply increased precision. These features create an impression of impersonal, impartial and rational authority behind the judgment, signal its distance and power, and hence impose judgments and make them less contestable. Other CJEU-specific features include lower lexical richness, ca. 20% fewer verbs (in particular past tense verbs), adverbs and subordinators, which when combined with the frequent use of complex prepositions reduce their dynamicity and increase analytic constructions, which may be a side effect of translation. Certain features, such as fewer verbs, but more phrasal verbs, more complex prepositions and numerals, are shared by all Eurolect corpora, including regulations. Against this background, UKSC judgments seem much more personal, dynamic, conversational, hypothetical and subjective.

Finally, despite these similarities, our data demonstrate that CJEU judgments show a considerable internal variation, which may be attributed to different types of cases dealt with by the GC and the CJ. With respect to a range of features, GC judgments are more similar to UKSC than CJ judgments. In particular, they have an identical average length (CJ judgments being twice as short); use more adverbs and past tense verbs due to an increased reliance on reported speech; *it [verb] [adjective]* argumentative pattern; and fewer gerunds. Additionally, GC judgments have more personal pronouns, subordinators, determiners, more occurrences of the hypothetical modal *would*, significantly more inference and addition markers, and 20% more contrast/concession markers. On the other hand, CJ judgments have more distant determiners, the performative *hereby* and other formal *here-* and *there-* compounds, as well as ca. 25% more complex preposition with inter- and intratextual framing. Thus, further studies into the judicial Eurolect could account for the different types of cases dealt with by the CJ and the GC, separating preliminary rulings, direct actions and appeals at the corpus design phase to better understand their internal variation.

This study lays the groundwork for future research into the judicial variety of the EU English Eurolect, as well as other judicial Eurolects and their linguistic distance to the Member States' national judicial styles, which seems to be a promising area for further work. As a final note, this study raises the question of how such distances impact the reception and interpretation of hybrid judicial texts, as well as attitudes towards CJEU case law.

Acknowledgement

We wish to thank Marcin Wilkowski from the Digital Competence Centre of the University of Warsaw for harvesting files for the CJEU and EU_Reg corpora.

References

Albors-Llorens, A., 2017. Judicial protection before the Court of Justice of the European Union. *In:* C. Barnard & S. Peers, eds., *European Union law*. 2nd ed. Oxford: Oxford University Press.

Baker, M., 1996. Corpus-based translation studies: The challenges that lie ahead. *In:* L.H. Somers, ed., *Terminology, LSP and translation: Studies in language engineering in honour of Juan C. Sager*. Amsterdam: John Benjamins.

Bhatia, V.K., 1993. *Analysing genre – language use in professional settings*. London: Longman.

Biel, Ł., 2014. *Lost in the Eurofog. The textual fit of translated law*. Frankfurt: Peter Lang.

Biel, Ł., 2015. Phraseological profiles of legislative genres: Complex prepositions as a special case of legal phrasemes in EU law and national law. *Fachsprache*, 37, 139–160.

Biel, Ł., 2020. Eurolects and EU legal translation. *In:* M. Ji & S. Laviosa, eds., *The Oxford handbook of translation and social practices*. Oxford: Oxford University Press.

Biel, Ł., Biernacka, A., & Jopek-Bosiacka, A., 2018. Collocations of terms in EU competition law: A corpus analysis of EU English collocations. *In:* S. Marino, L. Biel, M. Bajčić, & V. Sosoni, eds., *Language and law: The role of language and translation in EU competition law*. Cham: Springer International.

Biel, Ł., Koźbiał, D., & Mũller, D., 2021. Corpus data set for the judicial English Eurolect. https://doi.org/10.18150/JOQPG1.

Bobek, M., 2015. The Court of Justice of the European Union. *In:* A. Arnull & D. Chalmers, ed., *The Oxford handbook of European Union law*. Oxford: Oxford University Press.

Derlén, M., 2015. A single text or a single meaning: Multilingual interpretation of EU legislation and CJEU case law in national courts. *In:* S. Šarčević, ed., *Language and culture in EU law. Multidisciplinary perspectives*. Farnham: Ashgate.

Kilgarriff, A., Baisa, V., Bušta, J., Jakubíček, M., Kovář, V., Michelfeit, J., Rychlý, P., & Suchomel, V., 2014. The Sketch Engine: Ten years on. *Lexicography*, 1, 7–36.

Koźbiał, D., 2018. Phraseological profile of judgments: Complex prepositions in EU competition law judgments. *In:* S. Marino, L. Biel, M. Bajčić, & V. Sosoni, eds., *Language and law: The role of language and translation in EU competition law*. Cham: Springer International.

Koźbiał, D., 2020. *The language of EU and Polish judges: Investigating textual fit through corpus methods*. Berlin: Peter Lang.

Kuijper, P.J., 2018. *The Court of Justice of the European Union*. Cambridge: Cambridge University Press.

Mazzi, D., 2007. The construction of argumentation in judicial texts: Combining a genre and a corpus perspective. *Argumentation*, 21, 21–38.

Mcauliffe, K., 2012. Language and law in the European Union: The multilingual jurisprudence of the ECJ. *In:* P.M. Tiersma & L.M. Solan, eds., *The Oxford handbook of language and law*. Oxford: Oxford University Press.

Mcauliffe, K., & Trklja, A., 2019. Formulaic metadiscursive signalling devices in judgments of the Court of Justice of the European Union: A new corpus-based model for studying discourse relations of texts. *International Journal of Speech, Language and the Law*, 26, 21–55.

Modiano, M., 2017. English in a post-Brexit European Union. *World Englishes*, 36, 313–327.

Mori, L., ed., 2018. *Observing Eurolects: Corpus analysis of linguistic variation in EU law*. Amsterdam, Philadelphia: John Benjamins.

Robertson, C., 2015. EU multilingual law: Interfaces of law, language and culture. *In:* S. Šarčević, ed., *Language and culture in EU law. Multidisciplinary perspectives*. Farnham: Ashgate.

Sandrelli, A., 2018. Observing Eurolects: The case of English. *In:* L. Mori, ed., *Observing Eurolects: Corpus analysis of linguistic variation in EU law*. Amsterdam, Philadelphia: John Benjamins.

Šarčević, S., 2010. Creating a Pan-European legal language. *In:* M. Gotti & C. Williams, eds., *Legal discourse across languages and cultures*. Frankfurt: Peter Lang.

Slapper, G., & Kelly, D., 2017. *The English legal system*. London: Routledge.

Szczyrbak, M., 2014. *The realisation of concession in the discourse of judges. A genre perspective*. Kraków: Wydawnictwo Uniwersytetu Jagiellońskiego.

Trklja, A., 2018. A corpus investigation of formulaicity and hybridity in legal language. A case of EU case law texts. *In:* S. Goźdź-Roszkowski & G. Pontrandolfo, eds., *Phraseology in legal and institutional settings. A corpus-based interdisciplinary perspective*. London, New York: Routledge.

Woods, L., Watson, P., & Costa, M., 2017. *Steiner & Woods EU law*. Oxford: Oxford University Press.

Wright, S., 2016. The language of the law in multilingual contexts – unpicking the English of the EU courts' judgments. *Statute Law Review*, 37, 156–163.

2 Evidentiality in US Supreme Court opinions

Focus on passive structures with *say* and *tell*

Magdalena Szczyrbak

1 Introduction

Judicial opinions differ in many ways from other types of discursive or persuasive prose (Garner 1995, p. 621). What differentiates them from other kinds of legal writing is that they conform to judges' "notions of what justice dictates" (Garner 1995, p. 621), or, as some believe, their intuitive sense of what is right or wrong (Frank 1930). This holds true also for opinions issued by the Supreme Court of the United States, addressing some of the most fundamental problems of society and presenting the Court's final determination based on legal reasoning and judicial philosophy. Seen from a linguistic perspective, the Court's argumentation accommodates not only disciplinary values and practices but also the "judge-like" expression of epistemic modality and evidentiality, or, put differently, it is reflective of the judicial "mode of thought" and "mode of knowing" (Chafe 1986).

As demonstrated in earlier studies on stance-related and evaluative strategies inherent in judicial opinion writing, judges prefer certain phraseologies which reveal the beliefs and disciplinary values of the judicial community (Goźdź-Roszkowski and Pontrandolfo 2013). It has also been shown that recurrent semantic sequences provide useful "entry points" into the study of the judicial argumentative style (Goźdź-Roszkowski 2018, p. 158). It has likewise been noted that various aspects of lexical choice, among other linguistic resources, determine the degree of personality or impersonality in the text and "project the epistemological premises of the discipline and the value system that operates within it" (Breeze 2011, p. 94). Specifically, it has been found that certain high-frequency adjectives and adverbs, together with their semantic preferences, embody values held by the legal community and convey attributes and qualities, such as reasonableness, that have particular importance in the field of law (Breeze 2011, p. 94).

With that in mind, this chapter draws attention to reporting verbs which – like stance-denoting nouns, adjectives and adverbs – are the building blocks of judicial narrative and which are central to the construction of judicial voice and authority. While the relevance of reporting verbs to legal writing in general has been recognised in earlier work (Breeze 2017, 2018), the study reported here

DOI: 10.4324/9781003153771-3

focuses on a single genre. Its aim is to trace long-term trends in the use of *it is said (that)* and the present-tense variants of the *BE said to* and *BE told (that)* constructions, and to demonstrate their evidential and discourse-organising role in judicial opinions.

2 Evidentiality and passive structures with reporting verbs

Little need be said about the attention that evidentiality has attracted in recent linguistics scholarship. Some describe it as a grammatical category subsuming a finite number of markers indicating information source in languages in which evidential coding is obligatory (Aikhenvald and Dixon 2014), whereas those studying languages which lack grammaticalised evidentiality adopt a broader view (Mushin 2001) and define it as a functional category which refers to "the perceptual and/or epistemological basis for making a speech act" (Cornillie 2009, p. 45). In the latter approach, evidential marking includes functional, lexical and nonverbal devices as well as implicit references to evidentiality realised in the form of salient discourse patterns (Fetzer 2014, p. 336). It should also be noted that a conceptual differentiation is commonly made between epistemic modality and evidentiality, where "the former refers to a category in which some hypothetical state of affairs is indexed and evaluated", while "the latter refers to a visual, sensorial, hearsay or inferential mode of knowing" (Fetzer 2014, p. 333). Put differently, it is argued that "evidential expressions indicate that there are reasons for the assumption made by the speaker and epistemic expressions evaluate that assumption" (Cornillie 2009, p. 57).

Against this background, passive structures with reporting verbs, representing hearsay evidentiality, have been shown to play a role in marking information source (Noël and van der Auwera 2009; Breeze 2017). The passive voice itself has been the subject of the ongoing debate on the use of impersonal structures in scientific writing which, like judicial discourse, is largely expected to show emotional neutrality, impartiality and objectivity (Gross et al. 2002). The passive construction has also been discussed in studies focusing on the verb phrase and recent language change, pointing to a decline in the use of BE-passives in certain registers (including general prose and academic writing) and the concurrent rise in GET-passives, especially in general prose and fiction (Smith and Leech 2013).

As regards specifically formal written genres, passivised structures with reporting verbs have been noted to redistribute information within the sentence, to mark thematic progression, to avoid repetition and, most importantly, to give credence to the author's claims without specifying their source (Breeze 2017). In agreement with this, the constructions *it is said (that), BE said to* and *BE told (that)* give a semblance of objectivity to the writer's assertions, although they are linked to an unnamed source. Likewise, in its evidential use, *BE expected to* calls in "an unspecified source, from whose implied existence the relative factuality of the statement can be inferred" (Noël 2001, p. 270), and mindsay *BE supposed to*, similarly, helps the author to background the source and convey evaluative overtones.

As to legal texts, they are notorious for heavy reliance on the passive, which, if used injudiciously, results in wordier sentences and "disrupts the ordinary sequence of events in the reader's mind" and also may lead to vagueness and purposeful obfuscation (Garner 1995, p. 643). One could even argue, following Garner (1995, p. 643), that the "otiose" passive "subverts the English-speaking reader's reasonable expectation of a direct actor-action-consequence sequence, unless a departure from that sequence is somehow an improvement". Still, although active structures do animate style, in some contexts the writer may prefer the passive when the actor/agent is immaterial or when the active would shift the emphasis or even change what the writer wishes to say (Garner 2002, pp. 41–42). In line with this, as Alcaraz Varó and Hughes (2002, pp. 19–20) note, the passive construction allows the author to suppress "the identity of the agent responsible for the performance of the act" and to keep "the stress on the action, rule or decision rather than on the personality of the doer". This applies also to passives with reporting verbs which typically allow the writer to de-emphasise information source while implying its existence, thus adding credibility to the writer's claims.

3 Data and method

As noted earlier, this study centres on present-tense passives with *say* and *tell* in judicial opinions issued by the US Supreme Court over the past 200 years (1790s–present). In the study, evidence from the 130-million word SCOTUS corpus (Davies 2017) is used to trace long-term trends in the distribution of reporting structures with the two hearsay verbs and to explore their evidential and other discourse functions. The analysis focuses specifically on *it is said (that)*, *BE said to* (*be said to; is said to; are said to*) and *BE told (that)* (*we are told (that); I am told (that)*) constructions. It explores the frequency and distribution of these forms from a Modern Diachronic Corpus-Assisted Discourse Studies perspective (Partington et al. 2013)[1] and demonstrates their evidential and discourse-organising role. The functional description is based on an examination of a random sample of concordance lines representing different decades (in most cases, at least 50 instances of individual structures were scrutinised, except for several low-frequency items, in the case of which all occurrences were examined). The results of the study are reported in Section 4.

4 Passive structures with *say* and *tell* in SCOTUS

As the decade-by-decade analysis of the SCOTUS data reveals, passive structures with *say* and *tell* were employed with varying frequencies, and they took different diachronic paths between the end of the 18th century and the beginning of the

1 The raw data have been normalised to reflect frequencies per million words (pmw).

21st century (Figures 2.1–2.3). Of all the realisations under study, *be said to* and *it is said that* proved most common, with *is said to* and parenthetical *it is said* taking the third and fourth positions, respectively. In the following sections, I discuss the most noteworthy trends and, where relevant, I provide contexts of use of individual structures to explain their evidential and discourse-organising role. The examples represent 20th- and 21st-century opinions, except for those illustrating structures which were attested in earlier writing but which have fallen out of use.

4.1 *It is said (that)*

The first observation about *it is said* is that even though it has the greatest overall frequency in the corpus, currently the structure is no longer in fashion. Figure 2.1 confirms the long-term decline of *it is said*, with an unexpected peak in the 1910s when the structure rose to a frequency of around 140 occurrences pmw, only to dwindle away over the following decades. As to the individual realisations, *it is said* followed by a *that*-complementiser proved most common, and its long-term trend generally mirrored that of *it is said*, similarly to parenthetical *it is said* (which was however much less frequent, with its greatest normed frequency in the region of 40 occurrences pmw at the turn of the 19th century). As to *it is said by*, it was attested chiefly in the 19th century, when its normed frequency did not exceed 10 occurrences pmw, and so even then its occurrence was marginal. An interesting discovery was that of *it is said* with a *that*-complementiser preceded by a comma, which was in use only from the end of the 18th century to the mid-19th century. In brief, what Figure 2.1 demonstrates is the relative popularity of *it is said* in the 19th century and its dramatic decline in the 20th century.

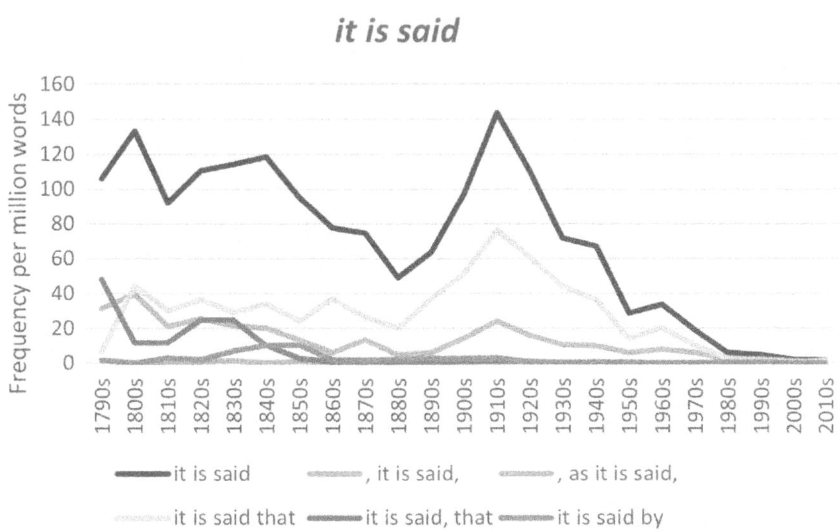

Figure 2.1 Frequency of variants of *it is said (that)* in SCOTUS

To demonstrate the effect that the use of *it is said* has in discourse, I present several examples which aptly illustrate the way in which the phrase was used in context. Given the limits set to this chapter, only selected excerpts can be presented.[2]

To begin with, (1) throws more light on the text-structuring role of *it is said that*. Here the phrase is used in a summary of third-party argumentation and to mark progression in the text. We can also see that although *it is said that* – which focuses on the message rather than the sayer – seems to call in an unspecified source of information: it is followed by a detailed list of legal authorities. Thus, rather than convey information from an unnamed source, *it is said that* introduces claims whose origin may be precisely located. The references are provided within the sentence (as in *it is said on the part of the government* or *In Dealy v. United States it is said that . . . . [225 U.S. 347, 359]*), or immediately following the sentence, as in (1), or even much earlier in the same stretch of text (not shown here).

(1) **It is said that** members of the public may lawfully proceed along a walkway leading to the front door of a house because custom grants them a license to do so. *Breard v. Alexandria*, **341 U.S. 622, 626 (1951);** *Lakin v. Ames*, **64 Mass. 198, 220 (1852); J. Bishop, Commentaries on the Non-Contract Law § 823, p. 378 (1889).** [2013]

In a similar vein, parenthetical *it is said* in (2) operates as a metacomment paraphrasable as "it is argued" or "as X argues". Its goal is to structure the account of third-party argumentation and to avoid repetition of other reporting structures (e.g. *as the argument continues; it is contended; it is further argued*). Again, although *it is said* is a hearsay evidential, when used in the opinions, it co-occurs with identifiable sources.

(2) **EPA encourages us to view** the situation not as a taking of Monsanto's property interest in the trade secrets, but as a "pre-emption" of whatever property rights Monsanto may have had in those trade secrets. Brief for Appellant 27–28. **The agency argues that** the proper functioning of the comprehensive FIFRA registration scheme depends upon its uniform application to all data. Thus, **it is said,** the Supremacy Clause dictates that the scheme not vary depending on the property law of the State in which the submitter is located. Id., at 28. This argument proves too much. [1984]

2 The examples shown in the qualitative analysis have been selected from a representative sample of concordances. In the case of high-frequency items, 50 concordances were analysed for each item, while in the case of low-frequency items (e.g. *I am told* having only 12 occurrences), all concordances were studied.

Though marginal in terms of frequency (see Figure 2.1), two more realisations warrant a mention here. The first one is shown in (3), where a comma is used before a *that*-clause (as in *it is said, that* and *the adverse counsel admits, that*). Such uses were identified only in the opinions issued in the 18th century and the first half of the 19th century. Later occurrences were also attested, but they were either historical quotations or instantiations of the demonstrative *that*, and not a *that*-clause (as in *because, it is said, that is an issue of contract interpretation*).

(3) **In Carthew 26, it is said, that** bills of exchange are attachable, according to the custom of London; and **the adverse counsel admits, that** the note was attachable, while it remained in the hands of Duer. [1799]

Finally, (4) illustrates the use of *it is said by*, which was found mainly in the first half of the 19th century in the pattern *it is said by [NAME] in [SOURCE] (that) [QUOTE]*. An interesting discovery was that while in 19th-century opinions *it is said by* was followed either by the name of an individual (e.g. *Mr. Starkie*, *Mr. Justice Miller*) or a designation of their role in the proceedings (e.g. *counsel/court/solicitor/appellee*), those issued in the first decade of the 20th century mentioned the cited authorities' institutional roles, and not their names.

(4) **It is said by Mr. Justice Strong in** *Braun v. Sauerwein,* **10 Wall. 218:** "It seems therefore to be established that the running of a statute of limitation may be suspended by causes not mentioned in the statute itself". [1889]

At this point, one more observation is in place about the data analysed but not presented here, and it concerns the most common collocates of *it is said (that)*. As the corpus queries revealed, contrastive *but* was the most frequent L5-L1 collocate of both *it is said* and *it is said that* (745 occurrences in each query; as in *But it is said that there is no proof that any such purchase was ever made*), whereas *however* turned out to be the most frequent R1-R5 collocate of *it is said* (250 occurrences; as in *It is said, however, that this case is controlled by the ruling*). Both *but* and *however* are argumentative devices (cf. Fetzer 2014), whose co-occurrence with *it is said (that)* provides more support for the claim that in the data at hand, this reporting structure is used to organise arguments and to signal text relations, and not only to report hearsay.

Summing up, from all the examples scrutinised for the purpose of the qualitative description, it is clear that the main role of *it is said (that)* in the opinions is to organise discourse, that is, to mark argumentative progression and to enhance cohesion as well as to avoid repetition of other reporting verbs.

4.2 *BE said to*

Regarding the *BE said to* construction, its individual realisations took different diachronic paths. For reasons of clarity, in Figure 2.2, only the three most

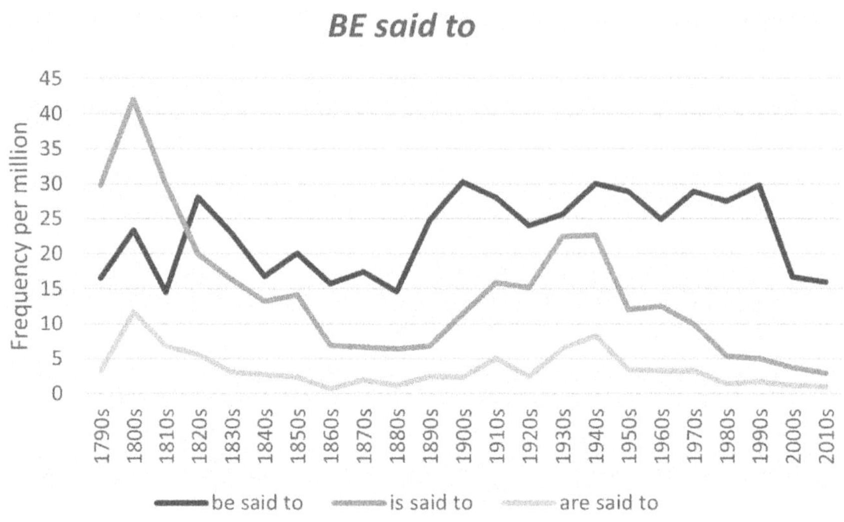

Figure 2.2 Frequency of *BE said to* in SCOTUS

frequent realisations are shown: *be said to, is said to* and *are said to.* As can be seen, *be said to* suffered moderate fluctuations, with a noteworthy rise from the 1880s onwards and a sharp decrease at the beginning of the 21st century. On the other hand, *is said to* was subject to the most dramatic development: it started with a peak at the turn of the 19th century (and a frequency of about 40 occurrences pmw) and then experienced a steady decrease which continued until the second half of the 19th century, when it took off, rising to the level of about 20 occurrences pmw in the third and fourth decades of the 20th century. Subsequently, from the 1950s onwards, it continued to decline. In contrast to that, *are said to* showed a low and fairly regular frequency over the whole studied period.

Unlike *it is said* discussed earlier – used to structure discourse and to attribute arguments without any epistemic overtones – *be said to* co-occurred most frequently with the modals *can* and *may* as well as negation, and it did convey the writer's subjective, inference-based assessments. For reasons of space, only one instance is provided here, but it suffices to illustrate the manner in which *can/ may be said to* was used alongside other markers of subjectivity. In (5), we can find such expressions as *seems intrinsically burdensome* and *certainly cannot be said to be unreasonable.* Also noteworthy is the co-occurrence of *fairly* and *be said to* (as in *may fairly be said to*), which is somewhat surprising given that it indexes more subjectivity than do, for example, *reasonably* and *properly*, typically linked to logical reasoning and the judicial mode of thought (cf. Breeze 2011), but not found to be significantly correlated with *be said to.* In sum, as the evidence shows, *can/may be said to* is deployed to convey epistemic meaning, signalling the arguer's subjective assessment rather than used to mark evidentiality based on external sources.

(5) Neither requirement **seems intrinsically burdensome**; and they **certainly cannot be said to be unreasonable** as applied to appellant, who included in his advertisement no information whatsoever regarding costs and fee rates. [1985]

Finally, the discourse role of *is said to*, differing from that of *be said to*, also deserves a mention. Similarly to *it is said*, the phrase *is said to* denotes reliance on hearsay, that is, it implicitly indicates the source which is outside the self, but which is not explicitly named. Structures of this kind (*is/are said to; is/are thought to*) may in fact be seen as standing "mid-way between straightforward attributions and averrals" (Breeze 2017, p. 298).[3] This is illustrated in (6), where the arguer refers to what trademark law stipulates, even though the latter is not explicitly evoked. The data also provide evidence of the structure *is said to* being followed by a past participle (as in *is said to have "aged out"... under § 1153(d)*), where the source of the claim is explicitly mentioned.[4] Thus, again, unlike less formal contexts, in judicial opinions, evidentials with *say* report information which can be unambiguously linked to the source and, as such, they are not associated with unattributed hearsay.

(6) Rights in a trademark are determined by the date of the mark's first use in commerce. The party who first uses a mark in commerce **is said to have priority** over other users. [2015]

To recapitulate this portion of the analysis, some of the realisations of the *BE said to* construction convey epistemic meaning based on the writer's inference (*can/may be said to*), whereas others (*is/are said to (have)*) serve as evidentials reporting information without any epistemic overtones.

4.3 BE told (that)

While in the previous sections the focus was on passive structures with *say*, the following part centres on present-tense passives with *tell* anchored to first-person subjects. Since *I am told* proved marginal (12 occurrences in total),

3 Attribution refers to a piece of language which is presented "as deriving from someone other than the writer", whereas in the case of averral, the writer speaks himself or herself (Hunston 2000, p. 178; drawing on Sinclair 1988). At the same time, as Hunston (2000, p. 179) notes, "every attribution is also averred" (i.e. the writer is the ultimate source responsible for the attributed information).

4 The SCOTUS data corroborate the low frequency of *is said to have* + PP and its decline over time identified in other corpora (cf. Breeze 2017).

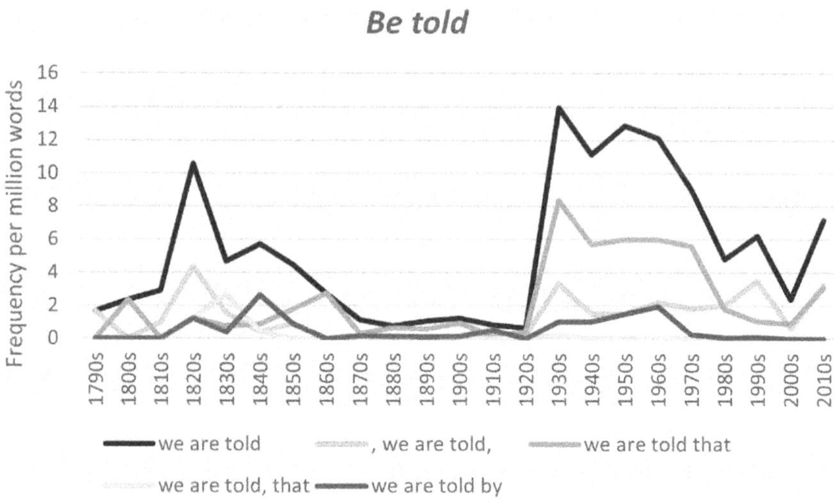

Figure 2.3 Frequency of *we are told (that)* in SCOTUS

Figure 2.3 shows trends only for variants of *we are told (that)*. The first thing to note is the much lower frequency of *we are told (that)* as compared with those of *it is said (that)* (Figure 2.1) and *BE said to* (Figure 2.2), and its rather erratic development over time. The phrase seemed to enjoy some popularity in the 1820s but declined afterwards, and its level remained low until the 1920s when *we are told* unexpectedly increased. In the 20th century, its use was much more frequent than in the 19th century; however, around the 1960s the phrase embarked on a steady decline, only to rise slightly again at the turn of the 21st century. As for the variants, *we are told that* was generally favoured over parenthetical *we are told*, except for the first decades of the 19th century when parenthetical *we are told* and *we are told, that* (cf. *it is said, that* in Figure 2.1) were more common. All in all, the most visible feature in Figure 2.3 is the rising popularity of *we are told* in the 20th century.

When examined more closely, concordance lines with *we are told (that)* revealed certain regularities. By analogy to *it is said that*, the structure *we are told that*, similarly, focused on the message rather than the sayer and, despite being associated with unattributed hearsay in non-legal contexts, in the data at hand, it was followed by references (as in [7]).

(7) The Court justifies its result today with several additional reasons – or, rather, sentiments in reasons' clothing. **We are told, ante, at 126–127, that** "the Great Writ entails significant [456 U.S. 107, 147] costs. [1982]

On the other hand, parenthetical *we are told* seemed to perform the same text-organising function as parenthetical *it is said* (cf. the excerpts shown in [7] and

[2]). Interestingly, parenthetical *it is said* started to decline roughly at the time (in the 1910s) when parenthetical *we are told* began to rise (in the 1920s). As the examples suggest, both structures are used to organise discourse, to ensure cohesion and to avoid repetition of other reporting verbs (e.g. *stress* and *conclude* in [8]), and they are both associated with an identifiable source.

(8) **It[5] stresses that** the subject of the expert's testimony must be "scientific . . . knowledge," and points out that "scientific" "implies a grounding in the methods and procedures of science" and that the word "knowledge" [509 U.S. 579, 3] "connotes more than subjective belief or unsupported speculation." **Ante, at 9. From this it concludes that** "scientific knowledge" must be "derived by the scientific method." **Ante, at 10.** Proposed testimony, **we are told,** must be supported by "appropriate validation." **Ante, at 10.** [1993]

Another thing that emerged during the analysis was that *we are told by* was followed either by names of individuals, as in (9), in the few examples identified in the first half of the 19th century, or by references to various types of authorities, as in *we are told by the Attorney General/counsel/the state/the dissent/the scientists/the IRS* – noted in more recent opinions (cf. the trend observed for *it is said by*).

(9) **We are told by Lord Coke, Co. Lit. 352, that** recitals are reciprocal. Such too is the law of New York. Lansing vs. Montgomery, 2 Johns. Rep. 382. . . . [1830]

Overall, as the study reveals, the distribution and the functions of *we are told (that)* resemble those of *it is said (that)*. Both constructions are used to introduce third-party arguments, to avoid repetition and to structure judicial opinions.

As mentioned earlier, with only 12 attestations, *I am told* was marginal in the data and so there are too few examples for one to notice any clear trends. However, one excerpt is provided in (10) to illustrate the context of represented speech. What can be seen here is that *I am told* does not belong to the judicial register but rather to spoken genres which are embedded in judicial opinions, as is the case with the letter sent by a defendant from prison and included in the court's argumentation in (10).

(10) "**I am told**, sir, there is a United States attorney in Vermont whose duty it is to investigate such matters, and I respectfully ask, sir, if the matter is within your jurisdiction, that he be directed to bring me to trial, and if the government is not ready for trial, I can find any number of respectable people who will become my bail until such time as the government is ready to try me". [1878]

5 The Court.

5 Discussion and conclusions

As the qualitative part of the analysis has revealed, passives with *say* and *tell* organise judicial argumentation in a patterned manner. They serve both as hearsay evidentials and discourse-organising devices, and in some cases (*can/may be said to*) they convey epistemic assessments, too.

In terms of general frequency, the SCOTUS data indicate that in the period under study the structures *can/may be said to* and *it is said (that)* were the most preferred ones, while *is/are said to* and *we are told (that)* were much less common, with *I am told (that)* having a marginal presence in third-party discourse quoted in the opinions. A more detailed examination of trends noted for individual verb patterns and decades shows that there was significant variation in frequency, with some structures gaining prominence (e.g. *we are told (that)*) and others steadily declining (e.g. *it is said (that); . . . , it is said, . . . ; is said to*).

In terms of functional flexibility, and in agreement with earlier studies, the SCOTUS data suggest that passive structures with *say* and *tell* – apart from their primary role of calling in unnamed sources and providing a semblance of factuality and objectivity – help opinion writers to repackage information within the sentence and to establish structural links, thus enhancing cohesion and ensuring smooth thematic progression. Importantly, contrary to non-judicial communication, in the opinions, evidentials like *it is said, is said to* or *we are told* are linked to references, and consequently the sources can be easily traced. This reflects the nature of judicial discourse and the weight that the judicial discipline attaches to factuality and rationality, leaving no room for unreliable or unattributed hearsay. At the same time, *can/may be said to* serves to convey subjective assessments relying on the justices' inferences and not on external sources, which means that this structure is associated with epistemicity, rather than evidentiality.[6]

On the other hand, the move away from citations of individuals in favour of references to institutional authorities might be indicative of a shift towards greater objectivity. Concurrently, the rise of *we are told* in the 20th century may be seen as marking a shift towards a less detached and more personal style of writing foregrounding the Court's perspective. This seems plausible given the continual reduction in the frequency of impersonal passives.[7] Obviously, it should be borne in mind that the findings presented in the current study reflect the use of two reporting verbs only, and so they cannot account fully for how the Court exploits other reporting verbs to structure its argumentation. To reach this goal, one would have to examine a wider range of hearsay (e.g. *argue, report, contend*) and mindsay (e.g. *think, believe, expect*) verbs as well as

6 It should be reiterated, though, that – as noted by Fetzer (2014, p. 337) – the expression of evidentiality and epistemicity in English is thought to be of a scalar nature.

7 However, it may not be ruled out that the surge in the use of *we are told* may be attributable to the justices' idiosyncratic styles of writing.

compare the distribution of active and passive structures (e.g. *(as) we say/have said, the Court say/says, the Court has said/have said* vs *it is said, we are told*) with a view to explaining their role in the positioning of the Court's reasoning against third-party arguments.

What may be observed at this point, however, is that the decrease in the frequency of agentless passive structures (*it is said (that)*) runs parallel to the increase in the frequency of hearsay forms anchored to the animate subject (*we are told (that)*). This, in turn, agrees with diachronic developments noted in other types of discourse which are becoming more author-centred, including general written English (Hou and Smith 2018) and modern scientific writing (Leong 2020). That said, a caveat needs to be made that in the current study no differentiation was made into majority opinions and separate opinions. These, as earlier research indicates, show marked differences with regard to stance-related and evaluative patterns (Szczyrbak 2014), and so a fine-grained analysis might reveal different trends in the use of the focal structures in the opinions representing the collective voice of the Court and those issued by dissenting or concurring justices.

Still, irrespective of the above limitation, it may be posited that the patterns with the passive of the reporting verbs *say* and *tell* point to the discipline- and genre-specific construction of stance and authority reflecting the judicial mode of thought and mode of knowing, and the way in which judges "put the world into words", making visible concepts such as objectivity, factuality and rationality.

References

Aikhenvald, A.Y., & Dixon, R.M.W., 2014. *The grammar of knowledge. A cross-linguistic typology*. Oxford: Oxford University Press.

Alcaraz Varó, E., & Hughes, B., 2002. *Legal translation explained*. Manchester: St. Jerome.

Breeze, R., 2011. Disciplinary values in legal discourse: A corpus study. *Ibérica*, 21, 93–116.

Breeze, R., 2017. Exploring evidential uses of the passive or reporting verbs through corpus analysis. *In:* J.I. Marín Arrese, G. Haßler & M. Carretero, eds., *Evidentiality revisited: Cognitive grammar, functional and discourse-pragmatic perspectives*. Amsterdam: John Benjamins, 297–313.

Breeze, R., 2018. Giving voice to the law: Speech act verbs in legal academic writing. *In:* S. Goźdź-Roszkowski & G. Pontrandolfo, eds., *Phraseology in legal and institutional settings. A corpus-based interdisciplinary perspective*. London: Routledge, 221–239.

Chafe, W., 1986. Evidentiality in English conversation and academic writing. *In:* W. Chafe & J. Nichols, eds., *Evidentiality: The linguistic coding of epistemology*. Norwood, NJ: Ablex, 261–272.

Cornillie, B., 2009. Evidentiality and epistemic modality. On the close relationship between two different categories. *Functions of Language*, 16(1), 44–62.

Davies, M., 2017. *The corpus of US Supreme Court opinions (SCOTUS): 130 million words, 1790s–present.* [online] Available from: www.english-corpora.org/scotus/.

Fetzer, A., 2014. Foregrounding evidentiality in (English) academic discourse: Patterned co-occurrences of the sensory perception verbs *seem* and *appear*. *Intercultural Pragmatics*, 11(3), 333–355.

Frank, J., 1930. *Law and the modern mind.* New York: Brentano's Inc.

Garner, B.A., 1995. *A dictionary of modern legal usage.* 2nd ed. Oxford: Oxford University Press.

Garner, B.A., 2002. *The elements of legal style.* 2nd ed. Oxford: Oxford University Press.

Goźdź-Roszkowski, S., 2018. Facts in law: A comparative study of *fact that* and its phraseologies in American and Polish judicial discourse. *In:* S. Goźdź-Roszkowski & G. Pontrandolfo, eds., *Phraseology in legal and institutional settings. A corpus-based interdisciplinary perspective.* London: Routledge, 143–159.

Goźdź-Roszkowski, S., & Pontrandolfo, G., 2013. Evaluative patterns in judicial discourse: A corpus-based phraseological perspective on American and Italian criminal judgments. *International Journal of Law, Language and Discourse*, 13(2), 9–69.

Gross, A.G., Harmon, J.E., & Reidy, M., 2002. *Communicating science: The scientific article from the seventeenth century to the present.* Oxford: Oxford University Press.

Hou, L., & Smith, D.A., 2018. Modeling the decline in English passivization. *Proceedings of the Society for Computation in Linguistics (Scil)*, 34–43.

Hunston, S., 2000. Evaluation and the planes of discourse: Status and value in persuasive texts. *In:* S. Hunston & G. Thompson, eds., *Evaluation in text: Authorial stance and the construction of discourse.* Oxford: Oxford University Press, 176–207.

Leong, A.P., 2020. The passive voice in scientific writing through the ages: A diachronic study. *Text & Talk*, 40(4), 467–489.

Mushin, I., 2001. *Evidentiality and epistemological stance. Narrative retelling.* Amsterdam: John Benjamins.

Noël, D., 2001. The passive matrices of English infinitival complement clauses. Evidentials on the road to auxiliarihood? *Studies in Language*, 25(2), 255–296.

Noël, D., & van der Auwera, J., 2009. Revisiting *be supposed to* from a diachronic constructional perspective. *English Studies*, 90, 599–623.

Partington, A., Duguid, A., & Taylor, C., 2013. *Patterns and meanings in discourse. Theory and practice in corpus-assisted discourse studies (CADS).* Amsterdam: John Benjamins.

Sinclair, I., 1988. Mirror for a text. *Journal of English and Foreign Languages*, 1, 15–44.

Smith, N., & Leech, G., 2013. Verb structures in twentieth-century British English. *In:* B. Aarts, J. Close, G. Leech & S. Wallis, eds. *The verb phrase in English. Investigating recent language change with corpora.* Cambridge: Cambridge University Press, 68–98.

Szczyrbak, M., 2014. Stancetaking strategies in judicial discourse: Evidence from US Supreme Court opinions. *Studia Linguistica Universitatis Iagellonicae Cracoviensis*, 131, 91–120.

3 Standardisation in the judicial discourse

The case of the evolution of the French *Arrêts de la Cour de Cassation* and the use of forms in European procedural law

Margarete Flöter-Durr and Paulina Nowak-Korcz
Translated from French by Claudia Schnier

1 Introduction

Standardisation in judicial discourse can be analysed on two levels, linguistic and legal, with regard to concepts pertaining both to positive law and to procedural law. In reality, these two levels are not distinct but entwined, since law as a discursive phenomenon is part of the language (Galdia 2017). The approach on such a twofold level reflects the two dimensions of standardisation: the speciality, which is systematically linked to a discipline of reference, on the one hand, and, on the other hand, the linguistic and discursive dimension which can be assessed by analysing texts (Gautier 2019).

In order to assess the place and role of standardisation in the judicial discourse in a context of increasing complexity of the discourse itself and its subject matter, it is important to first focus on the notion of *standard*. Etymologically, the term refers, on the one hand, to the notion of a rule or criteria and, on the other hand, to the notion of a standard (Cassin 2019, p. 1212). Standard was expressly defined by Hume in his essay *Of the Standard of Taste* (2019, p. 27) as a general rule derived from empirical observation and not fixed a priori (Babich 2019, p. 78). In this sense, the term "standard" determines how to act in order to carry out an activity and serves as a rule of conduct (Babich 2019, p. 82). A rule established in such a way enables one to assess human conduct and to measure any deviation from what is considered normal or acceptable. Standard as an assessment criterion can therefore be used as a unit of measurement and, as a result, has a normative value (Babich 2019, p. 87). In the common use of language, a standard, in the sense of a norm, refers to a pre-constituted model, type or manufacturing standard (Bernard 2010, p. 8). This notion of model underlies both the linguistic notion of standard (Milroy 2001, p. 133) and the legal notion of standard (Bernard 2010, p. 8). However, if the linguistic notion of standard

DOI: 10.4324/9781003153771-4

implies uniformity and invariance and therefore leads to a certain fixation of language (process that leads to fixed expressions), the legal notion of standard leads, on the contrary, to more flexibility, because it allows the individualisation of solutions (Bernard 2010, p. 9). In this chapter, we will take a look at the linguistic standardisation within the judicial discourse, on the one hand, and on the other hand, at the legal standardisation and the difficulties it raises in linguistic terms. Methodologically, this chapter is firmly placed within the French doctrine. We will therefore apply a method of analysis typically used within the French school of discourse analysis (with particular reference to Krieg-Planque 2009) and adopt an approach which has been developed within the French doctrine and which refers to the notion of standard as a legal formulation technique. Consequently, this methodological approach is also reflected in the references mentioned in this chapter and explains our bibliographic choice. Ultimately, it is another way of understanding the phenomenon of standardisation in language in general and the repetitive and somewhat fixed ("formulaic") nature of legal language (Trklja and McAuliffe 2019, p. 22).

2 Standardisation from the linguistic point of view

From the linguistic perspective, standardisation is a familiar concept in sociolinguistics (Labov 1972; Milroy 1987). It consists in postulating the existence of a standardised form of language (Milroy 2001, p. 133). The essential characteristic of linguistic standardisation is therefore its uniformity. Aiming at uniformity, standardisation is an exclusionary process because it tends to eliminate any other variation, considered unacceptable, and it imposes only one form as acceptable. Linguistic standardisation leads to the emergence of a norm or standard in the sense of "a variety propagated by education, codified in books and favoured by non-regional speakers in a society" (Hickey 2012). Standardisation is a way to reduce complexity and avoid vagueness and ambiguity. In fact, its significance is growing not only in the technical field but also in the legal field, where clarity remains a supreme ideal. But just like clarity, uniformity remains an ideal that cannot be fully achieved in practice (Milroy 2001, p. 134), since, as Milroy and Milroy point out, "the only fully standardised language is a dead language" (1985).

2.1 Standardisation in the judicial discourse of the Cour de Cassation

In judicial discourse, linguistic standardisation can be observed in the use of specific expressions and phrases that give a judicial decision its unique structure and style. As far as the French judicial discourse is concerned, this phenomenon will be illustrated by analysing the decisions of the *Cour de Cassation* and their evolution after the reform in October 2019, which changed the rules for drafting such decisions. Methodologically, in order to assess the phenomenon of standardisation, it seems appropriate to use the notion of formula proposed by Krieg-Planque (2009) in the discourse analysis. Indeed, this notion constitutes an interesting tool for analysing the different forms of fixation within the judicial discourse stylistically, terminologically and syntactically. This methodological framework will be used to determine in what way the focus on formulas allows a better understanding of the judicial discourse and in what way typical linguistic expressions of such discourse can be considered as formulas.

Generally speaking, the term "formula" is defined as "a set of formulations which, because of their use at a given time and in a given public space, crystallise political and social issues that these expressions in turn help to construct" (Krieg-Planque 2009, p. 7). A formula is defined by four main characteristics: its fixation, its discursive character, its role as a social referent and its polemical nature. With regards to fixation, Krieg-Planque distinguishes the formula from other types of formulations, in so far as it is expressed using "a meaningful form of relative stability" (Krieg-Planque 2009, p. 63). Fixation requires formulas which are concise and anchored in the specific context they appear in. The use of formulas is therefore systematically linked to specific corpora and concrete situations (Krieg-Planque 2012, p. 99). In this sense, the formula is tied to the context in which it is used (Simon 2016). Formulas can take various linguistic forms. They can be a simple lexical unit (e.g. "globalisation"), a complex lexical unit, a lexical-syntactic unit[1] or an autonomous sequence[2] (Krieg-Planque 2009, p. 64). The discursive character of formulas stems from the specific situations in which they are commonly used (Krieg-Planque 2009, p. 84). The formula being a social referent "displays its dominant character, at a given time and in a given socio-political space" (Krieg-Planque 2009, p. 93). This is why the formula is "a sign that evokes something for everyone at a given moment" (Krieg-Planque 2009, p. 97). Finally, the polemical nature of the formula is determined by the morphology and syntax as well as the lexical components of the formula on the one hand, and, on the other hand, by the specific situation in which the formulas are commonly used (Krieg-Planque 2009, p. 109).

In its legal sense, the formula is defined as "a model of how a statement has to be formulated. Only respecting its standardised form can guarantee its validity" (2009, p. 114). Defining the formula as a model brings this notion closer to the notion of standard as defined by Hume (i.e. a rule or standard to be followed). Therefore, the notion of formula is an interesting approach regarding the analysis of the judicial discourse because it allows the assessment of some of its specific aspects, in particular the linguistic fixation (process leading to fixed expressions)

1 Lexical-syntactic unit refers to the co-presence of one or more lexical elements and a particular syntactic operation, such as coordination, complementation or negation.

2 According to Krieg-Planque, slogans such as "La France aux Français", short sentences such as "La France ne peut accueillir toute la misère du monde" (France cannot take in all the misery of the world) or any other sentence anchored in the collective memory, such as "Plus jamais ça!" (Never again!; 2009, p. 66).

and the model-like character of specific formulations. In view of the four characteristics of the formula mentioned above, it seems to us that formula-like expressions which are frequently used in the judicial discourse, such as *par ces motifs* (*on these grounds*), *sur ce, la Cour* (*thereupon, the Court*) or *attendu que* (*given that*), can be described as having a fixed and discursive character and as being a social referent as defined above.[3] On the other hand, they are devoid of any polemical character. It is true that the characterisation of these expressions as formulas is only partially correct; their discursive use, however, responds to a strong need to structure the judicial discourse.

In the decisions of the *Cour de Cassation* a number of linguistic expressions are used that can be described as formulas. These decisions reflect a discourse which can be considered as an archetype of the discourse delivered by a judge when applying the law: a discourse taking the form of a judgment. Indeed, the judicial decision represents a specific type of discourse that is catalogued, validated and standardised and, as such, should be distinguished from all the other "thousand discourses in the judicial world" (Cornu 2005, p. 333). With regard to the structure of the linguistic communication underlying the judgment, it should be noted that its sole official and formal issuer is the judge. In this respect, it seems important to point out that the judge's decision is a mixed discourse that incorporates many other discourses. In the decision, other discourses are recounted, summarised and analysed before rendering judgment (Cornu 2005, p. 333). Thus, in formal terms, the judgment refers to other discourses either by way of quotation, by using another modality of the verb or by way of linguistic borrowing. This is why the decisions of the *Cour de Cassation* are characterised by "a typical reproduction of the jurisdictional discourse" (Cornu 2005, p. 354). This discourse is therefore, by its very nature, "intrinsically dialogical" (Sobieszewska 2014, p. 293).

Since the establishment of the *Cour de Cassation* in 1790, the technique of writing judgments has been refined to a sophisticated style characterised by conciseness, terminological precision and logical rigour (Weber 2009). According to the standards derived from the case law of the *Cour de Cassation*, the grounds for a decision must "exist, be real, relevant, sufficient, devoid of any ambiguous or hypothetical character and must consider the arguments brought forward" (Castillo-Wyszogrodzka 2014, p. 4). The rigid structure of the judgments is determined by the syllogism and the conciseness with which the requirement of being succinct is met. It should be noted that such a rigid structure "establishes a discursive routine" (Sobieszewska 2014, p. 2909) and imposes the use of stylistic rules, precise formulas and typical structures in order to achieve the constitutionally valid objective of clarity. However, it must be noted that the achievement of this objective depends on the knowledge available to the reader of the judgment.

3 The translation of the French expressions is a literal translation and is provided for informational purposes only to readers who do not speak French. As these expressions stem from the French legal system, no comparison can be made with similar English legal expressions.

Indeed, it turns out that, in the end, a judgment is often difficult for a layperson to understand. This is why the judgments and grounds of judgment have been the subject of much criticism because of their monophrastic structure (consisting of a single phrase) and their very laconic, even cryptic style. Traditionally, form and style of the grounds of judgment reflected the role given to the French judge, who was merely conceived as the "mouth of the law". Thus, the intention behind drafting the grounds of judgment was always to eliminate any element of subjectivity, to give the impression of a unitary and coherent decision and to base a decision exclusively on the very letter of the law without taking into account a wider context (e.g. socio-economic considerations; Castillo-Wyszogrodzka 2014, p. 2). In 2019, a new method of drafting judgments was introduced, which established new objectives for the grounds of judgment rendered by the *Cour de Cassation* in order to make them more comprehensible and more accessible to the defendant. New objectives were included, such as justifying the decision, convincing the reader and gaining their support, or enabling the judge to participate in national and international debates on important legal issues.

In order to achieve these objectives, various proposals have been made regarding the drafting of the grounds of judgment in order to improve the structure and form of the judgment regarding the language and, above all, syntax and style. In particular, it was recommended (a) to refrain from starting the legal opinion with *attendu que* (*given that*) and from writing the judgment in a single sentence; (b) to favour a direct style with logical connectors to ensure greater readability; (c) to introduce a standardised structure with paragraph numbering and insertion of subheadings to make the presentation of the judgment clearer for the reader; (d) to quote relevant case law; (e) to explain the reasons why the Court interprets or applies the rule of law in a particular sense; and (f) to give explicit reasons for reversals of case law (cf. Lacabarats 2018, p. 72; Lacabarats 2016, p. 2).

All these changes contribute not only to modifying the structure and the discursive and stylistic characteristics of the judgments, but also to changing the conception of the judge's role and their rendering of judgments. At present, editorial practices reflecting the traditional conception of the role of a judge are officially abandoned. In order to justify their decisions to the defendant in a clear and comprehensible manner, judges now seek to use all the lexical and stylistic means at their disposal, including the use of formulas. Indeed, as Sourioux and Lerat (1975, pp. 69–70) observe, "the law is expressed in formulas, the decisions of the judge are formulas and professionals drafting legal instruments instinctively feel the need . . . to stipulate rules regarding the form and to use formulas".

The decisions of the *Cour de Cassation* provide a fertile ground for linguistic examinations. As the decisions have evolved over time, we can observe that certain linguistic expressions used in the decisions of the *Cour de Cassation* serve as formulas. Stylistically, the standardisation of such judgments can be observed in the implementation of certain drafting principles, such as the principles regarding the justification of judgments or in the implementation of stylistic rules or in the use of specific fixed expressions. Indeed, the linguistic expressions used in judgments are characterised by the use of formulas, such as simple or complex fixed phrases (e.g. *Faits et procédure*) or autonomous sequences (*Par ces motifs* or *Le tribunal statuant*).[4] Moreover, formulas are not "resistant to change" (Sourioux and Lerat 1975, p. 70), since it is possible to replace them with other formulas or to abandon them altogether (e.g. the formula *attendu que* was discarded after the reform). This demonstrates that a formula can only be used within its limited scope. It fully depends on the discourse in which it is used. Indeed, the linguistic markers used in the form of stereotyped formulas can only be observed in decisions of the *Cour de Cassation*. Regarding their discursive functioning, these stereotyped formulas are part of a multifaceted discourse, and their repeated use leads to changes in style (Cornu 2005, p. 350).

The decisions of the *Cour de Cassation* have been frequently criticised because of the cryptic style in which the grounds of judgment are written. This is due to the use of pre-written formulas and standardised types of grounds justifying the decision. The recent reform of the drafting rules regarding the judgments of the highest French court responds, on the one hand, to this criticism; on the other hand, it helps French judges to better justify their legal decisions (Chassagnard-Pinet et al. 2015, p. 229), which is all the more important when taking into account the impact globalisation has on law, the standardisation of EU law and its jurisprudence. Indeed, national judges are automatically exposed to the influence of decisions rendered by the courts of other Member States. Likewise, European courts are equally interested in the decisions rendered by national supreme courts. Such mutual influence encourages the development of a common standard which, as an "instrument of dialogue between judges" (Malhière 2013, p. 12), enables the harmonisation of drafting principles for decisions and creates a standard within the discourse of judges.

3 Standardisation at the legal level

To begin with, it should be noted that standardisation is a response to the growing complexity of social life on the one hand and the "increasing legal value of expertise" on the other hand (Ouedraogo 2013, p. 156). Therefore, neither the common language nor the legal language can escape standardisation. In law, the use of specific terminology in positive and procedural law is mainly, but not exclusively, subject to standardisation. Contrary to the positivist approach based on the ontology of nominalism, various linguistic forms can be considered as a standard.

The standard may take the form of a noun (e.g. *subsidiarity*), but it may also come in the form of adjectives (e.g. *important, high, reasonable*, etc.), adverbs (e.g. *normally, reasonably*) or adnominal phrases (e.g. *reasonable time*). Furthermore,

4 The following translation of French fixed phrases is a literal translation and is provided for informational purposes only to readers who do not speak French. As these phrases stem from the French legal system, no comparison can be made with similar English legal expressions. Faits et procédure – Facts and procedure; Par ces motifs . . . – On these grounds. . . ; Le tribunal statuant . . . – The Court rules. . . ; Attendu que . . . – Given that.

semantic prosody also plays a role in the standardisation of legal language and judicial discourse, because drafting principles or stylistic rules can also be subject to standardisation. This is why standards are being described as "notions that are almost instinctively understood" (Bernard 2010, p. 521). Such linguistic diversity makes the identification of a standard so difficult.

Even though the standard is originally a term from the common law,[5] it is not alien to the legal systems rooted in the civil law tradition (Bernard 2010, p. 581). Thus, in Roman law, the notion of *bonus pater familias* is a standard. Without necessarily using the term, legal systems based on the Romano-Germanic tradition also know this standard as an instrument of legal technique. It takes the form of a "soft norm based on an intentionally indeterminate criterion . . . which has to be applied by the judge on a case-by-case basis" (Cornu et al. 2020, p. 979) or in the form of notions such as, for example, *bon père de famille* (*good family father*) or *bonne foi* (*good faith*) (Bernard 2010, p. 169) or phrases such as *dans les meilleurs délais* (*as soon as possible*) and so forth (Bodin 2011). In the law of the European Union, standards are widely used as a legislative technique (Bernard 2010) and as a means of harmonising procedural law in both civil (Hess 2010) and criminal matters, particularly through the use of forms (Gréciano 2016). EU standards are either a sui generis notion (e.g. *subsidiarity* or *proportionality*), or they are the result of a deviation from a national standard (e.g. *abuse of rights*; 2010, p. 242) or the transposition of a national standard (e.g. *force majeure* or *proper administration of justice*; 2010, p. 277). As "the particular expression of a rule of law" (Bernard 2010, p. 54; Ouedraogo 2013, p. 173), EU standards are present in almost all areas of law. Thus, in economic law we can cite the standard of the *average consumer* (Bernard 2010, p. 473), in competition law the jurisprudential standard of *abuse of rights* (2010, p. 243) and of *legitimate expectations* (2010, p. 258) or, in administrative law, the EU standard of *manifest error of assessment*, which was inspired by the French administrative law (2010, p. 292). As far as international law is concerned, the standard is considered as an instrument to harmonise law (Ouedraogo 2013, p. 179). Finally, it seems appropriate to underline the important role standards have in the transition to postmodern law, which is more flexible and characterised by the development of a polynormativity that tends to blur the line between fact and law (Bernard 2010, pp. 563–564).

3.1 The standard in positive law: definition and characteristics

Defining the notion of standard poses a major difficulty for several reasons. First, this concept is of an ambiguous and elusive nature (Bernard 2010, p. 2) on the one hand, and, on the other hand, it has a more functional than conceptual

5 It seems that the term standard first appeared in 1881 in Olivier Wendell Holmes's book *The Common Law* (cf. Ouedraogo 2013, p. 161).

character (2010, p. 4). The fact that the legal technique of applying standards without actually using the term "standard" leads to a potential rift that makes the definition of this notion even more difficult. Second, translating a notion that was initially conceptualised within the North American doctrine is difficult. In this respect, "attempts to translate this term, in particular, have failed, even more than all those often failing attempts to translate other notions deeply rooted in a living tradition" (2010, p. 581).[6] Numerous translations for the term "standard" have been proposed (e.g. *directive, criterion, flexible standard, concept with indeterminate content, elastic concept, word with multiple meanings*, etc.; 2010, p. 5). They almost genetically inherit the undetermined character of the original term and therefore remain just as vague. The difficulty of translating and adopting the notion of standard in civil law lies in the specific meaning the term has adopted in the North American doctrine. There, the term standard is traditionally defined by referring to Dean Roscoe Pound's definition: "The standard is a measure of proper social conduct" (1925, p. 118). Pound's conception of the standard has therefore the same defining elements established by Hume (i.e. a unit of measurement whose calibration is set by the rule of conduct). Since the notion of standard is deeply rooted in the specific tradition of common law, the particular connotations of this term are difficult to translate into French or into other languages given the polysemy and anisomorphism of linguistic universes and legal systems. In addition, the difficulty of translating the term *standard* correlates with the difficulty of translating the notion of *rule*, another typical notion of the common law. The French translation of this term as *règle de droit* (rule of law) seems to be meaningless (without any relevance). The concept of *rule*, however, is in so far crucial when defining standards, as the North American doctrine makes the specific distinction between *standard* and *rule*. According to Elsa Bernard, differentiating between the standard and the rule of law is equivalent to denying the legal power of the standard and to degrading the standard to a mere "sub-rule" (Bernard 2010, p. 7). This, however, would be incompatible with its normative value and the fact that the standard is an element of the rule of law (2010, p. 54). With reference to Pound's definition, various French definitions have been proposed. Thus, for example, one author has defined it as "a formulation technique for the rule of law which aims at an *a priori* indeterminacy".[7] There are many criteria defining the standard, but only on the criterion of indeterminacy has a widespread consensus been reached.

The standard has the following main characteristics: being a priori undetermined, used for assessing normalcy on the basis of references outside law, revealing its concrete meaning only when being applied to a specific case and, due to its relational character, having different variations depending on the time and field of use. Being intentionally formulated in an a priori undetermined way is considered

6 Cf. H.A. Schwarz-Libermann von Wahlendorf, Idéalité et réalité du droit. Les dimensions du raisonnement judiciaire. Paris, LGD, 1980: 130; quoted by Elsa Bernard, p. 581, n. 1764.

7 This is a definition of S. Rials quoted by Elsa Bernard (2010, p. 9, n. 38).

to be the decisive characteristic of a standard. Therefore, the standard can be defined as "an intentionally indeterminate legal notion, which allows to measure the normalcy of behaviour and situations using references outside law" (Bernard 2010, p. 53). According to this author, the standard differs both from the rule of law, which has an a priori determined content, and from indeterminate notions, which are defined by having both an unlimited and an illimitable meaning. With regard to the rule of law, the standard is in so far different, as its meaning can only be determined by applying criteria such as normality, exogeneity and intention (Bernard 2010, p. 60). With regard to indeterminate notions, excluding their common feature of a priori indeterminacy, the standard is in so far different, as indeterminate notions do not require an analysis in terms of normalcy and intention (2010, p. 65). Finally, the standard also differs from the general principle of law. In fact, such a principle has an abstract meaning which does not vary regarding the specific case at hand. In contrast, the meaning of the standard is more concrete and depends on the specific case to which it is applied. The respective functions of the standard and the general principle of law are different as well. In fact, the principle aims to ensure the completeness and consistency of the law, whereas the standard aims to make rigid rules more flexible so that they can better be adapted to societal developments.

The functions of the standard are defined by its very own characteristics. The standard underpins the indeterminacy of the rule of law and enables law to be adapted to the facts at hand. Regarding community law, the functions of standards such as subsidiarity or proportionality reflect the specific structures within the law of the European Union (Bernard 2010, p. 580). In the process of lawmaking, the standard plays a unifying role since a consensus on a norm can be reached based on commonly accepted values. In the community legal order, the standard serves as an instrument to overcome divergences, which are rooted in the fact that Member States belong to different legal cultures, and as an instrument to harmonise law in order to make the different legal systems of the Member States compatible (2010, pp. 575–576).

3.2 *The standard in community procedural law: language risk management*

Generally speaking, it can be observed that in terms of procedure, the standardisation of documents through the use of standardised forms is a way of managing European multilingualism. The status of multilingualism in the European Union is a paradox. Multilingualism is enshrined in the Treaty of Lisbon and the Charter of Fundamental Rights of the European Union and although multilingualism is seen in the doctrine as an opportunity (Gréciano 2016), within this very same doctrine and from the perspective of practice multilingualism is considered as a risk and a major obstacle to the effectiveness of procedures within the European Union (Hess 2010, p. 121). The use of standardised forms in civil and criminal proceedings therefore aims to manage multilingualism by minimising the linguistic risk and aims to avoid translation as much as possible.

In the Area of Freedom, Security and Justice (AFSJ), provided for in the Treaty of Amsterdam of 1997 and enshrined in the Treaty of Lisbon in 2009, standards play a major role in the harmonisation of procedural law. For instance, numerous procedures and procedural standards have been developed by European legislators in the field of civil and criminal procedure to enable the rapid and effective implementation of common principles such as mutual trust, allowing the automatic recognition of judicial decisions without assessing their merits and the associated abolition of exequatur procedures (Hess 2010, p. 67) in order to facilitate judicial cooperation between Member States. Harmonisation in this area is mainly achieved by using standardised forms available in all EU languages. An example in civil matters would be the declaration of enforceability pursuant to Article 18(1) of Regulation (EC) No 1896/2006 of the European Parliament and of the Council creating a European order for payment procedure, or the European Enforcement Order for uncontested claims pursuant to Regulation (EC) No 805/2004. Examples in criminal matters would be the instrument of the European Investigation Order for the purpose of gathering evidence established by Directive 2014/41 EU of the European Parliament and of the Council of 3 April 2014, or the European Arrest Warrant established by the Council Framework Decision of 13 June 2002 on the European Arrest Warrant and the surrender procedures between the Member States. In day-to-day reality, however, the use of forms does not really solve the problem of translation. Instead, the problem will resurface at a later stage within the procedure. Indeed, and contrary to the assertion of certain representatives of the legal profession, court clerks, when drawing up certificates using a European form, always draw it up in their native language and the court clerks receiving such certificates want to read it in their own language without having to bother with juxtaposing the different language versions of the same form (Hess 2010, p. 125). In addition, as certain entries in the certificate are specific to each individual case, in particular regarding the disposition of a judgment, they are always written down in the original language. This is why, in the end, translation will always be necessary.

4 Conclusion

In conclusion, several observations can be made. From the linguistic point of view, standardisation, in the sense of using predetermined norms, creates a certain linguistic and discursive fixation, as it gives specific textual elements a more or less rigid form. Depending on the degree of fixation of linguistic expressions, legal language acquires a more or less "formulaic" character.

From the legal point of view, the role of standardisation appears to be more nuanced depending on whether standardisation is analysed from the perspective of positive law or from the perspective of procedure. From the perspective of positive law, standardisation, in the sense of using standardised concepts, allows for greater flexibility when applying the law. Furthermore, a legal standard provides a basis for overcoming differences and reaching consensus. As such, it is therefore an instrument for the unification of law.

From the perspective of procedural law, standardisation, in the sense of using standardised forms in certain types of proceedings, is an instrument of language risk management, on the one hand, and procedural harmonisation on the other.

References

Babich, B., ed., 2019. *Reading David Hume's "Of the standard of taste"*. Berlin: De Gruyter.

Bernard, E., 2010. *La spécificité du standard juridique en droit communautaire*. Bruxelles: Bruylant.

Bodin, M., 2011. *Les notions relatives en droit civil*. Thèse de doctorat, Université de Bordeaux IV.

Cassin, B., ed., 2019. *Vocabulaire européen des philosophies. Dictionnaire des intraduisibles*. Paris: Le Robert and Seuil.

Castillo-Wyszogrodzka, S., 2014. *La motivation des décisions de justice: Perspective comparatiste*. [online] Available from: www.dalloz-actualite.fr/revue-de-presse/motivation-des-decisions-de-justice-perspective-comparatiste-20140929#.XMk-uqTgqM8 [Accessed September 29, 2020].

Chassagnard-Pinet, S., Duchy, S., & Dauchy, S., eds., 2015. *La fonction communicationnelle de la motivation des décisions de justice. Droit, justice et politiques communicationnelles. Permanence et rupture // Droit, justice et politiques communicationnelles. Permanences et ruptures*. Lille: Editions mare&martin and Mare & Martin.

Cornu, G., 2005. *Linguistique juridique*. Paris: Editions Montchrestien.

Cornu, M., Ghozi, A., & Goré, M., eds., 2020. *Vocabulaire juridique*. 13th ed. Paris: Presses universitaires de France.

Galdia, M., 2017. *Lectures on legal linguistics*. Frankfurt: Peter Lang Edition.

Gautier, L., 2019. La recherche en "langues-cultures-milieux" de spécialité au prisme de l'épaisseur socio-discursive. *In:* M. Calderón & C. Konzett, eds., *Dynamische Approximationen*. Berlin: Peter Lang, 369–387.

Gréciano, P., 2016. Droit de l'Union Européenne et Médiation Linguistique. *International Journal for the Semiotics of Law – Revue internationale de Sémiotique juridique*, 29(3), 511–523.

Hess, B., 2010. *Europäisches Zivilprozessrecht: ein Lehrbuch*. Heidelberg: Müller.

Hickey, R., ed., 2012. *Standards of English. Codified varieties around the world*. Cambridge: Cambridge University Press.

Hume, D., 2019. Of the standard of taste. *In:* B. Babich, ed., *Reading David Hume's "Of the standard of taste"*. Berlin: De Gruyter, 25–40.

Krieg-Planque, A., 2009. *La notion de "formule" en analyse du discours. Cadre théorique et méthodologique*. Besançon: Presses universitaires de Franche-Comté.

Krieg-Planque, A., 2012. *Analyser les discours institutionnels*. Paris: A. Colin.

Labov, W., 1972. *Sociolinguistic patterns*. 11th ed. Philadelphia: University of Pennsylvania Press.

Lacabarats, A., 2016. *Synthèse sur la motivation des arrêts de la Cour de Cassation*. [online] Available from: www.courdecassation.fr/IMG/37_LACABARATS_Synthese_motivation_1116.pdf [Accessed September 29, 2020].

Lacabarats, A., 2018. La motivation des arrêts de la cour de Cassation. *In:* Malhière Fanny, ed., *Comment rédiger une décision de justice au XXI siècle.* Paris: Dalloz, 67–72.

Malhière, F., 2013. *La brièveté des décisions de justice. (Conseil constitutionnel, Conseil d'État, Cour de cassation); Contribution à l'étude des représentation de la justice.* Paris: Dalloz.

Milroy, J., 2001. Language ideologies and the consequences of standardization. *Journal of Sociolinguistics*, 5(4), 530–555.

Milroy, J., & Milroy, L., 1985. *Authority in language. Investigating language prescription and standardisation.* London: Routledge and Kegan Paul.

Milroy, L., 1987. *Language and social networks.* 2nd ed. Oxford: B. Blackwell.

Ouedraogo, A., 2013. Standard et standardisation: la normativité variable en droit international. *Revue québécoise de droit international*, 26(1), 155–186 [Accessed September 12, 2020].

Pound, R., 1925. *An introduction to the philosophy of law.* New Haven, CT: Yale University Press.

Simon, J., 2016. *Formule. Publictionnaire. Dictionnaire encyclopédique et critique des publics.* [online] Available from: http://publictionnaire.huma-num.fr/notice/formule/ [Accessed September 29, 2020].

Sobieszewska, M., 2014. Procédés référentiels dans le discours juridictionnel: cas des arrêts de la Cour de cassation. *SHS Web of Conference*, 8(2014), 2899–2916. [online] Available from: www.researchgate.net/publication/307728112_Procedes_referentiels_dans_le_discours_juridictionnel_cas_des_arrets_de_la_Cour_de_cassation [Accessed September 29, 2020].

Sourioux, J.L., & Lerat, P., 1975. *Le langage du droit.* Paris: Presses universitaires de France.

Trklja, A., & McAuliffe, K., 2019. Formulaic metadiscursive signalling devices judgments of the Court of Justice of the European Union: A new corpus-based model for studying discourse relations of texts. *International Journal of Speech, Language & the Law*, 26(1), 21–55.

Weber, J.F., 2009. *Comprendre un arrêt de la Cour de cassation rendu en matière civile.* [online] Available from: www.courdecassation.fr/publications_cour_26/bulletin_information_cour_cassation_27/bulletins_information_2009_2866/no_702_3151/communication_3153/.

4 The consensus case law of the European Court of Human Rights in light of the Court's legitimacy over time

A corpus-linguistic perspective

Anne Lise Kjær

1 Introduction

The purpose of this chapter is to shed new light on the meaning and use of the concept of consensus in the case law of the European Court of Human Rights (ECtHR). I do so by conducting a corpus-based linguistic analysis of consensus terms and phrases in the judgments of the Court. Consensus is an interpretive tool used in the legal reasoning of the Court in cases which are not clearly covered by the European Convention on Human Rights (ECHR) and which call for an evolutive interpretation of the Convention.[1]

The consensus instrument has attracted widespread attention in legal research (see e.g. Helfer 1993; Heringa 1996; Benvenisti 1999; Wildhaber et al. 2013; Letsas 2014; Dzehtsiarou 2015; Kapotas and Tzevelekos 2019; O'Hara 2021). However, as I will show, the consensus case law is interesting also from a linguistic perspective. It illustrates the intricate relationship between lexical and pragmatic meaning as well as the difference between legal concepts and legal terms, and thus goes to the heart of what law and language scholarship is about.

The question soon arises as to what the Court means by consensus. For several reasons, the answer to that seemingly simple question is more complicated than one should think.

First, the notion of consensus has been superimposed by doctrine on a variety of different terms and phrases applied by the Court (e.g. *European consensus, international trend, common ground, common denominator, uniform approach, commonly accepted standard*). Second, legal scholars and commentators have maintained that the meaning of the different terms and phrases does not affect the meaning of the legal concept. Thus, in a recent article by the Editorial Board of the Human Rights

1 In the following, I use *italics* to refer to the term *consensus*, while the concept of consensus, is referred to without any highlighting. This applies to other cases where I need to distinguish between terms and concepts, e.g. the term *trend* vs. the concept of trend.

DOI: 10.4324/9781003153771-5

Education for Legal Professionals (HELP),[2] it is argued that "these variations in terminology" do not affect the legal meaning of consensus. At the same time, however, the observation is also made that "there is a slight tendency to approach [i.e. assimilate] the meaning to the term 'trend', given that 'consensus' may imply, from the linguistic perspective, an identity in behavior and opinions between all parties".

From the point of view of lexical semantics, the two words are obviously not synonymous. However, a dictionary definition of the meaning of *consensus* and *trend* is not helpful in identifying the meaning that the Court actually attaches to them. According to the language theory of Wittgenstein, which underlies my argument, the only way to establish the semantics of the consensus phrases is to investigate their use in the language of the Court, as "the meaning of a word is its use in the language" (*Philosophical Investigations* 1953, p. 43). Even if it does not seem probable that the Court uses the words as randomly as suggested by HELP in the aforementioned article and the majority of legal scholars (see Section 3.1), it may be true. The point is, we cannot know for sure unless we investigate the context in which the various words and phrases are used.

I hypothesise that the terminology varies over time in accordance with the balance of power between the Court and the Member States. In other words, I assume that the way consensus arguments are phrased and used to a certain extent mirrors the authority that the Court believes to enjoy vis-à-vis the Member States at any given time and hence its legitimacy among the Member States.

In the following, I first present an overview of what, legally speaking, constitutes the consensus case law of the ECtHR and then explain why consensus cases are also relevant to study from a linguistic perspective. On this basis, I present my corpus-based analysis of different consensus phrases applied by the Court in Grand Chamber judgments over time. Subsequently, I present my results and show that a change is detectable both in terms of an increase in the number of judgments in which the Court discusses a possible consensus between the Member States and in terms of the consensus terminology that the Court prefers over time (an increasing use of *consensus* rather than *trend*). Finally, I reflect on the relevance of my results to broader legal and sociopolitical debates, especially as regards the relationship between the Court and the Member states and the authority and legitimacy of the Court.

2 The consensus case law of the European Court of Human Rights

The consensus case law refers to the body of decisions by the ECtHR in which the Court has felt the need to adopt an evolutive interpretation of the European Convention on Human Rights. Consensus specifically refers to the level of uniformity present in the legal frameworks of the Member States of the Council of Europe on a particular topic at a given point in time. It is closely related to

2 The Human Rights Education for Legal Professionals (HELP), Interpretative Mechanisms of ECHR Case-law: The Concept of European Consensus, Council of Europe. www.coe.int/en/web/help/article-echr-case-law (accessed April 11, 2021).

another interpretative principle, namely the doctrine of the Member States' so-called margin of appreciation.

Consensus reasoning involves a comparison of the laws of the Member States; it measures the development (the present-day-conditions) of human rights protection in Europe and helps the Court decide the degree of diversity that it will allow in the Member States' human rights protection and, hence, a particular State's margin of appreciation in a given case at a given point in time. If, for example, the Court establishes a broad consensus among the Member States that transgender rights should be respected and recognised, the margin of appreciation will be narrow. If, on the other hand, a consensus cannot be established, the margin of appreciation will be broad. Thus, consensus reasoning goes hand in hand with the balance that the Court will always have to strike between the need for a uniform interpretation of the Convention at European level and the freedom to choose individual legal solutions in the legal systems of the Member States.

The Court uses the consensus tool both to justify a wide margin of appreciation given to the Member States in the absence of consensus, thus stagnating the development of case law, and to impose new standards, where there is a clear trend in most Member States to protect the contested right, thus advancing the interpretation of the Convention.

In order to understand the consensus tool, it is necessary to consider the ideas behind the Convention when it was drafted by some Western European countries after World War II. The Preamble of the Convention sets out the intention of the contracting Parties at that time and stipulates the ground rules for interpretation of the Convention (paragraph 3):

> Considering that the aim of the Council of Europe is the achievement of greater unity between its members and that one of the methods by which that aim is to be pursued is the maintenance and further realisation of Human Rights and Fundamental Freedoms.

Paragraph 4 of the Preamble also stresses that

> those fundamental freedoms . . . are best maintained . . . by an effective political democracy and . . . by a common understanding and observance of the Human Rights upon which they depend.

The Preamble shows that the intention of the contracting Parties clearly was to strive both for a "greater unity" between the Member States and a "common understanding" of the convention rights and a "further realisation" (development) of the rights.

In several cases, the Court has referred to the role that consensus has played in the realisation of the Convention rights.

> Beginning with *Tyrer v. the United Kingdom* (25 April 1978, § 31, Series A no. 26), "[t]he existence of a consensus has long played a role in the development and evolution of Convention protections, . . . the Convention being considered a 'living instrument' to be interpreted in the light of present-day

conditions. Consensus has therefore been invoked to justify a dynamic interpretation of the Convention".

(*A, B, and C v. Ireland*, No 25579/05, § 234, December 16, 2010)

Moreover, as explained by one of the judges at the Court at the Dialogue between Judges conference in 2011, it lies in the nature of fundamental rights that they can be applied only through a process of interpretation, as rights are abstract in nature and acquire a concrete meaning only in the particular context in which they are invoked (Tulkens 2011, p. 6). Thus, the interpretation of the Convention cannot be based on the meaning that those rights had when the Treaty was drafted. On the contrary, as the Court states in an early judgment:

> Given that [the Convention] is a law-making treaty, it is . . . necessary to seek the interpretation that is most appropriate in order to realise the aim and achieve the object of the treaty, not that which would restrict to the greatest possible degree the obligations undertaken by the Parties.
>
> (*Wemhoff v. Germany*, No 2122/64, As to the Law, § 8, June 27, 1968)

But it seems there are limits to the evolution of the Convention and to the legitimacy of the Court to continue the "further realisation" of the Convention right. In recent years the Court has met a growing reluctance among the Member States to accept its authority to further the development of the Convention rights. Since the beginning of the century, and especially since the adoption of the Brighton Declaration in 2012,[3] the governments of the Member States have become increasingly sceptical about the dynamic interpretation style of the Court. The States now stress the need to take into account the historical, cultural and social conditions in the individual Member States when adjudicating citizens' claims of violated Convention rights. In other words, the Member States call for a broader margin of appreciation, a demand that culminated with the adoption in May 2015 of Protocol No 15. According to Protocol 15, Art. 1, an explicit reference to the principle of subsidiarity and the margin of appreciation shall be added to the final paragraph of the Convention's preamble:

> Affirming that the High Contracting Parties, in accordance with the principle of subsidiarity, have the primary responsibility to secure the rights and freedoms defined in this Convention and the Protocols thereto, and that

3 Since the Court was set up in 1959, the Council of Europe's Member States have adopted Protocols to the Convention, aimed at reforming it. In addition, several "high-level conferences" on reform of the Convention system have been held, organised by the Committee of Ministers and resulting in several political declarations. These high-level conferences are commonly referred to as the Interlaken process, named after the first conference in Interlaken in 2010. Especially since Brighton 2012, the reform process has increasingly reflected the Member States' attempt to delegitimize the Court's authority (cf. Madsen 2016, Madsen et al. 2018, and Helfer & Voeten 2020).

in doing so they enjoy a margin of appreciation, subject to the supervisory jurisdiction of the European Court of Human Rights established by this Convention.

This change in the way Member States view the Court's role is reflected in the case law of the Court; thus, the existence or non-existence of consensus between the contracting parties on the interpretation of a particular Convention right has been the object of attention in an increasing number of judgments since around 2010. As I will comment on in more detail below, my research shows that the percentage of Grand Chamber judgments in which consensus considerations are included has experienced a steep growth since 2010. Thus, 29.2% of the judgments passed in the time span between 2001 and 2010 addressed consensus; this grew to a staggering 68.5% of the judgments between 2011 and 2020.

3 The consensus case law from a law and language perspective

The consensus case law of the ECtHR has attracted widespread attention in international law (IL) and international relations (IR) studies (e.g. Helfer 1993; Heringa 1996; Benvenisti 1999; Wildhaber et al. 2013; Letsas 2014; Dzehtsiarou 2015; Kapotas and Tzevelekos 2019; O'Hara 2021).

IL scholars are primarily interested in the Court's reference to consensus as a method of international interpretation and engage in normative debates on how it should be applied by the Court. IR scholars, on the other hand, view the consensus cases as balancing acts between the European and national levels of human rights protection and discuss the attempts made by the Court to strike a fair balance between individuals' rights and nation states' interests.

I concentrate on another contested issue: the divergent linguistic expressions used by the Court, believing that the debates in IL/IR research would benefit from input from linguistics.

3.1 The relevance of the consensus case law for law and language research

Before we can focus more on the language perspective on the case law, it is important to note that the Court has not defined the concept itself. This has provoked a debate in legal scholarship on what is meant by consensus and what it should mean (Wildhaber et al. 2013). Thus, in an early article on the topic, Helfer (1993) analyses "the ambiguity in the tribunals' current consensus methodology and its effect on the development of a coherent European human rights jurisprudence" (p. 135).

The ambiguity of the concept is still a prevailing point of criticism and occurs as a recurring theme in recent research. In an article from 2019, Christian Djeffal makes an attempt at defining the consensus concept based on a continuum of

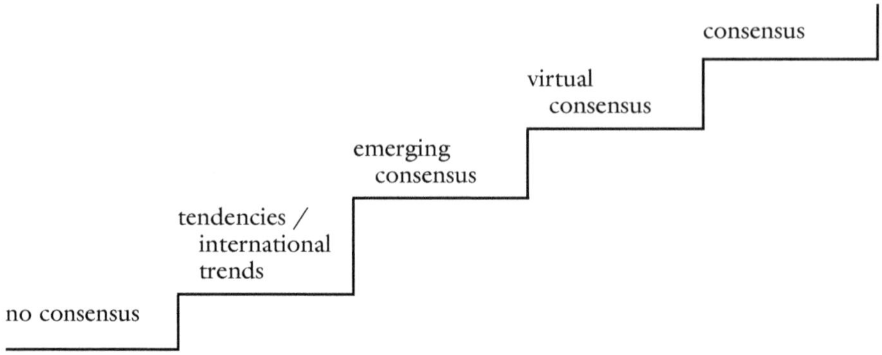

Figure 4.1 Consensus steps according to Djeffal (2019, p. 77)

expressions from "no consensus" to "consensus". He points out that the Court does not treat consensus in a binary fashion and suggests that the Court graduates the degree of consensus along the steps shown in Figure 4.1.

Even though Djeffal's consensus steps seem logical, based on the lexical meaning of the terms, they are merely postulated and do not reflect the Court's actual use of terms and phrases.

Except for a recent article by Vetrovsky (2019), the consensus cases have not been the topic of much law and language research. As Vetrovsky (2019, p. 121) rightly points out, legal scholars fail to distinguish between the *concept* of consensus and the different *terms* that the Court has applied in its case law. They imply or state explicitly that variations in terminology are of no relevance to the content of the concept, and it is widely presumed that the phrases should be considered synonymous:

> Although they have slightly different nuances of linguistic meaning it does not change their nature; all these titles refer to the European consensus argument. They indicate the Court's acknowledgement of commonly accepted values or procedures. These and similar phrases should be considered as synonyms.
>
> (Dzehtsiarou 2009, p. 2)

From a linguistic point of view, the claim of identity of referential meaning provokes interesting research questions about the relationship between law and language and calls for an in-depth analysis of the language of the consensus case law of the Court.

A linguistic analysis is not only of academic interest, as the claim of identity of meaning is also made on the Council of Europe website, Human Rights Education for Legal Professionals, as I commented on in Section 1. To recall, it is argued that the variations in terminology do not affect the legal meaning of consensus, and that there is a tendency for the Court to assimilate the meaning to trend.

The HELP article is meant for judges, lawyers and prosecutors in the 47 Member States and it aims at enhancing their capacity to apply the Convention in the national legal systems. However, the guidelines are not clear. On the one hand, readers are advised *not* to pay attention to the linguistic level of the consensus concept. On the other hand, they are encouraged to assimilate the content of the concept to the linguistic meaning of the word *trend*, as the word *consensus* implies an identity in opinion which is not required, so it is maintained. Not only do the authors fail to distinguish clearly between the lexical and the conceptual levels of language, but they also adopt inconsistent theories as to how the meanings of words are identified. Is meaning inherent in the words themselves? Is it established in language use? Is meaning anchored in the minds of individual language users? Is it derived from the intention of the writer? Or is it determined normatively by certain authoritative language users, such as the experts advising the national legal professionals on the Council of Europe website?

Usually, it is for the Court to determine the meaning of words and phrases used in the ECHR and the Court's own case law. In fact, authoritative meaning making by courts is the norm rather than the exception. The ECtHR's failure to define consensus and explain when an evolving European approach acquires consensus status has forced others to try to fill the gap. However, while the Court itself has the institutional authority to define the concepts that it uses, others should base their definition on thorough analyses and arguments that may be accepted or not. HELP and legal scholars so far have not explicated the basis of their claims of synonymy of the various consensus terms and phrases.

3.2 *The consensus case law analysed from a pragmatic theory of meaning*

My analysis is based on the pragmatic theories of meaning that emerged from English-language philosophy and linguistics of the mid-20th century. Prominent representatives are the philosophers Austin (1962), Searle (1969), and Wittgenstein (1953), and within linguistics Firth and his so-called Neo-Firthian followers, including the founder of corpus linguistics Sinclair, see e.g. Sinclair (2004).

Firth's pragmatic theory entails that it is impossible to measure the meaning of a word objectively and independently from language users' use of the word in context – semantics is a function of "the context of situation" (Firth 1935, p. 29). Hence, from the point of view of pragmatics, a semantic distinction between the consensus phrases applied by the ECtHR and an accompanying conclusion that certain phrases are more or less fitting to the intended meaning or more or less synonymous is not feasible. It all depends on the actual use of the phrases in the context of the judgments.

In other words, as long as the judges at the ECtHR do use the terms and phrases interchangeably and the community of human rights lawyers, non-governmental organisations, national authorities and legal scholars agree, they do have the same meaning.

This leads us to the next step in the considerations. We need to ascertain whether the Court uses the phrases interchangeably. In order to do so, we need to identify the meaning of the consensus terms in use. To that end, I employ corpus linguistics to uncover how the terms are used in the context of collocations. To supplement the analysis of context, I additionally track the comparative use of the individual consensus phrases over time, especially the comparative use of *consensus* and *trend*. Corpus and methods are described in more detail in the following.

4 Corpus and method

4.1 Corpus

It was no easy task to select the relevant judgments, knowing that the Court has used a variety of different consensus phrases. I based my selection on the terminology which has been described in English language journal articles, books and case law commentaries. I then supplemented the consensus terms and phrases mentioned there with additional searches in the Court's HUDOC database which includes all judgments and decisions passed by the Court.

As not all Chamber and Committee judgments are published in both official languages, I made the search in both English and French. In that way, I got a fuller picture of the total number of consensus judgments.

4.1.1 Search terms

The selected English search terms were as follows:

> *Consensus, trend, common approach, European approach, uniform approach, common denominator, common ground, common standard, European standard, international standard,* and *commonly accepted.*

The search results showed some false positives; especially, *common ground* returned many false positives, the most frequent context turning out to be *it is common ground* in the sense "it is undisputed". In the results commented on below, I have therefore chosen to disregard *common ground*. An example of the kind of context that I was looking for is the following:

> Turning to prisoners' social cover, the Court reiterates that when defining the breadth of the margin of appreciation, a relevant factor may be *the existence or non-existence of common ground between the laws of the Contracting States.*
> (*Stummer v. Austria*, No 37452/02, § 104, July 7, 2011; emphasis added)

Among the other selected consensus phrases, some turned out to be used only a few times and therefore have been left out in the analysis below. This applies to *common denominator, European approach, international standard*, and *commonly accepted*.

The terms *tendency, development[s]*, and *evolution* could have been chosen as search terms as well; however, they returned so many false positives that I decided to leave them out of the analysis. Tests show that most of the relevant instances of the three terms co-occur with *consensus* or *trend*; hence, ignoring them seems to have limited impact on the search results.

4.1.2 Search period

The search period stretches from the beginning of the Court's practice until the end of 2020. The resulting corpus consists of a total number of 1850 judgments, of which 307 judgments exist only in French. The corpus covers judgments from the Committee (formed by three judges deciding routine cases), the five Chambers (formed by seven judges), and the Grand Chamber (formed by 17 judges; previously called the Plenary Court).

I focus on judgments passed by the Grand Chamber, because they are likely to present the most relevant consensus cases. The purpose of the Grand Chamber is to decide exceptional cases or cases in which a question is raised that affects the interpretation of the Convention. Thus, when the Court is faced with contested issues which involve a possible evolutive interpretation of the Convention, they are likely to be brought before the Grand Chamber.

4.1.3 Sub-corpora

Based on the full corpus of Grand Chamber consensus judgments, I formed three sub-corpora to allow me to conduct a diachronic analysis of the number and relative frequency of the various consensus phrases over time. The three phases were chosen with the aim of reflecting the sociopolitical and historical developments of the Court and its interplay with the Member States. Phase 1 (until 2000) roughly represents the first phase of the Court's existence until it was turned into a full-time Court as of 1998. Phase 2 (2001–2010) covers the period of the overburdened Court, which had difficulties coping with the immense workload caused by its tremendous success. Phase 3 (2011–2020) includes judgments from the time of contestation of the Court's authority from increasingly sceptical governments in the Member States (the post-Interlaken era).

I expected that an increasing number of judgments would include consensus considerations and that the term *consensus* would increase more than *trend*, especially in phase 3. A decrease in the support of the Member States is likely to force the Court to be more alert to Member States' interests than in the early years of widespread national support. In other words, I anticipated that the more backlash the Court experiences from the Member States, the less inclined the Court will be to interpret the Convention text dynamically without being able to refer to a widespread consensus among the Member States.

4.2 Method

The method of analysis mixes computer-assisted empirical approaches and manual analyses of individual judgments. Based on computational searches in the HUDOC database of the ECtHR, I traced the absolute and relative frequency of Grand Chamber judgments which included one or more of the selected consensus phrases. In addition, I conducted corpus-linguistic searches for collocations to the individual consensus terms. The software programme applied was Sketch Engine. Finally, I added a manual analysis of the concordance lines identified by Sketch Engine with the aim of uncovering typical lexico-grammatical patterns of use.

5 Analysis

5.1 Quantitative analysis of the use of the consensus terms

The automated diachronic analysis gives a first insight into the Grand Chamber's use of the various consensus terms and phrases (see Tables 4.1 and 4.2). A quick look at the numbers supports my expectation that consensus terms would be used more frequently over time. First, there is clear evidence of an increase in the use of all consensus phrases. Second, it is obvious that *consensus* and *trend* are the Court's favourite lexical choice compared to the other consensus phrases and that they experience a steep rise entering the post-Interlaken period. In the following, I will therefore concentrate mostly on those terms.

Table 4.1 Number of Grand Chamber judgments in which one or more consensus terms are applied over time

AGGREGATED, **ABSOLUTE VALUES**	Until 2000	2001–2010	2011–2020
consensus	7	38	89
common approach	4	6	8
uniform approach	1	1	10
common standard	3	3	15
European standard	1	13	15
trend	9	35	70
Total number of Grand Chamber Judgments	130	171	174

Table 4.2 Percentage of Grand Chamber judgments in which one or more consensus phrases are used over time

AGGREGATED, **RELATIVE VALUES**	Until 2000	2001–2010	2011–2020
consensus	5.4	29.2	68.5
common approach	3.1	4.6	6.2
uniform approach	0.8	0.8	7.7
common standard	2.3	2.3	11.5
European standard	0.8	7.6	11.5
trend	6.9	26.9	53.8

In relative terms, *consensus* appears in only seven (or 5.4%) of the judgments passed until 2000, whereas 89 (or 68.5%) of the judgments in the post-Interlaken period include *consensus.*

The use of *trend* exhibits a similar development, with *trend* increasing from being applied in only nine judgments until 2000 to 70 judgments post-2011 or, in relative terms, from 6.9% to 53.8% of the judgments.

A comparison of *consensus* and *trend* shows that the growth in the use of *consensus* is more pronounced. This is indicative of the fact that the two terms are not used interchangeably by the Court as claimed in HELP's learning material for national legal professionals and in several legal studies (see Section 3). If that had been the case, one would expect that the relative frequency of *consensus* and *trend* would have been stable over time.

However, we still need to ascertain whether the claim made in legal research that *consensus* and *trend* are synonymous is correct. To do so, we first need to elucidate the immediate context of their use, their most salient modifiers and other collocates.

5.2 Collocations

To identify the most salient modifiers to the lemmas *consensus* and *trend*, I applied the Sketch Difference tool in Sketch Engine, which is designed to compare the use of two different lemmas by contrasting their collocations. I set the minimum frequency to five. The results are based on the LogDice score, thus reflecting the typicality of the collocation (as opposed to the mere frequency). The collocates with a high difference in co-occurrence with *consensus* or *trend* are placed at the top or the bottom, the collocates with a small difference appear in the centre.

As neither *consensus* nor *trend* was used frequently in the early case law of the Court, the following results are based only on judgments from 2001 and onwards. Moreover, I constructed an additional sub-corpus, dividing the post-Interlaken time frame (2011–2020) into two (2011–2015 and 2016–2020). I did so because the calculation of the frequency of consensus judgments accounted for in Table 4.1 showed a considerable growth from 2011; splitting the 2011–2020 sub-corpus into two would give room for more immediate comparisons with the earlier case law and at the same time give valuable insights into the most recent developments.

Generally, the results show clear differences between collocates of the two terms. First, *trend* has no strong collocates; only *current, clear*, and *international* are calculated as typical collocates. Second, except for *international* in the most recent period, *consensus* and *trend* have generally no overlapping modifiers. Based on those observations alone, it is fair to say that the two terms are not used as synonyms in the judgments.

This becomes even more obvious when one looks more closely into the concrete modifiers (all adjectives). Most conspicuous is the use of *European*. In no period does *European* co-occur with *trend*, whereas it is the most dominant collocate to *consensus* over time. Moreover, *European* and *international* collocate almost equally with *consensus* in the case law between 2001 and 2010. This changes dramatically particularly in the period 2011–2015, immediately after the introduction of the Interlaken process in 2010. This is probably no coincidence, and it seems to support my expectation that the Court would be more alert to Member States' sentiments in the aftermath of Interlaken, Brighton and beyond. With the increasing contestation of the Court's authority among the Member States, reference to an "international" consensus can be expected to be less persuasive than reference to a "European" consensus on a particular issue, given the general neo-nationalist outlook in the Member States.

A comparison of the adjectives *clear, broad*, and *general* also shows interesting developments in the meaning of *consensus* in context. Until 2010, the Court did not consider it particularly relevant to measure the "breadth" or "generality" of a consensus among the Member States. The "clarity" or lack of such "clarity" was the more typical parameter applied by the Court. Again, this seems to support my expectation that the Court would be increasingly concerned with the national outlook on human rights protection and be reluctant to interpret the Convention dynamically, unless it could refer to a "broad" or "general" consensus among the Member states. For details, please compare Tables 4.3, 4.4, and 4.5 below.

Table 4.3 Modifiers of *consensus* vs. *trend* in Grand Chamber judgments 2001–2010

Modifiers	*consensus*	*trend*
European	23	0
clear	11	0
international	21	0
current	0	6

Table 4.4 Modifiers of *consensus* vs. *trend* in Grand Chamber judgments 2011–2015

Modifiers	*consensus*	*trend*
European	70	0
broad	18	0
general	17	0
international	5	0
clear	0	0

Table 4.5 Modifiers of *consensus* vs. *trend* in Grand Chamber judgments 2016–2020

Modifiers	*consensus*	*trend*
European	59	0
broad	13	0
international	9	16

5.3 *Manual analysis of concordance lines*

The next step in the investigation is the manual analysis of the concordance lines in which the identified *consensus* and *trend* collocations are embedded. What does the broader textual context reveal about the meaning and use of *consensus* and *trend*?

In the Sketch Difference results, I particularly noticed the prepositional pattern *of consensus/trend*, which again showed that *consensus* exhibits a more conspicuous collocational behaviour than *trend*, with *lack*, *existence* and *absence* being typical collocates of *consensus*, whereas *trend* is not represented at all, see Table 4.6 below.

Table 4.6 Prepositional pattern of *consensus/trend* in Grand Chamber judgments 2011–2015

Prepositional patterns of	*consensus*	*trend*
lack	30	0
existence	19	0
absence	11	0

The concordance lines of those collocations uncover an almost exclusively negated context of use and give an impression of the kind of reasoning that the consensus case law involves; see the following examples:

> The *lack of complete consensus* on this issue meant that the High Contracting Parties were to be granted a wide margin of appreciation. (*Perincek v. Switzerland*, no. 27510/08, § 170, 15 October 2015.)

> The Court considers that the narrowness of this sample is such that no conclusions can be drawn as to *the existence of a possible consensus* among Council of Europe member States. (*X and Others v. Austria*, no. 19010/07, § 149, 19 February 2013.)

> In *the absence of a European consensus* and taking into account that the case at stake undoubtedly raises sensitive moral or ethical issues, the Court considers that the margin of appreciation to be afforded to the respondent State must still be a wide one (see *X, Y and Z v. the United Kingdom*, cited above, § 44). (*Hämäläinen v. Finland*, no. 37359/09, § 75, 16 July 2014.)

The predominantly negative context of *consensus* is reflected also in the fact that *no* is among its collocates, more precisely in the lexico-grammatical patterns "there is no [European] consensus" and "no [European] consensus exists"; see the following examples:

> It also appears from the comparative-law material at the Court's disposal that *there is no European consensus* on this issue. (*Barbulescu v. Romania*, no. 61496/08, 2017, § 118, 5 September.)

> The survey concludes that *no consensus currently exists* among the member States of the Council of Europe, or in the other countries surveyed, regarding the authorisation of assisted suicide or euthanasia. (*Lambert and Others v. France*, no. 46043/14, § 78, 5 June 2015.)

Trend, in contrast, is almost exclusively used in a positive context. As evidenced by the following examples, *trend* is also often combined with words that express "development" and "change" (*towards, gradually, consolidating*):

> This suggests *a certain trend towards a European standard* which must be seen as a relevant consideration in the present case. (*Biao v. Denmark*, no. 38590/10, § 132, 24 May 2016.)

> *This trend is gradually reducing the margin of appreciation* which States may enjoy in this area. (*Stummer v. Austria*, no. 37452/02, Joint Partly Dissenting Opinion of Judges Tulkens, Kovler, Gyulumyan, Spielmann, Popović, Malinverni and Pardalos, § 5, 7 July 2011.)

> *This trend has been consolidating* not only in the civil and constitutional laws of several countries, but also in international human rights law and international environmental law. (*Herrmann v. Germany*, no. 9300/07, Partly Concurring and Partly Dissenting Opinion of Judge Pinto De Albuquerque, 26 June 2012.)

The concordance lines of *consensus* and *trend* reveal two other interesting patterns, which combine and contrast *consensus* and *trend*. They can be put in the following formula: (1) "no consensus, but a trend", (2) "a clear trend, and therefore an emerging consensus":

> The Court observes that *although there is no European consensus on the matter, there is an evolving trend.* (*Stummer v. Austria*, no. 37452/02, § 105, 7 July 2011.)

> The Court would conclude that *there is now a clear trend* in the legislation of the Contracting States towards allowing gamete donation for the purpose of in vitro fertilisation, *which reflects an emerging European consensus.* (*S.H. and Others v. Austria*, no. 57813/00, § 96, 3 November 2011.)

Examples like those indicate the Court's contrasting use of the two terms, which is in line with my expectation that *consensus* and *trend* are not used interchangeably in the case law. This is further supported by the views expressed in the following dissenting opinions, where ECtHR judges comment on the Court's use of the two terms. In the first quotation, the judges refer to *consensus* as a "restrictive notion" and suggest that *trend* be used instead, as a simpler and more appropriate way of speaking about "the current state of international law".

> Furthermore, and moving from methodology to terminology, should we always adhere to *the somewhat restrictive notion of "consensus"*, which is rarely encountered in real life? Would it not be *more appropriate and simpler to speak in terms of a "trend"*? These observations lead us into a more detailed examination of *the current state* of international law in this regard. (*X and Others v. Austria* (GC) no. 19010/07, Joint Partly Dissenting Opinion of Judges Casadevall, Ziemele, Kovler, Jočienė, Šikuta, De Gaetano and Sicilianos, § 15, 19 February 2013.)

In the following quotation from a dissenting opinion by Judge Pinto de Albuquerque, he states that "the terminology is unsubstantial". At the same time, however, he contrasts the two terms, indicating that *consensus* implies a higher degree of convergence between the national legal systems than *trend* ("at least a significant trend").

> I would not hesitate to call this a consensus, but this terminology is unsubstantial: in similar cases, the Court has consistently recognised findings of this kind as, at least, a significant "trend", with normative consequences. (*Correia de Matos v. Portugal*, (GC) no. 56402/12, Dissenting Opinion of Judge Pinto de Albuquerque Joined by Judge Sajó § 20, 4 April 2018.)

To give the full picture, it is important to highlight that, in few cases, it would be possible to substitute *consensus* for *trend* and vice versa without changing the meaning of the text. This is evidenced also by the fact that the Sketch Difference results show overlapping collocations as regards *emerge* and *reflect* (see Table 4.7).

Table 4.7 Grand Chamber judgments (all years)

Verbs as object	*consensus*	*trend*
grow	13	0
reach	10	0
exist	5	0
be	162	34
emerge	35	8
reflect	8	11

The following concordances show typical contexts of the collocations:

> Moreover, *this trend is reflected* in the relevant Council of Europe materials. (*Vallianatos and Others v. Greece*, nos. 29381/09 and 32684/09, § 91, 7 November 2013.)

> In their view, neither the "living instrument" approach, nor the existence of *a European consensus reflected* in the adoption of freedom of information acts in the domestic legal systems could justify such a right being read into Article 10 of the Convention. (*Magyar Helsinki Bizottság v. Hungary*, no. 18030/11, § 76, 8 November 2016.)

> The report appended to the 1991 Draft Articles stated that the rules formulated in Article 11 appeared to be consistent with *the emerging trend* in the legislative and treaty practice of a growing number of States . . . (*Cudak v. Lithuania*, no. 15869/02, § 29, 23 March 2010.)

> *That emerging consensus* is not, however, based on settled and long-standing principles established in the law of the member States. . . . (*S.H. and Others v. Austria*, no. 57813/00, X, § 96, 23 March 2010.)

6 Results

As regards the practical meaning of the term *consensus*, the context indicates that *consensus* is used to describe, at a given point in time, the degree of virtual agreement among the Member States as regards a certain human rights issue. Thus, it makes sense to examine whether a consensus exists which, as we saw above, is reflected in the lexico-grammatical patterns in which consensus is often embedded: "there is no consensus" and "no consensus exists".

Trend, on the other hand, is used to describe the development in the laws of the Member States or in international law more generally in a diachronic perspective. The reasoning underlying the use of *trend*, then, is fundamentally different from the *consensus* reasoning, the raison d'être being that societies and laws are continuously changing and that the Court must identify their stage of development. This is reflected in the fact that *trend* is often combined with words that express "development" and "change".

As regards modifiers, the most dominant collocate of *consensus* is *European*, whereas *trend* co-occurs more often with *international.*

Based on the results of my analysis, I believe that it is safe to conclude that the variations in terminology *do* affect the meaning of the consensus concept contrary to what is asserted in many legal studies and in learning material for national legal professionals.

My expectations were confirmed: *consensus* and *trend* are not used interchangeably by the Court, they are not synonymous, and the use of *consensus* increases more over time than *trend.* I do not believe that the terminological choices made in the judgments are as innocent as it sometimes appears in the literature. In the aftermath of the reform process and the growing scepticism among the Member States towards the European human rights regime, the Court focuses more on the sentiments of the national governments and is reluctant to apply the evolutive interpretation style originally adopted to develop the human rights protection in Europe.

Judge Pinto de Albuquerque expressed what I believe explains the reason behind the rise of consensus reasoning in the Court's case law. He explicitly states that "some domestic courts have not resisted the current lurch towards the populist scapegoating of the Court for all the evils of Europe" and "have called into question the legal force of the Court's inconvenient judgments, by advocating a State-centred Westphalian interpretation of human rights, giving priority to regulatory discretion of governments over fundamental rights of citizens". Therefore, "the Court has a shrinking amount of wiggle room within which to react" (dissenting opinion in *G.I.E.M. S.R.L. and Others v. Italy*, nos. 1828/06 and 2 others, § 68 and § 69, 28 June 2018).

He pinpoints the legitimacy crisis that the ECtHR is experiencing in the present time. With populism spreading across European nation states in both Eastern and Western Europe, the "unelected bureaucrats" at the Strasbourg Court no longer enjoy immediate support in the Member States of the Council of Europe. They are under attack from national governments to have taken over the role of law-making that should rightly be the task of national parliaments, so the argument goes. This has caused the Court to show "self-restraint" by allowing a broader margin of appreciation to the national authorities and preferring a consensual interpretation of the ECHR rather than an evolutive interpretation in accordance with the present-day conditions in the societies of the Member States. The development in the use of the various consensus terms shows this change in a nutshell.

References

Austin, J.L., 1962. *How to do things with words.* Oxford: Clarendon Press.

Benvenisti, E., 1999. Margin of appreciation, consensus and universal standards. *New York University Journal of International Law and Politics*, 31(4), 843–854.

Djeffal, C., 2019. Consensus, stasis, evolution. reconstructing argumentative patterns in evolutive ECHR jurisprudence. *In:* P. Kapotas & V.P. Tzevelekos, eds., *Building consensus on European consensus: Judicial interpretation of human rights in Europe and beyond.* Cambridge: Cambridge University Press, 71–95.

Dzehtsiarou, K., 2009. *European consensus: A way of reasoning.* University College Dublin Law Research Paper No. 11/2009, 1–18.

Dzehtsiarou, K., 2015. *European consensus and the legitimacy of the European Court of Human Rights.* Cambridge: Cambridge University Press.

Firth, J.R., 1935. The technique of semantics. *Philosophical Society*, 34(1), 36–73.

Helfer, L.R., 1993. Consensus, coherence and the European convention on human rights. *Cornell International Law Journal*, 26, 133–165.

Helfer, L.R., & Voeten, E., 2020. Walking back human rights in Europe? *European Journal of International Law*, 31(3), 797–827.

HELP, The Human Rights Education for Legal Professionals, *Interpretative mechanisms of ECHR case-law: The concept of European consensus.* Council of Europe. [online] Available from: www.coe.int/en/web/help/article-echr-case-law [Accessed April 11, 2021].

Heringa, A.W., 1996. The consensus principle – the role of common law in the ECHR case law *Maastricht Journal of European & Comparative Law*, 3(2), 108–145.

Kapotas, P., & Tzevelekos, V.P., eds., 2019. *Building consensus on European consensus: Judicial interpretation of human rights in Europe and beyond.* Cambridge: Cambridge University Press.

Letsas, G., 2014. The truth in autonomous concepts. How to interpret the ECHR. *European Journal of International Law*, 15, 279–305.

Madsen, M.R., 2016. The challenging authority of the European Court of Human Rights: From cold war legal diplomacy to the Brighton declaration and backlash. *Law and Contemporary Problems*, 9, 167–175.

Madsen, M.R., Cebulak, P., & Wiebusch, M., 2018. Backlash against international courts: Explaining the forms and patterns of resistance to international courts. *International Journal of Law in Context* (Special Issue 2: Resistance to International Courts), 14(2), 197–220.

O'Hara, C., 2021. Consensus, difference and sexuality: Que(e)rying the European Court of Human Rights concept of European consensus. *Law and Critique*, 32, 91–114.

Searle, J.R., 1969. *Speech acts.* Cambridge: Cambridge University Press.

Sinclair, J., 2004. *Trust the text: Language corpus and discourse.* London: Routledge.

Tulkens, F., 2011. What are the limits to the evolutive interpretation of the convention? *In: Dialogue between judges, European Court of Human Rights.* Strasbourg: Council of Europe, 6–11.

Vetrovsky, J., 2019. Determining the content of the European consensus concept: The hidden role of language. *In:* P. Kapotas & V.P. Tzevelekos, eds., *Building consensus on European consensus.* Cambridge: Cambridge University Press, 120–140.

Wildhaber, L., et al., 2013. No consensus on consensus? The practice of the European Court of Human Rights. *Human Rights Law Journal*, 33, 248–269.

Wittgenstein, L., 1953. *Philosophical investigations.* G.E.M. Anscombe, trans. Oxford: Blackwell.

5 Spider Woman beats Hulk

Baroness Hale and the prorogation of Parliament

Ruth Breeze

1 Introduction

On September 24, 2019, the president of the Supreme Court of the United Kingdom, Baroness Hale, declared Prime Minister Boris Johnson's suspension of Parliament to be unlawful. Johnson's measure was widely interpreted at the time as a means to forestall further debating of the Brexit deal, and the Supreme Court's ruling – a unanimous judgment by 11 Supreme Court justices – appeared to confirm this interpretation. Baroness Hale herself described this ruling as "a source of not pride, but satisfaction". Given the heated political climate at the time, the court's decision proved extremely controversial. Johnson himself proclaimed that the court had got it "wrong" and his attorney general, Geoffrey Cox, hinted that "there may very well need to be parliamentary scrutiny of judicial appointments" in the future.

The interest of this case thus lies not only in its immediate relevance within the ongoing Brexit saga, but what the political and media manifestations surrounding it reveal about wider societal attitudes towards and representations of the judiciary at a time when populism was on the rise. It is significant that a large amount of the positive and negative commentary surrounding this issue centred on Baroness Hale in person. Her prominent spider brooch worn when delivering the ruling led the press to call her "Spider Woman", a name which she herself then appropriated with pride in her subsequent public appearances. Over the next few weeks, heated controversy raged on both sides in the press and social media, with attacks against the Law Lords, the Supreme Court, and Baroness Hale in particular. As in many cases of public controversy, various different narratives or "frames" started to emerge concerning what this incident meant, how it was to be interpreted, and how it fitted into the broad panorama of public debate concerning Brexit (in particular) and the nature of democracy (in general).

This chapter addresses the framing that emerged from the reporting of and reactions to this incident, investigating how representations of the Supreme Court ruling and Baroness Hale herself were subsumed into ongoing controversies in public discourse, and, arguably, lent particular force by recourse to deeply

DOI: 10.4324/9781003153771-6

engrained cultural patterns. In methodological terms, this chapter shows how a corpus-assisted discourse analytical approach can shed light on both the rational and symbolic framing of controversial issues.

2 Framing and corpus assisted discourse analysis

The classical theory of framing, formulated by Goffman (1974) and later applied to media and social communication (Entman 1993), postulates that people organise their knowledge according to schemata or frameworks that enable them to perceive, identify, label and interpret what is going on around them. This theory has been criticised for its intrinsic indeterminacy and fragmentation (Entman 1993), but it remains one of the most compelling approaches to understanding media coverage of events and phenomena (Van Gorp and Vercruysse 2012). Media frames, in their most developed form, provide people with a full narrative concerning the type of phenomenon in question: for example, people's rational framing of terrorism at a given moment may include suppositions about the causes, motivation and means of operation, the moral judgment to be applied and the possible solutions (Jiménez-Yáñez 2018). Moreover, such frames are not closed systems: people's framing of terrorism is quite likely to fit into and overlap with even larger frames concerning their conceptualisations of right and wrong and even the meaning of human life, which they are likely to share with many other people on grounds of education, culture, religious or ethical beliefs. At this point, the rational framing tends to merge with the symbolic order, as the "story" present in the frame meshes with universal narratives of right and wrong.

In order to have narrative consistency and to make sense, then, news stories are shaped to fit into frames employed by journalists that reflect their worldview, which they probably share with a proportion of their readers (Scheufele 2000). The sociopolitical worldview within which the journalist and his/her publication operate thus determines whether a factory closure is framed as a crime of capitalism against the workers, or as a necessary measure to preserve the company's economic viability in the marketplace, with the implicit demonisation of bosses or unions in the symbolic order. Such frames rarely need to be stated in full, since the readers of the newspaper are practised at picking up the fragments on offer and piecing them together with the help of shared underlying master frames about how the world works.

Most previous research on framing has been conducted either in purely qualitative terms, or (more frequently) with the help of quantitative content analysis, a technique that relies on assistants trained to code large quantities of text in terms of a number of predetermined categories. However, keyword analysis has been found to compare favourably with content analysis to measure political ideologies (Rooduijn and Pauwels 2011), and previous authors have used keyword and concordance analysis to detect frames inductively, by identifying "important concepts in a text which may help 'diagnose' and 'nominate' central ideas around which the frame is constructed" (Touri and Koteyko 2015, p. 606). Like these authors,

I consider that the frames in texts should be explored inductively, because the framing that pertains to a specific issue under investigation is a dynamic phenomenon that can take many twists, even though it also inevitably overlaps with broader, more generic frames about wider issues. In my analysis I apply keyword and concordance analysis to dig more deeply into the discourses surrounding the ruling, in order to detect the frames being applied, and then investigate the overlap with other societal discourses current in late 2019 (e.g. populist and anti-elitist discourses, misogynist discourse directed at women in public life).

3 Corpus and method

A corpus of 71 newspaper texts (128,629 words) published over the following four weeks was assembled from a search in Nexis Uni for articles including the search terms "Hale" and "parliament". Twitter and social media searches were conducted, and around 4000 commentaries on the YouTube video containing the BBC report on the ruling (39,595 words) were collected. These corpora were uploaded to Sketch Engine for lexical processing, including analysis of keywords and collocations. The comments corpus was also uploaded to Wmatrix4 for semantic analysis, and relevant themes were then further investigated using qualitative discourse analytical methodology of significant examples (Rayson 2008).

4 Framing analysis of articles

To illustrate the general trends, three representative examples of each major tendency from three popular news sources are presented, in order to examine the framing in each case.

4.1 Overview of framing

The overview of the 71 articles revealed three main approaches to covering the Supreme Court ruling, with most British newspapers initially either presenting a neutral factual account of the decision (e.g. *Financial Times*, BBC) or inserting this episode into their habitual stance on Brexit (e.g. *Daily Mail, Daily Telegraph* on the pro-Brexit side; and *Guardian* on the Remainer side). The following examples illustrate the framing in each camp. For reasons of space, only the most significant parts of the text are presented in each case. Framing in news genres is clearly related to the foregrounding/backgrounding of different elements within the text (Breeze 2020). The principal textual means through which foregrounding is achieved are the headlines, subheadings and inserts, and the order of the information in the text – in multimodal terms, the use of images, hyperlinks, and so on – also has an important potential influence on the way readers are intended to understand the story. In this analysis, I concentrate on the textual strategies, mentioning multimodal elements where relevant.

4.2 *Balanced framing:* BBC

> *Boris Johnson's decision to suspend Parliament for five weeks was unlawful, the Supreme Court has ruled.*
>
> [Video of Lady Hale reading the key points in the ruling]
>
> Judges said it was wrong to stop MPs carrying out duties in the run-up to the Brexit deadline on 31 October.
>
> The PM, who has faced calls to resign, said he "profoundly disagreed" with the ruling but would "respect" it.
>
> . . . It comes after the court ruled it was impossible to conclude there had been any reason "let alone a good reason – to advise Her Majesty to prorogue Parliament for five weeks".
>
> (BBC, September 24, 2019)

The BBC report adopts a balanced approach by alternately placing Johnson and the judges in first position. The headline itself is interesting in two senses. First, it actually foregrounds Boris Johnson, but does so to stress that his decision was "unlawful". Second, it uses the term "suspend Parliament" rather than the more technical "prorogue", in order to make the message clear. The text itself foregrounds the judges by mentioning them in first position, and through the image of Lady Hale in the video presented between the headline and the text. Moreover, it reproduces the gist of their conclusions twice, once in simple language ("wrong to stop MPs carrying out duties") and then again in the more technical, legal terms used by the judges themselves (there had been no reason "to advise Her Majesty to prorogue Parliament"). So despite the prominence given to Johnson in the headline, the authoritative role is accorded to the judges. Moreover, the text repeats a conciliatory aspect of Johnson's comments, namely the fact that he is prepared to "respect" the ruling, rather than the (many) defiant remarks he made in the same context. In a sense, this article seems to downplay and neutralise what was a highly controversial decision, rather than to dramatise it and thus throw more fuel on the fire. In this framing, the Supreme Court ruling is an authoritative legal decision that strikes down the Prime Minister's attempt to suspend Parliament; the Prime Minister is displeased about this, but will do what the court says.

4.3 *Negative framing:* Daily Telegraph

> *Boris Johnson hits back at Supreme Court ruling saying people want to "frustrate Brexit" and "stop this country coming out of the EU"*
>
> [Video of Lady Hale delivering her conclusions with superimposed foreground image of Johnson in a despairing pose]

> Boris Johnson hit back at the Supreme Court's ruling that suspending Parliament was unlawful as he accused people of wanting to "frustrate Brexit" and "stop this country coming out of the EU".
>
> Responding to the verdict from New York, the Prime Minister said: "I strongly disagree with what the justices have found".
>
> Mr. Johnson added that while he did not "think that it's right", he would respect the decision and that Parliament would return.
>
> He reiterated his stance on Brexit that the "most important thing" was to deliver Brexit on Oct 31. "Clearly the claimants in this case are determined to frustrate that and to stop that", he added.
>
> "I think it would be very unfortunate if Parliament made that objective, which the people want, more difficult but we will get on".
>
> (*Daily Telegraph*, September 24, 2019)

This article, published on the *Daily Telegraph* live feed almost immediately after the ruling had been announced, is entirely framed as a response to the ruling rather than a report about it. The newspaper itself thus positions itself very clearly on the side of the Prime Minister and, of course, on the side of Brexit. The initial image in the inserted video shows Johnson in the foreground, his hand to his head in an attitude of despair, superimposed over Lady Hale reading her ruling. The reader is thus very clearly positioned to understand that Johnson is the important figure in this story and that the newspaper aligns itself with him. The text foregrounds Johnson in every sentence, placing him in an active role ("Boris Johnson hit back") and echoing his words linking the Supreme Court ruling to the notion of a conspiracy to "frustrate Brexit". This article thus gives scarcely any prominence to the judges or their reasoning, offering an entirely political interpretation of the ruling, and presenting the setback as another obstacle to be overcome on the route to leaving the EU. In this framing, the main point is that Johnson defies the judges, who are depicted as "causing problems" for him, and for Brexit. However, this tedious setback will not let it stop him from "delivering Brexit".

4.4 *Positive framing:* Guardian

> *Johnson's suspension of Parliament unlawful, Supreme Court rules*
>
> [Video image showing protesters carrying placards with "Misled the Queen", "Defend democracy" and "Don't silence our MPs"]
>
> Judges rule unanimously that PM's decision to prorogue Parliament can be examined by judges.
>
> The Supreme Court has ruled that Boris Johnson's advice to the Queen that Parliament should be prorogued for five weeks at the height of the Brexit crisis was unlawful.

> The unanimous judgment from 11 justices on the UK's highest court followed an emergency three-day hearing last week that exposed fundamental legal differences over interpreting the country's unwritten constitution.
>
> The momentous decision was read out by Lady Hale, president of the supreme court.
>
> (*Guardian*, September 24, 2019)

The headline of the *Guardian* report bears a strong similarity to that of the BBC report, but the image between the headline and text immediately situates the reader in the world of the protesters with their colourful, crisply worded placards, proposing a positive framing of the judges' ruling and a negative view of the Prime Minister. The text places the judges and their decision in first position throughout the initial section reproduced above, suggesting strong alignment with the judges through the repetition of the term "unanimous", through the assertion of legal authority in the first line, and through the framing of the ruling as a "momentous decision". The third sentence in the text is particularly interesting, in that it both reinforces the credibility of the judges and their ruling ("unanimous judgment from 11 justices") and alludes to problems in the system ("fundamental legal differences over interpreting the country's unwritten constitution"), thus pointing to the underlying issue that is not mentioned in the other two reports here but which helps the educated reader to understand the nature of the problem at hand. The main framing offered here is that the Supreme Court has defeated the Prime Minister, and, if we attend to the multimodal evidence, that this is a victory for democracy.

5 Corpus analysis of comments

5.1 Keyword analysis applied to framing

The keywords function in Sketch Engine was used to determine the keywords in the 4000 commentaries on the YouTube video associated with the BBC report (422,247 views), as a way to process the comments and bring out the main themes in the comments. The enTenTen15 corpus (consisting of 13,191 million words from a wide range of Internet sites in English; see Jakubíček et al. 2013) was used as the most appropriate reference corpus. This consists of linguistically valuable material obtained by web-scraping, and is thus likely to contain more of the generic features of digital texts than, say, the British National Corpus (BNC), which consists of conventionally published material (fiction, news, academic texts), conversation and so forth.

Tables 5.1 and 5.2 display the keywords and key two-word combinations and their respective keyness scores calculated through Sketch Engine using the Simple Maths method (roughly speaking, the frequency/million of the item in the

Table 5.1 Top 12 keywords in the Comments corpus

Word/item	*Keyness score*
Brexit	2018
Remainer	784
Bojo	732
Boris	703
Prorogue	558
Prorogation	553
Brooch	414
Hale	181
Unlawful	159
Brexiteer	256
Remoaner	236
Unelected	116

Table 5.2 Top 12 key two-word combinations in the Comments corpus

Two word/item combination	*Keyness score*
Spider brooch	335
Supreme court	244
Democratic vote	184
Black widow	153
Referendum result	151
Second referendum	80
Huge spider	79
Widow spider	77
Giant spider	76
Conference season	72
Suspending Parliament	59
Spider pin	59

focus corpus, divided by its frequency/million in the reference corpus, so the larger the keyness score the more "key" the word or combination is; see Kilgarriff 2009).

Table 5.1 illustrates the predominantly political focus of the comments, and the way the ruling is popularly conceptualised as a dispute between Boris Johnson (Boris, Bojo) and Baroness Hale, in the immediate sense, and between Brexiteers and Remainers or pejoratively "Remoaners" in the wider sense. The term "unlawful" echoes the wording of the ruling. The occurrence of "unelected" is worthy of comment, however. When the ruling was announced, the (then) Labour leader Jeremy Corbyn told cheering delegates that "this unelected prime minister should now resign". This term was thus launched into currency and picked up by the pro-Boris contingent, so that the lead story in the Sun blasted "unelected judges", while Brendan O'Neill, the editor of online libertarian, pro-Brexit magazine *Spiked* characterised the ruling as "a vile assault on the democratic order" and "a decisively political act by 11 *unelected judges* who have taken sides against the government of the day, and this opens up a new, dark era in British political life" (O'Neill 2019). Despite Corbyn's launching of the term to describe the (then) unelected Prime Minister, all the instances of "unelected" in the comments are used to describe the judges, who are variously denigrated as "unelected silver spooners", "unelected scum" and a "supposedly unbiased unelected judiciary". Taken up in later pronouncements by various Conservative representatives and echoed throughout the right-wing media, the stereotype of "unelected judges" blocking "the will of the people" became a leitmotif of Johnson's first year in office.

The word combinations identified as "key" allow us to glimpse the language used in the comments themselves. It is certainly significant that six of these two-word combinations refer to Baroness Hale herself and her most noticeable accessory, the spider brooch that she wore on her black dress when she read out the Supreme Court ruling. The term "widow" refers to a type of spider, the venomous black widow spider, mentioned in association with the brooch (Lady Hale herself was not a widow at that time, but wore black, as is mandatory for judges in the UK). This theme was explored further through semantic analysis and will be discussed in more depth below.

The other keyword combinations allude mainly to the Brexit referendum, which is presented by commenters as the immediate background to the issues at stake: the underlying logic here is that since "the people" voted "leave" in the referendum, anything that delays leaving (like the present ruling) must be anti-democratic.

A brief overview of this keyword analysis shows how it enhances our understanding of the framing of this incident in the popular imagination. First, the keyword analyses bring out its framing as an episode in an ongoing battle between two sides simplistically lined up as pro-Brexit and anti-Brexit. Second, they provide further evidence of the framing of the judges, by the pro-Brexit side, as members of the elite ("silver spooners"), and thus as antagonists of the people (see Breeze 2018, on the framing of the High Court judges in *Miller v. Secretary of State* for exiting the European Union as "enemies of the people", for a wider discussion of this point). Finally, they point to the popular framing of this dispute as a conflict between two prominent individuals, Boris Johnson and Baroness Hale. Further aspects of this will be discussed in the analysis of key semantic areas below.

5.2 Semantic keyness applied to framing

Semantic processing with Wmatrix4 brought out the semantic areas listed in Table 5.3 as being particularly prominent in the comments (BNC spoken used as reference corpus).

Table 5.3 Top 12 key semantic areas in the Comments corpus

Semantic area	*Log likelihood*
Politics	1417
Geographical names	1284
Law and order	1070
Government	998
Evaluation: good	351
In power	208
Unethical	157
Crime	149
Living creatures: animals, birds	127
Evaluation: false	87
Failure	54
Hindering	47

The frequency of "politics", "government", "law and order" and "in power" are perhaps unsurprising, given that the issue of the court's decision concerning the prorogation of Parliament lay in the intersection between these areas, with matters of "democracy" and "constitution" being handled by judges explaining the limits of governmental power. "Evaluation: good" and "evaluation: false" also seem to fit loosely with the subject matter. However, other areas are more surprising. These will be analysed below, in the context of four emergent themes: populism, conspiracy, win-lose drama, and witchcraft.

5.2.1 *Populism*

The lexical items associated with "unethical" and "crime" turned out to be particularly highly charged (*traitors, corruption, cheat, wicked, trick*, etc. in the first case, and *treason, renegade, gangster, criminal*, etc. in the second). The comments using these terms are almost entirely pro-Brexit, and tend to have a heavily patriotic emphasis with frequent references to the Queen and other national institutions:

(1) Her Majesty IS the law and these false justices are now in open rebellion against the Kingdom. Her Majesty should send her guards to execute these traitors immediately.

It is interesting, however, that this national-populist tone is often linked with an appeal to the "common people", following the populist principle of anti-elitism that has been so successfully exploited in recent years by leaders on the right like Trump, Johnson and Salvini (see Moffitt 2016 on populist performances of anti-elitism).

(2) The gilded spider is appropriate, signifies the well to do poisoning common folks chance of real democracy.

5.2.2 *Conspiracy*

Another closely related theme emerging from the semantic analysis, associated with the areas "unethical" and "crime", is particularly interesting because of the way it draws on other aspects in the public imagination, shedding light on the process of myth-making surrounding the highly inflammatory issue of Brexit and the multiple cultural forces involved. The conspiracies, in this case, involve entities thought to have "betrayed Brexit", including Blair, the BBC, and "the establishment" in general.

(3) Those Judges are traitors hand picked by Tony Blair.
(4) Propaganda, lies, and treason brought to you by the masters of deception the BBC.
(5) What's the point in voting anymore? I said the day after the referendum result the establishment would never allow us to leave the EU!

5.2.3 *Win-lose drama*

The areas "failure" and "hindering" suggest a frequent framing of the issue as a heightened win-lose drama rather than as merely the clarification of the constitutional position. Brexit supporters tended to frame the ruling as a deliberate obstruction, but one that would ultimately be overcome:

(6) Brexiteers have been the silent majority until now but this will not last and a hefty price will be exacted from those who have obstructed the will of the proletariat.

However, the anti-Brexit side was equally vocal about what they felt to be "their" victory. Example (7) exudes exultation at Johnson's defeat:

(7) Boris and the Brexit leadership tried to side step democracy but shutting it down and they lost and have now been labeled anti-democratic by their own supreme court. When is Boris going to face the Queen and apologize to her for lying to her?

5.2.4 *Witchcraft*

The semantic area of "religion and the supernatural" was also key in this corpus, and the list of words in this category is thought-provoking: *witch, hell, unicorn, spectre, spirit, angel, devil, dragon, freemason, witchcraft, satanic, ghost* and *coven*. These items are surprising if we consider that the report is about a Supreme Court ruling on what was essentially a constitutional issue. Such associations seem to have been chiefly inspired by Baroness Hale's spider brooch, which gave rise to a large number of playful and not-so-playful contributions speculating as to her reason for wearing it and linking it to other aspects of the case, her role or the judges in general. Almost all of the negative comments in this sense had misogynistic undertones; some were offensive and condemnatory (8), while (9) and (10) are representative of decidedly more troubling trends:

(8) This woman looks like the old Wicked Witch with a black widow spider on her sweater; what a bizarre choice of clothing . . . like her bizarre reasoning in interfering with the democratic vote.

(9) That spider is a clear signal of her witchcraft. The Elites are past hiding it and are openly taunting us with their symbols. Vile. Degenerate. Satanic filth.

(10) The Westminster system falls prey to the BLACK WIDOW

Table 5.4 presents the "wordsketch" obtained from Sketch Engine for the search term "spider", and gives some idea of the range and variety of metaphors and connotations associated with the spider.

The association with witchcraft is particularly interesting in cultural terms – although wearing a spider brooch on such a high-profile occasion must be seen as an act of provocation, and what Baroness Hale herself intended is by no means clear. As the more sinister comments and associations reported above in (9) and (10) and Table 5.4 show, the witch still appears to be an archetype that serves to discredit women, particularly powerful women, in the popular *imaginaire* (Goodare 2016). Like its parallel, the "whore", the "witch" is a time-honoured label used for policing and denigrating women (Miller 2018), which has recently been applied liberally to Hillary Clinton ("the wicked witch of the left"), Nancy Pelosi and Theresa May, and undoubtedly has undertones of both ageism and sexism.

Table 5.4 WordSketch for "spider" in comments corpus

Modifiers of spider	Nouns modified by spider	Verbs with spider as object	Verbs with spider as subject	Spider and/or
giant	brooch	wear	crawl	giant
huge	pin	love	represent	roach
black	woman	get	tote	bug
widow	design	have	hide	boris
massive	outfit	jewel	creep	
big	flex	be	wait	
gilded	queen	come	be	
glittery	granny	ignore	do	
decorative	bug		have	
pimp	lady			
blinged out				
roach				
itsy bitsy				
illuminati				

Interestingly, however, some comments also presented the spider in a more positive light: Baroness Hale appears as a symbolic counterweight to the figure of Boris Johnson (in fact, Hale was represented in cartoons of the moment as "Spider Woman" vs. "Hulk"). Her spider brooch was to be presented graphically in cartoons and reproduced in social media as a symbol of resistance to Brexit, as an assertion of female power, or both. One commenter posted:

(11) Spider woman just battered the lying womanizing racist the incredible Sulk, love it.

6 Discussion

The framing analysis and corpus-assisted discourse analysis presented here have allowed us to observe a broad intersection of discussions of the Supreme Court ruling with the nationalist-populist discourses familiar from the Brexit campaign. The framing of the incident in terms of ideological and/or personal conflict is fully in line with previous research on the representation of Brexit-related issues (Eatwell and Goodwin 2018; Bennett 2019). In line with previous trends concerning an establishment conspiracy to block Brexit, Baroness Hale and her fellow Supreme Court judges are here represented as part of a sinister establishment conspiracy to undermine democracy. In this perspective, the spider and its "web" take on ideological undertones as part of an ominous, underhand attempt to undermine the will of the people – a "will" presented as unanimously directed towards achieving Brexit. In this context a nexus is constructed with previous episodes in the Brexit saga, particularly the highly polarised reporting of Gina Miller's challenge to the government's bid to sidestep a parliamentary vote on Article 50 and the themes aired in the controversial *Daily Mail* article "Enemies of the People" (Breeze 2018). Investigation of the intense media interest surrounding these events sheds light on emergent conspiracy discourses about how the establishment is "betraying Brexit". As Browning has recently analysed (2019), the populist discourses surrounding Brexit became so heavily invested with such high hopes (or indeed, fantasies) that disappointment was inevitable, and it is highly likely that conspiracy theories surrounding incidents such as these provided one outlet for the ontological anxieties and insecurities upon which populist politics preys.

On examining the representation of this case in more detail, we can clearly appreciate that the digital viewer comments that displayed this tendency offer a symbiosis of discourses directed against the judiciary, with the familiar range of pervasive anti-elite discourses associated with the Brexit campaign and its aftermath (Clarke and Newman 2017) which could be loosely characterised as populist. Digital media, including user comments and discussion boards, have been shown to be particularly influential as a means of spreading radical populist, anti-elitist and conspiracy-oriented ideas (Demata 2018), and in this case the messages found in the digital space were considerably more extreme than those in the mainstream media sources consulted.

Moreover, it is not coincidental that these digital sources also abound with manifestations of misogynist discourses, in this case, attacks on one of the few women in a prominent position within the legal establishment. There is evidently some confluence here with the replication of real-world gender inequalities in the digital sphere (KhosraviNik and Esposito 2018; Esposito forthcoming), and the frequent social media representation of women in public life as outsiders or in some sense other, documented by previous researchers (Southern and Harmer 2019; Esposito 2021). In the comments on this incident, the spider theme provides a focal point for social media users to develop metaphors or comparisons that combine negative representations of a powerful woman (the spider queen) with other negative symbolic representations of the ruling and its sinister "conspiratorial", "treacherous" or "unpatriotic" status.

Analysis of this episode thus brings to light further dimensions of the interface between politics, law and the media in the post-referendum United Kingdom, with ongoing repercussions that seem to bode ill for the separation of powers as the judiciary itself is positioned as opposing "the people". The digital media afterlife of this episode on the comments pages offers clues to understanding the reconfiguration and revitalisation of populist discourses in the years after the Brexit referendum, and the increasing confluence of post-Trumpian right-wing politics, anti-establishment conspiracy-oriented discourses and persistent misogynistic attitudes in social media discourses. Investigation of the seemingly trivial details of this incident and their media and social media repercussions thus adds to our understanding of the workings of ideology in social media, and provides further insights into their power to shape the political landscape.

References

Bennett, S., 2019. Standing up for "real people": UKIP, the Brexit, and discursive strategies on Twitter. *In:* J. Zienkowski & R. Breeze, eds., *Imagining the peoples of Europe. Populist discourses across the political spectrum.* Amsterdam: John Benjamins, 229–256.

Breeze, R., 2018. "Enemies of the people": Populist performances in the daily mail reporting of the Article 50 case. *Discourse, Context & Media*, 25, 60–67.

Breeze, R., 2020. Don't let the facts spoil the story. Foregrounding in news genres versus scientific rigour. *Lingue e Linguaggi*, 34, 167–189.

Browning, C., 2019. Brexit populism and fantasies of fulfilment. *Cambridge Review of International Affairs*, 32(3), 222–244.

Clarke, J., & Newman, J., 2017. "People in this country have had enough of experts": Brexit and the paradoxes of populism. *Critical Policy Studies*, 11, 101–116.

Demata, M., 2018. "I think that maybe I wouldn't be here if it wasn't for Twitter". Donald Trump's populist style on Twitter. *Textus*, 31(1), 67–90.

Eatwell, R., & Goodwin, M., 2018. *National populism. The revolt against liberal democracy.* London: Penguin.

Entman, R., 1993. Framing: Toward clarification of a fractured paradigm. *Journal of Communication*, 43(4), 51–58.

Esposito, E., 2021. Introduction: Critical perspectives on gender, politics and violence. *Journal of Language Aggression and Conflict* (Special Issue on Critical perspectives on violence against women in politics), 9(1), 1–20.

Esposito, E., forthcoming. The Continuum of Violence: Gender-based Violence Online. *In:* E. Bjarnegård & P. Zetterberg (eds.) *Gender and Violence against Political Actors.* Philadelphia: Temple University Press.

Goffman, E., 1974. Frame analysis: An essay on the organization of experience. London: Harper and Row.

Goodare, J., 2016. *The European witchhunt.* London: Routledge.

Jakubíček, M., Kilgarriff, A., Kovář, V., Rychlý, P., & Suchomel, V., 2013. The TenTen corpus family. *In: 7th international corpus linguistics conference CL*, Lancaster: Lancaster University. 125–127. https://www.sketchengine.eu//wp-content/uploads/The_TenTen_Corpus_2013.pdf

Jiménez-Yáñez, R.M., 2018. El programa electoral: el análisis desde la teoría del framing. *In:* C. Llamas Saíz, ed., *El análisis del discurso político: géneros y metodologías.* Pamplona: EUNSA, 103–129.

KhosraviNik, M., & Esposito, E., 2018. Online hate, digital discourse and critique: Exploring digitally mediated discursive practices of gender-based hostility. *Lodz Papers in Pragmatics*, 14(1), 45–68.

Kilgarriff, A., 2009. Simple maths for keywords. *In:* M. Mahlberg, V. González-Díaz, & C. Smith, eds., *Proceedings of corpus linguistics conference CL2009.* Liverpool: University of Liverpool.

Miller, M., 2018. *Circe.* London: Bloomsbury.

Moffitt, B., 2016. *The global rise of populism: Performance, political style and representation.* Stanford, CA: Stanford University Press.

O'Neill, B., 2019. A tyranny of judges. *Spiked.* September 24. [online] Available from: www.spiked-online.com/2019/09/24/a-tyranny-of-judges/.

Rayson, P. 2008. From key words to key semantic domains. *International Journal of Corpus Linguistics*, 13(4), 519–549. DOI: 10.1075/ijcl.13.4.06ray.

Rooduijn, M., & Pauwels, T., 2011. Measuring populism: Comparing two methods of content analysis. *West European Politics*, 34(6), 1272–1283.

Scheufele, D., 2000. Agenda-setting, priming, and framing revisited: Another look at cognitive effects of political communication. *Mass Communication & Society*, 3, 297–316.

Southern, R., & Harmer, E., 2019. Othering political women: Online misogyny, racism and ableism towards women in public life. *Online Othering*, 187–210.

Touri, M., & Koteyko, N., 2015. Using corpus linguistic software in the extraction of news frames: Towards a dynamic process of frame analysis in journalistic texts. *International Journal of Social Research Methodology*, 18(6), 601–616. http://doi.org/10.1080/13645579.2014.929878.

Van Gorp, B., & Vercruysse, T., 2012. Frames and counter-frames giving meaning to dementia: A framing analysis of media content. *Social Science & Medicine*, 74, 1274–1281. http://doi.org/10.1016/j.socscimed.2011.12.045 www.theguardian.com/books/2018/apr/07/cursed-from-circe-to-clinton-why-women-are-cast-as-witches.

Part II

Judicial argumentation and evaluative language

6 Making a corpus-linguistic U-turn in multilingual adjudication

Martina Bajčić

1 Introduction

Koen Lenaerts (2011, p. 212), current president of the Court of Justice, openly acknowledged the threat for the quality of the reasoning of judgments posed by the overload of cases and the speed with which they have to be resolved. In light of the corpus-linguistic turn in jurisprudence, it is fascinating to contemplate whether using corpora could support the judges in their reasoning and expedite their decision-making. What type of corpora should best be used to accomplish this? Another pressing issue in this regard concerns the users' (lack of) expertise in linguistics, enabling them to genuinely use corpus data (cf. Dörk and Knight 2015, p. 84) and leverage corpus-based argumentation. Addressing these questions, it is necessary to provide not only a general account of corpora and corpus linguistics' methods with emphasis on multilingual parallel corpora of EU law, but also of legal interpretation methods in the context of multilingual EU law by means of an analysis of settled case law. Emphasis is put on language cases which have retained piquancy and relevance and which allow us to hypothesise on the use of corpus linguistics' methods in multilingual interpretation of EU law. Operationalised by translation, EU legislation is a multilingual legislative instrument of equal authoritative status in all 24 official languages of the EU. Irrespective of its equal status, there are divergences between the different language versions of EU legislation that lie at the heart of the language cases.[1]

Corpus linguistics methodology has forayed into empirical studies of law and language, that is, legal linguistics (e.g. Hamann and Vogel 2017; Trklja and McAuliffe 2018) and legal translation (Biel 2014; Prieto Ramos 2019). Insightful, comparative corpus-driven analyses of judgments have not only illustrated the usefulness of corpus methodology for legal practitioners (Koźbial 2018; Pontrandolfo 2018); they have also provided a deeper understanding

1 EU translation as a type of institutional translation can be described as an amalgamation of different steps including drafting, translating, and legal revision (Mori 2018, p. 6). Leaving aside the complex procedures involved, it is a matter of fact that legal translation is inherently imperfect, thus resulting in divergences between the 24 authentic texts of EU legislation (Šarčević 2013, p. 1).

DOI: 10.4324/9781003153771-8

of linguistic framing of rationales in judgments (Goźdź-Roszkowski 2020). Despite groundbreaking research into using corpus methods in interpretation of statutes (Solan and Gales 2017; Hessick 2018), their application in the context of multilingual legal reasoning and the relationship between adjudication and multilingual legislation is still suffused by many questions that are not restricted to the philosophical reflections of jurists and invite further interdisciplinary investigation.

2 Corpora as a springboard for legal interpretation

Corpus linguistics as the study of language based on examples of real-life use today applies many different approaches, such as corpus-informed, corpus-assisted, corpus-based and corpus-driven.[2] Following the first monolingual corpora, since the 1990s parallel corpora-assisted research has revolutionised all linguistic disciplines. In light of the rapid development of parallel corpora, some scholars speak of a parallel corpus linguistics (Doval and Sánchez Nieto 2019, p. 2). Likewise, both parallel and comparable corpora have been growing in terms of their potential application. Although the technical tasks of compiling corpora have become much easier, parallel and multilingual corpora are still lagging behind their monolingual counterparts (Mikhailov et al. 2019, p. 183). Not only are they smaller than monolingual corpora, but their use is often limited to parallel concordancing, while other query functions are less popular (Mikhailov et al. 2019, p. 183).

Usually, research into parallel corpora is conducted for investigating linguistic phenomena, or, parallel corpora are a source of data in computational linguistics (Doval and Sánchez Nieto 2019, p. 3).[3] Accordingly, parallel corpora can be approached either from the process or the product perspective. The latter perspective can be utilised as a tool for translation error detections or for identifying differences in the meaning of different language versions, or for resolving these differences. The CJEU has consulted collections of multilingual EU legislation to this end in many cases as will be analysed in the second part of this chapter. However, multilingual corpora in the field of corpus-based legal translation studies are still scarce (Prieto Ramos 2019, p. 2). What is more, at present, the corpus analysis software for multilingual corpora is underdeveloped, making it necessary for corpus methods to integrate not only quantitative but also qualitative (legal)

2 Greatly simplified, corpus-based approach refers to a methodology that avails itself of the corpus to expound, test or exemplify theories and descriptions (Tognini-Bonelli 2001, p. 65), whereas a corpus-driven approach uses a corpus beyond the selection of examples to support linguistic argument or validate a theoretical statement (Tognini-Bonelli 2001, p. 84). Researchers nowadays often combine corpus-based and corpus-driven approaches. See also Biel (2018).

3 In general, corpora are said to have four main areas of application: basic research in contrastive linguistics and translatology, translation practice, lexicography and the teaching of foreign language and translation (Doval and Sánchez Nieto 2019, p. 3).

parameters into corpus-building criteria (Prieto Ramos 2019, p. 1) tailored to the specific needs of the national courts of EU Member States.

2.1 Multilingual parallel corpora of EU law

The multilingual parallel language resources of the European Union represent perhaps the most important parallel corpora to date. Some of the largest freely available multilingual parallel corpora today comprising legislative and administrative texts from the European Union are DGT-Acquis, JRC Acquis and Europarl v7.[4] DGT-Acquis, as a family of several multilingual parallel corpora extracted from the Official Journal of the EU, consists of documents from the middle of 2004 to the end of 2011 in 23 languages (see Steinberger et al. 2014).[5] Europarl v7, as a corpus collected of parallel texts in 11 languages from the proceedings of the European Parliament, is widely used for the purpose of statistical machine translation (Koehn 2005), as is DGT-TM.[6] Together with EUR-Lex and DCEP, the latter corpora have been integrated into the language corpus management and query system Sketch Engine (Biel 2018).

Worth mentioning is the recently compiled European Union case law corpus (EUCLCORP) as a multilingual parallel corpus of the case law of the CJEU (Trklja and McAuliffe 2018). Since it includes case law of eight EU Member States' constitutional/supreme courts, it is a comparable corpus as well. Unlike parallel corpora, comparable corpora include original texts in more than one language or variety. EUCLCORP allows users to pull up different language versions of a particular term to investigate translation consistency or errors. While it could be argued that the online database of EU legislation EUR-Lex, available in 24 official languages, has been used for this purpose, it does not contain national case law. In contrast, EUCLCORP makes it possible to investigate the meaning of terms by observing their typical patterns in CJEU judgments and the judgments of the relevant national constitutional/supreme courts (Trklja and McAuliffe 2018). Owing to various options regarding frequency, collocations and n-grams, one can examine the senses of ambiguous terms, the influence of national legal languages on EU case law (and vice versa), discourse relations and formulaic expressions which can contribute to the understanding of the textual organisation of judgments (Trklja and McAuliffe 2018). Other scholars have conducted comparative corpus-driven analyses of judgments underscoring the usefulness of corpus methodology for translators and legal practitioners

4 Available from: http://opus.lingfil.uu.se/ (Accessed September 8, 2020). However, many texts are not available in Croatian, although it is an official EU language as of 2013. For an overview of legal corpora in general, see Pontrandolfo (2012) and Biel (2018) for the use of corpora in institutional legal translation.

5 Available from: https://ec.europa.eu/jrc/en/language-technologies/dgt-acquis (Accessed September 8, 2020).

6 This multilingual translation memory in 22 languages is freely accessible since 2007. Available from: DGT-Translation Memory EU Science Hub (www.europa.eu) (Accessed October 30, 2020).

(e.g. Koźbial 2018; Pontrandolfo 2018). Highlighting the importance of the context of use of "crucial language items" helps legal practitioners to properly understand EU judgments and produce texts resembling the established conventions of the genre (Koźbial 2018, p. 355). Furthermore, some studies probe into the usefulness of corpora for legal interpretation from the perspective of judges and courts (e.g. Goldfarb 2019), thereby profiling legal practitioners as a new generation of users of corpus methods. This raises the pressing issue of whether users of corpora should have expertise in linguistics in order to be able to genuinely use corpus data. Dörk and Knight (2015, p. 84) point out that many existing corpora are aimed mainly at people with expertise in linguistics. Despite the fact that judges in some jurisdictions use general language corpora (e.g. in the US jurisprudence for searching for ordinary meaning), we argue that judges working in the multilingual EU environment require special parallel corpora comprising legislative texts and designed to fit the purpose of preserving the unity of a single instrument in all authentic texts with the aim of promoting the uniform interpretation and application of EU legislation by the national courts in all Member States (Šarčević 2012, pp. 86–87). For this purpose, more metadata should be included in corpora such as EUCLCORP; for example, limiting searches to specific legal issues and sections of judgments, as well as comprehensive national case law (not just of supreme/constitutional courts). This is instrumental, as despite the growing number of multilingual resources, corpora designed for judges only, and not terminologists and translators, are still lacking.

3 CJEU's multilingual interpretation

Considering potential benefits of utilising corpus methods in multilingual legal reasoning, it is important not to conceptualise the law as (merely) legal texts. According to legal realists, while legal texts are sources of law, law is a set of normative meanings which are ascribed to legal texts by interpreters, either by means of interpretation or legal construction (Guastini 2015, p. 49). Hence, the law is said to arise from the interaction of legislators and interpreters (Guastini 2015, p. 50). As regards the interpretative methods of the CJEU, over the years it has developed dynamic methods of multilingual interpretation, with the requirement to compare all language versions of a provision as its starting point (Šarčević 2013, p. 11). In its judgment in the *Van der Vecht* case of 1967, the Court has for the first time stated that, in cases of doubt, a provision should be interpreted and applied in accordance with other versions.[7] What's more, in other cases[8] it held that even when a language version is clear and unambiguous, courts, including national courts of Member States, need to interpret and apply EU legislation

7 Case 19-67, Bestuur der Sociale Verzekeringsbank v. J.H. van der Vecht [1967] ECR 00345.
8 Case C-219/95, Ferriere Nord SpA v. Commission of the European Communities [1997] ECR I-04411.

in accordance with other versions.[9] Therefore, the requirement to compare all language versions applies to all cases, not just to instances of discrepancy or doubt (i.e. to the so-called language cases) and is now considered as well-established case law, as the following analysis confirms.

3.1 Case law analysis

CJEU's interpretive methods in language cases have been examined by a quantitative empirical study of judgments and opinions of Advocates General in the period from January 1 until December 31, 2019, retrieved from the online case law database e-curia.[10] The search was conducted using the keyword "language version" in the indicated period. Subsequently, by content analysis inferences were made about the quantitative data. Initially, the search generated a dataset of 22 opinions and 21 judgments. Following the content analysis,[11] actual comparison of languages was identified in 18 judgments and 19 opinions.[12] From a pool of 1620 cases decided by both the Court of Justice and the General Court in 2019, it is questionable whether language cases warrant investigation. However, if national courts need to interpret and apply EU legislation in accordance with other versions, it follows that linguistic comparison should be widely used to support interpretation (cf. Pacho Aljanti 2015). The fact remains that there is profound opportunity for inconsistencies among the various language versions (Solan 2007, p. 2), so that it can be assumed that many discrepancies, ambiguities and inconsistencies in case law of national courts remain unnoticed. Therefore, exploring the potential of parallel corpora in this context merits attention.

The present analysis corroborates previous findings in that actual linguistic comparison is carried out less frequently,[13] in so far as the Court today doesn't compare all languages,[14] but a few. For instance, in the case C-477/17 the Court

9 This prompted claims that linguistic comparison serves as a method to support interpretation by the court beyond issues of language discrepancies (e.g. Pacho Aljanti 2015), thereby encouraging linguistic reflections on multilingual judicial reasoning and attempts to illuminate the nature of linguistic comparison conducted by the court (e.g. Kjær 2010; Bajčić 2020).

10 http://curia.europa.eu/juris/recherche.jsf?language=en

11 In some cases, "language version" is referred to in relation to the knowledge of languages and language discrimination, such as C-621/16 P, therefore, such cases were not included in the analysis.

12 Similarly, Baaij (2018, p. 75) reports that the Court compared language versions in merely 4.2% of preliminary rulings between 1960 and 2010. Furthermore, in the same period the Court compared all language versions only in 1.4% of all judgments (2018, p. 74).

13 For a detailed discussion of the role of linguistic comparison in CJEU's decision-making, see Bajčić (2020).

14 An exception is the judgment in joined cases C-115/16, C-118/16, C-119/16 and C-299/16, in which all language versions are consulted: as is apparent from paragraph 10 above, some language versions of Article 1(1) of Directive 2003/49, such as the Bulgarian, French, Latvian and Romanian versions, use the term "beneficiary"/"recipient"; other versions have recourse to expressions such as "beneficial owner"/"actual beneficiary" (the Spanish, Czech, Estonian, English, Italian, Lithuanian, Maltese, Portuguese and Finnish

of Justice dealt with the concept of *legal residence* within the meaning of the Directive 2011/98. The referring court took the view that the exact scope of the concept of *legal residence* within the meaning of that provision is uncertain, given the divergence between the language versions of the directive. Whereas the Dutch version uses the term *verblijven*, which appears to refer to a stay which is not necessarily long-term, the versions in German or English, which respectively mention *rechtmässiger Wohnsitz* and *legally resident*, could be understood as referring to a stay, entailing a degree of permanence (para. 55). In case T-108/17, the English and German version were compared in order to determine if two French terms are synonyms. Sometimes, comparisons are conducted to refer to a translation error (cf. T-760/15). Similarly, only French and German were consulted in the case C-477/18; English and French in C-195/18, C-516/17; English (which was at odds with), French, German, Dutch, Spanish, Italian, Danish, Finnish and Czech versions in T-607/15. Dutch, Polish and Romanian were juxtaposed with German, English, Italian and Spanish in C-383/8. In case C-391/16 it was established that the French version differs from Spanish, German, English, Portuguese and Swedish versions, while the Hungarian language version was brought into question in the case C-361/18.

Although the Court does compare language versions, it does not resolve a legal issue based on the results of the conducted comparison, as is especially apparent in the following two cases. In case C-649/17, the Court explicitly stated that the issue in question is not resolved by the analysis of different language versions of Article 6(1)(c) of Directive 2011/83. While it does compare language versions, and states that the majority – in particular, the versions in English (*where available*), French (*lorsqu'ils sont disponibles*), Dutch (*indien beschikbaar*), Italian (*ove disponibili*), Polish (*o ile jest dostępny*) and Finnish (*jos nämä ovat käytettävissä*) – suggest that the obligation imposed on traders to inform consumers of their telephone and fax numbers applies only where those traders have such means of communication. Other versions of that provision, in Spanish (*cuando proceda*) and German (*gegebenenfalls*), do not allow the circumstances to be determined in which that obligation does not apply (para. 36). To resolve the issue, the Court states that it is necessary to interpret the provision in question by reference to the context in which it occurs and the objectives pursued by the rules of which it is part (para. 37).

Analogously, in C-519/18 the referring court raised the issue of the interpretation of the concept of being "dependent" within the meaning of Directive 2003/86, since in the version of the language of the case, Article 10(2) of that directive is directed at the family members who are supported by the refugee (*a menekült eltartottjai*), whereas in the English-language version, that provision refers to those members who are in a relationship of dependence with the

---

versions), "owner"/"person entitled to use" (the German, Danish, Greek, Croat, Hungarian, Polish, Slovak, Slovenian and Swedish versions) or "person entitled in the end" (the Dutch version). Para. 89.

refugee (*dependent on the refugee*; para. 18). The referring court hence brought into question whether those expressions are fully equivalent. In parallel to the previous case, the Court doesn't answer this question but resolves it by referring to the need to interpret concepts independently (of national law provisions) and uniformly Union-wide.[15]

Similarly, the analysed opinions of Advocates General demonstrate that the comparison of language versions is prompted by ambiguities, inconsistencies or translation mistakes in one language version or to support their interpretation. Advocates General tend to concentrate on defining legal concepts and explaining their elements and scope to deduce from that analysis the resolution of a case (Barcelo 1997). Furthermore, they set forth policies and doctrinal choices open to the court (Perju 2009, p. 338). Much like in the analysed judgments, the comparison of language versions in the analysed opinions is not pertinent for resolving the legal issue. This is perhaps more apparent in opinions of Advocates General, who tend to frame the legal issue more clearly and transparently, whereas their opinions are considered as the functional equivalent of a judgment of a court of first instance (Perju 2009, p. 354).[16] For example, Advocate General Saugmandsgaard Øe detected variations in the English language version ("clear and comprehensible information") and the German language version (*in klarer und verständlicher Weise informieren*), whereas the French language version of Recital 34 of Directive 2011/83/EU expresses the comprehensibility of information to be given more apparently (*informations claires et exhaustives*). Despite the noted variations, he deems that all of the differing terms highlight the same need, namely that consumers must be fully informed before concluding a contract (*Ibid.*).

Summarising, while it was not possible to discuss the facts of these cases in detail due to space limitations, the analysis demonstrates that the Court's view of divergences between language versions has remained unaltered since 1969, when the signature case on linguistic divergences *Stauder*[17] was adjudicated, and in which all four authentic language versions were compared. The Court reiterates that the wording used in one language version of a provision of EU law

15 See para. 44, case C-519/18:
Secondly, as regards the meaning to be given to the condition of being "dependent" on the refugee, it must be borne in mind that the need to ensure a uniform application of EU law and the principle of equality require that the terms of a provision of EU law which makes no express reference to the law of the Member States for the purpose of determining its meaning and scope must normally be given an independent and uniform interpretation throughout the European Union (Judgment of July 29, 2019, Spiegel Online, C 516/17, EU:C:2019:625, para. 62 and the case law cited).

16 This assertion must be observed in the context of the preliminary ruling mechanism pursuant to Article 234 EC Treaty, whereby national courts refer questions to the Court of Justice pertaining to the interpretation of the Treaties, as well as questions regarding the validity and interpretation of secondary legislation. In this context the Court of Justice has a special role of a court of original jurisdiction and not of an appeals court (Perju 2009, p. 351).

17 Case 29/69 Stauder [1969] ECR 419, ECLI:EU:C:1969:57.

cannot serve as the sole basis for the interpretation of that provision or be made to override the other languages. Accordingly, provisions of EU law must be interpreted and applied uniformly in the light of the versions existing in all languages and by reference to the general scheme and purpose of the rules of which they form part (see para. 31, case C-477/17).[18]

4 Discussion

The comparison of different language versions does not serve the purpose of resolving the legal issue in question, neither in judgments nor in opinions of Advocates General. This exposes a general shortcoming of using parallel corpora as a supportive method of resolving language cases by "looking for law in 24 different places" (cf. Schilling 2010) that concerns the centrality of reason for judicial decision-making. Judicial decision-making includes stating the reasons on which a decision is based.[19] The Court of Justice has a duty to give reasons for its decisions[20] in keeping with the need that a legitimate exercise of powers is one justified by reason (Perju 2009, p. 313). What matters is not only that the parties are explained why they lost or won a case[21] but also to justify the outcome to multiple audiences, among them national courts and law practitioners Union-wide. Stating of reasons and understanding the *Sinnzusammenhang* (Wank 1985, p. 134) as the means-end connection between facts and the statement of the law demystify multilingual adjudication of the Court of Justice that has in the past been criticised for low public visibility (cf. Perju 2009). However, as illustrated by analysed case law, parallel corpora of EU legislation (as presently used) do not serve the purpose of adjudicative interpretation (in the sense of Guastini 2015, p. 46), as they are not used to ascribe a definite meaning to a text, while rejecting the others. In light of the fact that such interpretation is a matter of decision (Ibid.), the Court's reasoning is grounded in a non-linguistic context including the objective and scheme of a legal provision. As demonstrated, in pursuing the task of adjudicative interpretation, the Court makes no use of the results of comparisons of language versions, as opposed to cognitive interpretation. Directed at identifying possible, plausible meanings, cognitive interpretation, just like

18 Judgments of 24 January 2019, Balandin and Others, C-477/17, EU:C:2019:60.

19 Treaty of Nice Amending the Treaty on European Union, the Treaty Establishing the European Communities, and Certain Related Acts art. 36, Feb. 26, 2001, 2001 O.J. (C 80) 1, http://eur-lex.europa.eu/LexUriServ/ LexUriServ.do?uri=OJ:C:2001:080:0001:0087:EN :PDF. Accessed August 5, 2020.

20 Treaty of Nice Amending the Treaty on European Union, the Treaty Establishing the European Communities, and Certain Related Acts art. 36, Feb. 26, 2001, 2001 O.J. (C 80) 1, http://eur-lex.europa.eu/LexUriServ/LexUriServ.do?uri=OJ:C:2001:080:0001:0087:EN :PDF. Accessed August 5, 2019.

21 Justice will not be done if it is not apparent to the parties why one has won and the other lost. English v. Emery Reimbold and Strick Ltd (Practice Note) (2002) 1 W.L.R. 2409, per Lord Phillips MR.11.

language comparison, reveals the ambiguity of normative formulations. While law is a set of normative meanings from an ontological perspective, it is also a set of interpretative practices (cf. Guastini 2015, p. 49). Hence, in the legal ambit we can depict meaning in the sense of the aforementioned means-end connection between facts and the statement of the law (cf. Bajčić 2017). Laying proof of the centrality of this to legal adjudication is the claim that judgments must be reasoned.

Nevertheless, in our opinion parallel corpora can be used to conduct language comparisons as part of the practice of cognitive interpretation. Cognitive interpretation consists of identifying the possible meanings of a normative text, namely meanings admissible on the basis of shared linguistic rules and accepted methods of legal interpretation and existing juristic theories (Guastini 2015, p. 52). In stark contrast to adjudicative interpretation that is described as a matter of decision, in cognitive interpretation ambiguity is revealed, but no meaning (of the identified possible meanings) is chosen (Guastini 2015, p. 52). Similarly, from the perspective of the linguistic theories of meaning, there is no standard by which to compare (cf. Kjær 2010), assuming there is no predetermined meaning in any of the language versions, for the meaning of a certain norm always depends on the interpreter and the context (Engberg 2004; Ćapeta 2009). Indeed, pursuant to the mainstream cognitive linguistics' approaches, the meaning of a concept depends on its conceptual structure and on our perception of the concept (Ostroški Anić 2019, p. 9). By the same token, legal reality too depends on observation (cf. Ćapeta 2019). In consequence, interpretation of an article cannot be based only on its wording, which reinforces the claim that adjudicative interpretation as a matter of decision constitutes the most important task of legal scholars (Guastini 2015, p. 52).

5 A proposal: parallel corpora for national courts of Member States

In order to understand the role of the comparison of language versions in the CJEU's decision-making, we have analysed the moves of its judges and Advocates General in selected case law. This has allowed us to reflect on employing parallel corpus methods in the context of multilingual adjudication. While the requirement to compare language versions as construed by the CJEU poses a risk to legal certainty, in that it undermines the right of individuals to ascertain their rights in their language, and in turn impacts full effect of EU law (cf. Bajčić 2020), our analysis points to its rather limited contribution to the reasoning of cases. A shortcoming of using corpus tools in this context concerns the centrality of reason for judicial decision-making which invites further investigation into the appropriateness of corpus-based judicial reasoning, primarily from the perspective of legal theory. Notwithstanding the truism that a problem is easier to state than to resolve, the findings of this study do allow for some cautious remarks about future parallel corpora, which could be used by national judges of the Member States and lead to more uniform case law Union-wide.

Putting the spotlight on the national courts in this context is important as they apply and interpret EU law on a daily basis and are expected to compare language versions, despite the fact that the CJEU failed to provide them with any guidance as to how to implement that requirement in practice (e.g. Derlén 2009). What is more, national courts are required to interpret national law in the light of the wording and the purpose of a directive, that is, in conformity with EU law.[22] Conducting keyword searches in several languages would ensure more clarity when faced with potential language discrepancies, but also lead to more uniform application and interpretation of EU law by allowing judges to conform to the relevant case law of the CJEU, in line with the latter principle of consistent interpretation.

Needless to say, judges should be provided with adequate training in order to be able to efficiently employ parallel corpora designed specifically to fit their purpose. This task calls for joint efforts of corpus linguists and legal scholars to develop corpus tools that integrate both quantitative and qualitative legal parameters. While EUCLCORP does offer functionalities not present in any of the existing legal databases, it does not contain comprehensive national case law.[23] Further specific metadata should be integrated in multilingual case law corpora, including both EU and national case law, tailored to the needs of national judges and not terminologists or translators. Legal scholars in particular are called upon to provide more insight into rules for judicial decision-making which should be considered in the design of corpora, for at the moment, there is a lack of "clear legal prescripts one might teach an intelligent machine to enable it to 'learn' how to decide in judicial cases" (Ćapeta 2019). Marking a shift towards more pronounced datafication in multilingual adjudication, with appropriate parallel corpora judges of national courts would finally be provided with genuine instructions for implementing the requirement to conduct language comparison and to ensure consistent interpretation in their (cognitive) interpretive practice.

References

Baaij, C.J.W., 2018. *Legal integration and language diversity. Rethinking translation in EU lawmaking*. New York: Oxford University Press.

Bajčić, M., 2017. *New insights into the semantics of legal concepts and the legal dictionary*. Amsterdam: John Benjamins.

Bajčić, M., 2020. Linguistic comparison within CJEU's decision-making: A debunking exercise. *International Journal for the Semiotics of Law*. [online] Available from: https://doi.org/10.1007/s11196-020-09751-4 [Accessed October 28, 2020].

22 The principle of consistent interpretation was introduced in the case 14/83 Von Colson and Kamann v. Land Nordrhein-Westfalen [1984] ECR 1891. National courts are required to interpret their national law in the light of the wording and the purpose of the directive (para. 26).

23 Available from: http://www.euclcorp.bham.ac.uk/#!/ (Accessed May 28, 2021).

Barceló, J.J., 1997. Precedent in European community law. *In:* D.N. MacCormick & R.S. Summers, eds., *Interpreting precedents: A comparative study.* Aldershot: Dartmouth Applied Legal Philosophy Series. 407–436.

Biel, Ł., 2014. *Lost in the Eurofog: The textual fit of EU translated law.* Frankfurt: Peter Lang.

Biel, Ł., 2018. Corpora in institutional legal translation: Small steps and the big picture. *In:* Fernando Prieto Ramos, ed., *Institutional translation for international governance: Enhancing quality in multilingual legal communication.* London: Bloomsbury, 25–36.

Ćapeta, T., 2009. Multilingual law and judicial interpretation in the EU. *Croatian Yearbook of European Law and Policy*, 5(5), 1–17.

Ćapeta, T., 2019. Do judicial decision-making and quantum mechanics have anything in common? A contribution to realist theories of adjudication at the CJEU. *In:* M. Belov, ed., *The role of courts in contemporary legal orders.* The Hague: Eleven International.

Derlén, M., 2009. *Multilingual interpretation of European Union law.* Alphen aan den Rijn: Kluwer Law International.

Dörk, M., & Knight, D., 2015. WordWanderer: A navigational approach to text visualization. *Corpora,* 10(1), 83–94.

Doval, I., & Sánchez Nieto, M.T., 2019. Parallel corpora in focus: An account of current achievements and challenges. *In:* I. Doval & M.T. Sánchez Nieto, eds., *Parallel corpora for contrastive and translation studies. New resources and applications.* Amsterdam: John Benjamins, 1–11.

Engberg, J., 2004. Statutory texts as instances of language(s): Consequences and limitations on interpretation. *Brooklyn Journal of International Law*, 29. [online] Available from: https://brooklynworks.brooklaw.edu/bjil/vol29/iss3/6 [Accessed August 5, 2020].

Goldfarb, N., 2019. *Corpus linguistics in legal interpretation: When is it (In)appropriate? SSRN.* [online] Available from: http://doi.org/10.2139/ssrn.3333512 [Accessed September 10, 2020].

Goźdź-Roszkowski, S., 2020. Move analysis of legal justifications in constitutional tribunal judgments in Poland: What they share and what they do not. *International Journal for the Semiotics of Law.* [online] Available from: https://doi.org/10.1007/s11196-020-09700-1 [Accessed May 27, 2020].

Guastini, R., 2015. A realistic view on law and legal cognition. *Revus*, 27. [online] Available from: http://doi.org/10.4000/revus.3304 [Accessed April 19, 2020].

Hamann, H., & Vogel, F., 2017. Evidence-based jurisprudence meets legal linguistics-unlikely blends made in Germany, 2017. *BYU Law Review*, 1473(2018).

Hessick, C.B., 2018. Corpus linguistics and the criminal law, 2017. *BYU Law Review*, 1503(2018).

Kjær, A.L., 2010. Nonsense: The CILFIT criteria revisited: From the perspective of legal linguistics. *In:* H. Koch et al., eds., *Europe: The new legal realism: Essays in honor of Hjalte Rasmussen.* København: Djøf Forlag, 297–319.

Koehn, P., 2005. *Europarl: A parallel corpus for statistical machine translation, MT summit.* [online] Available from: europarl-mtsummit05.pdf (ed.ac.uk) [Accessed February 1, 2021].

Koźbial, D., 2018. Phraseological profile of judgments: Complex prepositions in EU competition law judgments. *In:* S. Marino et al., eds., *Language and law. The role of language and translation in EU competition law.* Cham: Springer, 163–179.

Lenaerts, K., 2011. The unity of European law and the overload of the ECJ – the system of preliminary rulings revisited. *In:* I. Pernice et al., eds., *The future of the European judicial system in a comparative perspective*. Baden-Baden: Nomos-Verl.-Ges, 211–239.

Mikhailov, M., Santalahti, M., & Souma, J., 2019. Pest: A parallel electronic corpus of state treaties. *In:* I. Doval & M.T. Sánchez Nieto, eds., *Parallel corpora for contrastive and translation studies. New resources and applications*. Amsterdam: John Benjamins, 183–195.

Mori, L., 2018. *Observing Eurolects*. Amsterdam: John Benjamins.

Ostroški Anić, A., 2019. *Metafora u terminologiji*. Zagreb: Institut za hrvatski jezik i jezikoslovlje.

Pacho Aljanati, L., 2015. *The Court of Justice of the European Union's case law on linguistic divergences (2007–2013): Interpretation criteria and implications for the translation of EU legislation*. Thesis (PhD). Université de Genève. [online] Available from: https://archive-ouverte.unige.ch/unige:76529 [Accessed August 9, 2020].

Perju, V., 2009. Reason and authority in the ECJ. *Virginia Journal of International Law*, 49(2).

Pontrandolfo, G., 2012. Legal corpora: An overview. *Rivista Internazionale di Tecnica della Traduzione*, 14, 121–136.

Pontrandolfo, G., 2018. Sensibly and appropriately the judge considered. . . . A corpus-based study of sentence adverbs in judicial language. *Linguistik Online*, 92(5/18). [online] Available from: https://doi.org/10.13092/lo.92.4511 [Accessed October 10, 2020].

Prieto Ramos, F., ed., 2019. Corpus-based research in legal and institutional translation. *Translation Spaces*, 8(1).

Šarčević, S., 2012. Coping with the challenges of legal translation in harmonization. *In:* C.J.W. Baaij, ed., *The role of legal translation in legal harmonization*. Alphen aan den Rijn: Wolters Kluwer, 83–107.

Šarčević, S., 2013. Multilingual lawmaking and legal (Un)certainty in the European Union. *International Journal of Law, Language & Discourse (IJLLD)*, 2013, 1–29.

Schilling, T., 2010. Beyond multilingualism: On different approaches to the handling of diverging language versions of a community law. *European Law Journal*, 16(1), 47–66.

Solan, L.M., 2007. Interpretation of multilingual statutes by the European Court of Justice. *Brooklyn Journal of International Law*, 34, 277–301.

Solan, L.M., & Gales, T., 2017. Corpus linguistics as a tool in legal interpretation, 2017. *BYU Law Review*, 1311(2018). [online] Available from: https://digitalcommons.law.byu.edu/lawreview/vol2017/iss6/5 [Accessed October 5, 2019].

Steinberger, R., Ebrahim, M., Poulis, A., et al., 2014. An overview of the European Union's highly multilingual parallel corpora. *Language Resources and Evaluation*, 48, 679–707.

Tognini-Bonelli, E., 2001. *Corpus linguistics at work*. Amsterdam: John Benjamins.

Trklja, A., & McAuliffe, K., 2018. The European Union case law corpus (EUCLCORP): A multilingual parallel and comparative corpus of EU court judgments. *In:* A.U. Frank et al., eds., *Proceedings of the second workshop on corpus-based research in the humanities: CRH-2*, Vol. 1, Vienna, Austria.

Wank, R., 1985. *Die juristische Begriffsbildung*. München: Verlag C.H. Beck.

Analysed judgments

C-34/18, Lovasné Tóth, [2019] ECLI:EU:C:2019:764
C-115/16, N Luxembourg 1 and Others, [2019] ECLI:EU:C:2019:134
C-163/17, Jawo, [2019] ECLI:EU:C:2019:218
C-195/18, B.S. (Malt in composition of beer), [2019] ECLI:EU:C:2019:197
C-347/17, A and Others, [2019] ECLI:EU:C:2019:720
C-361/18, Weil, [2019] ECLI:EU:C:2019:473
C-383/18, Lexitor, [2019] ECLI:EU:C:2019:702
C-391/16, M (Révocation du statut de réfugié), [2019] ECLI:EU:C:2019:403
C-420/16, P Izsák and Dabis v. Commission, [2019] ECLI:EU:C:2019:177
C-477/17, Balandin and Others, [2019] ECLI:EU:C:2019:60
C-477/18, Exportslachterij J. Gosschalk, [2019] ECLI:EU:C:2019:1126
C-516/17, Spiegel Online, [2019] ECLI:EU:C:2019:625
C-519/18, Bevándorlási és Menekültügyi Hivatal, [2019] ECLI:EU:C:2019:1070
C-634/17, ReFood, [2019] ECLI:EU:C:2019:443
C-649/17, Amazon EU, [2019] ECLI:EU:C:2019:576
T-108/17, ClientEarth v. Commission, [2019] ECLI:EU:T:2019:215;
T-607/15, Yieh United Steel v. Commission, [2019] ECLI:EU:T:2019:831
T-760/15, Netherlands v. Commission, [2019] ECLI:EU:T:2019:669;

Analysed opinions of advocates general

C-34/18, Lovasné Tóth, [2019] ECLI:EU:C:2019:245
C-163/18, Aegean Airlines, [2019] ECLI:EU:C:2019:275
C-213/18, Guaitoli and Others, [2019] ECLI:EU:C:2019:524
C-302/18, X (and suffisantes), [2019] ECLI:EU:C:2019:469
C-363/18, Organisation juive européenne and Vignoble Psagot, [2019] ECLI:EU:C:2019:494
C-381/18, G.S. (Menace pour l'ordre public), [2019] ECLI:EU:C:2019:608
C-420/16 P, Izsák and Dabis v. Commission, [2019] ECLI:EU:C:2018:816
C-423/17, Warner-Lambert Company, [2019] ECLI:EU:C:2018:822
C-449/17, A & G Fahrschul-Akademie, [2019] ECLI:EU:C:2018:791
C-450/17 P, Landeskreditbank Baden-Württemberg v. ECB, [2019] ECLI:EU:C:2018:982
C-465/17, Falck Rettungsdienste and Falck, [2019] ECLI:EU:C:2018:907
C-477/18, Exportslachterij J. Gosschalk, [2019] ECLI:EU:C:2019:759
C-483/17, Tarola, [2019] ECLI:EU:C:2018:919
C-487/17, Verlezza and Others, [2019] ECLI:EU:C:2018:915
C-634/17, ReFood, [2019] ECLI:EU:C:2019:61
C-649/17, Amazon EU, [2019] ECLI:EU:C:2019:165
C-681/17, slewo, [2019] ECLI:EU:C:2018:1041
C-688/17, Bayer Pharma, [2019] ECLI:EU:C:2019:324

7 Evaluative language and strategic manoeuvring in the justification of judicial decisions

The case of teleological-evaluative argumentation

Stanisław Goźdź-Roszkowski

1 Introduction

The Supreme Court in Poland ruled in 2018 against a print shop employee who refused to print banners for an LGBT business group because he did not want to "promote" the gay rights movement. The court's decision was based on a legal rule contained in article 138 of the Code of Misdemeanors, which provides that "whoever, . . . willfully and without a reasonable reason refuses to provide a service to which s/he is obligated, is liable for a fine".[1] In the cassation appeal, the Attorney General who filed for the cassation (an appeal on a point of law) for the benefit of the defendant argued that this legal provision, unamended since 1972, was "anachronistic" and its application infringed the service provider's right to express their disagreement with conduct that is conflict with his conscience and value system. In its justification, the Supreme Court chose to resort, inter alia, to teleological-evaluative argumentation (MacCormick and Summers 1991) to refer to the consequences of applying the rule in the context of the goal and values the rule had been envisaged to realise.[2] A seemingly clear case involving a mere misdemeanour turned into a hard case (Dworkin 1986), at the heart of which is the need to resolve a dispute that revolves around competing rights and interests.

This case is one of a number of similar cases involving the conflict between the principle of non-discrimination and the freedoms of conscience, religion and speech.[3] While jurisprudence has at its disposal various legal methods (e.g. balancing and proportionality) to compare incommensurable constitutional

1 The full text of the provision in Polish can be found at https://sip.lex.pl/akty-prawne/dzu-dziennik-ustaw/kodeks-wykroczen-16788218/art-138 (viewed December 2, 2020). The English translation was provided by the author.

2 See Feteris (2017, pp. 237–242) for a discussion of teleological-evaluative argumentation, its prototypical patterns and different levels of argumentation.

3 See, for example, Masterpiece Cakeshop Ltd. et al. v. Colorado Civil Rights Commission et al. in the United States, Brockie v. Dilinger in Canada, or Bull & Bull v. Hall & Preddy in the UK.

DOI: 10.4324/9781003153771-9

principles (da Silva 2011), the questions remain as to the way in which Supreme Court judges manoeuvre strategically in their role as the highest appellate court and the court of cassation to resolve the difference of opinion regarding competing principles with the rhetorical goal of steering the discussion towards the promotion of a particular legal development (cf. Feteris 2012). In doing so, judges carry out different types of assessments, which, coded variously in language, form an integral part of their argumentation. This chapter attempts to integrate the linguistic study of evaluation into the model of strategic manoeuvring embraced within the pragma-dialectic approach (van Eemeren 2010, 2018) in order to shed more light on the discursive practices adopted by judges in the justifications of their decisions.

2 Evaluation and legal justification

Justification is pervasive in most, if not all, forms of legal discourse. Advancing a legal standpoint inevitably involves presenting justifying arguments if it is to be accepted. The quality of justification becomes particularly vital in the process of judicial decision-making. Whether drafting a majority or dissenting opinion, judges are expected to support their decisions with sound arguments "to make it acceptable to the parties involved as well as to other judges and the legal community as a whole" (Feteris 2017, p. xv). Clearly, the acceptability of judicial decisions in both legal and social contexts involves persuading a multiple audience. Thus, one of the basic premises of this study is that legal justification is both a communicative and argumentative activity type (cf. Feteris 2017; Goźdź-Roszkowski 2020). It is communicative because judges aim to persuade a diverse audience ranging from the parties to a given dispute, lower-court judges (in appeal cases) and the legal community to the media and the public in high-profile and controversial cases. Legal justification is also argumentative because judges are required to provide arguments supporting their decisions. As Feteris aptly comments, "legal justification is part of a dialogue, a *critical discussion* aimed at the resolution of a dispute between the court and the multiple audience that must be convinced" (2017, pp. 2014–15; emphasis added).

The central question of what determines or contributes to the soundness of legal argumentation has been researched extensively by legal theorists, legal philosophers and argumentation theorists.[4] The concept of evaluation has remained at the forefront of these perspectives. Argumentation theorists have for a long time been interested in developing methods for the analysis and evaluation of legal argumentation (e.g. Walton 2016). They tend to assess the merits of legal argumentation based on certain norms of rationality which serve as a basis for establishing whether an argument is sound and rational. However, argumentation

4 For an up-to-date survey of theories on the justification of judicial decisions, see Feteris (2017). See also Mazzi, Chapter 8 in this volume.

scholars seldom pay attention to specific linguistic resources used by legal actors to construct their assessments.[5]

In contrast, linguists are not only interested in identifying recurrent language patterns in the expression of evaluation, but they also focus on the complex relationships of (dis)alignment between the speaker/writer, their interactants and the evaluated object.[6] Despite a considerable variation regarding the way the concept of evaluation is conceptualised and the different corresponding methodologies, most linguistic studies of evaluation in judicial discourse are corpus-based, that is, they start with a predefined language form associated with evaluative meanings, which is then identified and investigated in electronic text corpora with the use of computer tools.[7] For example, in a recent study Pontrandolfo (2018) uses a trilingual corpus to study sentence adverbs in Italian, English and Spanish judicial discourse. The results are intended to demonstrate that, although judges' attitude is supposed to be impartial, adverbs ending in *mente* and *-ly* (e.g. *coerentemente, surprisingly*) are one of the pragmatic vehicles used to code evaluative meanings and signal stances, and these adverbs are said to contribute to judicial argumentation.

Such linguistically oriented studies are limited in that they do not usually take into account the macro-context of the institutional environment in which argumentative discourse occurs. This means that the results of such investigations are not grounded in the argumentative reality of judicial discourse, and the linguistic account of legal justification may appear fragmented and inconclusive because they tend to focus on the microlevel of discrete language items. Instead, legal justification should be perceived as an argumentative activity type which imposes constraints unique to the institutional context of the law.

3 The method: integrating the study of evaluative language into the argumentative reality of legal justification

Set against this background, it is argued here that any meaningful study of evaluative language in legal justification should take into account the macro-context of an institutional environment in which it is located. Further, such investigations should be embedded within a theory of legal argumentation. In a series of publications (e.g. 2009, 2012, 2015), Feteris has demonstrated the relevance of the pragma-dialectic theory to account for the complexities of argumentative practices in the justifications of judicial decisions (see also Goźdź-Roszkowski 2021 for a study of evaluative language in legal argumentation informed by the

5 However, it should be borne in mind that there is extensive research concerned with the interaction of language and argument. See Hinton (2019) for an overview.

6 This aspect of construing evaluation is usually explored using the related concept of stance-taking (Englebretson 2007).

7 See Goźdź-Roszkowski (2018) for an overview of linguistic research into evaluation in judicial discourse.

pragma-dialectical theory of argumentation). At the heart of this theory is the concept of strategic manoeuvring (van Eemeren 2010, 2018), which is adopted to account for the fact that in real-life, argumentative discourse two objectives are simultaneously pursued: aiming for effectiveness and maintaining reasonableness. Those two aims must be kept in balance, which implies that arguers manoeuvre strategically in order to keep those two aims in balance. The core of the pragma-dialectical theory consists of an ideal model for critical discussions and a code of conduct for reasonable discussants.

The ideal model specifies the stages which must be passed through to facilitate the resolution of a dispute, and the various speech acts which contribute to the process. In the *confrontation* stage the focal point of dispute is established; in the *opening* stage the participants reach agreement concerning the discussion rules, starting points and evaluation methods. In the *argumentation* stage the point of view at issue is defended against critical reactions and the argumentation is evaluated; and in the *concluding* stage the final result is determined. This means that only one stage actually involves the exchange of arguments, suggesting that a far more holistic approach to the nature of argumentative discourse and the accompanying evaluative language must be taken. It is further argued in this study that each of these stages involves the use of evaluative language which underpins the dialectical goal of the discussion, albeit in different ways. To this end, the analysis is organised around these stages of critical discussion to demonstrate the main structure of the argumentation of the Supreme Court justification. The argumentation is interpreted in terms of the argumentative moves which correspond to the different stages of the critical discussion. The aim is to show how the Supreme Court judges in their opinion steer the discussion in the desired direction within the boundaries of the rules prescribed for cassation proceedings. This part of the analysis is combined with close reading of the text to identify and explore how specific language items imbued with evaluative function contribute to this strategic manoeuvring.

4 The analysis of the discussion strategy of the Supreme Court

The aim of cassation procedure before the Supreme Court in Poland is to ensure the consistency, uniformity and legality of decisions given by courts in Poland. There are two measures routinely undertaken to that effect: cassation (for criminal cases) and cassation complaint (for civil cases). These are treated as extraordinary legal remedies (Jabłońska-Bonca 2004). In order to meet the formal eligibility criteria, the application for cassation must demonstrate that the decision of a lower court is in violation of a specific legal provision by failing to respond to the charges and arguments raised by one of the parties.

In the present case, the Court of Appeals upheld the decision of the District Court (*Sąd Rejonowy*) in which the defendant, in his capacity as a print shop employee, was found guilty of a deliberate and unjustified refusal to perform a service under article 138 of the Code of Misdemeanors. The cassation appeal was filed by the Attorney General (*prokurator generalny*) for the defendant and against the decision of the Appeals Court. The Appeals Court decision was attacked on the grounds that it had violated certain provisions of the Polish law of procedure in misdemeanour cases by failing to duly consider arguments brought up in the appeal by the defence counsel.

The argumentative space of the Supreme Court is thus constrained, in that it must focus on whether and how the Court of Appeal responded to the charges and arguments advanced by the Attorney-General and whether the rules of law applied by the Court of Appeals had been applied correctly. In light of the concept of strategic manoeuvring, the dialectical goal of the argumentation in this case is to establish whether the protagonist in the cassation case, the Court of Appeals, defended its decision successfully against the attacks of the antagonist, the plaintiff in cassation (the Attorney General), or whether it was attacked successfully.

4.1 The confrontation stage

This stage of the critical discussion consists of realising the dialectic goal of establishing the difference of opinion. This is achieved by reporting the decisions of the court of first instance (the District Court) and the Court of Appeals and then specifying the grounds on which the cassation was brought by the Attorney General in which the objections against the decision of the Court of Appeal are listed. The introductory part of the Supreme Court's justification reiterates two objections. First, the Attorney General challenged the Court of Appeal's ruling on the grounds that there was an obligation on the part of the defendant to provide a service because no valid contract had been made. Second, the Attorney General challenged the Court of Appeal's ruling that the defendant's refusal to provide a service based on his religious convictions was not justified under article 138. As already signalled, it is the plaintiff that determines the content and scope of the difference of opinion in cassation proceedings. The Supreme Court has little or no space to manoeuvre strategically at this discussion stage. The evaluative language can be found in the specific charges made in the cassation complaint and the corresponding negative assessment of the Appeals Court's decision, attributed to the Attorney-General at the beginning of the Supreme Court's legal justification:

(1) The Attorney General appealed for cassation for the benefit of the defendant . . . alleging that the Court of Appeal's decision constituted a *flagrant violation* of procedural law provisions (art. 433 § 2 of the Code of Criminal Procedure in connection with article 109 § 2 of the Code of Procedure in Misdemeanor Cases and article 107 § 3 of the Code of Procedure in Misdemeanor Cases) which had *adversely affected* the outcome of the decision by *failing* to duly consider the charges and the corresponding argumentation filed in the appeal for the benefit of A.J. [the defendant] by the prosecutor and the defense counsel.

As can be seen in (1), the negative assessment of the Court of Appeal's decision is expressed through overtly negative, value-laden lexical items such as *flagrant violation, adversely affected* and *failing*, and it is clearly attributed to the Attorney-General. The way this negative assessment is worded mirrors a legal provision contained in the Code of Criminal Procedure (article 523 § 1).[8] This means that the way the evaluation is expressed is by no means idiosyncratic. Rather, it reflects the intention to ensure that the cassation appeal fulfils formal criteria for acceptance by reproducing key phrases from the legislative provision. It should be noted that no assessments are made by the Supreme Court at this stage. The negative assessment is attributed to the Attorney General to signal the difference of opinion.

4.2 The opening stage

This stage serves the purpose of preparing the way in which the subsequent argumentation stage is managed. To that end, the Supreme Court chooses procedural and material starting points for the ensuing critical discussion. The rhetorical element requires that the common starting points are selected with a view to the final goal, which in this case amounts to dismissing the appeal in cassation and maintaining the decision of the Appeals Court. In addition, the Supreme Court intends to ensure that a particular development of law is promoted. There are usually certain procedural conventions which, to some extent, dictate the rules of discussion, such as codes of procedure (cf. Feteris 2017). In this case, these are the rules contained in the Code of Criminal Procedure, especially chapter 55 (titled "Cassation") and the rules included in the Code of Procedure in Misdemeanor Cases.

Example (2) shows how the Supreme Court first organises the argumentation stage by specifying that the cassation focuses on two major issues:[9]

(2) The Attorney-General in the cassation appeal alleged that the Court of Appeal flagrantly violated article 433 § 2 of the Code of Criminal Procedure in connection with article 109 § 2 of the Code of Criminal Procedure and article 107 § 3 of the Code of Misdemeanor Cases by failing to duly consider charges which focus on two groups of issues.

Admittedly, there is considerable overlap between (1) and (2), which incidentally shows a certain degree of repetitiveness in the language of justification. Yet, the

8 The provision contained in Art. 523 § 1 reads as follows: "Cassation may be filed only on the grounds listed in article 439 or based on other flagrant violation of law, if such violation could have a significant impact on the outcome of the case" (author's translation based on the original text available as of November 20, 2020, at https://isap.sejm.gov.pl/isap.nsf/download.xsp/WDU19970890555/U/D19970555Lj.pdf).

9 In all excerpts, author's emphasis is indicated in italics. The excerpts come from the justification of the Supreme Court decision available in Polish www.sn.pl/sites/orzecznictwo/Orzeczenia3/II%20KK%20333-17.pdf. Their translation is literal and it may cover only parts deemed relevant for the analysis.

function of each excerpt is different. While the former indicates the area of discord between the Appeals Court decision and the Attorney General's complaint, the latter serves a text-organising function.

Example (3) illustrates how the Supreme Court relies on the procedural law to steer the discussion in the desired direction by specifying which parts of the lower courts' decisions cannot be challenged:

(3) It should be emphasized that these findings of the two courts [the court of first instance and the Court of Appeal] could not be and will not be challenged in view of the *restricted cassation grounds* under article 523 § 1 of the Code of Criminal Procedure.

Further, another example (4) shows how this move, made in response to the Attorney General's first challenge that there was no obligation on the part of the defendant to provide a service contributes to narrowing down the area that is subject to judicial review in this case:

(4) Therefore, the fact of concluding a contract for a specific task (Pol. *umowa o dzieło*) . . . remains *outside the scope of Supreme Court judicial review.*

In addition, the Supreme Court judges are also responsible for establishing common factual starting points. Setting aside the disputed issue of whether a binding contract had been concluded, which would create an obligation to provide a service on the part of the defendant, the Court clearly signals its position:

(5) In consequence, the Supreme Court *accepts the view that* the source of obligation derived from article 138 of the Code of Misdemeanors is the mere *fact of rendering professional services.*

In (5) the judges establish as fact that being professionally engaged is sufficient as a source of obligation to provide a service, and article 138 does not stipulate that a contract must be concluded to create an obligation on the part of a service provider.

Finally, the opening stage is exploited by the Supreme Court to signal the method it adopts for evaluating argumentation related to the crucial provision, which, as we recall, served as the legal basis for convicting the defendant:

(6) Therefore, this provision [article 138] must be interpreted using the *teleological method of interpretation* from the perspective of contemporary trends in civilization and social needs, taking into account the protection of consumers' interests and the rights of service providers (*dynamic interpretation*).

In (6) the Supreme Court explicitly indicates the method to be adopted in analysing and interpreting the disputed legal provision of Article 138. According to legal theory, it adopts the objective purposive approach to indicate the "intention of the law" judged under present conditions (cf. Małolepszy and Głuchowski 2021). In pragma-dialectic terms, the Supreme Court selects those starting points that it perceives as essential for the subsequent argumentation stage, in which it evaluates the attack of the Attorney-General negatively and it defends the standpoints of the Appeals Court. The provision contained in article 138 was originally enacted in 1972 in radically different socio-economic realities, as a measure to counteract profiteering. The Attorney-General in the cassation appeal challenged its relevance referring to it as "anachronistic". The Supreme Court establishes the common starting point by acknowledging that this provision is still relevant because it has now acquired an anti-discriminatory and protective attribute. In other words, the prolonged application of this provision can be justified on the basis of reasonableness and fairness (cf. Feteris 2012). This is a common form of argumentation in hard cases "in which a court refers to the consequences of applying a legal rule in a particular interpretation in light of the goal and values the rule is intended to realize" (Feteris 2017, p. 237). Legal rules are regarded as means to carry out legal, but also economic and social goals. In addition, a legal rule enshrined in a specific provision is viewed as a way to promote goals and values deemed desirable from the perspective of justice or the public good (ibid.). In this case, the Court effectively applies teleological-evaluative argumentation because, in their justification, the judges refer to the consequences of applying the rule contained in article 138 and they treat it as an instrument for realising specific social and economic goals.

At this stage of the critical discussion, evaluative language is found in the value-oriented justification of the choice of the teleological method of interpretation. The justification relies on value-laden words to refer to principles and values underlying the legal rule enshrined in the contested article 138 (e.g. *protection of consumers' interests, rights of service providers*). In addition, the evaluative resources used at this stage are stance-oriented to indicate the standpoint adopted by the Supreme Court and to establish legal and factual starting points regarding the existence and content of procedural law and the method of interpretation.

4.3 The argumentation stage

The dialectical goal of this stage consists in determining the acceptability of the argumentation in view of the common starting points and evaluation methods (Feteris 2017, p. 222). The discussion strategy amounts to providing a positive evaluation of the argumentation of the Court of Appeals in light of the attacks by the plaintiff (Attorney General) and a negative assessment of the plaintiff's arguments. The discussion strategy can be seen in a selection of statements arranged according to the object of evaluation (i.e. the argumentation of the Attorney General and the argumentation of the Appeals Court). Given the limited space, the discussion focuses on the Supreme Court's argumentation regarding the

1. The claim of the plaintiff that the print shop employee was under no obligation to perform a service because no valid contract had been made must be dismissed.

↑

1.1

Article 138 does not stipulate that an obligation to perform a service results from a contract.

1.2

The very fact of being engaged in professional provision of services leads to an obligation to perform under article 138 of the Code of Misdemeanors.

2. The claim of the plaintiff that article 138 is obsolete and it limits the freedom of conscience must be dismissed.

↑

2.1 It was the intention of the legislator not to amend article 138.

2.2 Article 138 has become anti-discriminatory in nature in view of the absence of other legal measures to that effect.

Figure 7.1 Overview of the main argumentation structure of the Supreme Court's justification

Attorney General's first claim that the defendant (the printer) was not obliged to provide a service because no valid contract had been concluded, and the related claim that article 138 is anachronistic and could effectively restrict the service provider's right to refuse to act against his conscience and his value system. For ease of reference, an overview of the main structure of argumentation of the Supreme Court regarding these claims is provided in Figure 7.1.

In response to the first claim, the Supreme Court accepts the view of the Court of Appeals that professional performance of service is the source of obligation under article 138 of the Code of Misdemeanors. In other words, the mere fact of operating a business entity creates an obligation. Even if there is no contract, the defendant is under an obligation to serve his client.

Regarding the second claim, the Supreme Court focused on defending the validity and currency of article 138. Adopting the teleological (goal-oriented) and dynamic interpretation, the Supreme Court argued that the Court of Appeals was correct in analysing the defendant's conduct under article 138 in the context of contemporary socio-economic reality. The plaintiff's argument that article 138 is anachronistic was rebutted by arguing that despite the fact that the Code of Misdemeanors had been amended several times, the legislator chose not to amend article 138 for a reason. In consequence, article 138 must be interpreted using the teleological method of interpretation, which interprets legislative provisions in light of the purpose, values, legal, social and economic goals these provisions have been envisaged to fulfil.

4.4 Negative evaluation of the attorney general's argumentation

The link between evaluative language and argumentation is highlighted in the next two sections. First, the discussion strategy can be seen in the statements in which the Supreme Court focuses on the evaluation of the charges brought by the Attorney-General:

(7) To demonstrate the legitimacy of the charge, the Attorney General analyzed at length whether the email correspondence between A.H. and "M. s.c." [the litigants] led to the closing of the contract under article 627 of the Civil Code, concluding that it had not because the correspondence stopped during the negotiation stage. *This charge does not deserve to be taken into account.*

In (7), the Court first adopts reporting language to present the argument made by the Attorney General in the cassation complaint, which, as we recall, amounted to the claim that since no valid contract had been concluded between the litigants, the defendant was under no obligation to provide service. The last sentence (italicised) has the function of "encapsulating" the foregoing argument (*this charge*) and it contains an explicit negative evaluation of this argument by adding "value-judgement" to the ensuing proposition (*does not deserve to be taken into account*). The reason for the negative assessment is provided in the following:

(8) This cassation charge is *incorrect* because article 138 of Code of Misdemeanors does not stipulate that the obligation to provide service should arise from a contract.

The negative assessment is made in light of the previously established starting point that a contract is not required to establish an obligation on the part of a service provider. In other instances of the Supreme Court evaluation, the claims made in the cassation grounds are assessed as *contradictory* and *tenuous.* The overt expression of negative evaluation focuses on the Attorney General's charges contained in the cassation. In textual terms, it signals where the Supreme Court argumentation starts regarding the claims made in the cassation. These assessments made by the Supreme Court in its justification imply that the attack of the plaintiff included in the argumentation supporting the first charge against the Court of Appeal's decision has failed.

4.5 Positive evaluation of the appeals court argumentation

Second, the positive assessment of the Court of Appeal's conduct, regarding its response to the charges in the cassation grounds, results from a positive evaluation of the argumentation of the Court of Appeal in light of the attacks by the Attorney-General. In (9) the Supreme Court evaluates the Court of Appeal's argument as consistent with that of the District Court.

(9) *This position* adopted by the Court of Appeals *remains in line with* the argumentation of the Court of first instance because it [Court of

> Appeals] *correctly reconstructed* those factual circumstances that led to the conclusion of the contract. However, the Court of Appeals did not examine this issue closely acknowledging that the fact of concluding the contract is not important in view of what amounts to misdemeanor under article 138.

In terms of evaluative language, the Supreme Court's justification uses an extremely limited range of evaluative adjectives to assess the Court of Appeals' argument:

(10) The Court of Appeals, when making a legal assessment of the defendant's conduct, *was correct* to refer to the present-day reality rather than to the economic reality at the time when article 138 was enacted.

(11) Both the courts of first instance and the Appeals Court *were correct* to establish that article 138 had effectively become an anti-discriminatory measure and non-discrimination, which is also constitutionally protected under article 32 section 2 of the Polish Constitution, was rightly perceived as a reason for limiting the service provider's right to cite religious convictions as a basis for conscientious objection.

This shows the role of the Supreme Court, which manoeuvres strategically in its capacity as court of cassation to uphold and promote a particular development of law according to which article 138 has been construed as an anti-discriminatory measure. In other words, the Supreme Court attributes a different argumentative role to the legal principle originally contained in article 138. Rather than counteracting profiteering, article 138 should be now assigned the role of an anti-discriminatory measure.

4.6 The concluding stage

This stage brings the result of the critical discussion based on the Supreme Court's argumentation. The Supreme Court judge establishes the decision specifying which of the different positions in the dispute is justified in light of the common legal and factual starting points. Adhering to the argumentative space imposed by the cassation rules, the Supreme Court concluded this part of its justification by insisting that the Appeals Court responded adequately to the charges brought by the Attorney General, and the Supreme Court judges accept the Appeals Court argumentation:

(12) Therefore, it is not possible to agree that, regarding these issues [issues included in the objections to the decision given by the Court of Appeal], the Court of Appeal flagrantly violated article 433 § 2 of the Code of Criminal Procedure in connection with article 109 § 2 of the Code of Criminal Procedure and article 107 § 3 of the Code of Misdemeanor Cases since the Court of Appeal *responded to the charges in the appeal.*

The discussion strategy led to the fulfilment of its main goal, that is, the Supreme Court determines that the argumentation of the Court of Appeals withstood the Attorney General's attacks specified in the cassation. The use of evaluative language boils down to the positive evaluation of the appellate court's conduct. By responding to the complaints specified in the appeal proceedings, the appeals court fulfilled the formal and procedural criteria.

5 Conclusions

The findings documented in this chapter demonstrate the interaction and interreliance of language and argument by combining a study of evaluative language with an analysis of legal argumentation. The ideal model of a critical discussion was adopted to reconstruct the different stages of the judicial justification, which, unlike the judgment itself, shows low levels of formulaicity and text-internal organisation. Thanks to it, the justification was framed as an exchange of arguments and counterarguments, where the Court, as the protagonist, defends standpoints against the reactions of the antagonist, the Attorney-General. The qualitative approach has led to a more holistic analysis contextualised within the institutional constraints of the Polish cassation procedure going beyond the argumentative stage.

The analysis brings to light the impact of the institutional environment, which seems to be most conspicuous in the confrontational and opening stages. In the former, the use of evaluative language has been found to be motivated institutionally, when the Supreme Court reiterates and attributes to the Attorney-General, the negative assessment of the Appeals Court's decision in order to signal a difference of opinion and to establish the compliance of the cassation appeal with the formal requirements of cassation procedure. In doing so, it relies on intertextual links with external statutory instruments and their wording. The analysis of the latter reveals the presence of value-laden words (e.g. *protection of consumers' interests, rights of service providers*) which signal that more emphasis is put on moral, social and economic deliberations. The use of evaluative language is fused here with the choice of a teleological-evaluative argumentation in line with the hierarchy of interpretation methods (cf. Małolepszy and Głuchowski 2021). In addition, the evaluative resources used at this stage point towards stance-taking concerns necessary to present and defend specific standpoints.

Clearly, the occurrence of evaluative lexis has proved to be particularly salient in the argumentation stage, where it served the purpose of expressing a positive assessment of the Court of Appeal's argumentation in light of the attacks by the Attorney-General. The attacks of the Attorney-General were evaluated negatively in order to finally dismiss the appeal. These assessments were carried out using an extremely limited word choice (e.g. *this cassation charge is incorrect, the Appeals Court was correct to*), suggesting that judges tend to favour tried and tested evaluative resources rather than indulging in more varied and idiosyncratic ways of signalling their attitudes.

Further, the results of this study corroborate the initial hypothesis that the Supreme Court in its justification manoeuvres strategically to resolve both the difference of opinion regarding the presence of obligation to provide a service by the print shop employee and to determine the argumentative role of the legal rule contained in the challenged article 138. The latter was achieved by resorting to teleological-evaluative argumentation as a counterargument to reject an interpretation proposed by the Attorney-General. In doing so, the Supreme Court in its justification referred to the reconstructed will of a rational legislator rather than to the actual will of the historical legislator. The court signalled its dynamic stance by means of value-laden language, such as *contemporary trends in civilisation, social needs, the protection of consumers' interests* and *the rights of service providers.* This type of evaluative language is used to determine the axiological framework in which the identified value (the social and economic goal) is adopted to construct the basis for the judicial decision.

It is hoped that this chapter has made the point that the combination of techniques and theories from both linguistics and argumentation perspectives can add to our understanding of how judges motivate their decisions and how legal justification is constructed and construed. Future research could be extended to include more cases and find out how the choice of various evaluative language resources corresponds to different types of argumentation and their patterns.

Acknowledgements

The research documented in this chapter was funded by National Science Centre Poland. Grant No. UMO-2018/31/B/HS2/03093.

References

da Silva, V.A., 2011. Comparing the incommensurable: Constitutional principles, balancing and rational decision. *Oxford Journal of Legal Studies*, 31(2), 273–301. https://doi.org/10.1093/ojls/gqr004.

Dworkin, R., 1986. *Law's empire*. London: Fontana.

Englebretson, R., ed., 2007. *Stancetaking in discourse. Subjectivity, evaluation interaction*. Amsterdam: Benjamins.

Feteris, E.T., 2009. Strategic maneuvring in the justification of judicial decisions. *In:* F.H. van Eemeren, ed., *Examining argumentation in context. Fifteen studies on strategic maneuvering*. Amsterdam: John Benjamins, 93–114.

Feteris, E.T., 2012. Strategic manoeuvring in the case of the "Unworthy spouse". *In:* Frans H. van Eemeren & Bart Garssen, eds., *Exploring argumentative contexts*. Amsterdam: John Benjamins, 149–164.

Feteris, E.T., 2015. The role of pragmatic argumentation referring to consequences, goals, and values in the justification of judicial decisions. *In:* B.J. Garssen, D. Godden, G. Mitchell, & A.F. Snoeck Henkemans, eds., *International society for the study of argumentation: 8th international conference on argumentation*, July 1–4, 2014. University of Amsterdam, The Netherlands, Amsterdam: Sic Sat, 414–425.

Feteris, E.T., 2017. *Fundamentals of legal argumentation. A survey of theories on the justification of judicial decisions.* Dordrecht: Springer.

Goźdź-Roszkowski, S., 2018. Counting the uncountable? Quantitative and qualitative methods of analyzing evaluative language in institutional discourse. A corpus linguistics perspective. In Łukasz Bogucki & Piotr Cap, eds., *Explorations in language and linguistics.* Berlin: Peter Lang, 145–158.

Goźdź-Roszkowski, S., 2020. Communicating dissent in judicial opinions: A comparative, genre-based analysis. *International Journal for the Semiotics of Law*, 33, 381–401. https://doi.org/10.1007/s11196-020-09711-y.

Goźdź-Roszkowski, S., 2021. Hostility to religion or protection against discrimination? Evaluation and argument in a case of conflicting principles. *In:* J. Giltrow & F. Olsen, eds., *Legal meanings and language rights international, social and philosophical perspectives.* Boston/Berlin: De Gruyter Mouton.

Hinton, M., 2019. Language and argument: A review of the field. *Research in Language*, 17(1), 93–103. https:/doi.org/10.2478/rela-2019-0007.

Jabłońska-Bonca, J., 2004. *Introduction to law.* Warsaw: LexisNexis.

MacCormick, N., & Summers, R., 1991. *Interpreting statutes. A comparative study.* Aldershot: Dartmouth.

Małolepszy, M., & Głuchowski, M., 2021. Argumentation and legal interpretation in the criminal decisions of the Polish Supreme Court and the German federal Court of Justice: A comparative view. *International Journal for the Semiotics of Law.* https://doi.org/10.1007/s11196-021-09843-9.

Pontrandolfo, G., 2018. Sensibly and appropriately the judge considered. A corpus-based study of sentence adverbs in judicial language. *In:* Anna-Maria De Cesare, Ana Albom, Doriana Cimmino, & Marta Lupica Spagnolo, eds., *Formal and functional perspectives on sentence adverbials in the Romance languages and beyond*, Vol. 5. Bern: Linguistik Online, 92, 215–233. https://doi.org/10.13092/lo.92.4511

van Eemeren, F.H., 2010. *Strategic manoeuvring in argumentative discourse. Extending the pragma-dialectic theory of argumentation.* Amsterdam: John Benjamins.

van Eemeren, F.H., 2018. Strategic manoeuvring in argumentative discourse. *In: Argumentation theory: A pragma-dialectical perspective. Argumentation library*, Vol. 33. Cham: Springer. https://doi.org/10.1007/978-3-319-95381-6_7

Walton, D., 2016. *Argument evaluation and evidence.* Cham: Springer.

8 "Without proof of negligence or a causative connection"

On causal argumentation in the discourse of the Supreme Court of Ireland's judgments on data protection

Davide Mazzi

The aim of this study is to provide a discourse perspective on the use of causal argumentation in the context of a corpus of Supreme Court of Ireland's judgments on the topical issue of data protection. The Supreme Court (SCI) is the Republic's court of last resort and its jurisprudence has attracted sustained scholarly attention for a number of reasons. First, some of the most distinguished scholars in the country have served as its justices, and in such capacity their authoritative voices have been a living embodiment of the kind of progressive or conservative views reflecting Irish society (Mac Cormaic 2016). Second, some of the Court's judgments turned out to be landmark decisions that brought about nothing short of a revolution in Irish constitutional jurisprudence. This was, for instance, the notion that the Constitution implicitly safeguards citizens' rights "over and above those specifically enumerated in one or other article", so that "the courts were entitled to identify such latent rights . . . by reference to their understanding of a standard such as 'the Christian and democratic nature of the State'" (Kelly 1988, p. 168).

Judicial argumentation itself has been a classic, favourite subject of investigation, particularly in relation to the complex issue of the justification of judicial decisions. This is briefly reviewed in Section 1, which is devoted to argumentation in judicial settings. In Section 2, corpus design is discussed and the research methodology is outlined. In Sections 3 and 4, the findings of the study are presented in detail, while Section 5 is designed to assess their overall significance.

1 The justification of judicial decisions in argumentation studies

In States based on democratic accountability enhanced by checks and balances, courts are expected to both settle disputes and justify their decisions. As they outline the reasons underlying their verdict, judges advance argumentation. By doing so, they have been observed by legal theorists to address a multifaceted audience including the parties and their legal representatives, fellow judges and

DOI: 10.4324/9781003153771-10

courts higher up in the judicial hierarchy, for the purpose of showing them that their decision was made on legitimate grounds (cf. Perelman 1980).

From the perspective of mainstream argumentation theory, the issue of how to justify judicial decisions has been addressed by pragma-dialecticians, who examine argument structure in the resolution of differences of opinion on the merits. Of the wide range of argument schemes drawing their attention, causal argumentation has always been prominent. By definition, causal argumentation is postulated to occur when "the argument is presented as if what is stated in the argumentation is a means to, a way to, an instrument for or some other kind of causative factor for the standpoint or *vice versa*" (Van Eemeren and Grootendorst 1992, p. 97).

More specifically, a number of studies have elucidated the role of pragmatic argumentation, a sub-type of causal argumentation (Van Eemeren et al. 2007, p. 166), in judicial decision-making. Pragmatic argumentation is inherently consequentialist argumentation in that "judges often defend a decision by referring to the consequences of application of a particular legal rule in the concrete case" (Feteris 2002, p. 349). Interestingly, Feteris distinguishes two main variants: a positive variant, whereby the acceptability of an act, decision or interpretation is defended by envisaging its positive future consequences; and a negative variant, in which conversely the unacceptability of the act is argued to derive from the negative effects it would produce.

The articulation of causality in the form of pragmatic argumentation has been thoroughly examined in recent research by Feteris (2016). In legal justification, the general argument scheme of pragmatic argumentation may be observed to be embedded in an argumentative pattern of complex argumentation. The complexity of the argumentation is related to the contribution of pragmatic argumentation to justification in cases where the acceptability of the application of a legal rule in a specific interpretation is defended. In order to investigate the argumentative patterns developing from the extension of pragmatic argumentation in response to critical questions, Feteris (2016) argues that the desirability or undesirability of a specific decision tends to be assessed in the light of the goal of the rule.

Since legal rules can be seen as a means to reach objectives that are desirable from a legal, social or economic perspective, an interpretation that relates to the goal of the rule may be identified as a relevant form of justification. The most authoritative source to reconstruct the goal of the rule is the historical legislator's original intention when they laid down the rule. The goal of the rule may ultimately rest on the explicit intention of the legislator, as can be assumed from legislative documents, which Feteris (2016, p. 67) refers to as "subjective teleological interpretation of the meaning of the rule". Alternatively, the court may opt for the objective goal of the rule, which requires going back to the rationale of the rule in the context of the law as a whole.

To maintain that the application of the rule is acceptable in a subjective teleological or objective teleological interpretation, a second level of subordinate argumentation should be identified. In turn, this denotes the argumentation that the desirability or undesirability of the consequences in relation to the purpose or goal of the rule can be asserted. In legal theory, the argumentation referring to the goal or purpose is typically advanced as argumentation from coherence with a range of legal approaches, purposes, policies, principles and values. The centrality of such components to judicial reasoning may vary according to the legal system under analysis.

The attempt to identify the discursive configuration of causal argumentation in a jurisdiction not covered by previous studies of this kind (i.e. the Republic of Ireland) has been a strong motivation for this research. As is shown in the next section, the study begins with a preliminary overview of phraseology as a key to data-mine and explore the complexity of corpus data. Second, it undertakes a qualitative investigation of a more restricted sample of judgments, to assess how causal argumentation unfolds in text with a view to the norms and values underpinning the Irish legal order.

2 Materials and methods

The study is based on a small corpus of SCI's judgments on data protection. The issue of data protection was considered by virtue of its centrality to Irish public debate over the last few years. In Ireland, Kearney (2018, p. 136) shows, public discussion has recently seen increasing emphasis laid on data protection and privacy, where "an accord must be struck between the individual's right to privacy and an organisation's right to examine an individual's personal information for its given commercial, contractual or social media activities". The relevance of data protection to Irish jurisprudence is established by Kearney at two main levels. The first is legislation, whereby the Office of the Data Protection Commissioner has been given statutory empowerment, and transparency has tended to focus on awareness of the obligation of registration on the part of certain controllers and processors who are participating in collecting personal data. The second level is that of case law, since Irish Superior Courts have often referred questions of significant importance to the Court of Justice of the European Union, which eventually resulted in some seminal decisions within the area of data protection law.

For the purpose of the present investigation, the corpus judgments were retrieved from the Supreme Court's official website (www.supremecourt.ie, accessed October 31, 2019) when corpus design was completed. The advanced-search function allowing one to insert any string in the quest for judgments was used. In particular, the item ***data protection*** was inserted as the search term. In order to compile the corpus, the judgments delivered by the Court between 2017 and 2019 were selected to generate the so-called *DP_SCI_Corpus*. In total, the corpus includes 29 texts and amounts to 347,927 words.

From a methodological perspective, the study consisted of two main stages (Mazzi 2016). The first one was a preliminary data-mining phase. The underlying notion is that corpora as large repositories of authentic data stored in electronic form are interrogated through exploratory-analysis queries: these can then reveal suggestive patterns useful for the purpose of knowledge elicitation (Tognini Bonelli 2001). In order to data-mine the corpus (Section 3), 4- and a 5-gram frequency lists were created through the linguistic software package *AntConc* (Anthony 2006). These lists allow analysts to visualise the most recurrent phraseology of a corpus. The most salient items in each list were then concordanced (Römer and Wulff 2010), with the aim of identifying their most common usage patterns in context. In the main, this first stage of the analysis allowed for a preliminary quantitative survey of corpus data.

The importance of phraseology for the study of specialised texts has been thoroughly explored in legal contexts (cf. Pontrandolfo 2013), where strong emphasis was laid on "lexical bundles" as a prime example of phraseological patterns. These are aptly defined by Breeze (2013, p. 230) as "multi-word sequences that occurred most frequently in particular genres, regardless of whether or not they constituted idioms or structurally complete units". Bundles were taken as a case in point in light of recent scholarly research (Goźdź-Roszkowski 2011), whereby the adoption of corpus-driven methods and multidimensional analysis pointed to their frequency as evidence of their operative function in communicating key procedural aspects of judicial decisions.[1]

The second stage of the investigation (Section 4) was more of a qualitative kind. Its scope was thus restricted to the judgments where the usage patterns established through the first stage of the analysis were observed to be most frequent. The manual study of the judges' argumentative discourse revealed the use of causal argumentation to be rather extensive. As a result, the textual sequences embedding causal argumentation were reconstructed to determine how causal reasoning supported the Court's standpoint in light of the relevant legal provisions, their intended goals and the underlying values in controversial cases on data protection in the Republic of Ireland.

3 A preliminary survey of corpus data: insights from phraseology

By generating a frequency list for both 4- and 5-grams in the *DP_SCI_Corpus*, two trends can be established. First of all, there is a prevalence of prepositional elements among the most widely used 4-grams, whereas verbal elements can be documented to prevail among their 5-gram counterparts, as shown in Tables 8.1 and 8.2.

Table 8.1 Most frequent 4-grams from the *DP_SCI_Corpus* and related word frequency

4-grams	*Frequency*	*4-grams*	*Frequency*
in the context of	152	*on the basis of*	79
in relation to the	139	*to the effect that*	77
for the purposes of	108	*in accordance with the*	76
in the course of	96	*on behalf of the*	76
in respect of the	84	*in the case of*	45

1 For the sake of simplicity, please note that, in the following sections of the chapter, terms such as "phraseology", "n-gram", "cluster" or "bundle" are synonymous.

Table 8.2 Most frequent 5-grams from the *DP_SCI_Corpus* and related word frequency

5-grams	*Frequency*	*5-grams*	*Frequency*
it seems to me that	45	*is to be found in*	16
it can be said that	28	*I am not satisfied that*	11
it will be necessary to	23	*I am satisfied that the*	11
it is clear that the	22	*It might be said that*	11
it does not seem to	18	*is important to emphasise that*	10

By analysing the salient co-occurrence patterns of each element in context, a remarkable regularity can be associated with many of them. In more detail, the n-grams appear to fulfil three main functions, which can roughly be described as "aboutness", interpretation and argumentation. Each one of these will be documented in this section.

As could be expected, first of all, there are a number of n-grams that uncover information in terms of corpus aboutness, namely the subject matter underlying the corpus itself. This is apparent from a bundle such as *for the purposes of*, the second most frequent in the *DP_SCI_Corpus*. In the main collocational pattern associated with the item, *for the purposes of* is preceded by a description of operations conducted on data (e.g. *DNA profile, collection of data, review of the data* and *seize electronic data*). In addition, the 4-gram is followed by verbal tools sharing a semantic preference of "discovery", notably *assessing, determining, establishing, identifying* and *discovering*. In a nutshell, therefore, these occurrences of *for the purposes of* broadly define the scope of the Supreme Court's jurisprudence in the matter of facts related to data protection. This applies to 13.8% of the corpus entries of *for the purposes of*, as illustrated in (1):[2]

(1) It would have been impracticable to carry out a *review of the data* **for the purposes of** *identifying* the documentation concerned during the search. (*CRH et al. v. The Competition and Consumer Protection Commission*)

Moving on to interpretation, second, the n-grams provide evidence of the Supreme Court's activity in setting core aspects of the case at hand against the appropriate legal background. Thus, for instance, the main collocational surroundings of *in accordance with the* are as follows: in 68.4% of its tokens, the 4-gram is introduced by evaluative statements pointing to the correct interpretation of legislation (e.g. *legislation properly construed, legislation must be interpreted, Act must be construed*) while it is followed by a specification of the relevant legal source – cf. *Constitution, Act, Article, search warrant*, as in (2). In a similar

2 In all of the numbered examples of this section, the case the passage is taken from is indicated in brackets. Furthermore, the n-grams under analysis are in bold typeface, while relevant collocates are italicised.

vein, 43.7% of the concordance hits of *is to be found in* appear to be embedded in passages where the Court associates what they see as the relevant aspects of the dispute as a whole with the legal source to be taken into account, once again. The 5-gram was therefore detected to be preceded by such items as *the background to this case* or *the definition of the test of relevance*, as can be seen in (3):

(2) Such a re-consideration is simply a matter that is contemplated by *the legislation properly construed* **in accordance with the** *Constitution* and does not involve a challenge to the validity of the original decision to go down the SID route in the first place. (*John Callaghan v. An Bord Pleanála and the Attorney General*)

(3) For present purposes, *the core of the decision* of the ECtHR **is to be found in** *para. 78 of the judgment*, where it stated: "The Court then observed that, during the conduct of the operations, the Applicants were unable to take note of the content of the seized documents or to discuss the need for them to be seized". (*CRH et al. v. The Competition and Consumer Protection Commission*)

Reasonable interpretations of valid legal sources predictably go hand in hand with argumentation, which is the third major dimension provided by the n-grams under scrutiny. The relationship between n-grams and the unfolding of argumentation in text develops in three respects. First and foremost, not surprisingly, the Court considers the parties' arguments by both pointing out at what stage in the proceedings they were put forward and, needless to say, attributing arguments to the person responsible for advancing them.

The first function is performed through n-grams such as *in the course of*: in 33.3% of its entries, the item is preceded by reporting verbs referring to somebody else's views (e.g. *reference was made to, was pointed out, described*) and followed by an indication of the judicial stage at which the views were expressed (i.e. *judgment, evidence, submissions, hearing*, as in [4]). The second function predictably lies with *on behalf of*: in 21.1% of its occurrences, the prepositional bundle is preceded by items sharing a semantic preference of "argumentation", such as the verb *argue* or the noun *submission*, while it is followed by the name of the person in whose name the argument in question was articulated (cf. [5]):

(4) *Reference was made* **in the course of** *the submissions* to the standard form Dublin III Regulation Information Leaflet in relation to "right to information" which has to be given to individuals affected by the Dublin III Regulation. (*B.S. and R.S. v. The Refugee Appeals Tribunal et al.*)

(5) *It was argued* **on behalf of the** *accused* that samples could only be taken from a suspect pursuant to the statutory regime and that the manner in which the prosecution had obtained this evidence was unfair. (*The People v. Keith Wilson*)

In addition, judges are invariably expected to express their points of view about the admissibility of arguments or rulings from lower courts. In 28.6% of its concordance hits, *it can be said that* is attested in passages where the Court evaluates the validity of arguments in the form of embedded questions introduced by *whether* or *to what extent* (see [6]). Furthermore, judges consider other courts' verdicts by dealing with the aspects they see as having been conclusively demonstrated by learned colleagues down the country's judicial hierarchy, as in 36.4% of the tokens of *I am satisfied that* (7). Finally, judges appear to engage in dialogue with other voices, real or imagined, in the process of dispute resolution. In 54.5% of the entries of *it might be said that*, Supreme Court judges anticipate and take into account potential competing interpretations before actually refuting them through putatively stronger arguments, as in (8). In this excerpt, Clarke C.J. weighs up the merits in the view that judges may find themselves in a particularly insidious position in cases such as that under review. However, he then moves on to point out that there is a fundamental principle in Irish law that leads him to rule differently (*But there is in Irish law what appears to me to be an equally potent principle to the effect that . . .*):

(6) Having indicated the proper approach it seems to me to follow that the first question which arises on this appeal is as to *whether* **it can be said that** Mr. Rowland had established that the process embarked on by An Post had, as at the time of the trial, clearly gone irremediably wrong. (*Thomas Rowland v. An Post*)

(7) For those reasons **I am satisfied that the** *overall and ultimate conclusion of the trial judge*, which was to the effect that that Becker test had not been met, *was correct*. (*Thomas Rowland v. An Post*)

(8) On one view, **it might be said that** a judge being required to review for legality an administrative decision, without having access to some of the information which informed that decision, is placed in a difficult position in being able properly to assess the legality of the challenged decision. *But* there is in Irish law what appears to me to be an equally potent principle to the effect that it is wrong for a judge to make a decision when influenced by evidence which was not available to a party and which, therefore, the party concerned was not able to challenge in any meaningful or effective way. (*A.P. v. The Minister for Justice and Equality*)

The trends identified in this section and instantiated in (1)–(8) may be said to refer to features of judicial decision-making, such as the interpretative and argumentative nature of the Court's discourse, that conform to widespread expectations about judgments. However, this part of the investigation only served as a first step to data-mine the corpus. At the same time as the quantitative analysis was completed, it was noted that the above features were most conspicuous in a number of judgments. These were then examined in more detail to focus on any widely used argumentative strategy. In such cases, not only were a number of 4- and 5-grams observed to be used, but in fulfilling the functions documented earlier on the bundles established a network of cross-references that was considered indicative of a crucible in the Court's argumentation.

In *Alan Shatter v. Seán Guerin*, for instance, the bundle *is to be found in* occurs in a passage where the Court appears to identify a key aspect of the dispute (i.e. "the legal protection of a person's good name") in association with a relevant legal source, as we saw earlier in (3): "the legal protection of a person's good name as required by the Constitution **is to be found in** the law of defamation". By looking at the wider co-text, as allowed for by the manageable size of corpus data, two occurrences of *in the context of* were detected. In both cases, the bundle is correlated with the Justice's attempt to express his view on the admissibility of an argument raised by the appellant, consistent with the argumentative dimension explored above (in [6]–[8]). In particular, testing the validity of the appellant's overall line of argument is said to be "more difficult . . . *in the context of* the right to a good name of a citizen".

It is important to note that bundles are not taken here as signals of argumentation per se, nor of specific argument schemes as such. Rather, phraseology is assumed to perform discourse functions that unfold in relation to the major theme eventually shaping up the Court's argumentative strategy. In the above case, this was the right to have one's good name vindicated, whereas in others it was "an adequate level of [data] protection" or "respect" for one's "private or family life", to name a few. The recurrence of bundles and their tendency to cluster around a key theme served as the starting point of the manual analysis reconstructing the Court's reasoning in a way that shed light on the persistence of causal argumentation in the forms highlighted in the upcoming section.

4 Causal argumentation in context: a case study from the corpus

Among the cases in which the phraseological patterns in Section 4 were most frequent were *Peter Murphy v. Gary Callinan et al.* [Appeal No. 435/2012]; *The Data Protection Commissioner v. Facebook Ireland et al.* [Appeal No. 2018/68]; *CRH et al. v. The Competition and Consumer Protection Commission* [Appeal No. 65/16]; and *Alan Shatter v. Seán Guerin* [Appeal No. 51/2017]. The manual analysis of each showed that the articulation of causal argumentation was not only associated with the letter of legal norms per se but also with legal principles and values behind statutory or constitutional rules. Owing to space constraints, only two of the cases are discussed in detail in this section.

The combination of causal argumentation with the relevant normative background, to begin with, is apparent from *Peter Murphy v. Gary Callinan et al.* Mr. Murphy, the appellant, filed the action after his motor insurance policy with ARB Underwriting Ltd., the third named respondent, was cancelled as he was considered to have falsely stated on the policy application form that he had never been convicted of any motoring offence or of any criminal non-motoring offence. The information on the grounds of which the policy was cancelled came to the attention of ARB from the first respondent, a member of *an Garda Síochána* [the Republic of Ireland's national police and security service] who, at all material times, acted in his professional capacity. Although Mr. Murphy never contested the cancellation of the motor insurance policy and accepted the returned premia, he exercised his right of access pursuant to the then operative data protection legislation, the Data Protection Act 1988. As he did so, Mr. Murphy identified inaccuracies in the databases held by *an Garda Síochána*, and he pointed to the fact that some of those records were of such antiquity as to amount to stale convictions. He therefore had grounds argued as deriving from what he described as "incompetent record keeping" of the Garda Commissioner, and requested that the respondents should be held accountable by a competent court for their breaches of his rights as a data subject.

In his majority judgment, Baker J. referred to section 7 of the 1988 Act, in which claims for damages may be observed to be rooted. As can be appreciated from (9), the burden of proof lies on plaintiffs, who are required to prove that there has been a breach, and that in turn this led to a loss:

(9) A plaintiff claiming breach of a duty of care in the management or processing of data is not relieved of the obligation to show that there has been a breach and to establish a causative connection between the breach and a loss.

Going back to the High Court judgment by MacMenamin J., Baker J. eventually dismissed the appeal by reason of the fact that the appellant failed to both provide evidence of any negligence in the processing of his personal data, and establish any loss, as shown in (10):

(10) MacMenamin J. . . . was correct in his primary determination that the plaintiff had not established a *prima facie* case on the evidence. In regard to the claim in negligence and for breach of the duty of care under s.7 of the 1988 Act, because the appellant had not shown any negligence or unfairness in the processing of his personal data, nor had he established any loss . . ., I conclude that the appeal must fail.

Underlying Baker J.'s conclusion is the argument that the lack of evidence of negligence as well as the missing link between the alleged negligence and any loss incurred by the appellant is what ultimately causes him to lose the appeal. In Table 8.3, both the norm in the 1988 Act and its application to the concrete case are illustrated:

Table 8.3 Causal argumentation in the legal rule vs. the concrete case

Causal argumentation	
Data Protection Act, 1988	*Murphy v. Callinan et al.*
Evidence has been provided of unfairness or negligence.	No evidence of unfairness or negligence has been provided.
Unfairness or negligence caused loss or damage.	No loss or damage have been established.
The appellant is entitled to compensation.	The appellant has no right to compensation.

In (10), causal argumentation applies to the letter of statutory law. In other cases, however, it may involve invoking principles (e.g. "adequate level of data protection" in *The Data Protection Commissioner v. Facebook Ireland et al.*) or values behind legal norms, whether from binding international law (e.g. the European Convention on Human Rights as in *CRH et al. v. The Competition and Consumer Protection Commission*) or the Constitution of Ireland, as in *Alan Shatter v. Seán Guerin.*

The latter made the front pages of national newspapers because Mr. Shatter was not only a well-known solicitor but also a successful politician who held office as Minister for Justice as of February 2014. At the time, there was considerable public controversy about allegations made by a member of *an Garda Síochána* (Sergeant Maurice McCabe) in relation to putative Garda mismanagement, and the manner in which those allegations and complaints had been dealt with. By reason of the scale of the public discussion around these matters and their implications for confidence in the administration of justice in the country, the Irish Government asked an independent and objective legal expert, Mr. Seán Guerin SC, to examine and access all the relevant papers. On Mr. Guerin's recommendation, the Guerin Inquiry was established for the purpose of interviewing Sergeant McCabe and any other such person as was considered necessary and capable of providing relevant and material assistance to the review process.

Based on the documentation available to him, Mr. Guerin produced a report where serious allegations were made about the way Sergeant McCabe's statements had been handled by both the Garda Commissioner and the Department of Justice. Among other things, the report implied that the Garda Commissioner's response was not probed or tested in any reasonable way, and surprise was expressed that the Minister was apparently satisfied with a brief summary of the conclusions of the investigation, rather than seeking a copy of the report of the investigation itself. After the report was delivered to the *Taoiseach* (prime minister) yet before it was published or laid before the *Oireachtas* (Parliament), Mr. Shatter was summoned to the *Taoiseach*'s office. On that occasion, the *Taoiseach* pointed to certain passages in the report. More than anything else, he indicated that, in the light of such passages, he would have difficulty expressing confidence in the Minister for Justice, after which Mr. Shatter tendered his resignation.

A few months later, a commission of investigation chaired by O'Higgins J. was established following advice from the Guerin report itself. In the O'Higgins Report, Mr. Shatter was exonerated from any criticism in respect of his dealings with the complaints made by Sergeant McCabe. Mr. Shatter therefore pointed to this fact as illustrating the substantive merit of his complaints in the proceedings he subsequently decided to initiate against Mr. Guerin. If Mr. Guerin had chosen to consult him as thoroughly as O'Higgins J. did, he claimed, he would have come to the same conclusions, and Mr. Shatter's ministerial career would not have ended as abruptly as it did. While the High Court dismissed

Mr. Shatter's claim on all grounds, the Court of Appeal allowed the appeal, before the case came to the attention of the Supreme Court upon Mr. Guerin's own appeal.

In the Supreme Court, O'Donnell J. was adamant that Alan Shatter's resignation was not a reflection on the lack of fair procedures in the Guerin Report, but rather on the fact that the *Taoiseach* may dismiss a minister without any process of inquiry, hearing or subsequent review or appeal. Furthermore, it was significant that the Court was far from critical of Mr. Guerin's conduct, given the short timescale and ambiguous nature of the role he was asked to perform, while the difficulty of his task was compounded by ***a surprising lack of communication*** within the Department of Justice. The core of O'Donnell J.'s argumentation eventually lay in the causal reasoning in (11):

(11) A closely related issue arises in relation to question of the opportunity for ***vindicating the applicant's good name.*** Of course, if the Guerin Report was the State's final word on the applicant's reputation, then it could also be said that he did not have the opportunity of vindicating his good name. But the O'Higgins Commission, recommended by the respondent and established by the government in due course, not only offered the possibility of vindicating the applicant's good name, but provided a more comprehensive and complete remedy than anything that could be provided by way of judicial review of the report for failure to follow particular procedures. [emphasis added]

The right to vindicate one's good name is protected as a fundamental value by Article 40.3.2 of the Constitution (2018 [1937], p. 154), which reads as follows: "The State shall, in particular, by its laws protect as best it may from unjust attack and, in the case of injustice done, vindicate the life, person, good name, and property rights of every citizen". In (11) above, the causal link would be between the Guerin Report's status as ***the State's final word on the applicant's reputation*** and a breach of Mr. Shatter's right to vindicate his good name. No such link could be established in the case, because the O'Higgins Commission allowed Mr. Shatter a distinct possibility to have his good name vindicated, which he eventually did. As far as this ground of appeal was concerned, therefore, Mr. Guerin succeeded in proving his credentials as the Report did not restrict but rather safeguarded the respondent's right to vindicate his good name, as schematised below:

1 Mr. Guerin's credentials have been proved.

1.1a The Guerin Report did not jettison the respondent's right to vindicate his good name.

1.1b Each and every citizen's right to vindicate their good name is safeguarded by the Constitution.

5 Discussion and conclusions

The findings presented across Sections 3 and 4 helped address the research question posed at the outset about the use of causal argumentation. Not only did the preliminary analysis of phraseology contribute to identifying the judgments where the patterns in Section 3 were most frequent, but the qualitative study of the cases in Section 4 shed light on the flexibility of causal argumentation as a reasoning tool that ties in with valid legal norms at two main levels.

The first is the fact that causality may be combined with more literal approaches to legal text, as we saw with case *Peter Murphy v. Gary Callinan et al.* in relation to "unfairness", "negligence", "loss" and "damage". The second level is represented by more schematic or teleological approaches to legal text, as was observed with the necessity to embrace principles or uphold values underlying domestic statutes, international law or the Constitution (see *The Data Protection Commissioner v. Facebook Ireland et al.*, *CRH et al. v. The Competition and Consumer Protection Commission* and *Alan Shatter v. Seán Guerin*). For each text under analysis, the factual background was outlined and the steps involved in the articulation of causal argumentation were briefly schematised.

From an analytical perspective, the significance of bundles lies in their capability to both "cut across grammatical structures" and "have identifiable discourse functions" (Biber 2006, p. 155). It is proof of their flexibility as a discourse tool that bundles span a diverse range of syntactic and semantic categories. From a syntactic point of view, they may incorporate verb phrase fragments (e.g. *it does not seem to*), dependent clause fragments (*to the effect that*) or prepositional phrase fragments (*in the context of*) (Biber et al. 2004, p. 381). In semantic terms, moreover, bundles have been detected to, among others, denote abstract concepts (*on the basis of*) and serve as indicators of "stance expression" (*I am not satisfied that*) (Breeze 2013, p. 245). To these usage patterns, clues to the textual sites where argumentation unfolds may be added.

As suggested in Section 3, this is not to say that bundles act as "argumentative indicators" as "words and expressions that directly refer to *argumentation*" or "to *any of the moves* that are significant to the argumentative process" (Van Eemeren et al. 2007, p. 2). After all, Van Eemeren et al. (2007, p. 189) themselves concede that the indicators in their own inventory do not automatically identify specific argument schemes but rather "may occur in more than one type of argumentation", or else their use may not in itself be indicative of argumentation at all (Mazzi 2016). Rather, what is argued here is that bundles broadly converge towards the focal point of judgments, and as such they guide the analyst to the prime sites around which judges' argumentative discourse will gravitate.

From a methodological point of view, the study has a number of merits. To begin with, it used a corpus-driven method to data-mine the texts and identify those judgments worth analysing in more detail owing to their tendency to exhibit the phraseological regularities documented in Section 3. In this regard, the investigation expanded the coverage of both legal theoretical and argumentation studies with a more broad-based corpus background. Unlike in legal theory including research on the Irish legal system (cf. Byrne et al. 2014), the emphasis here was more on discourse than procedure per se. Unlike in argumentation research such as Feteris (2016), furthermore, the study included more than a single text and it clarified how causal argumentation was more specifically interwoven with the affirmation of principles and values enshrined in the Irish legal order.

As a path of further research, it would be desirable to extend the methodology utilised here to small corpora including judgments from other subject areas from the Irish legal order. This would allow one to ascertain whether other argumentative strategies are as widely used as causal argumentation has been reported to be in the *DP_SCI_Corpus*. In addition, the identification of the most salient texts in each corpus, again based on the methods in Section 2, would enable one to perform a more detailed analysis of the argument patterns in each text with a view to the critical questions testing the validity of argument schemes in context.

References

Anthony, L., 2006. *AntConc 3.2.1.* [online] Available from: www.laurenceanthony.net [Accessed December 2, 2019].

Biber, D., 2006. *University language: A corpus-based study of spoken and written registers.* Amsterdam: Benjamins.

Biber, D., Conrad, S., & Cortes, V., 2004. If you look at. . . : lexical bundles in university teaching and textbooks. *Applied Linguistics*, 25(3), 371–405.

Breeze, R., 2013. Lexical bundles across four legal genres. *International Journal of Corpus Linguistics*, 18(2), 229–253.

Byrne, R., Mccutcheon, P., Bruton, C., & Coffey, G., 2014. *The Irish legal system.* Dublin: Bloomsbury.

Constitution of Ireland., 2018 [1937]. *Bunreacht na hÉireann.* Dublin: The Stationery Office.

Feteris, E.T., 2002. A pragma-dialectical approach of the analysis and evaluation of pragmatic argumentation in a legal context. *Argumentation*, 16, 349–367.

Feteris, E.T., 2016. Prototypical argumentative patterns in a legal context: The role of pragmatic argumentation in the justification of judicial decisions. *Argumentation*, 30, 61–79.

Goźdź-Roszkowski, S., 2011. *Patterns of linguistic variation in American legal English: A corpus-based study.* Bern: Peter Lang.

Kearney, S., 2018. Data protection and privacy for media and individuals under Irish and EU law. *Irish Communications Review*, 16, 136–146.

Kelly, J.M., 1988. Fundamental rights and the constitution. *In*: B. Farrell, ed., *De Valera's constitution and ours.* Dublin: Gill & Macmillan, 163–173.

Mac Cormaic, R., 2016. *The Supreme Court.* London: Penguin.

Mazzi, D., 2016. *The theoretical background and practical implications of argumentation in Ireland.* Newcastle-upon-Tyne: Cambridge Scholars.

Perelman, C., 1980. *Justice, law and argument.* Dordrecht: Reidel.

Pontrandolfo, G., 2013. La fraseología como estilema del lenguaje judicial: El caso de las locuciones prepositivas desde unap contrastiva. *In*: L. Chierichetti & G. Garofalo, eds., *Discurso profesional y lingüística de corpus. Perspectivas de investigación.* Bergamo: CELSB, 187–215.

Römer, U., & Wulff, S., 2010. Applying corpus methods to written academic texts: Explorations of MICUSP. *Journal of Writing Research*, 2, 99–127.
Tognini Bonelli, E., 2001. *Corpus linguistics at work*. Amsterdam: Benjamins.
Van Eemeren, F.H., & Grootendorst, R., 1992. *Argumentation, communication, and fallacies*. Hillsdale, NJ: Lawrence Erlbaum Associates.
Van Eemeren, F.H., Houtlosser, P., & Snoeck Henkemans, A.F., 2007. *Argumentative indicators in discourse. A pragma-dialectical approach*. Dordrecht: Springer.

9 A corpus-based comparative analysis of the evaluative lexicon found in judicial decisions on immigration

María José Marín Pérez

Most of the scholarly work devoted to the characterisation of legal language has traditionally been accomplished from a rather prescriptive angle (Mellinkoff 1963; Alcaraz 1994, 2001; Tiersma 1999), being frequently based on a reduced number of language samples and on the authors' extensive experience and intuition. Concerning the actual description of the legal lexicon, we may come upon such features as the presence of Latin borrowings and Old French phrases, synonyms, archaisms and redundancy, as well as the widespread use of common words with uncommon meanings (Mellinkoff 1963, p. 11); nevertheless, little reference is made to the expression of appraisal.

In recent years, there has been an increasing tendency to scrutinise legal texts in search for linguistic evidence of the expression of stance (Finegan 2010; Mazzi 2010; Goźdź-Roszkowski and Pontrandolfo 2013; Goźdź-Roszkowski 2017). As Goźdź-Roszkowski and Pontrandolfo (2013) acknowledge, the relevance of the expression of subjectivity in legal discourse should not be underestimated, as it is paramount to legal argumentation, particularly in common law legal systems where judges interpret or show agreement or disagreement with other decisions that might be relevant to a specific case at trial.

"The notion of attitude understood as a cover term for the expression of the speaker or writer's . . . stance towards, viewpoint on, or feelings about the entities or propositions that he or she is talking about" (Thompson and Hunston 2000, p. 5), which Eggins and Slade (1997) or White (1999) and Martin (2000) conceptualise as *appraisal*, has been explored in connection with the legal context as the explicit verbalisation of the speakers'/writers' stance through the scrutiny of single lexical items or phrases obtained from legal text collections. Mazzi's research (2010) illustrates this trend by examining the expression of attitude via the use of verbs or adjectives like *disagree* or *incorrect* and syntactic patterns (demonstratives + nouns such as *opinion, argument* or *conclusion*) which, according to the author, might have been used by US Supreme Court judges to subtly persuade readers and listeners to interpret the facts from a very specific angle.

Evaluative language has also been analysed in judicial opinions in connection with the concept of "disciplinary values" (Breeze 2011, Goźdź-Roszkowski (2018), whereby values or qualities which define what is prized or stigmatised by different professional communities (Breeze 2011, p. 94) relate to the linguistic

DOI: 10.4324/9781003153771-11

strategies deployed by US Supreme Court judges to express approval or disapproval of same-sex marriages.

However, the amount of research devoted to the cross-linguistic scrutiny of the linguistic mechanisms used to convey the speakers'/writers' stance towards the propositional content of legal text is scarce, as only few authors analyse the legal texts produced in different languages to that end. The work by Goźdź-Roszkowski and Pontrandolfo (2013), Pontrandolfo and Goźdź-Roszkowski (2014) and, more recently, Orts Llopis (2018), evidence the presence of vocabulary and expressions that reveal the significance of this feature of language and the disparities found across legal systems.

In that vein, as stated by Marín (2019), the presence of vocabulary which could potentially signal the attitude of the speakers/writers in two corpora of British and Spanish judicial decisions is not anecdotal. Roughly 20% more vocabulary items falling under the category *affect*, one of the four classes embraced by the *appraisal* system (Eggins and Slade 1997; White 1999; Martin 2000), were found in a British corpus as opposed to a Spanish one.

Following from the above and given the scarce number of comparative corpus-based studies circumscribed within the legal field, this research was designed to try and fill that gap. To that end, based on the results obtained by Marín (2019), two corpora of British and Spanish judicial decisions related to the topic of immigration were processed to obtain the lexical networks of some of the terms contained in the category *affect*, as illustrated in Tables 9.3 and 9.4.

By doing so, this study aims at comparing both legal systems in an attempt to shed some light on the picture of immigration in Spain and the UK as seen through the lens of the judiciary. This comparison will be carried out using the framework of corpus-based discourse analysis (CBDA) by means of the observation of the context of usage of the collocates and co-collocates of some of the terms in the category *affect* in both languages.

As regards the structure of this research, it was organised as follows: Section 1 presents the theoretical and empirical background provided by Marín's work (2019) that was used as the point of departure for this analysis. In Section 2, an explanation of the methodology applied is given. The results are shown and discussed in Section 3, followed by the conclusion to this research.

1 Background to the study

As already stated, this study departs from the findings by Marín (2019), where the recurrence of evaluative lexicon is evidenced and compared across legal systems. Marín identifies the evaluative vocabulary retrieved from two legal corpora obtained from British and Spanish sources, which was classified following the theoretical framework of systemic linguistics, specifically, as defined by Eggins and Slade (1997) White (1999), Rothery and Stenglin (2000) and Martin (2000).

The *appraisal* system is part of this linguistic model of analysis whereby language is understood as a whole network of systems which are interconnected and available for the speaker to choose so as to express meaning. In language usage, speakers are presented with a whole array of language options which arise from the environment of other options (Halliday 2003, p. 8). In systemic linguistics, those options, often identified as language functions, are defined as systems, one of those systems is *appraisal*. This linguistic model was implemented by Marín (2019) to scrutinise the way in which information is presented on the part of the writer/speaker in legal texts. As defined by Eggins and Slade (1997) and later on revisited by White (1999) and Martin (2000), the appraisal system comprises four major categories or systems, namely, *affect*, *appreciation*, *judgment* and *amplification*. The category *affect* embraces those linguistic items which appeal or make reference to emotion (Eggins and Slade 1997; White 1999; Martin 2000). After processing the two corpora and obtaining two frequency Spanish and English word type lists, Marín (2019) finds different examples which were included within this group such as *suplicar (beg)*, *preocupado (worried)*, *vulnerable* or *fearful*. When using the term *appreciation*, Eggins and Slade (1997, p. 125) state that it marks the speakers' reactions to and evaluations of reality. Words like *arbitrario (arbitrary)*, *controvertido (controversial)*, *nice* or *helpful* fall within this class. The *judgment* system comprises those terms which present a speaker's assessment of other people's ethics, morality or social values (Kaltenbacher 2006, p. 272), for instance, *indebido (wrongful)*, *legítimo (legitimate)*, *discriminatory* or *unfair*.

From a quantitative perspective, the comparison between both corpora in Marín (2019) shows certain differences in the proportion of evaluative vocabulary extracted the British corpus as opposed to the Spanish one. It is observed that the total percentage of lexical items falling under the system *appraisal*, which, as stated, is composed of four major thematic groups, namely, *appreciation*, *judgment*, *affect* and *amplification* (Eggins and Slade 1997; White 1999; Martin 2000), was higher in the British corpus than in the Spanish dataset. Actually, 1.08% of the most frequent 2500 words extracted from the English text collection belonged in any of those four categories, as opposed to the Spanish set, where 0.72% were identified (33% less). In fact, the difference was even more noticeable within the group of terms embraced by the category *affect*, which contained 20% more items than the Spanish corpus.

Marín (2019) links the results of her comparative analysis to the very nature of the legal systems the texts in the corpora stemmed from, assuming that the Spanish system, which is circumscribed within the realm of the civil law, tends to be less open to interpretation than case law systems, such as the British one, which is said to be judge made, hence the lesser amount of evaluative items found in the former corpus.

The rationale behind the decision made to resort to Marín's (2019) findings as a point of departure for the following analysis was driven by our belief that those terms falling within the category *affect* (which appeal to the reader's/listener's emotions or express those of the speaker) may relate at a time to others which could reflect the emotional state of migrants going through legal processes, or at least, unveil sensitive topics and the speakers'/writers' attitude towards them that might enhance our perception of the phenomenon of immigration as reflected on judicial decisions.

2 Methodology

2.1 Corpus description

As shown in Table 9.1, two corpora were employed in this study which include 600 judicial decisions each. The size of both texts collections differed considerably as the Spanish corpus had 2.4 million tokens (or running words), while the British one was noticeably bigger, containing 3.7 million. Two major sources were employed to obtain the texts, which were produced between 2016 and 2017: the *CENDOJ*[1] (Spanish legal documentation centre) and the *BAILII*[2] (British and Irish Legal Information Institute). Both databases offer free access to judicial decisions from Spanish and British courts as well as to other legal texts. As regards the search setting themselves and the type of texts retrieved from both databases, the search engine on the *BAILII* website was configured to only resort to case law datasets. This decision implied that no legislative texts or any other sort of legal text would be singled out by the system but rather judicial decisions issued by courts and tribunals from the UK, including England and Wales, Northern Ireland, Scotland and those courts whose jurisdiction is exercised over the whole of the UK territory regardless of their level within the judiciary.

Similarly, the *CENDOJ* search engine was configured practically without any restrictions with respect to the type of court or tribunal (ranging from the Spanish Supreme Court to first-tier local courts/tribunals). Unlike *BAILII*, the *CENDOJ* database comprises basically two types of texts which were filtered, namely, *sentencias* and *autos*. In this case, only the former were considered for the study as the more approximate equivalent of the British texts.

The query terms used to retrieve the Spanish texts included *inmigración* (immigration), *inmigrante* (immigrant), *extranjero* (literally *foreigner*) and *extranjería* (this term is employed in Spanish to refer to the laws and regulations on immigration, for instance, the Ley de Extranjería 4/2000 [Immigration Act 4/2000]). In English, the search terms were *immigration, migration, immigrant* and *migrant*.

Table 9.1 Corpora description

Corpora	Texts	Tokens	Types
Spanish corpus *CENDOJ*	600	2,396,985 (**2.4 m**)	20,236
British corpus *BAILII*	600	3,723,587 (**3.7 m**)	25,268

1 www.poderjudicial.es/search/indexAN.jsp
2 www.bailii.org/

The selection of the query terms was carried out in advance using as reference the Spanish Ley de Extranjería 4/2000 and the British Immigration Act 2014 (ch. 22), which were processed in search for the keywords that might facilitate the selection of the query terms themselves and subsequently guarantee their significance in text retrieval. The words "foreign" and "foreigner" (directly related to the Spanish *extranjero* and *extranjería*) were discarded as they were not statistically relevant in the British corpus, in fact, the term "foreign" was not included in the word-type list.

2.2 *Procedure*

The study by Marín (2019) served as a point of departure for the present analysis, as stated earlier, using those terms singled out in it which ranked the highest within the category *affect* in both languages, as shown in the first column of Tables 9.3 and 9.4, so as to obtain the collocate networks of such terms, displayed in the third and fifth columns of both tables. For the purpose of this research, the terms in the category *affect* were ranked according to their keyness value, as also illustrated in Tables 9.3 and 9.4 (column 2). As for their collocates and co-collocates, the statistical measure used for their identification and ranking was Mutual Information (MI) in combination with log-likelihood (LL) in column 4. All the collocates and co-collocates which form the networks of the terms selected and whose contexts of usage will be scrutinised below have been introduced for the first time in this chapter and were not included in Marín (2019).

As far as the selection of the contexts of usage of some of the collocates below is concerned, a closer and exhaustive examination of the concordance lines associated to them was accomplished. In order for those samples to be representative of the corpora at hand and for the qualitative analysis not to be skewed or biased, at least half if not all of the occurrences of each of the collocates (it always depended on the total number of hits obtained) was manually examined. This was a time-consuming task, yet it guaranteed that the interpretation of the results and the selection of the excerpts used as samples would be based on solid ground.

Table 9.2 displays some of the vocabulary items extracted by Marín (2019) from both corpora and classified according to the four major categories within the *appraisal* system; *affect* is one of them.

The application *Graphcoll*, included in the package *Lancsbox* (Brezina et al. 2018), was used to obtain the lexical networks of some of the terms in the *affect* category, which is the one that displayed the greatest differences between the two corpora. *Graphcoll* deserves special attention as it not only manages to obtain a word's network very quickly, but it also represents the network visually through a graph that displays the node's collocates. Likewise, *Lancsbox* is capable of producing the lexical network of a term on the fly, which, on its own, is a major improvement. Brezina et al. (2015) emphasise that the main potential of this software is

Table 9.2 The appraisal theory framework: examples from both corpora (Marín 2019, p. 153)

	SPANISH	ENGLISH
AFFECT		
Dis/inclination	*Exigir* (demand), *suplicar* (beg)	Expectation, opportunity
Un/happiness	*Feliz* (happy), *obligado* (obliged)	Free, forced, satisfied
In/security	*Preocupado* (worried), *ansioso* (anxious)	Vulnerable, emotional, fearful
Dis/satisfaction	*Harto* (fed up)	Like, hate
APPRECIATION	–	
Reaction	*Arbitrario* (arbitrary), *controvertido* (controversial)	Nice, adequate, harsh
Valuation	*Preciso* (accurate), *Correctamente* (correctly)	Helpful, difficult, essential
Composition		Detailed, precise, complex
JUDGMENT		
Social sanction	*Indebido* (wrongful), *legítimo* (legitimate)	Discriminatory, unfair, true
Social esteem	*Constante* (tenacious), *inteligente* (intelligent)	Determined, capable
AMPLIFICATION	–	–
Enrichment	*Mucho* (much), *más* (more), *muy* (very)	Entirely, much, highly
Augmenting	*Reducido* (reduced), *simplemente* (simply)	Sole, shortly, mere
Mitigation		

its capability to unveil the semantic interaction among the words in a corpus by extending a word's context beyond the word itself, thus avoiding the painstaking and time-consuming process of doing it manually, as Baker (2016) and Marín (2016) also acknowledge.

3 Results and discussion

This research was thus conceived as an attempt to account for the different mechanisms deployed in two corpora of judicial decisions issued by British and Spanish courts for the expression of appraisal in relation to such a sensitive topic as immigration. To that end, this section was structured into two main blocks. In Section 3.1, a presentation and analysis of the data retrieved from the British text collection is introduced, whereas Section 3.2 comprises the interpretation of the results obtained from the Spanish text collection as compared with its British counterpart.

Table 9.3 displays the lexical networks of four terms automatically retrieved from the British corpus that belong in the category *affect* and ranked the highest in terms of their keyness score. These terms' collocates were selected and organised according to their collocational robustness, evidenced by the score displayed in column 4 of Tables 9.3 and 9.4, which was calculated through the automatic implementation of the mutual information and log-likelihood algorithms. The degree of robustness of the collocational link established between second-level collocates (in column 5) and the nodes in column 4 (first-level collocates) has not been included in the tables for the sake of clarity; however, it is mentioned whenever needed in the following analysis.

As reflected in Tables 9.3 and 9.4, the networks have two hierarchical levels: on the one hand, the first level collocates of the selected term; and on the other hand, the collocates of those collocates, that is, its co-collocates. Exploring these lexical networks in detail might provide an in-depth insight into the picture of British and Spanish judicial decisions project of the figure of migrants and immigration in general, as all the texts revolve around this topic.

3.1 British corpus

On a first approach, some of the collocates in the British corpus strike us as particularly significant, since they point at the distressful circumstances that migrants experiment throughout the migration process. We are told about human *trafficking* or sexual *exploitation* in relation to *women* as well as about *abduction* or *cruelty*, which are found among the co-collocates of the term *child*. According to the texts, migrants are presented as *miserable, inferior* and *vulnerable* and concerned about family issues, particularly about children, since parenthood and other related terms appear in the collocate networks shown below.

The terms themselves already reveal the conditions migrants encounter in their voyages to European soil. *Distress* strikes us as particularly significant through its association with *demoralisation, humiliation, harassment, suffering* and *mother*, and points towards a clear direction in the interpretation of the data extracted by the software. Nevertheless, a deeper analysis of the context of usage of some of these lexical items is needed to ratify our initial perception.

As evidenced in Table 9.3, the terms *trafficking* and *exploitation* are closely linked in the British corpus and the situations described in the texts always have a common thread. As a matter of fact, the statistical relevance of the term *trafficking* is noticeable, as it is comprised within the networks of the adjective *vulnerable* and the noun *fear* (as co-collocates of these terms), displaying, for instance, an average collocational strength of 12.95 (a measure which combines the mutual information and log-likelihood algorithm, as stated earlier) within the network of the term *fear*, as opposed to the average for the whole network, which is 8.97. The degree of collocational robustness between the term *exploitation* and other elements comprised in the network of the adjective *vulnerable* is also remarkable. Its score is beyond the average for the whole network (7.37), standing almost 2 points above it.

Let us remind the reader that we are reflecting upon the picture of migration in the UK and Spain as depicted in legal texts, which is not a comprehensive picture of the phenomenon as a whole but rather a portrait of the legal difficulties

Table 9.3 Lexical networks of the English terms *fear, happy, miserable* and *vulnerable*

Terms	Keyness	Main Colls	MI-likelihood ($p < 0.05$)	Co-collocates
Fear	5689.88	persecution	13.221	trafficking, attack, victim, fear, family
		distress	11.042	demoralisation, humiliation, harassment, suffering, mother
		abduction	10.501	coercion, retention, custody, deception, irrational
		reprisal	9.030	network, trafficking, attacks
		anguish	8.001	inferiority, humiliating, feelings
Happy	3745.05	settled	16.252	workforce, migrant, job, calm, relatives
		contact	14.332	father, confining, distressed, apprehension, supervisor
		child	12.256	cruelty, abduction, cares, parents, blame
		excited	11.876	Saddam, pleased, suspicion, Iraq, prospect
		wary	9.450	proof, allegation, statement, child, British
Miserable	2487.65	feelings	15.418	motivation, suffocation, fatherly, anguish, disorientation
		mother	10.210	stepfather, threaten, suing, intimidating, incapacitating
		house	9.206	raid, demolition, explosives, footpath, bedroomed
		children	9.108	asylum-seeker, non-dependent, single-parent, unaccompanied, devastated
		life	8.006	ruptured, private, shortened, family, insurmountable
Vulnerable	1056.87	females	13.251	young, inferior, vulnerable, risk
		exploitation	13.201	prostitution, sexual, slavery, forced, trafficking
		women	11.008	stereotypes, punished, equal, pregnant, discrimination
		harm	11.002	irreversible, bodily, persecution, reoffending psychological
		witness	9.005	statement, intimidation, averment, credible

migrants have to face either as members of an ethnic minority living in a foreign country or as asylum seekers. In this respect, migrant women are often held against their will by criminal organisations (see [1]), which force them to prostitute themselves by taking advantage of their lack of language skills among other things, as shown in (2). These stories are recurrently told throughout the corpus in connection with the attempts by these women to claim asylum in the UK, which is often the legal issue that brings them to court for one reason or another. From the perspective of statistical data, both *trafficking* and *exploitation* stand out, as they occur on 899 and 131 occasions respectively and are considerably well distributed, the former appearing in 52 texts and the latter in 18.

(1) Her report began by breaking down what she characterised as the claimant's *trafficking* experience into three: *trafficking* within Albania for sexual exploitation . . . and travel from Albania to the UK as a result of previous sexual *exploitation*.

(2) Victims are generally moved to a place where there is a market for their services, often where they *lack language skills* and other basic knowledge that would enable them to seek help. . . . these actions can all take place within one country's borders . . . they can also take place across borders . . . and the act of receiving the victim and the *exploitation* taking place in another.

Nevertheless, after examining many of the concordances and extended contexts of usage of the term *abduction*, which the software associates with the word *child*, they reveal migrant parents taking their children away from their partners without their consent either to their home countries or to the UK, where they seek asylum, as evidenced in (3). The data associated to *abduction* also make it stand out as statistically relevant, repeating itself 96 times and being used in 20 out of the 600 texts in the corpus. The collocational link established between the term *abduction* and the noun *child* is also noticeable, as the score associated to it is 9.87, 4.5 points above the average for the whole collocate network (6.53).

(3) The fact that he was issued with a child *abduction* notice . . . but I accept that the issue of the notice does link the Claimant with the child's disappearance over a number of days.

The collocate *cruelty* also called our attention and we decided to delve into its context of usage, which unveils two opposed scenarios. On the one hand (as (4) illustrates) migrant parents are accused of inflicting harm on their children, on the other hand, we are informed of the ill-treatment migrant children may have received in detention centres, as shown in (5). Even so, the figures associated to *cruelty* are low, as it only occurs seven times in the corpus, hence its lesser significance from a statistical perspective.

(4) Both the Claimant and the Interested Party were sentenced on the same indictment to prison sentences for child *cruelty*. The Claimant was sentenced to concurrent sentences.

(5) The traumatic and disturbing nature of being subject to deliberately inflicted severe ill-treatment at child detention centers and the consequential suffering that deliberate *cruelty* entails.

The situation changes if we explore the contexts where the term is used in its plural form, *children*. The word *children* is strongly linked to the distressful conditions faced by unaccompanied infants seeking asylum who, as illustrated by (6), do not often obtain it. The texts also provide an eloquent insight into the family backgrounds in the children's home countries, as evidenced in (7). From a quantitative perspective, the collocate *unaccompanied* is used 83 times in 24 texts. Concerning the collocational bond between *children* and *unaccompanied*, as measured by the software, it is also 3.2 points higher than the average for the whole network of the noun *children*, in its plural form (5.88).

(6) The appellant is a citizen of Afghanistan born in 1997. He arrived in the UK on 25 March 2011 as an illegal entrant. . . . This was refused on 22 June 2011 and he was granted discretionary leave as an *unaccompanied* asylum-seeking child until 20 June 2014.

(7) As it concerned the return of unaccompanied children. . . . and he would be returning *unaccompanied* and the judge's finding was that he had lost touch with his family. . . . He would, therefore, be an unaccompanied child in Kabul.

As a final remark, the term *vulnerable*, whose statistical salience is noticeable (it occurs on 367 occasions in 87 texts), reinforces our general perception of the portrait of migration in the UK. In the first place, (8) graphically portrays the background in the appellant's home country, Sudan, where he was the victim of political persecution, feeling forced to escape and to try to enter the UK. On a different note, (9) informs on a child involved in the black market and probably exploited by his own fellow countrymen, whereas (10) depicts the vulnerable position of a migrant woman due to her irregular situation in the country and her fragile health.

(8) But a few have been kept incommunicado, outside the protection of the Sudanese law and *vulnerable* to torture and other forms of ill-treatment.

(9) He would have had little choice but to work on the black market. . . . He was a child surrounded by adults from his own country he was *vulnerable* to exploitation.

(10) Nevertheless, the Court considered that that applicant was in a *vulnerable* position, not only . . . because of her specific past and her personal emotional circumstances . . . but also because of her fragile health.

3.2 *Spanish corpus*

The detailed examination of the Spanish collocates and co-collocates within the category *affect* reveals that it shares common thematic areas with its British counterpart such as the relevance of the family environment. In that vein, *familia* stands at the top of the first collocational level of the term *deseo* (*wish/desire*), displaying

13.08 collocational strength with this term. Nonetheless, other topics are identified among the most salient collocates within these networks, for instance, *shipwrecks* (*naufragios*) or *racial hate* (*odio*), which stand at 4.2 and 2.74 points above the average for the whole network, respectively. Let us explore the data in greater detail.

In Table 9.4, the lexical networks of the Spanish terms *deseo* (wish), *riesgo* (risk), *feliz* (happy) and *odio* (hate) are presented. As stated above, they ranked the highest within the list of keywords retrieved from the Spanish corpus which could be identified with the category *affect.*

Table 9.4 Lexical networks of the Spanish terms *deseo* (wish), *riesgo* (risk), *feliz* (happy) and *odio* (hate)

Terms	**Keyness**	**Collocates**	**MI–log-likelihood ($p < 0.05$)**	**Co-collocates**
Deseo (desire)	7632.24	*familias* (families)	13.087	*monoparental* (single-parent) *emparentado* (related) *sacrificios* (sacrifices) *sufren* (suffer) *víctimas* (victims) *reunificación* (reunification)
		atender (assist)	12.592	*acuciante* (compelling) *imperiosa* (urgent) *necesidades* (needs)
		residir (reside)	12.350	*España* (Spain) *deseo* (desire), *familias* (families) *entrar* (enter)
		inquietud (concern)	10.459	*desazón* (discomfort) *zozobra* (uneasiness) *perjuicio* (damage)
Riesgo (risk)	5430.89	*naufragio* (shipwreck)	11.809	*rocosa* (rocky) *proximidad* (proximity), *riesgo* (risk) *consecuencia* (consequence)
		escarmiento (chastisement)	11.798	*sufrido* (suffered) *existe* (exists) *familia* (family) *riesgo* (risk)
		desarme (disarmament)	11.487	
		clandestinos (clandestine)	10.007	*encubrir* (conceal) *ocultos* (hidden), *policías* (policemen/ women), *sometidos* (subject to)
		hundimiento (sinking)	9.867	*flotación* (flotation) *choque* (crash), *inminente* (imminent) *rocosa* (rocky), *señalización* (signalling)

Terms	Keyness	Collocates	MI–log-likelihood ($p < 0.05$)	Co-collocates
Feliz (happy)	4331.12	*contenta* (happy)	18.471	
		tranquila (calm)	17.157	
		chica (girl)	16.890	
Odio (hate)	3887.45	*antisemitismo* (antisemitism)	17.201	*racial* (racial) *xenofobia* (xenophobia) *odio* (hate)
		propagación (spread)	16.206	*proscrito* (outlaw) *odio* (hate) *incitación* (inducement) *violencia* (violence)
		racial (racial)	15.880	*incitar* (incite) *xenofobia* (xenophobia) *promover* (promote)
		hostilidad (hostility)	10.654	*minorías* (minorities) *violencia* (violence) *incitación* (inducement)
		intolerancia (intolerance)	10.002	*mostrar* (show) *rechazo* (refusal) *odio* (hate)

From a quantitative perspective, the proportion of such items in the Spanish corpus, less inclined towards the expression of appraisal, as affirmed by Marín (2019), was lower (175.28 raw frequency as opposed to 448.35 in the British corpus), hence their lesser capacity to establish a statistical bond with other terms and the lesser amount of collocates and co-collocates found in the networks. The collocate frequency threshold was thus lowered (from >5 to >3) to try and compensate for this fact; even so, the divergence between both corpora can be clearly appreciated. Such scarceness also affects the image projected of migrants as reflected on the Spanish text collection, less comprehensive than the one observed in the British corpus.

In spite of the coincidences across corpora, we do not find any reference to shipwrecks or racial hate in the British corpus when delving into the link between the vocabulary in the category *affect* and its collocates. This does not necessarily imply that racial hate is not associated with the phenomenon of immigration the UK; it simply does not stand out as a salient topic in the corpus at hand. However, the statistical significance of these topics in the Spanish corpus is considerable. Once more, as stated above, a closer scrutiny of the contexts of usage of these and other terms may add to the depiction of the circumstances that surround migrants in their relationship with courts and in the voyage, both physical and mental, towards a better life in Europe.

After examining the context surrounding some of the items comprised in the collocate networks displayed in Table 9.4, the Spanish corpus clearly reinforces the image of migrant families projected in the British one, in the sense that migrant children are shown as helpless and in need of protection from their parents, who often resort to this argument to claim asylum in European soil. In (11), a Syrian family willing to enter Spanish territory asks the authorities permission to access the country due to the ill-treatment they are exposed to in Moroccan soil (*es pública y notoria la discriminación que los inmigrantes sirios y . . . sus familias sufren en Marruecos*).

Similarly to the British corpus and as depicted in (12), migrant women are subject to criminal organisations who, in this case, threaten them to do harm to their families (*amenazadas con causar mal a sus familias*) if they do not accept to be exploited sexually in Spain to return the money they owe them (*saldar la deuda que había contraído con el viaje mediante el ejercicio de la prostitución*).

On the contrary, we also find a connection between the term families (*familias*) and the unethical use of the argument of reunification, as illustrated by (13). In it, the father alleges the need to reunify a family he has no contact with, judging by the words of the prosecution, who states that he never worried about the life of his 15-year-old daughter (*el Sr. XXX no se preocupa por la vida de su hija adolescente de 15 años*).

Once more, the statistical significance of the term *family/families* is high, being found in 187 texts (almost a third of the corpus) and occurring on 573 occasions; however, from a quantitative perspective, we only found one instance of the situation presented in the third extract, whereas the first two repeat themselves throughout the corpus. Its keyness score is also the highest within the category, and it can be found not only as a first-level collocate of the term *deseo* (displaying 13.087 MI+LL score, the highest in the network) but also as a co-collocate of *riesgo*, as illustrated in Table 9.4 above.

(11) *Hay un bebé de 10 meses necesitado de protección . . . es pública y notoria la discriminación que los inmigrantes sirios y, por ende, sus* ***familias*** *sufren en Marruecos.*

(12) *que las víctimas fueron presionadas y coaccionadas, . . . amenazadas con causar mal a sus* ***familias****, en caso de no saldar la deuda que había contraído con el viaje mediante el ejercicio de la prostitución.*

(13) *Dado que la reagrupación* ***familiar*** *aboga por la reunificación de las* ***familias*** *¿por qué el Sr. XXX no se preocupa por la vida de su hija adolescente de 15 ños?*

On a different note, something that appears to be statistically salient in the Spanish corpus, as opposed to the British one, is the presence of the terms *clandestino (clandestine)* or *oculto (hidden)*, which allow us to picture the poor working conditions that migrants often suffer and also the way they access Spanish territory through the Moroccan border, being hidden in trucks and other vehicles and risking their lives in doing so.

The term *clandestino* displays a strong collocational bond with *riesgo*, whose score (10.007) stands 4.56 points above the average for this network. Likewise, *oculto*, one of the co-collocates of the term *riesgo* (risk), also displays a noticeably high robustness score, much higher than the average for its collocational level, at 5.24 points above the average for its whole network.

Samples (14) and (15) refer to two clandestine sweatshops found by the Spanish police where migrants were being abused, ill-treated (*trato denigrante, desconsiderado y abusivo*) and exploited illegally (*explotación . . . en los talleres clandestinos*). Along these lines, excerpts (16) and (17) depict the dangerous conditions for migrants to cross the border, being hidden inside two vehicles, one under a seat (*debajo del asiento trasero*) and another inside the dashboard (*oculto en la zona situada en el salpicadero*). Although the identity of the defendant has been hidden, (17) informs on a Spanish criminal organisation which brings two minor migrants of sub-Saharan origin into Spanish territory, also hidden inside a vehicle (*llevando ocultos a dos menores de edad, subsaharianos*).

(14) *Poniendo al descubierto las condiciones de explotación . . . en los talleres* ***clandestinos***.
(15) *Ya que para encubrirlo (talleres* ***clandestinos****) era usual . . . que tales actividades ilícitas se llevaron a cabo en domicilios particulares.*
(16) *Que es sorprendido . . . transportando* ***ocultos*** *en un habitáculo . . . debajo del asiento trasero, a un inmigrante de origen subsahariano. . . . Así mismo, transportaba* ***oculto*** *en la zona situada en el salpicadero, . . . a otro inmigrante.*
(17) *XXX, acompañado de otra persona. . . . Entró en Melilla procedente de Marruecos, llevando* ***ocultos*** *a dos menores de edad, subsaharianos.*

Although their statistical relevance is not as high as that of other collocates examined above (i.e. *family*), the terms related to shipwrecks, *naufragio* and *hundimiento* (whose collocational strength with the term *riesgo* stands at 1.3 and 3.08 points below *family*, as displayed in Table 9.4), might deserve specific attention, as they complement what has already been said about the way in which migrants cross the Spanish land borders. In this case, criminal organisations embark migrants on sea voyages which often end up fatally, and force them to pay large sums of money to be taken onboard yet without the necessary safety conditions. The scenes included in (18) and (19) vividly depict the moment when the illegal boats are spotted by the police. In the former, we are told about the danger of shipwreck (*peligro inminente de humdimiento*) after the pilot cuts the rubber surface of the boat (*procede a rajar la embarcación*), unleashing panic among the passengers (*creó el pánico entre los ocupantes*). The latter is particularly interesting as it narrates how migrants pay the illegal voyage organisers large sums (*habían abonado una cantidad de dinero por salir de Marruecos*) while they are totally neglected during the journey, not being provided with any food or water (*no les dieron comida ni bebida*) and feeling terrified and lost at sea (*pasaron miedo porque estaban perdidos en el mar*).

(18) *Que pilotaba la nave . . . procede a rajar la embarcación. . . . Acción que genera un peligro inminente de* **hundimiento**, *que a su vez creó el pánico entre los ocupantes de la embarcación neumática.*
(19) *Con riesgo inminente de* **hundimiento** *por el choque con dichas rocas . . . manifestaron cómo habían abonado una cantidad de dinero por salir de Marruecos, . . . añadiendo que no les dieron comida ni bebida, y pasaron miedo porque estaban perdidos en el mar.*

To conclude this analysis, it would also be worth mentioning, although in passing due to it lesser relevance in quantitative terms (it occurs on 58 occasions in the corpus and has the lower keyness of the four terms selected for analysis), the presence of the term *odio* (*hate*) in the corpus at hand, which does not appear as a collocate of any of the items identified or as an item itself in the British corpus. In this case, we observe two different contexts where the term it is used. On the one hand, and on most occasions, reference is made to the Spanish criminal code as well as to the decisions made by the Supreme Court which set precedent together with European directives where the limits between freedom of expression and hate speech are established or where the crime *incitación al odio* (incitement to hatred) is defined before its application to specific cases, as seen in (20) and (21). On a different note, sample (22) portrays the case of a migrant involved in a terrorist attack connected with the Islamic State, which represents the other side of the coin. Once more, and particularly in comparison with other terms analysed herein, this particular context has only been observed in three texts out of the 600 that are included in the Spanish corpus.

(20) *De una parte . . ., las acciones de* **incitación al odio** *o la violencia contra grupos o individuos por motivos racistas.*
(21) *La libertad de expresión no puede ofrecer cobertura al llamado "discurso del* **odio**", *esto es, . . . que supongan una incitación directa a la violencia . . . o contra determinadas razas o creencias en particular.*
(22) *Este acusado tenía en su domicilio numeroso material multimedia de incitación al* **odio** *. . ., así como fotografías con iconografía referente al grupo terrorista Estado Islámico.*

4 Conclusions

This research has explored the association between the evaluative vocabulary automatically extracted from two corpora of judicial decisions (obtained from Spanish and British sources), which fell under the category *affect* as defined by systemic linguistics, and the way in which the phenomenon of immigration is depicted in both text collections.

Using the vocabulary items included in the category *affect* found in Marín (2019) as a point of departure in both languages, the collocate networks of a selection of these items were obtained by focusing on the first and second collocational levels. Such selection always implied quantitative criteria as regards both the main terms' keyness (those taken from Marín (2019)), as well as their collocational robustness as measured by *Lancsbox* (Brezina et al. 2015), the software used to process both corpora.

The observation of the context of usage of terms such as *child/children* or *vulnerable* in the British corpus and *familias* (*families*) in its Spanish counterpart led us to the conclusion that we are faced with one of the major issues which the texts in both corpora revolve around (their statistical salience reinforces our perception) and, basically, one of the key concerns for migrants regardless of their origin or destination. Migrants struggle to reunite their families, and we are often informed on the vulnerable situations of unaccompanied children, who are prey to criminal organisations. In connection with familiar issues, the texts also point at fraud and crime, finding evidence of parents who are accused of child abuse or who employ the argument of reunification to their own advantage. However, from a quantitative perspective, these contexts are not as relevant, as they appear at a lower rate than others such as the ones mentioned above.

Similarly to familiar concerns, human trafficking stands out as a chief topic in the British corpus, the data highlight its significance in it. Trafficking is always linked to migrant women, who are the victims of sexual exploitation in return for the debts they hold with those who organise their illegal journey to British soil.

In regard to the Spanish corpus, in spite of the lower general incidence of the collocates in the Spanish lexical networks, the evidence found also reveals the methods employed by criminal gangs to cross the land borders with Morocco, risking the life of those who are desperately trying to reach Spanish territory and hiding them inside tiny vehicle compartments, often poorly ventilated. On a similar note, the corpus vividly depicts the circumstances surrounding illegal sea voyages where migrants try to reach the Spanish coast. Once more, as presented in the legal texts examined, they are seen as victims of criminals who charge them with large sums of money for a journey that may end fatally and causes distress and fear, as evidenced in the excerpts provided.

References

Alcaraz Varó, E., 1994. *El inglés jurídico: textos y documentos.* Madrid: Ariel Derecho.

Alcaraz Varó, E., 2001. La investigación oracional y supraoracional en el inglés profesional y académico. *In:* G. Aguado de Cea & P. Durán Escribano, eds., *La investigación en lenguas aplicadas: enfoque multidisciplinar.* Madrid: Fundación Gómez Pardo UPM, 25–46.

Baker, P., 2016. The shapes of collocation. *International Journal of Corpus Linguistics*, 21(2), 139–164.

Breeze, R., 2011. Disciplinary values in legal discourse: A corpus study. *Ibérica: Revista de la Asociación Española de Lenguas para Fines Específicos*, 21, 93–115.

Brezina, V., Mcenery, T., & Wattam, S., 2015. A new perspective on collocation networks. *International Journal of Corpus Linguistics*, 20(2), 139–173.

Brezina, V., Timperley, M., & Mcenery, T., 2018. *LancsBox* v. 4.x [software]. [online] Available from: http://corpora.lancs.ac.uk/lancsbox.

Eggins, S., & Slade, D., 1997. *Analysing casual conversation*. London: Cassell.

Finegan, E., 2010. Corpus linguistics approaches to legal language: Adverbial expression of attitude and emphasis in Supreme Court opinions. *In*: M. Coulthard & A. Johnson, eds., *The Routledge handbook of forensic linguistics*. London: Routledge, 65–77.

Goźdź-Roszkowski, S., 2017. Facts in law. A comparative study of fact that and its phraseologies in American and Polish judicial discourse. *In*: S. Goźdź-Roszkowski & G. Pontrandolfo, eds., *Phraseology in legal and institutional settings: A corpus-based interdisciplinary perspective*. London: Routledge, 143–159.

Goźdź-Roszkowski, S., 2018. Values and valuations in judicial discourse. A corpus-assisted study of (dis)respect in US Supreme Court decisions on same-sex marriage. *Studies in Logic, Grammar and Rhetoric*, 53(66), 61–79.

Goźdź-Roszkowski, S., & Pontrandolfo, G., 2013. Evaluative patterns in judicial discourse: A corpus-based phraseological perspective on American and Italian criminal judgments. *International Journal of Law Language and Discourse*, 3(2), 9–96.

Halliday, M.A.K., 2003. Introduction. On the architecture of human language. *In*: M.A.K. Halliday & J. Webster, eds., *On language and linguistics*. London: Continuum.

Kaltenbacher, M., 2006. Culture-related linguistic differences in tourist websites: The emotive and the factual. A corpus analysis within the framework of appraisal. *In*: G. Thompson & S. Hunston, eds., *System and corpus. Exploring connections*. London: Equinox, 269–292.

Marín, M.J., 2016. Measuring the degree of specialisation of sub-technical legal terms through corpus comparison: A domain-independent method. *Terminology*, 22(1) 80–102. https://benjamins.com/catalog/term.22.1.04mar.

Marín, M.J., 2019. Exploring the unexpected in legal discourse: A corpus-based contrastive analysis of Spanish and British judgments on immigration. *ESP Today*, 7(2), 161–183. www.esptodayjournal.org/pdf/december_2019/2_Maria_Jose_Marin_Perez_abstract.pdf.

Martin, J.R., 2000. Beyond exchange: Appraisal systems in English. *In*: S. Hunston & G. Thompson, eds., *Evaluation in text: Authorial stance and the construction of discourse*. Oxford: Oxford University Press, 171–181.

Mazzi, D., 2010. This argument fails for two reasons. . . : A linguistic analysis of judicial evaluation strategies in US Supreme Court judgments. *International Journal for the Semiotics of Law*, 23(4), 373–385.

Mellinkoff, D., 1963. *The language of the law*. Boston: Little, Brown & Co.

Orts. M.A., 2018. A bilingual, bicultural approach to detachment and in the law: Tracing impersonality and interaction in English and Spanish legal op-eds. *International Journal for the Semiotics of Law*, 31, 1–24.

Pontrandolfo, G., & Goźdź-Roszkowski, S., 2014. Exploring the local grammar of evaluation: The case of adjectival patterns in American and Italian judicial discourse. *Research in Language*, 12(1), 71–91.

Rothery, J., & Stenglin, M., 2000. Interpreting literature: The role of appraisal. *In*: L. Unsworth, ed., *Researching language in schools and communities: Functional linguistics perspectives*. London: Cassell, 222–244.

Thompson, G., & Hunston, S., eds., 2000. *Evaluation in text: Authorial stance and the construction of discourse.* Oxford: Oxford University Press.
Tiersma, P., 1999. *Legal language.* Chicago: University of Chicago Press.
White, P.R.R., 1999. *The language of attitude, arguability and interpersonal positioning.* The Appraisal website. [online] Available from: www.grammatics.com/appraisal/

Part III

Judicial interpretation

10 Pedagogies of context

Language ideology and expression rights at the European Court of Human Rights

Jessica Greenberg

In 1971 a small publishing outfit in London distributed a little red book that sparked a firestorm and revolutionised European language politics. The *Little Red Schoolbook* was a translation of a popular Danish imprint. It was a frank and at times explicit handbook aimed at adolescents on issues ranging from drug use, relations with parents, and sex and sexuality. The book sparked a case, *Handyside v. The United Kingdom* (ECtHR 1976, Application no. 5493/72) that went all the way to the European Court of Human Rights (ECtHR) in Strasbourg. It addressed the standards for offensive speech in a society in which social norms were rapidly changing. The more subtle issue it addressed was the emerging power of pan-European judicial institutions, and their relationship to nationally specific definitions of democracy. The English courts held the book to be obscene and in violation of English law. The ECtHR upheld that decision in 1976. The judgment determined that seizure and destruction of the offensive publication was indeed necessary in a democratic society (Handyside 1976).

Handyside elaborated the basis for the doctrine of Margin of Appreciation. This critical doctrine reiterates that the Court's supervisory role must be balanced with respect for domestic legal systems, and the sovereignty of participating Member States. *Handyside* also established the principle that offensive speech should receive special protection in matters of freedom of expression. It thus affirmed the importance of freedom of expression in the name of democracy *and* curtailed those rights in the name of democracy. The case codified two paradoxical understandings of the European democratic order: protection for individual rights *and* the right of sovereign nation states to define the meaning of democracy in a given national (and cultural) context.

In examining ECtHR language ideologies (beliefs about the power and social significance of language), I argue that speech-based legal tests respond to this core tension between judicial supervision and democratic sovereignty. I take a methodological approach drawn from linguistic and legal anthropology that focuses on the contextual and ideological features of language rather than the denotational content (Irvine and Gal 2000; Mertz 2007; Ng 2009; Richland 2011). Forms of human communication convey meaning beyond content, such as social status, appropriate participant roles and relations of power (Irvine and Gal 2000). Judges' socially mediated beliefs about language shape

DOI: 10.4324/9781003153771-13

their interpretive practice (Philips 1998).[1] This includes whether and how they understand offensive speech as a legally sanctioned action. Because beliefs about language are so central to judicial interpretation, it is no coincidence that the foundational case of Handyside centres on language rights (Bernstein 2017). European Convention jurisprudence rests on a series of discursive operations that tack back and forth between the *content* and *context* of rights more broadly. *Handyside*'s approach to subsidiarity reveals how speech about speech is central not only to language rights but to how judges assess the power of language and whether it poses an actionable threat to the democratic order (Marmor 2014; Constable 2014). Such beliefs about the power of language shape how legal actors interpret and understand jurisdiction and the appropriate reach of court authority (Richland 2013).

1 Expression rights at the European Court of Human Rights

The ECtHR, based in Strasbourg France, interprets and adjudicates the European Convention on Human Rights, which came into force by treaty in 1953 (see also Brannan, Chapter 15 in this volume). Like other pan-European institutions, the ECtHR is bound by conflicting commitments to European integration and the principle of national sovereignty. Born of war and struggles against fascism, the post-war European project was premised on the idea that democracy must be nurtured and managed, through judicial intervention if necessary. This gave rise to a principle of militant democracy (Macklam 2006). Yet despite this commitment, the tensions between European and domestic judicial orders have sparked fierce debates (Spano 2014). This is particularly true in what many scholars have deemed an era of the judicialisation of politics in Europe (Stone Sweet 2012).

The Court's difficult charge is to balance national specificity and the universality of Convention rights among the 47 Council of Europe Member States. In Article 10, the Convention enshrines both protections and limits to free speech. It sets the task of the Court to balance domestic cultural contexts, meanings of democracy and individual human rights:[2]

1 Everyone has the right to freedom of expression. This right shall include freedom to hold opinions and to receive and impart information and ideas without interference by public authority and regardless of frontiers;

1 In the case of American jurisprudence, the idea that words can be distinguished from violent action is a classic language ideology made clear by the contrast in European law, in which words can have power merely by circulating widely and creating negative representations. This is an example of language ideologies – beliefs about the power of words to do things in the world – that underpin all human communicative systems and ethical orders, including law (Gal and Irvine 2000; Mertz 2007).

2 For the full convention see www.echr.coe.int/documents/convention_eng.pdf (accessed April 20, 2021).

2 The exercise of these freedoms, since it carries with it duties and responsibilities, may be subject to such formalities, conditions, restrictions or penalties as are prescribed by law and are necessary in a democratic society, in the interests of national security, territorial integrity or public safety, for the prevention of disorder or crime, for the protection of health or morals, for the protection of the reputation or rights of others, for preventing the disclosure of information received in confidence, or for maintaining the authority and impartiality of the judiciary.

As the Convention language makes clear, freedom of expression is not an absolute right. It requires a balancing of individual protections with domestic political, social and ethical concerns. The European Court's role is to assess whether a national legal system has adequately balanced the protected right with the limits set out in paragraph 2. Because freedom of expression is not a non-derogable right – such as freedom from torture or slavery – the domestic courts have more leeway for interpretation. This is especially true, if there is not a "European consensus" on a particular issue pertaining to morality, expression or religion (see Kjær, Chapter 4 of this volume). It is this tension that produced the method of margin of appreciation, which came of age as a legal doctrine in the judgment of *Handyside v. The UK* in 1976 (Spielman 2014).

2 Turning context into evidence

The *Little Red School Book* originally appeared in Denmark in 1969 and was translated into multiple languages across Europe. The English version, published by Mr. Handyside in his shoe-string, progressive publishing firm, Stage 1, ran to around 208 pages. The book included a 26-page section concerning "Sex" that included such subsections as Masturbation, Orgasm, Menstruation, Child-Molesters or "Dirty Old Men", Pornography, Homosexuality, and Venereal diseases. It was this stretch of 26 pages that got Mr. Handyside in trouble for obscenity. After going through Magistrates' Court, Mr. Handyside lodged an appeal before the Inner London Quarter Sessions. The judgment, delivered on October 29, 1971, upheld the lower court ruling on obscenity and ordered the applicant to pay 854 pounds. The remaining books were seized and destroyed. Mr. Handyside appealed to Strasbourg.

The English Court's ruling on obscenity hinged on two deceptively simple questions: (1) what effect would the material have on young readers? and (b) should the book be judged as obscene by reading it in part or in whole? Questions concerning the corrupting effect of the book were suggested by the original English statute that Mr. Handyside had violated: the Obscene Publications Act of 1959. This statute indicated:

> For the purposes of this act an article shall be deemed to be obscene if its effect is, if taken as a whole, such as to tend to deprave and corrupt persons who are likely, having regard to all relevant circumstances, to read, see or hear the matter contained or embodied in it.
>
> (*Handyside* § 25)

The language in the Obscenity Act is not absolute. It pinpoints the relationship between a text and specific readers in a cultural context. In other words, obscenity is an effect, it is not inherent in the text itself. One can determines the effect of a text through analysis of dynamic reading practices. The meaning of language is not about its content but its interactive force, creating a particularly located relationship between text and context. While the law focuses on "text", the object of legal scrutiny is the relationships and processes through which language is turned into text. Following linguistic anthropologists Michael Silverstein and Gregory Urban, "a text is a metadiscursive notion, useful to participants as a way of creating an image of a durable, shared culture immanent in or even undifferentiated from its ensemble of realized or even potential texts. . . [T]ext is one outcome of a process in which discourse metamorphoses and precipitates as form" (Silverstein and Urban 1996, p. 4).

The legal reasoning of the English courts rests heavily on such a process of "entextualization": the production of an image of durable shared culture out of text (ibid). Obscenity is an imagined relationship projected onto a piece of text. This emphasis on the relational significance of obscene speech is clear when the domestic court applies the Obscenity Act test to *Little Red Schoolbook*:

> The [domestic] court examined the background. For example, *looking at the book as a whole*, marriage was very largely ignored. . . . The [English] court reached the conclusion that, on the whole, and quite clearly through the mind of the child, the school was inimical to good teacher/child relationships. . . . Passing to the tendency to deprave and corrupt, the court considered *the atmosphere of the book looked at as a whole*, noting that the sense of some responsibility for the community as well as to oneself, if not wholly absent, was completely subordinated the development of the expression of itself by the child.
>
> (*Handyside* § 31; emphasis added)

The quality of offensiveness is an effect achieved through particular kinds of reading practices undertaken by the domestic court itself – practices that the court simultaneously enacts and then posits as those of the potentially corruptible child. In turn, the European Court's judgment foregrounds the *reading practices* of the domestic court and assesses the domestic judicial interpretation in light of Convention principles. The European Court creates authority by judging whether the domestic court read offensive speech in the right contextual frame, not only in terms of local cultural norms but in terms of principles of democracy more generally. As the judgment notes:

> The [ECtHR] attaches particular importance to a factor to which the judgment of 29 October 1971 did not fail to draw attention, that is, the intended readership of the schoolbook. . . . In these circumstances, despite the variety and the constant evolution in the United Kingdom of views on ethics and education, the *competent English judges were entitled . . . to think* at the

> relevant time that the Schoolbook would have pernicious effects on the morals of many of the children and adolescents who would read it.
>
> (*Handyside* § 52)

In this passage obscene speech is constituted as a *localised* relationship. English judges were "entitled" to read the book in light of their own local, cultural understanding of young English readers. The entire judgment is shot through with such references to cultural specificity. These serve as a limit to European supervision and trigger deference from the European Court. Indeed, this is the key: the English courts rely on a textually mediated notion of culture. But more importantly, in doing so, they trigger a particular *legal* relationship to obscene speech. The language in the judgment ties respect for cultural difference to nation state sovereignty. Invoking such specificity within the context of margin of appreciation demands deference from the European Court. The European Court notes:

> It is not possible to find in the domestic law of the various Contracting States a uniform European conception of morals. . . . By reason of their direct and continuous contact with the *vital forces of their countries*, State authorities are in principle in a better position than the international judge to give an opinion on the exact content of these requirements.
>
> (§ 48; emphasis added)

This paragraph points to the way that an assessment of obscenity is also an assessment of the Court's jurisdiction. Given that obscene speech is by definition shot through with localising frameworks, how can the European Court assess the significance of the speech in question? If national sovereignty rests in a bundle of reading practices defined as cultural context (e.g. "vital forces"), what role can the European court play?

3 Sovereignty and cultural context

The *Handyside* decision reflects the ECtHR's struggle to define what role a Court can play when it must also defer to processes of representation and sovereignty as they relate to national "culture". The tensions of multi-scaled democratic sovereignty are resolved through ideologies that link spatial proximity (community, nation) to the capacity to judge and read texts in more inherently truthful ways. As recent sociolinguistic theorists have argued, legal actors and others often figure socially mediated struggles over authority through metaphors of space and time (Carr and Lempert 2016). Scale is a folk category for apprehending and legitimating arrangements of power and authority. Competing jurisdictional authorities are mapped onto particular ideologies about how judicial actors read texts in more "concrete" versus more abstract contexts. The irresolvable question of obscenity can be resolved by relying on a doctrinal commitment to the authority of local (and state) communities to decide what is best in their particular social context.

Freedom of expression triggers two competing understandings of democracy both enacted in relationship to the question of *who determines the cultural impact of speech:* democracy as guaranteed by formal convention rights or democracy as a culturally specific expression of local norms grounded in national sovereignty. *Handyside* takes up the essential problem of who has (and who ought to have) the last word for reading and judging text in context. Across these cases, contradictory relationships to text map onto, and are argued in terms of, more fundamental jurisdictional questions that link locality to sovereignty. And indeed, subsequent use of the *Handyside* doctrine, via margin of appreciation, is precisely to adjudicate this tension between super-state European supervision through collective norms and domestic sovereignty through deference to unique cultural and historical contexts. One reason why expression cases are so good to think with – both in normative legal theory and sociolegal analysis – is because the slipperiness of speech objects can be productively mapped into the slipperiness of competing jurisdictional authorities. Talking about speech necessarily entails talking about scaled relationships of power and authority: Who has the power to judge and on what grounds? When does "cultural" knowledge supersede an integrated rights framework?

4 Pedagogies of context

The European Court skirts this problem by offering a counter-theory of the relationship between text and context to both maintain its authority and justify margin of appreciation. If the English courts are assessing obscenity in terms of a reader-text relationship, the European Court's role is to place that bundled relationship – a metadiscursive stretch that, in Silverstein and Urban's language, precipitates as form – into yet another set of interdiscursive relationships. First, in the following excerpt, the Court establishes its role in upholding principles of democratic necessity, grounded in a rights framework:

> The Court's supervisory functions oblige it to pay the utmost attention to the principles characterizing a "democratic society". Freedom of expression constitutes one of the basic conditions for such a society. . . . Subject to paragraph 2 of Article 10, it is applicable not only to "information" or "ideas" that are favourably received or regarded as inoffensive or as a matter of indifference, but also to those that offend, shock or disturb the State or any sector of the population. Such are the demands of pluralism, tolerance and broadmindedness without which there is no "democratic society".
>
> (*Handyside* § 49)

The ECtHR judgment establishes its supervisory authority through the framework of tolerance and pluralism. It weighs this attention to pluralism against a sovereign state's protection of the vital forces of its community; the framework of pluralism and tolerance. It goes on to state:

> It follows from this that it is in no way the Court's task to take the place of competent national courts. . . . However the Court's supervision would generally prove illusory if it did no more than examine these decisions in isolation; it must view them in light of the case as a whole, including the publication in question and the arguments and evidence adduced by the applicant in the domestic legal system and then at the international level.
>
> (*Handyside* § 50)

Offensive speech is always already an interpretative relationship, codified in statute, interpreted by Courts and reinterpreted yet again with each new jurisdictional level. In the preceding quote, the European Court's jurisdictional authority comes from a kind of "scaling up" of context. The judgment refers to a culturally specific interpretive practice and places it in the context of the European Convention. The Court recontextualises a prior link between text and context into a new framework of cosmopolitan or international perspectives.

This passage indicates an impasse. The European Court has deferred to the English judges' assessment of their own cultural surround, a central tenet of respect for popular and sovereign power. At the same time, this process produced a violation of expression rights. How is it possible to reconcile the competing principals at work? The judgment goes on to say: "The court [meaning the English court] stated that no doubt there were many features about the book which, taken by themselves, were good. The unfortunate thing was that so frequently the good was intermixed with things that were bad and detracted from it" (*Handyside*, § 34).

The ruling continues:

> Similarly, the treatment of the subject of homosexuality. . . *was a factual, very compassionate, understanding and valuable statement.* But again, no matter how good one assessed the value of this section, it was hopelessly *damning by its setting and context*. . . . Moreover, there was a very real danger that this passage would create in the minds of children a conclusion that that kind of relationship was something permanent.
>
> (*Handyside*, § 34)

The ECtHR, like the domestic courts, positions what is good about the book in relationship to the "hopelessly damning . . . setting and context". But the passage above also reveals the tension between the Court's embrace of tolerance and its deference to potentially intolerant local or cultural practices. It raises the problem: should the ECtHR be tolerant of English intolerance? The judgment gets around this problem by emphasising the compassionate elements of the initial UK ruling. The seeming contradiction between tolerance and violation of expression rights is papered over when the ECtHR judgment juxtaposes "very compassionate, understanding and valuable statements" and the idea that the Little Red School Book's language was *damning by its setting and context*" (*Handyside*, § 34).

Why characterise the *Little Red School Book* as having such value, if only to condemn it as hopelessly damning? The English court, and the European Court in turn, uphold the value of speech *even* as they curtail expression rights. What is at stake in noting the English court's positive reading of parts of the book? Strasbourg lauds the English courts as tolerant in relationship to the issue of sexual difference, a difficult and emerging area of political contestation at the time.[3] In characterising the English court's tolerance of social difference, the ECtHR also marks itself as an arbiter of tolerance: only a compassionate court can recognise the value of such approaches to difficult issues. This linkage between tolerance, democracy and speech is critical, because it establishes a basic requirement that the European Court itself not be intolerant. The European Court can have its cake and eat it too. It defers to national and parliamentary sovereignty (democracy 1) even as it produces evidence of the domestic Court's tolerance and "broadmindedness" (democracy 2). The judgment thus circumscribes speech in the name of sovereignty and at the same time distances the Court from the taint of intolerance – a foundational principle of the Convention itself. It is for this reason that the *Handyside* method is largely understood as a protection of offensive speech, even though it emerges from a case in which such speech was not protected. What was protected was the project of a European cosmopolitanism vis-à-vis domestic limitations of "moral necessity".

This double move also allows the European Court to pry open jurisdictional space to rule on such sensitive national matters. As an arbiter of tolerance, the Court has the authority to review national-level speech cases to ensure their consistency with core Convention principles. In this way, legal authority is produced even as the European Court defers to domestic judgments. Authority is created as a set of scaled relationships that establish both higher and lower courts – in a jurisdictional sense, through spatial metaphors of encompassment and perspective on text in context. Such an operation is not unlike the way anthropologists Akhil Gupta and James Ferguson have talked about the role of scale in establishing state power and authority: part-whole relationships expressed in metaphors of verticality, horizontality and encompassment (Gupta and Ferguson 2002). It is through such metaphors of space and hierarchy that relationships of higher and lower jurisdiction and legal authority are generated and sustained (Nakassis 2016; Philips 2016) Thus the European Court effectively teaches domestic courts to properly read their own cultural surround. What the European Court establishes in this case is the validity of its own textual hermeneutics, which I call pedagogies of context.

3 The Wolfenden Report came out in 1957, followed by the 1967 Sexual Offences Act. In 1981 ECtHr established the violation the criminalisation of male homosexuality a violation in Dudgeon v. UK. Six of the judges in Grand Chamber for Dudgeon also sat on Handyside.

5 From obscenity to hate speech: the danger of speech in motion

The *Handyside* approach to speech foregrounds the context of speech and its possible social effects. What kind of threat is speech when it is contextualised and recontextualised in mass mediated ways? In this section, I examine language ideologies that assume that mediatised speech is particularly dangerous and how the Court deals with language in motion. I suggest that the legal framework for free speech is as much about the forms and pathways of circulation that speech takes, as the perceived power of the speech itself.

In the European case law, *Jersild v. Denmark* is exemplary of the ECtHR's parameters for regulating racist speech and judicial attention to the context in which such speech occurs. The landmark 1994 case *Jersild v. Denmark* found a violation of Article 10 rights of the applicant, Jens Olaf Jersild. Jersild, a television journalist, produced a documentary about a group of racist youths called the "Greenjackets" that aired in 1985. The documentary was based on an extended interview which the applicant then edited into a several-minute segment. This segment was part of a larger news magazine program that covered a number of serious news items of interest to the public. Over the course of the segment, the young men made several explicitly racist comments. The applicant was charged and convicted of aiding and abetting the dissemination of these racist statements. The decision was upheld at the High Court of Eastern Denmark and the Danish Supreme Court. At issue was whether Mr. Jersild had sufficiently distanced himself from the remarks so that the interview would not be broadly interpreted as support or dissemination of racist utterances. The ECtHR eventually ruled 12–7 that this had been a violation of Article 10, that the conviction had not been necessary in a democratic society, and that the protection of the rights to reputation of racial minorities could not outweigh the right to impart information in this case.

The findings against Mr. Jersild were based on a penal code that prohibited "disseminating . . . to a *wide circle* . . . [statements that are] threatening, insulting or degrading a group of persons on account of their race, colour, national or ethnic origin" (§ 20, emphasis added). Like in *Handyside*, we can see the imagined reader built into the statutory language – the "wide circle". Like in *Handyside*, the question is less whether the speech itself is offensive on its own terms (it clearly was, and the Greenjackets were held legally liable for it). The question is whether the domestic courts sufficiently understand the context in which a stretch of speech comes to have meaning to a wider audience – the wide circle.

In effect, what the European Court argued is that the Danish courts did not understand how to adequately read text in relationship to context. They took too literally the content of speech and racist remarks without understanding the subtleties of framing that distanced a journalist's words from those of his interviewees. The Danish Court saw Jersild's actions as complicit in the wide circulation of racist speech, noting that "television was a powerful medium . . . and it was too subtle to assume that viewers would not take the remarks at face value" (Jersild at § 29). In contrast, the majority on the Court notes, "taken in the context of the broadcast as a whole, the offending remarks had the effect of ridiculing their authors rather than promoting racist views" (Jersild, at § 28).

The judgment applies the following method, reminiscent of the *Handyside* analysis: "The [European] Court's assessment will have regard to the manner in which the Greenjackets feature was prepared, its contents, the context in which it was broadcast . . . an important factor in the Court's evaluation will be whether the item in question, when considered as a whole, appeared from an objective point of view to have had as its purpose the propagation of racist views and ideas" (Jersild at § 31). The Court goes on to do precisely such an analysis of the framing context of the program, arguing in essence that the Danish Courts simply got the context clues wrong.

The European Court found that Jersild could not be held liable because the news program was intended to circulate information in a matter of public interest, and that he sufficiently distanced himself from the remarks. Through such pedagogies of context as established in *Handyside*, the European Court teaches the Danish courts to correctly read text in relation to context, arguing that the Danish Court's inability to scale up and gain sufficient perspective on the object of offensive speech meant that they read its significance incorrectly. Interestingly, in this case the Danish government attempts to out-context the European Court of Human Rights, by taking Jersild's stretch of interview and creating intertextual links, not with the European Convention of Human Rights principles but those of the International Convention on the Elimination of All Forms of Racial Discrimination. Indeed, the Danish government's argument was that "article 10 should not be interpreted in such a way as to limit, derogate from or destroy the right to protection against racial discrimination under the U.N. convention" (Jersild, at § 27).

Denmark argued that the ECtHR has gotten the UN convention wrong, and in fact lacks the true context or cosmopolitan perspective to understand the relationships among speech, context and democracy. This is a perfect illustration of how the discursive game of jurisdictional authority can be taken up by differently positioned actors, providing a kind of jurisdictional trump card that is mobilised by scaling up. And indeed a vigorous dissenting opinion in this case echoes the Danish Government's argument (see *Jersild v. Denmark*, Joint Dissenting Opinion of Judges Ryssdal, Bernhardt, Spielmann and Loizou).

When considered in this light, margin of appreciation is not normative doctrine as much as a method of reading speech rights alternately in terms of *content* versus *context*. The ECtHR *makes* its own authority by reading texts together: creating intertextual relationships that produce the effect of scale (higher and lower courts) and jurisdictional competence. Such pedagogies of context produce jurisdictional authority by creating cosmopolitan frameworks that discipline domestic courts for their parochial relationship to context-making practices. By teaching domestic courts how to read the complexity of their national social surround, the Court justifies intervention into domestic legal sovereignty in the name of protecting democracy.

Racist hate speech that rises to the level of judicial intervention is not defined by its content, or even its target per se. It is defined by the degree to which that speech circulates, forming a framework or anchor that links racist talk to past histories of violence and new racist imaginaries, utterances and stances. This concern about circulating language form is most evident in the Court's case law on Holocaust denial. The Court takes a strong stand on Holocaust denial, framing it as inherently undemocratic and therefore never worthy of speech projection. In a recent genocide denial case, ***Perinçek v. Switzerland***, the Court explains what conditions must obtain for such denial to be legally actionable. In this case, Mr. Perinçek, a Turkish national, spoke at three public events in Switzerland during which he denied the existence of an Armenian genocide. He was tried and fined for violating genocide denial provisions of the Swiss criminal code. Ultimately, the Grand Chamber found in 2015 that there had been an unlawful violation of Mr. Perinçek's freedom of expression. In paragraph 243 of the judgment the Court makes clear the danger of Holocaust versus other kinds of genocide denial:

> The Court has always been sensitive to the historical context of the High Contracting Parity concerned (Para 243): This is particularly relevant with regard to the Holocaust. For the Court, the justification for making its denial a criminal offence lies not so much in that it is a clearly established historical fact, but in that, in view of the historical context in the states concerned, its denial, . . . must invariable be seen as connoting an antidemocratic ideology and anti-Semitism. Holocaust denial is thus doubly dangerous, especially in States which have experience with the Nazi horrors. . .
>
> 244. By contrast, it has not been argued that there was a direct link between Switzerland and the events that took place in the Ottoman Empire . . . the only such link may come from the presence of an Armenian community on Swiss soil, but it is a tenuous one. . . . There is moreover no evidence that at the time when the applicant made his statements the atmosphere in Switzerland was tense and could result in serious friction between Turks and Armenians. 246. It is true that at present, especially with the use of electronic means of communication, no message may be regarded as purely local. . . . However, the broader concepts of proportionality inherent in the phrase "necessary in a democratic society" requires a rational connection between the measures taken by the authorities and the aim they sought to realize through these measures. . . . It can hardly be said that any hostility that exists toward the Armenian minority in Turkey is the product of the applicant's statements in Switzerland.

At issue in this stretch of legal argument is not the inherent violence of the denial itself, but the channels by which speech is mediated and the audience such speech hails. In other words, speech is violent when it entails a shared historical reference that then becomes the grounds for shared interpretative frameworks (Shoshan 2016). Holocaust symbols are widely recognised and thus form the basis for practices of orientation and community. The court draws a clear contrast between racist repertoires that inspire and cohere such hate publics, and those that are too far from home, or not sufficiently intelligible to be the basis of further discriminatory effect. In other words, the symbolic register of Armenian genocide was not widely shared enough to be threatening to a European democratic order.

6 Conclusion

I have hoped to show how the ECtHR *makes* its own authority by reading texts together: creating intertextual relationships that produce the effect of scale (higher and lower courts) and jurisdictional competence. Such "pedagogies of context" produce jurisdictional authority by creating cosmopolitan frameworks that discipline domestic courts for their parochial relationship to context-making practices. At the same time, as in *Handyside*, if a Member State can convincingly frame their interpretation of speech as authoritative (and closer to the vital forces of the people), they can in effect carve out space for discretion. Ideologies about language, the power it has and the social harm it can do when read, consumed and circulated are central to understanding these battles over sovereignty and jurisdiction.

References

Bernstein, A., 2017. Before interpretation. *University of Chicago Law Review*, 84(2), 567–654.

Carr, S.E., & Lempert, M., 2016. Introduction: Pragmatics of scale. *In:* E.S. Carr & M. Lempert, eds., *Scale: Discourse and dimensions of social life*. Oakland: University of California Press, 1–24.

Constable, M., 2014. *Our word is our bond: How legal speech acts*. Palo Alto, CA: Stanford University Press.

Ferguson, J., & Gupta, A., 2002. Spatializing states: Toward an ethnography of neoliberal governmentality. *American Ethnologist*, 29(4), 981–1002.

Irvine, J.S.G., 2000. Language ideology and linguistic differentiation. *In:* P. Kroskrity, ed., *Regimes of language*. Santa Fe: SAR Press.

Macklam, P., 2006. Militant democracy, legal pluralism, and the paradox of self-determination. *International Journal of Constitutional Law*, 4(3), 488–516.

Marmor, A., 2014. *The language of law*. Oxford: Oxford University Press.

Mertz, E., 2007. *The language of law school: Learning to "think" like a lawyer*. Oxford: Oxford University Press.

Nakassis, C.V., 2016. Scaling red and the horror of trademark. *In:* E.S. Carr & M. Lempert, eds., *Scale: Discourse and dimensions of social life*. Oakland: University of California Press, 159–184.

Ng, K.H., 2009. *The common law in two voices: Language, law, and the postcolonial dilemma in Hong Kong*. Stanford, CA: Stanford University Press.

Philips, S.U., 1998. *Ideology in the language of judges: How judges practice law, politics, and courtroom control*. New York: Oxford University Press, 112–132.

Philips, S.U., 2016. Balancing the scales of justice in Tonga. *In:* E.S. Carr & M. Lempert, eds., *Scale: Discourse and dimensions of social life*. Oakland: University of California Press.

Richland, J., 2011. Hopi tradition as jurisdiction: On the potentializing limits of Hopi sovereignty. *Law & Social Inquiry*, 36(1), 201–234.

Richland, J., 2013. Jurisdiction: Grounding law in language, *Annual Review of Anthropology*, 42, 209–226.

Shoshan, N., 2016. *The management of hate: Nation, affect, and the governance of right-wing extremism in Germany*. Chicago: University of Chicago Press.

Silverstein, M., & Urban, G., 1996. The natural history of discourse. *In:* M. Silverstein & G. Urban, eds., *Natural histories of discourse*. Chicago: University of Chicago Press, 1–17.

Spano, R., 2014. Universality or diversity of human rights? Strasbourg in the age of subsidiarity. *Human Rights Law Review*, 14, 487–502.

Spielman, D., 2014. Whither the margin of appreciation. *Current Legal Problems*, 67(1), 49–65.

Stone Sweet, A.L.E.C., 2012. A cosmopolitan legal order: Constitutional pluralism and rights adjudication in Europe. *Global Constitutionalism*, 1(1), 53–90.

Cases

ECtHR, *Handyside v. UK*, Appl. no. 5493/72, Judgment of 7 December 1976.

Jersild v. Denmark, GC, Appl. no. 15890/89, Judgment of 23 September 1994.

Perinçek v. Switzerland (application no. 27510/08) 2015.

11 Free speech, artistic expression and blasphemy laws within the ECHR margin of appreciation

Joanna Kulesza

1 Freedom of expression and its limits

The historical origins of the right to free expression have been disputed, with both sides of the Atlantic claiming it their own. However, the approach to free expression has substantially differed between the 1776 Virginia Declaration of Rights, pt. XII, which was later adopted into the US Bill of Rights and the European approach, as first expressed during the French Revolution. In the United States, freedom of expression has been referred to as "the freedom of the press is one of the greatest bulwarks of liberty [which] can never be restrained but by despotic governments".[1] Its framing in Europe has always been quite different: much more restrictive, binding individual freedom with the intrinsic obligation it carries for those willing to exercise it. The 1789 French Declaration of the Rights of Man and of the Citizen in Article 11 provided such a balanced perspective on the freedom of expression, one that looks at both the individual right and, respectively, the obligations restricting it towards third parties. It is this approach that has been universally adopted in international law on human rights, reflecting freedom of expression as a non-absolute right, one to be legally protected, yet with due regard to rights and interests of others.[2] As such, free expression is subject to legal restrictions substantiated by third-party or collective rights and carries with it a set of obligations and responsibilities.

It is this approach that has been reflected in the 1948 Universal Declaration of Human Rights (UDHR) and its Article 19. It grants "everyone . . . the right to freedom of opinion and expression", which includes "the freedom to hold opinions without interference and to seek, receive and impart information and ideas through any media and regardless of frontiers". Freedom of expression is comprised of four collective rights: (1) freedom to hold opinions; (2) freedom to seek information; (3) freedom to receive information and ideas; and (4) the

1 Constitution of the United States of America, First Amendment: "Congress shall make no law respecting an establishment of religion, or prohibiting the free exercise thereof; or abridging the freedom of speech, or of the press; or the right of the people peaceably to assemble, and to petition the Government for a redress of grievances".

2 For a discussion on the universal system on human rights, see, e.g., De Schutter (2019).

DOI: 10.4324/9781003153771-14

freedom to impart information and ideas. Collectively these are the substance of free expression. They must be granted collectively and only as such constitute the substance of this rights. The general framing of freedom of expression as a non-absolute right is reflected in Article 29 UDHR. As per its stipulations, "Everyone has duties to the community in which alone the free and full development of his personality is possible". Identifying the limits of free expression, UDHR states that "in the exercise of his rights and freedoms, everyone shall be subject only to such limitations as are determined by law solely for the purpose of securing due recognition and respect for the rights and freedoms of others and of meeting the just requirements of morality, public order and the general welfare in a democratic society". These provisions are fundamental to the understanding of the issue at hand: any restriction on the right to free expression may only be laid down in law and only when it is substantiated by the specific needs of a democratic society on one or more of the enumerated grounds: protection of morality, public order or the general welfare of such a society. Complementarily, the UDHR disallows individuals to make such use of their rights that may be "contrary to the purposes and principles" of international law, as per Article 14.

While today its provisions enjoy the status of binding customary international law, originally the UDHR was approved as a non-binding document, adopted by a majority vote of the 1948 United Nations General Assembly.[3] Forming universal consensus on a binding treaty reiterating the rights and obligations first phrased in the UDHR took the international community almost 20 more years. 1966 saw the introduction of two complementary human rights treaties: the International Covenant on Civil and Political Rights (ICCPR) and the International Covenant on Economic, Social and Cultural Rights (ICESCR). ICCPR Article 19 offers the very same safeguards for free expression as the UDHR, emphasising its limited character. The ICCPR grants everyone "the right to hold opinions without interference", that is, the right to "freedom of expression" understood as the "freedom to seek, receive and impart information and ideas of all kinds, regardless of frontiers, either orally, in writing or in print, in the form of art, or through any other media of his choice". ICCPR Article 19, para. 2 includes a limitative clause that refers to "special duties and responsibilities" laid upon those exercising it. As such, the right to free expression "may be subject to restrictions", provided by law and necessary for specifically detailed purposes, which include the respect of the rights or reputations of others and the protection of national security or of public order (*ordre public*), public health or morals. It this exact detailed legal construct that has served the universal community to better understand limits of free expression, allowing states to install national and regional safeguards aimed at protecting the collective and individual interests of others while protecting individual opinions and ideas.

3 The UDHR was adopted on December 10, 1948 (A/RES/217(III), during the 183rd plenary meeting of the General Assembly.

The UDHR together with the ICCPR have served as the fundamental standard for introducing freedom of expression laws around the globe. As any other human rights, freedom of expression places on states two kinds of obligations: negative ones, to refrain from violating their substance and scope beyond legally allowed limits; and positive ones, obliging states to take all necessary measures to ensure that individuals within their jurisdiction and control can fully enjoy their rights to the extent allowed by law. This latter part of any state obligation referring to human rights is a due diligence obligation. States must do what is at their disposal to ensure that individuals can freely enjoy their right to free expression. These duties imply the need to enforce effective safeguards against any public and private bodies attempting to restrict one's free speech. Any such restrictions may only be introduced through law and enforced accordingly. States are therefore under a direct obligation to do their utmost in preventing and/or disabling any attacks upon one's human right. The due diligence standard is a flexible one: it reflects circumstances of the case and actual, economic and political capability of the state. It is one of the numerous reasons why international human right protection remains highly politicised and challenging to fully enforce. While there hardly is a universal standard for free expression, certain regions have proven to be more effective in achieving that aim than others. Europe offers one of these unique examples.

In this contribution we examine two recent Polish cases in order to explore the link between legal dogmatic and linguistic semantics in the context of freedom of artistic expression and protection of the rights of third parties, in this case, their religious beliefs. Poland is one of the few countries in Europe which penalises blasphemy. Article 196 of the Polish Criminal Code provides for a fine, restriction of liberty or deprivation of liberty for up to 2 years for those who "offend the religious feelings of others by outraging in public an object of religious worship or a place dedicated to the public celebration of religious rites". Let us look at this provision and its active verb "offend" through the context of the jurisprudence of the European Court of Human Rights (ECtHR). This will be done with regard to two recent cases: one of a Wroclaw-based artist who gained notoriety through their work on *cipkomaryjki* ("vaginaMarys") in early 2019.[4] In this work, she replicated clay depictions of Mother Mary as to reference female genitalia. A similar case refers to a public display of banners with the Black Madonna against a rainbow background to draw attention to LGBTQ+ rights.[5] These two cases will serve as reference for the actual application of freedom of expression standards to linguistic interpretations of national law and its context.

The Council of Europe is home of arguably the most effective regional human rights document: the 1950 Convention for the Protection of Human Rights and Fundamental Freedoms (European Convention on Human Rights [ECHR]).

4 www.tvp.info/43670598/chciala-sprzedawac-teczowa-maryje-w-ksztalcie-waginy-bedzie-zawiadomienie-do-prokuratury

5 https://wiadomosci.dziennik.pl/wydarzenia/artykuly/611006,teczowa-matka-boska-obraza-uczuc-religijnych-lgbt.html

Drafted simultaneously with the UDHR, it reflects the same reasoning: Article 10 grants "everyone . . . the right to freedom of expression", as one that includes the freedom to "hold opinions and to receive and impart information and ideas without interference by public authority and regardless of frontiers". As noted above, free expression implies four complementary liberties: the right to 1) access, 2) seek, 3) receive and 4) impart both: information and ideas. These provisions, while constituting an individual right, are recognised as foundations for all European and national media law regulations, including those that cover artistic expression. As observed by the ECtHR in *Lingens v. Austria*:

> Whilst the press must not overstep the bounds set, inter alia, for the "protection of the reputation of others", it is nevertheless incumbent on it to impart information and ideas on political issues just as on those in other areas of public interest. Not only does the press have the task of imparting such information and ideas: the public also has a right to receive them.[6]

In *Mueller v. Switzerland* the court emphasised the need to protect all forms of artistic expression as well as communications that are of purely commercial nature.[7] Article 10 protects both the contents and the form of communications.[8] Most significantly, freedom of expression is applicable not only to information or ideas that are favourably received or regarded as inoffensive or as a matter of indifference but also to those that offend, shock or disturb. Such are the demands of that pluralism, tolerance and broadmindedness without which there is no "democratic society".[9]

With regard to setting limit for free expression, Article 10, para. 2 offers a comprehensive clause setting limits for individual freedoms and prerequisites for state interference. It indicates that the "exercise of these freedoms . . . carries with it duties and responsibilities" and as such may be "subject to such formalities, conditions, restrictions or penalties as are prescribed by law and are necessary in a democratic society, in the interests of 1) national security, 2) territorial integrity or public safety, for the 3) prevention of disorder or crime, for the 4) protection of health or morals, for the 5) protection of the reputation or rights of others, for 6) preventing the disclosure of information received in confidence, or for 7) maintaining the authority and impartiality of the judiciary". The European Court of Human Rights – the judiciary authority on enforcing the convention for all 47 CoE states – has described freedom of expression as "one of the basic conditions for the progress of democratic societies and for the development of each individual".[10]

6 Lingens v. Austria, Application No. 9815/82 (ECtHR, July 8, 1986), § 41.
7 Müller and Others v. Switzerland, Application No. 10737/84 (ECtHR, May 24, 1988); Markt intern Verlag GmbH v. Germany, Application No. 10572/83 (ECtHR, Nov. 20, 1989), § 26.
8 Hashmann and Harrup v. UK, Application No. 25594/94 (ECtHR, November 25, 1999), § 28.
9 Lingens v. Austria, Application No. 9815/82 (ECtHR, July 8, 1986), § 41.
10 Handyside v. UK, Application No. 5493/72, (ECtHR, December 7, 1976), § 49.

When enforcing restrictions, caution ought to be given when it is to impact political speech. In *Morice v. France*, the Court observed:

> There is little scope under art 10(2) of the Convention for restrictions on political speech or, on the debate on matters of public interest. Accordingly, a high level of protection of freedom of expression, with the authorities thus having a particularly narrow margin of appreciation, will normally be accorded where the remarks concern a matter of public interest.[11]

Similarly, artistic expression ought to be curbed only to the extent necessary in a democratic society, taking into account the special role it plays therein. The ECtHR observed in *Müller and Others v. Switzerland* that "creation and distribution of artistic works contribute significantly to the exchange of ideas and opinions, and as such is an essential component of any democratic society". In the same way, creative, literary and scientific expressions are covered by article 10.[12] Protection is granted not just to content, but also to the form of expression, as noted in *Lingens v. Austria*:

> Freedom of the press furthermore affords the public one of the best means of discovering and forming an opinion of the ideas and attitudes of political leaders. More generally, freedom of political debate is at the very core of the concept of a democratic society which prevails throughout the Convention.[13]

As per these broad safeguards, certain categories of communications are excluded from protection. As per a general guideline, any speech that is incompatible with the principles of the ECHR is not to be granted protection. This is the direct consequence of its Article 17 introducing the prohibition to abuse rights. Any exceptions thereto may only be established narrowly and explicitly.[14] Outside this scope of protection are statements that "spread, incite, promote or justify hatred based on intolerance" and "concrete expressions constituting hate speech".[15] This applies with regard to religious hate speech as in the case of *Pavel Ivanov v. Russia*, where the ECtHR observed that

> the applicant authored and published a series of articles portraying the Jews as the source of evil in Russia. He accused an entire ethnic group of plotting

11 Morice v. France, Application No. 29369/10 (ECtHR, April 23, 2015), § 125.
12 Müller and Others v. Switzerland, Application No. 10737/84 (ECtHR, May 24, 1988), § 22.
13 Lingens v. Austria, Application No. 9815/82 (ECtHR, July 8, 1986), § 42.
14 Chauvy and Others v. France, Application No. 64915/01 (ECtHR, September 29, 2004), § 63.
15 Delfi AS v. Estonia, Application No. 64569/09 (ECtHR, June 16, 2015), § 136; Lehideux and Isorni v. France, Application No. 55/1997/839/1045 (ECtHR, September 23, 1998); Garaudy v. France, Application No. 65831/01 (ECtHR, June 24, 2003); Norwood v. The United Kingdom, Application No. 23131/03 (ECtHR, Nov. 16, 2004); Witzsch v. Germany (2), Application No.7485/03 (ECtHR, Dec. 13, 2005).

> a conspiracy against the Russian people and ascribed the Fascist ideology to the Jewish leadership. Both in his publications and in his oral submissions at the trial, he consistently denied the Jews the right to national dignity, claiming that they did not form a nation. The Court does not doubt as to the markedly anti-Semitic tenor of the applicant's views and it agrees with the assessment made by the domestic courts that he sought through his publications to incite hatred towards the Jewish people. Such a general and vehement attack on one ethnic group is in contradiction with the Convention's underlying values, notably tolerance, social peace and non-discrimination. Consequently, the Court finds that, by reason of Article 17 of the Convention, the applicant may not benefit from the protection afforded by Article 10 of the Convention.[16]

Similar judgments have found legitimate the restriction put by states on statements denying the Holocaust,[17] justifying Nazism or linking all Muslims with a grave act of terrorism. ECHR identifies all forms of hate speech as outside its scope of protection, with the ECtHR observing in *Gündüz v. Turkey* that "tolerance and respect for the equal dignity of all human beings constitute foundations of a democratic, pluralistic society". That being so, as a matter of principle it may be considered necessary in certain democratic societies to sanction or even prevent all forms of expression which spread, incite, promote or justify hatred based on intolerance (including religious intolerance), provided that any "formalities", "conditions", "restrictions" or "penalties" imposed are proportionate to the legitimate aim pursued.[18] An expression is to be considered hate speech when it "incites . . . hatred".[19] At the same time, hate speech is to be distinguished from political expression, especially critical one.[20]

2 Margin of appreciation

As states significantly differ in interpreting the limitative prerequisites in Article 10 para. 2, especially when it comes to the "protection of morals", the ECtHR offers a "margin of appreciation" doctrine (see also Kjær, Chapter 4 in this volume). It presumes that the initial and primary responsibility for the protection of the human rights lies with the States, while the role of the ECtHR is to only monitor states' action, enforcing its power of review. As declared by the Court, the "domestic margin of appreciation goes 'hand in hand' with European supervision".[21] The doctrine of the margin of appreciation is applied differently

16 Pavel Ivanov v. Russia, Application No. 35222/04 (ECtHR, February 20, 2007).
17 Pavel Ivanov v. Russia, Application No. 35222/04 (ECtHR, February 20, 2007).
18 Gündüz v. Turkey, Application No. 35071/97 (ECHR, June 14, 2004), para 40.
19 Gündüz v. Turkey, Application No. 35071/97 (ECHR, June 14, 2004), para 40, at 51; Otegi Mondragon v. Spain, Application No. 2034/07 (ECHR, March 15, 2011).
20 Garaudy v. France, Application No. 65831/01 (ECHR, June 24, 2003).
21 Autronic AG v. Switzerland, Application No. 12726/87 (ECtHR, May 22, 1990), § 60.

among states. Its application depends on the degree of discretion allowed to the states according to the context of its application. States are allowed a considerable discretion where there is little common ground between the contracting parties, while the discretion is reduced almost to a vanishing point on the freedom of expression.

As the ECtHR pointed out in the *Handyside v. UK* judgment, the fundamental value of freedom of expression is beyond question. It reiterated that freedom of expression "refers not only to information and ideas, received favourably or perceived as harmless or indifferent, but also to those that offend, shock or disturb the state or any group of society. Such are the requirements of pluralism, tolerance and openness without which there is no democratic society. Therefore, the protection granted in Article 10 paragraph 1 of the Convention also refers to racist, pornographic, defamatory and offensive statements". However, one cannot forget that freedom of expression is not absolute, and (in accordance with Article 10, para. 2) authorities are allowed to subject it to restrictions and sanctions. It should be noted and emphasised that since the *Handyside* case, the Court has consistently assumed that in the event of restriction of freedom of expression with the reference to the argument for the protection of public morality, states have the widest "margin of appreciation", since it is not possible to establish a uniform European system of norms reflective of national laws and morality. In the case of the argument for the protection of public morals, usually combined with the arguments for the protection of public order and the rights of others, the state has wider possibilities of limiting freedom of expression and sanctioning, including in the field of criminal law the broadest sense, behaviours that violate the sanctioning norm. Therefore, the freedom of states to introduce restrictions on this freedom is greater, which the Court does not question. According to ECHR Article 10, para. 2, freedom of expression is subject to restrictions in accordance with the principles of the limitation clause of Article 31, § 3 of the Polish Constitution.

It should be noted that in the *Handyside* case, the Court found no violation by the United Kingdom of ECHR Article 10 in connection with the imposition of a criminal financial penalty on the publisher of the translation of a book for school children aged 12 and over, The *Little Red Schoolbook* (see Greenberg, Chapter 10 in this volume). The Court recognised the state's right to protect public morality, also by means of criminal law. This first judgment on ECHR Article 10 created guidelines that were followed consistently in later court decisions regarding the interpretation of the scope of protection of freedom of expression, including the aforementioned principle of the "margin of appreciation" of the state interference justified by the need to protect public morality. In turn, in the second judgment fundamental for balancing freedom of expression and public morality: the *Otto-Preminger-Institut v. Austria* case, the Court found no violation of Article 10 of the Convention in connection with preventive (before the first screening) film confiscation and criminal proceedings regarding "offending religious doctrine" (Article 188 of the Austrian Criminal Code). It indicated the irreplaceability of the feelings of people confronted with incriminated images. The protection of individual feelings of individuals in the context of the protection of morals and public order takes precedence over freedom of expression. The third fundamental judgment in which the argument for the protection of public morality appears is the case of *Müller et al. and Others v. Switzerland*. Here were not only images of sexuality and intimacy that were considered indecent, but also those which, having no sexual connotations, simply arouse disgust and resentment and were considered repulsive to the average observer (the so-called standard of the average recipient). Also in this case, the Court found no violation of freedom of expression and recognised the admissibility of punishing the accused with a fine. It should be emphasised that the display of these images did not cause public protests, the press supported the artist, and yet the punishment did not raise any reservations from the tribunal.

Based on the Court's case law thus far, it should be observed that when deciding if an interference is "necessary in a democratic society", the Court will consider local circumstances. With that, local lawmakers and judges are afforded quite a significant margin of appreciation in deciding upon introducing and enforcing measures that interfere with freedom of expression.[22] Margin of appreciation means that the court will assess whether an act of national law falls within the limits set by European supervision of the court. As in *Autronic Ag v. Switzerland*, the Court noted:

> The Contracting States enjoy a certain margin of appreciation in assessing the need for interference, but *this margin goes hand in hand* with European supervision, whose extent will vary according to the case. Where there has been an interference with the exercise of the rights and freedoms guaranteed in paragraph 1 of Article 10, the supervision must be strict, because of the importance of the rights in question; the importance of these rights has been stressed by the Court many times. The necessity for restricting them must be convincingly established.[23] [emphasis added]

When assessing these local measures, the Court will look into relevant European norms and standards. When doing so, the ECtHR

> notes on the outset that it is not for it to determine what evidence was required under Russian law to demonstrate the existence of the constituent elements of the offence of inciting to racial hatred. It is in the first place for the national authorities, notably the courts, to interpret and apply domestic law. The Court's task is mere to review under Article 10 the decisions they delivered pursuant to their power of appreciation.[24]

22 Prager and Oberschlick v. Austria, Application No. 11662/85 (ECtHR, May 23, 1991), § 35.
23 Autronic AG v. Switzerland, Application No. 12726/87 (ECtHR, May 22, 1990), § 60.
24 Pavel Ivanov v. Russia, Application No. 35222/04 (ECtHR, February 20, 2007), § 1.

Applying the margin of appreciation doctrine means that the court will assess (1) the proportionality of the measures when compared with the pursued aim and (2) the relevance and sufficiency of grounds used to justify the interference by national lawmakers. Any standards used to curtain free expression must fall in line with the principles of Article 10 and its jurisprudence while based on justifiable assessment of circumstances relevant to a specific case. This is relevant with regard to the freedom of media and political speech, where the interests of democratic society are deemed to prevail, solely when a "pressing social need" can be clearly identified and no other measures, short of limiting free speech, can prove effective.[25] As such, Article 10 para. 2 can be used to curb political speech only in the narrowest possible extent.[26] Political debate can only be curbed when certain circumstances are met. As noted in *Jerusalem v. Austria*: "Free elections and freedom of expression, particularly freedom of political debate, together form the bedrock of any democratic system. . . . The two rights are interrelated and operate to reinforce each other: for example, as the Court has observed in the past, freedom of expression is one of the 'conditions' necessary to 'ensure the free expression of the opinion of the people in the choice of the legislature' ".[27]

Attention needs to be paid when this political discourse is coloured with religious influence. The ECtHR advises highest caution when balancing the right to free speech and religious feelings of others. As is observed in *Gündüz v. Turkey*, "a certain margin of appreciation is generally available to the Contracting States when regulating freedom of expression in relation to matters liable to offend intimate personal convictions within the sphere of morals or, especially, religion".[28] It is in this context that the specific wording of Polish criminal law provisions limiting free expression with the aim to protect "religious feelings" are to be discussed.

3 Polish blasphemy law

> Polish Criminal Code, Article 196: Whoever offends the religious feelings of others, publicly insulting the subject of religious worship or a place intended for public performance of religious rites, is subject to a fine, the penalty of restriction of liberty or the penalty of deprivation of liberty for up to 2 years.[29]

25 Stoll v. Switzerland, Application No. 69698/01 (ECtHR, April 25, 2006), § 105.
26 Stoll v. Switzerland, Application No. 69698/01 (ECtHR, April 25, 2006), § 106.
27 Bowman v. The United Kingdom, Application No. 141/1996/760/961 (ECtHR, February 19, 1998), § 42.
28 Gündüz v. Turkey, Application No. 35071/97 (ECHR, June 14, 2004), § 37.
29 Art. 196. Obrażanie uczuć religijnych innych osób Dz.U.2019.0.1950 t.j. – Ustawa z dnia 6 czerwca 1997 r. – Kodeks karny Kto obraża uczucia religijne innych osób, znieważając publicznie przedmiot czci religijnej lub miejsce przeznaczone do publicznego wykonywania

Article 196 of the Polish Criminal Code, as is the case with other types of offenses, does not limit the content of the incriminating communication, does not censor it and does not subject it to evaluation. It limits freedom of expression only to the extent permitted by the Convention and the Court as to the form of the message, which is unacceptable in Polish society. The provisions of the article indicate a causative activity (i.e. the perpetrator is to "offend" religious feelings of others, rather than insult them, for example). Offending ("insulting feelings") is not the activity of the perpetrator but the result of his activities. For this offense to be committed, it must be demonstrated that at least two individuals felt harmed by having their religious feelings offended, thus narrowing the scope of criminality of the act. It should be noted that it is not difficult to find such two people in Poland. The offending effect is indisputable; that is, you cannot convince someone that they have not been offended, should not feel offended or are exaggerating. There is no objectivity in this respect (justification by circumstances, as in Article 148, para. 4 or Article 190, para. 1 of the Polish Criminal Code), and it is therefore not possible to examine whether another follower, tolerant, not devotional, would also feel offended. While "objectionable" as a causative act, it is strongly objectified to social assessment.

When looking at the phrasing of the article, hence at the actual scope of the crime, it is usually interpreted that "offending" feelings is equal to an abomination, an act of one who despises, insults, humiliates or abuses the religious feelings of others. It refers to a derision, dishonesty, dishonour, humiliation, profanity, insult, using epithets or invectives. "Offending" is therefore not simply "disregarding" (*lekceważenie*) as it fails to meet the criteria of Article 196. It does fall within the scope of Article 49 of the Polish Code of Offences, where "disregarding" is failing to take something into account, having something for nothing, paying no attention to someone or something, belittling, treating disrespectfully, ironizing or treating with reluctance. Article 196 requires two elements: (1) according to objectified assessments of the majority of the society, the behaviour is offensive and (2) the perpetrator intends to cause an insult – they want or agree thereto, where their reconciliation is contentious, whereas interpretation of these criteria should be restrictive, as with all criminal law provisions. The message is considered insulting when it is meant to be such as per the intention of the perpetrator. The justification of interference by means of criminal law may be disputable: it calls for striking a balance between the rights and freedoms of believers and freedom of expression. Effectively, the court needs to decide which legally protected interest should be given priority as it is closer to the dignity of the individual – the source of all human rights as per, for example Article 30 of the Polish Constitution, a reference derived from international human rights law.

Simultaneously, when trying to set the limit for free expression in Article 196, we could refer to "public morality" as indicated in Article 10 ECHR and try to

---

obrzędów religijnych, podlega grzywnie, karze ograniczenia wolności albo pozbawienia wolności do lat 2. English translation provided by the UN ODC www.imolin.org/

strike an equitable balance between the two. Public morality is understood in Polish constitutional law as a set of rules, norms, patterns of conduct and assessments allowing for the recognition of any conduct as accepted in a society. This term applies to moral principles concerning public life or regulating behaviour publicly available to an unlimited number of people. When contrasted with freedom of expression, as in the *Muller v. Austria* case, priority should be given to freedom of expression, because the principle *in dubio pro libertate* applies. In the *Muller* case, the ECtHR linked public morality with the protection of the individual. In this context, Article 196 PPC is questionable primarily because of its impending prison sentence and its freezing effect upon free expression. To meet the ECHR threshold for a compliant restriction of free speech, it would likely be sufficient to change the prosecution mode to a private complaint. What would make the application of Article 196 less questionable would be a strict interpretation of its provisions not only regarding the insults, but also the subject of the insults: the object of worship and its place. Finally, it begs the question on freedom of artistic expression and whether artists should enjoy more liberty, whether intentional offence can be justified by the freedom of artistic expression. These notions have recently been called to public attention with two creative works offered on public display. We shall use them to show practical application of these semantic considerations.

The first case, mentioned above, deals with a Wroclaw-based artist presenting a work called *cipkomaryjki* ("vaginaMarys") in early 2019.[30] She replicated popular clay depictions of Mother Mary with her coat opened as to, potentially, represent female genitalia, rainbow coloured inside. The artist wished to sell these with all proceeds going to the local non-governmental organisation protecting sexual minority rights (*Kampania przeciw homofobii*). A similar recent case deals with the public display of banners depicting the Black Madonna – an image of the Holy Virgin with particular religious significance to the predominantly Catholic Polish community – placed against a rainbow background. This image was used as a sign of protests against discrimination of the Polish LGBT community by the Polish Catholic Church, state and some local authorities.[31] These are to represent a potential exemplification of "offending" religious feelings of others.

Both of these cases represent speech intended by its authors as political: linking the deeply religious Polish society with the need to protect the LGBTQ+ community from discrimination. They both use the same religious symbol: Mother Mary as the main object of their expression. They are both examples of artistic expression. As such, they meet the prerequisite from Article 196 by addressing "subject of religious worship". As per the complaints received by state prosecutors, some members of the public felt these images offended their religious

30 www.tvp.info/43670598/chciala-sprzedawac-teczowa-maryje-w-ksztalcie-waginy-bedzie-zawiadomienie-do-prokuratury

31 https://wiadomosci.dziennik.pl/wydarzenia/artykuly/611006,teczowa-matka-boska-obraza-uczuc-religijnych-lgbt.html

feelings. As based on the first part of this chapter, it is up to state authorities to ensure a proper balance between these two competing rights: those of free political speech and those of religious followers.

In light of the considerations made above, it seems clear that regarding the ECtHR case law, political artistic speech calls for a higher, special level of protection from the state. Particularly when it is controversial, it should be granted specific safeguards. The meaning of the Polish word *znieważać* (offend) implies the intent of the author to put derogatory light on the subject used in their speech. The use of a rainbow cannot be understood as such by any standards – the use of rainbow colours fails to meet the standard of "offensive" as per linguistic or any other interpretation. As such, both of these cases should be seen as not falling within the narrow scope of penalisation as per Article 196. As of October 2020, only the first of the cited cases has been dismissed by the public prosecutor's office; proceedings against the Wroclaw artists are still pending.

4 Summary

National blasphemy laws are still popular around the world, if much less so in Europe.[32] In that context, Poland remains a minority with its Article 196 punishing those who offend religious feelings of others. The ECtHR has been reluctant to condemn blasphemy laws as such, largely leaving the balancing of these two competing rights: right to free speech and that to religious belief to states within their exclusive margin of appreciation. It has, however, emphasised the need to grant broad, effective protection to political and artistic expression. These two guidelines are to be used when Article 196 of the Polish Criminal Code is to be enforced.

When trying to anticipate the future of these challenging and ambiguous blasphemy provisions in Poland and elsewhere, it must be noted that international human rights soft law implies the need to refrain from criminal punishment of speech potentially offending religious convictions of others ("offending religion"). The 2011 UN Human Rights Council resolution on combating discrimination of persons based on their religion or belief rejects the concept of the so-called defamation of religions.[33] This document was prepared less with Europe in mind, and rather with regard to those regions of the world where blasphemy laws are often used as political tools to rid of competitors or curtail opposition.[34] It calls upon all UN states to "take . . . actions to foster a domestic environment

32 www.refworld.org/docid/4d5a7009c.html; www.france24.com/en/20181031-blasphemy-middle-east-asia-bibi-europe-law-religion-ireland, indicating 13 out of 46 European states have included provisions protecting religions from "offence" in their criminal legislations, including Russia, Italy, Turkey, Greece and Germany.

33 Human Rights Council, A/HRC/RES/16/18.

34 It explicitly references the "speech given by Secretary-General of the Organization of the Islamic Conference at the fifteenth session of the Human Rights Council". Human Rights Council, A/HRC/RES/16/18, para (a).

of religious tolerance, peace and respect". This is to be done by, among other things, "speaking out against intolerance, including advocacy of religious hatred that constitutes incitement to discrimination, hostility or violence" and fostering "religious freedom and pluralism by promoting the ability of members of all religious communities to manifest their religion, and to contribute openly and on an equal footing to society". It is in this context that the word "offends" should be read in the Polish Criminal Code Article 196.

Reference

De Schutter O., 2019. *International human rights law, cases, materials, commentary.* Cambridge. Cambridge University Press.

12 The US Supreme Court's language of racism

Kathryn M. Stanchi

1 Introduction

In *Law and Rhetoric*, Austin Sarat and Thomas Kearns (1996, p. 9) wrote this simple but powerful sentence: "Courts speak and how they speak matters". Legal language does not just resolve disputes, but "is a way of telling a story about what has happened in the world and claiming a meaning for it" (White 1985, pp. 691–692). Law does this by embedding into legal language "ideological and social presuppositions" about what things mean and what events "will count as true" (Andrus 2012, p. 590). Law as rhetoric, James Boyd White (1985, p. 684) wrote, is "the central art by which community and culture are established, maintained and transformed".

Sarat and Kearns's observation is particularly true of the US Supreme Court. That influential body has singular power, through its language, to create and structure American cultural beliefs. It has the power to instigate action or derail it. As Robert Cover (1986, pp. 1611–1613) wrote, "the judicial word is a mandate for the deeds of others", to the extent that "we expect judges' words to serve as virtual triggers for action". To paraphrase Sarat and Kearns (1996, p. 2), the Supreme Court's "words take on a seriousness virtually unparalleled in any other domain of human experience".

In this way, the Supreme Court's use of particular words to describe racism and white supremacy influences significantly what these terms mean in law and in broader American culture. The Court can make something racist by calling it so; it can also make something not racist by denying it is so or by failing to apply that label (Haney-López 2011, p. 815). The Court has always been at the centre of the law's approach to race, although it has not always been on the side of racial justice. For every decision heralded as an advancement of racial equality (e.g. *Loving v. Virginia* [1967], *Brown v. Board of Education* [1954]), there are other decisions that reveal the shameful complicity of the Court in upholding racism (e.g. *Plessy v. Ferguson* [1896], validating Jim Crow segregation laws; *Palmer v. Thompson* [1971], permitting Mississippi to close its public pools rather than integrate; *Korematsu v. United States* [1944], permitting the internment of Japanese citizens during World War II). All these decisions had – and continue to have – a significant impact on what is and is not considered racist in American culture.

DOI: 10.4324/9781003153771-15

Given the Court's history, one of the most important and significant steps the Court can take towards racial justice is to acknowledge and challenge its own role in institutionalising racism. For advocates, an explicit admission by the Court that a prior decision was racist opens the door for use of that reasoning and language to argue against a similar policy or law. For the Court (and really, all the federal courts), the Court's admission of racist complicity acknowledges the Court's power to perpetuate racism and so concedes the Court's power to correct it. Finally, the Court's admission that its decisions contributed to racism or white supremacy sends a strong cultural signal to the nation about what is and is not racist. For example, in *Plessy*, the Court decided that racial segregation was constitutional and the Court's reasoning referred uncritically to the white race as the superior and "dominant" race (Plessy 1896, p. 549–550). The Court has never referred to *Plessy* or its reasoning as "racist" or the product of "white supremacy". That is a signal to the nation that racial segregation is not deserving of the label. As a result, *Plessy*'s damaging decision and reasoning have had a broad impact on US law and culture that resonates to the current day (Harris 2005, pp. 867–868).

This chapter does not posit that the Supreme Court's using the words *racism, racist* or *white supremacy* is the only way that the Court can achieve or support racial justice or that use of these words is the only way that the Supreme Court can signal disapproval of racism. However, in prioritising the use of these particular words, the chapter argues that it is important to accept the position of critical race scholars that using the words *racist, racism* and *white supremacy*, while perhaps upsetting to white people, is singularly important to the cause of racial justice for the people who endure racial oppression (Cazenave 2015, p. xi). This chapter also is a more impressionistic approach to the Court's use of the words as opposed to a rigorous empirical argument. Rather, it makes the modest claim that the employment of the words by the justices has changed over time and this change reveals interesting shifts in the legal and cultural meaning of the words.

2 Overview and methodology

In this chapter, I treated the words *racist, racism* and *white supremacy* as cultural keywords. Cultural keywords are socially prominent words that contain a multitude of cultural meanings – meanings that can be contradictory, contested and changeable over time and across a wide range of audiences, disciplines and fields. By their nature, keywords present social and cultural problems precisely because of their shifting cultural meaning. Rhetoricians will not be surprised that the problems of the meaning of the keywords are "inextricably bound" to the problematic substance of the issues they are meant to describe (Williams 2015, p. xxvii).

To analyse the Supreme Court's use of these keywords, I searched the Supreme Court database on Westlaw, which includes over 10,000 Supreme Court opinions, for the words *racism*, *racist* and *white supremacy*.[1] I focused on 107 substantive uses of the keywords in Supreme Court opinions. By "substantive", I mean the Supreme Court uses the words in a way that connotes meaning; I did not count uses such as quotations from other sources, the names of litigants or the like.

I then looked for patterns. First, I looked at the overall timing of the references: when was the first reference? Were there significant gaps or upticks after that first use? I then narrowed the focus to look at two types of references: use of the keywords to criticise a Court decision or reasoning and use to deny the harms of racism. Use of the keywords to criticise the Court required calling a Court decision racist or criticising the Court for ignoring, allowing or constitutionalising a racist policy. Denying the harm of racism included any reference denying the existence of racism; denying that a law or policy was based in racism or the nation's racist history; and/or referring to white people as the "real" victims of racism. For example, if a justice used the phrase "reverse racism" to argue that white people were harmed by affirmative action or if a justice criticised the use of the label "racism" as uncivil or harmful to society, I considered those references as denial of racism.

Within these two groups, I next evaluated the rhetorical power of the references using several criteria. A reference was more powerful if it used clear, direct language instead of circumlocution and used the active voice and identified a racist actor as opposed to hiding the actor with the passive voice. A reference was less powerful if it used hedge language such as "possibly" or "it seems" or used a euphemism in referring to racism, such as calling racism "unfortunate". I also considered the placement of the reference. If it was in the main text, I considered it more powerful than if it appeared in a footnote or a parenthetical citation.

3 Overall timing

Of the 107 uses analysed, the overwhelming majority (92) are to "racism" or "racist". "White supremacy" is referenced only 15 times.

The first use of *racism* or *racist* in Supreme Court jurisprudence occurs in 1944 in Justice William Murphy's dissent in *Korematsu v. United States* (1944). After several uses of racism and racist in the 1940s (all by Justice Murphy), the words disappear from Supreme Court jurisprudence for almost 20 years, resurfacing only in 1966 in the majority opinion in *Brown v. Louisiana*, which held that civil rights protestors had a constitutional right to hold a peaceful sit-in at a segregated public library (Brown 1966, p. 142). Thus, during the height of Jim Crow segregation laws in the 1950s and early 1960s, none of the justices, in any opinion (majority, concurring or dissent), ever once used the keywords.

The phrase "white supremacy" appears much earlier. The Supreme Court's first use of this phrase was in 1928, in *New York ex rel. Bryant v. Zimmerman*.

1 Westlaw is one of the major online legal repositories for US law and legal materials. It is widely used in US legal research. https://legal.thomsonreuters.com/en/products/westlaw

Zimmerman represents one of the most common uses of the keywords by the Court: to describe the philosophy of the Ku Klux Klan (Zimmerman 1928, p. 76). Like racism/racist, this early use of "white supremacy" is followed by almost 40 years of silence. In 1965, a year before the case (*Brown v. Louisiana*) that broke the Court's silence on racism, "white supremacy" resurfaces in *Louisiana v. United States*, overturning one of Louisiana's effort to keep Blacks from voting, and then again in 1968 in the famous case of *Loving v. Virginia*, overturning Virginia's miscegenation law (Louisiana 1965, p. 149; Loving 1967, pp. 7, 11).

4 Use of the keywords to criticise Court decisions or reasoning

The Supreme Court never once, in a majority opinion, explicitly acknowledges that one of its decisions was racist or the product of white supremacy. The only use of the keywords to criticise the Court or its reasoning occurred in separate opinions (concurring or dissenting), and this was infrequent, occurring only 13 times out of 107. Moreover, the frequency of use of the keywords in separate opinions to criticise the Court has decreased over time (see Figure 12.1).

In terms of rhetorical strength, the strongest of the 13 opinions criticising the Court is Justice Murphy's 1944 dissent in *Korematsu* (also the very first use of the word "racism" by a Supreme Court justice). Since then, the rhetoric of the opinions criticising the Court has decreased in power (see Figure 12.1).

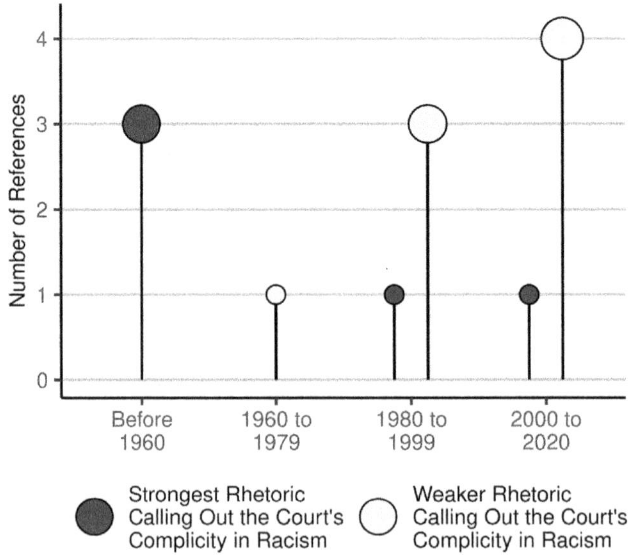

Figure 12.1 Decrease in strong rhetoric condemning racism/increase in weak

In *Korematsu*, Justice Murphy made the stark and powerful accusation that the Court had "legalized racism" and that the law had "descended into the ugly abyss of racism" (1944, p. 233). Since then, no other opinion has matched this dissent's power and clarity in calling out the Court's complicity in racism.

This is surprising considering the many times that the Supreme Court has been instrumental in legalising racism. *Plessy*, for example, was overturned in *Brown v. Board of Education* (1954), the famous case about school segregation. But the *Brown* Court never used the keywords to describe *Plessy*, even though by 1954 the words had appeared multiple times in Supreme Court decisions. Similarly, in 2018 the Court repudiated *Korematsu* in *Trump v. Hawaii* (2018), the Supreme Court case upholding former President Trump's Muslim travel ban, without once using the keywords.

Since Justice Murphy's dissent in *Korematsu*, the rhetoric criticising the Court's complicity in racism has weakened. *McCleskey v. Kemp* (1987) is a good example of this. In *McCleskey*, a Black defendant was sentenced to death for the murder of a white police officer by a jury composed of 11 white people and 1 Black person. The Court accepted as true the statistics offered by the defendant that showed defendants convicted of murdering white people were four times more likely to be sentenced to death than defendants convicted of murdering Black people. Nevertheless, the Court found that the Constitution afforded no remedy to the defendant, noting that the racial disparities shown by the statistics were an "inevitable part of our criminal justice system" (McCleskey 1987, p. 312).

The *McCleskey* decision inspired three dissents, none of which uses the keywords to indict the Court majority for its callous enabling of the racist death penalty law. Only one dissenter, Justice William Brennan, uses the word "racism" at all, and the word is not directed at the Court or the majority opinion. Justice Brennan calls the defendant's statistical evidence "disturbing . . . to a society that has formally repudiated racism" and admonished that "we ignore him at our peril, for we remain imprisoned by the past as long as we deny its influence in the present" (McCleskey 1987, p. 344). The target of Justice Brennan's use of the word "racism" here is not clear, but it is plainly not the Court or the *McCleskey* decision. Rather, it appears to be American society, or some hypothetical society, which Justice Brennan credits with formally repudiating racism. The use of the word "disturbing" is a shockingly mild description of the evidence in *McCleskey*, which showed that Georgia killed Black people convicted of murdering whites at 22 times the rate as Black people convicted of murdering other Black people.

The way Justice Brennan characterises the majority opinion is also oblique. Dissents are meant to be disruptive; their purpose is to illuminate the flaws of the majority decision and to hold the Court accountable for its errors (Hannah and Salmon 2020, pp. 943–944). But Justice Brennan's use of the word racism is meek, particularly as compared with Justice Murphy's use 33 years before. Justice Brennan's reference to "a society" is followed by an ambiguous reference to "we" who ignore the defendant's evidence. It is unclear to whom "we" refers. The Court? American society? Even if Justice Brennan was accusing the Court of ignoring the defendant's evidence, that characterisation significantly downplays the Court's responsibility. The Court in *McCleskey* went far beyond ignoring racism, though it certainly did that. To borrow Justice Murphy's phrase, *McCleskey* legalised the racist murder of Black criminal defendants. *McCleskey* said that a certain amount of racism in the administration of the death penalty was constitutionally acceptable. If judicial words are a "mandate for the deeds of others" (Cover 1986, pp. 1611–1613), *McCleskey* empowered police, prisons and prosecutors to continue to kill Black people, some of them innocent of the charged crime, at a shocking rate. The dissent's use of the term "racism" here dilutes the meaning of the term (if the *McCleskey* decision isn't racist, it is difficult to see what decision would be racist) and elides the Court's culpability.

There may be many legitimate reasons why Justice Brennan's rhetoric fell short of accusing the Court of racism. *McCleskey* was a deeply divided decision and Justice Brennan was a well-known dealmaker (Stern and Wermiel 2010, p. 545). He might have seen Justice Powell, a moderate centrist, as a potential swing vote to turn the case the other way. But whatever Justice Brennan's reasons – and they might have been very good ones – the issue is why the use of the word racism is so radioactive that Justice Brennan could use it only obliquely or risk losing Justice Powell's vote (which he famously lost in any event).

Justice Brennan's use of racism in *McCleskey* is emblematic of the Court's modern usage of the word. This type of understated, punch-pulling rhetoric surrounding the keywords characterises many of the 13 opinions in this category. In this way, the Court's language has mirrored its doctrine, shifting the meaning of the keywords to require an intentional "invidious use of race" and a "state of mind akin to malice" (Haney-López 2012, p. 1062; Cooper 2012, pp. 34–35). McCleskey is a stark example of this, but this usage is evident in many of the Court's decisions after the 1940s.

5 The Court's use of the keywords to deny the harms of racism

While the rhetoric challenging the Court on racism has become less frequent and weaker, the rhetoric of the justices denying racism and white supremacy has become more frequent. References denying racism have increased over time and have become rhetorically more powerful. This language is chipping away at the definition of the keywords, making their scope smaller and smaller, excluding from their definitions "even . . . disparities so wide that they are extremely hard to explain as anything other than a product of race" (Cooper 2012, pp. 34–35).

One example of this definitional evolution is the uptick in retaliatory language in response to use of the keywords to label racism by a member of the Court. This is a kind of "racial jujitsu" that deploys the power of the keywords to attack those who challenge racism as the "true racists" (Haney-López 2011, p. 817; Cooper 2012, p. 30). Since roughly the 1980s, the use of the keywords by the Court or a justice to label racist laws or decisions frequently causes other justices to decry the incivility of the rhetoric. The keywords have become fighting words in modern times (Cazenave 2015, p. xvi). A good example of this phenomenon is a comparison of the opinions in *Korematsu* and the 2020 opinions in *Ramos v. Louisiana*, a case about the constitutionality of non-unanimous juries in criminal cases. Both cases involved controversial issues of race and racism. Both cases included opinions that used the word racism to describe either the laws at issue or the Court's decision.

But the cases highlight some important differences. First, the *Ramos* majority is yet another example of the Court using a keyword to challenge the Court's racism in a rhetorically weak fashion. Second, the judicial reaction to the use of the keywords in the two decisions is pronounced. In *Korematsu*, Justice Murphy accused the Court majority of "legaliz[ing] racism", and yet the Court's reaction to the charge is at worst a mild rebuke. In *Ramos*, by contrast, the charge of racism is never directed at the Court or another justice. Nevertheless, the reaction is strident, excoriating the justices for use of the keywords.

In *Ramos* (2020), the Court confronted two state laws (Louisiana and Oregon) that permitted juries in criminal cases to be non-unanimous. These laws have a tarnished history in American jurisprudence; relics of the Jim Crow era, the laws were the state response to being required to include non-whites on criminal juries. The very purpose of non-unanimity laws was to dilute the influence of non-white jurors. The Supreme Court had found non-unanimity laws to be constitutional in 1972 in *Apodaca v. Oregon* (1972, pp. 413–414).

The Court finally overturned *Apodaca* almost 50 years later (Ramos 2020, p. 1408). The Ramos majority opinion uses one keyword (racist) one time, to describe the provenance of the state laws. The majority never calls *Apodaca* racist even though *Apodaca* helped legitimise and fortify racism into the criminal justice system of the United States by greatly increasing the risk of wrongful convictions for non-white defendants (Kaplan and Saack 2017, pp. 36–43).

Instead of calling the *Apodaca* decision racist, *Ramos* described the *Apodaca* Court's offense as a failure to "grapple with" the racism of the state laws (Ramos 2020, p. 1405). This characterisation is remarkably similar to Justice Brennan's description of the *McCleskey* Court and suggests that the only acceptable criticism is to accuse the Court of passively "ignoring" racism. And, as noted below, it seems that even accusing the Court of ignoring racism is becoming less acceptable.

Justice Kavanaugh's concurring opinion in *Ramos* is much more rhetorically powerful in its condemnation of the non-unanimity laws, calling them "pillars of a comprehensive and brutal program of racist Jim Crow measures" and "a practice that is thoroughly racist in its origins and has continuing racially discriminatory effects" (2020, pp. 1417–1419). But as impassioned and vehement as Justice Kavanaugh was in his opinion, he too avoided implicating the Court directly in racism.

These references provoked a strong reaction from Justice Alito. Although none of the opinions in *Ramos* directs the keywords at any member of the Court, Justice Alito calls the rhetoric "ad hominem" and criticises the language as "tar[ring] Louisiana and Oregon with the charge of racism" (Ramos 2020, p. 1425). Justice Alito's use of the metaphor "tars", which derives from the colonial (and feudal) punishment of painting a person with hot wood tar, shows he sees the use of the label racism as a form of mob vengeance.

It is worth quoting this longer passage from Justice Alito's dissent, as it shows quite clearly the modern, narrow definition of racism that is emerging in Supreme Court jurisprudence:

> Some years ago the British Parliament enacted a law allowing non-unanimous verdicts. Was Parliament under the sway of the Klan? The Constitution of Puerto Rico permits non-unanimous verdicts. Were the framers of that Constitution racists? Non-unanimous verdicts were once advocated by the American Law Institute and the American Bar Association. Was their aim to promote white supremacy? And how about the prominent scholars who have taken the same position? Racists all? Of course not. So all the talk about the Klan, etc., is entirely out of place. We should set an example of rational and civil discourse instead of contributing to the worst current trends. . . . Now to what matters.
>
> (Ramos 2020, p. 1427; footnotes omitted)

The import of this passage seems to be that unless all uses of the non-unanimous jury demonstrably have their roots in racism, then it is "entirely out of place" to discuss racism in the context of Louisiana's and Oregon's laws. In other words, a law cannot be called racist if we can imagine any possible non-racist reason for it.

The violence that this kind of rhetoric does to the cultural and legal definition of racism is significant. It reinforces the notion that the Court and its decisions cannot be racist because it suggests that Ku Klux Klan influence is the only way to show racism and that certain types of people (prominent scholars, the American Law Institute) are above charges of racism. Thus, passages like Justice Alito's construct a definition of racism that permits only a narrow swath of behaviour and people to be labelled "racist".

Justice Alito's words are, of course, part of a dissenting opinion with no precedential value. But his words are emblematic of a cramped definition of racism that is increasingly used in the Court's decisions. As Ibram Kendi (2019) notes, "denial is the heartbeat of racism", and "when racist ideas resound, denials that those ideas are racist typically follow". As a result, the modern trend is that describing something as racist, instead of being simply explicative, has become "radioactive" – a "slur", a "pejorative", "the worst word in the English language" (Kendi 2019, pp. 9, 46). The goal of this rhetorical trend is to undercut the work of racial justice by making it impossible to point out or identify racism.

This kind of denying language is becoming more common in Supreme Court decisions. As Figure 12.2 shows, this kind of rhetorical bullying surrounding the keywords did not exist in Supreme Court decisions prior to 1980 but has been on an upswing since then.

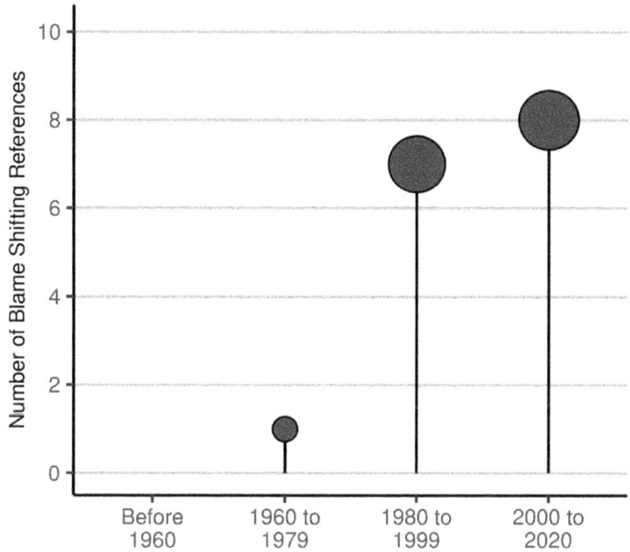

Figure 12.2 Increase in Racial Bullying Language

Now compare the *Ramos* opinions with the opinions in *Korematsu*. In *Korematsu* (1944), as noted above, Justice Murphy directly accused the Court of legalising racism. But in contrast to Justice Alito's reaction, the response of the Court majority in *Korematsu* is measured. The majority avoided engaging with Justice Murphy's charge of racism and treated it as a simple categorical disagreement: "To cast this case into outlines of racial prejudice, without reference to the real military dangers which were presented, merely confuses the issue" (*Korematsu* 1944, p. 223).

The difference in tone between Justice Alito's dissent and the *Korematsu* majority suggests that racism has shifted in meaning. The primary change is that in 1944, racism was not a "fighting word", and in 2020 it is. This could mean that the word racism has a more pejorative meaning in 2020 than it did in 1944, or it could mean that people in 2020 are more sensitive to the charge. The two sets of opinions also show that the Court majority is more willing to label laws racist. After all, the *Korematsu* majority specifically disclaimed that the Japanese internment law was racist, and in *Ramos* the Court majority was willing to acknowledge the racism of the jury non-unanimity laws.

But Justice Alito's dissent also shows the modern emergence of a definition of racism weaponised against the victims of racism. The use of the word racism to label victims who complain of racist behaviour did not appear in Court jurisprudence until very recently. Neither the change in meaning nor the difference in tone can be wholly explained by the difference between majority and dissenting opinions. We might expect dissents (like Justice Alito's) to be more passionate and strident than majority opinions, but recall that the strength of the dissenting rhetoric challenging the Court's racism (like Justice Brennan's in *McCleskey*) has become weaker. This suggests that it is the use of the keywords, not the type of opinion, that makes the difference.

6 Conclusion

Overall, the patterns show a Court that rarely accepts responsibility for its complicity in perpetuating racism. This avoidance of responsibility is increasingly enabled by dissenting or concurring justices who, though willing to challenge the Court, do so only with weak rhetoric, thereby soft-pedalling the Court's accountability for some of its most notoriously racist decisions. Layered over this decrease in accountability rhetoric is the increase in references that explicitly deny the harms of racism and oppose use of the keywords to label even the most racially discriminatory laws.

The language of the Supreme Court is highly influential beyond its power to say who won and who lost. The language of law is the "primary vehicle through which cultural and institutional ideologies are transmitted" (Ehrlich 2003, p. 4). The Supreme Court's way of talking about racism and white supremacy matters greatly to the task of racial justice. When the justices of the highest Court consistently fail to call things racist, those things become not racist legally and culturally. After all, if a decision were racist, wouldn't the Court say so? Wouldn't it be illegal? As Thomas Ross noted, "Rhetoric is a magical thing. It transforms things into their opposites. Difficult choices become obvious. Change becomes continuity. Real human suffering vanishes" (Ross 1990, p. 2).

This definitional distortion is worsened by the backlash rhetoric against labelling racism and white supremacy. The backlash perpetuates the idea that certain laws or actions are not truly racist and silences critics by making racism something that cannot be discussed or labelled. As Sarat and Kearns noted, for critical legal theorists, "the rhetoric of law is linked to its operation as a system of power in which power is defined in terms of what can be spoken and what is silenced" (1996, p. 13). The rise in Supreme Court rhetoric treating the words "racism" and "white supremacy" as slurs makes identifying of racism a violation of professionalism and civility. It silences those – whether judges or advocates – who wish to use those words. And so fewer things get labelled racist, and the definition of what is racist gets narrower and narrower. As the definition becomes narrower, the potential for correcting racism in law decreases.

When the problem is language, then the solution is language as well. According to Sarat and Kearns, "attending to rhetoric in law is a way of attending, albeit from a new and perhaps unrecognized angle, to questions of justice and injustice" (1996, p. 3). As Noel Cazenave notes, "Systems of oppression flourish when the language that camouflages their ideological core is accepted as a given and therefore goes both unexamined and unchallenged" (2015, p. 2). One step towards a solution must be for the Court to accept responsibility for its enabling of racism and for the justices – especially dissenting justices – to clearly label and identify racism, especially when perpetuated by the Court. To paraphrase Ibram Kendi, the "only way to undo racism is to consistently identify and describe it" (2019, p. 9). As the highest court in the United States, the Supreme Court should lead the way.

References

US Supreme Court cases

[1896] 163 U.S. 537 *Plessy v. Ferguson.*
[1928] 278 U.S. 63 *New York ex rel. Bryant v. Zimmerman.*
[1944] 323 U.S. 214 *Korematsu v. United States.*
[1954] 347 U.S. 483 *Brown v. Board of Education of Topeka, Shawnee County, Kansas.*
[1965] 380 U.S. 145 *Louisiana v. United States.*
[1966] 383 U.S. 131 *Brown v. Louisiana.*
[1967] 388 U.S. 1 *Loving v. Virginia.*
[1971] 403 U.S. 217 *Palmer v. Thompson.*
[1972] 406 U.S. 404 *Apodaca v. Oregon.*
[1987] 481 U.S. 279 *McCleskey v. Kemp.*
[2018] 138 S. Ct. 2392 *Trump v. Hawaii.*
[2020] 140 S. Ct. 1390 *Ramos v. Louisiana.*

Articles and books

Andrus, J., 2012. Language ideology, fractal recursivity, and discursive agency in the legal construction of linguistic evidence. *Language in Society*, 41(5), 589-614.

Cazenave, N., 2015. *Conceptualizing racism: Breaking the chains of racially accommodative language.* Lanham, MD: Rowman & Littlefield.

Cooper, F.R., 2012. Masculinities, post-racialism and the gates controversy: The false equivalence between officer and civilian. *Nevada Law Journal*, 11, 1–43.

Cover, R., 1986. Violence and the world. *Yale Law Journal*, 95(8), 1611-1629.

Ehrlich, S., 2003. *Representing rape: Language and sexual consent.* London: Routledge.

Haney-López, I., 2011. Is the post in post-racial the blind in colorblind. *Cardozo Law Review*, 32(3), 807–832.

Haney-López, I., 2012. Intentional blindness. *N.Y.U. Law Review*, 87, 1779–1877.

Hannah, M., & Salmon, S., 2020. Against the grain: The secret role of dissents in integrating rhetoric across the curriculum. *Nevada Law Journal*, 20(3), 935-966.

Harris, C.I., 2005. In the shadow of Plessy. *University of Pennsylvania Journal of Constitutional Law*, 7, 867–901.

Kaplan, A., & Saack, A., 2017. Overturning *Apodaca v. Oregon* should be easy: Non-unanimous jury verdicts in criminal cases undermine the credibility of our justice system. *Oregon Law Review*, 95(1), 37-52.

Kendi, I., 2019. *How to be an antiracist.* New York: One World.

Ross, T., 1990. The rhetorical tapestry of race: White innocence and black abstraction. *William & Mary Law Review*, 32(1), 1-40.

Sarat, A., & Kearns, T.R., 1996. *The rhetoric of law.* Ann Arbor: University of Michigan Press.

Stern, S., & Wermiel, S., 2010. *Justice Brennan: Liberal champion*. Boston: Houghton Mifflin Harcourt.
White, J.B., 1985. Law as rhetoric, rhetoric as law: The arts of cultural and communal life. *University of Chicago Law Review*, 52(3), 684-702.
Williams, R., 2015. *Keywords: A vocabulary of culture and society*. New York: Oxford University Press.

13 Do the words of the American Constitution still matter? The question of "the meaning of meaning" in current judicial argumentation

Anna Tomza-Tulejska and J. Patrick Higgins

1 Introduction

Interpretation is everywhere (Dilthey 1883). We interpret facts, words and human behaviours. We interpret even the weather before we go for a walk. Even if we are unaware of it, we are always interpreting, but that does not mean that our interpretation is always correct. When a man says or writes something, there are many ways in which his performances may be judged (Austin 1993). Wilhelm Dilthey claims that we understand correctly after we can interpret a word correctly. The fact that humans are incapable of reading each other's minds makes communication by outward signs necessary. By extension, we cannot ever escape the problem of interpretation, nor the fact that interpretation is necessary flawed (Lieber 1839).

The question of proper interpretation is one of the fundamental problems in the discourse of American jurisprudence and is connected to problems deriving from the philosophy of language concerning the meaning of words. American lawyers use the concept of language differently than their European counterparts (Hohfeld 1923). The American Constitution was written in a language for which no uniform definition has been presented to date, with scholars and researchers of American law noting that its language was not in common usage (see Balkin 2016). Baude and Sachs argues that legal texts may be written in a "specialized vocabulary and linguistic conventions that legally trained people use to talk to one another" (Baude and Sachs 2017, p. 1085). They try to convince that the standard picture of constitutional language is wrong, that an instrument's legal effect does not simply follow from the meaning of its language (Baude and Sachs 2017, p. 1085). The Founding Fathers' assumption about the concise nature of the Constitution was certainly related to the fact that the Constitution, as it formed the new nation, was to be understandable for all citizens (Bork 1991). The lack of a specialized legal language, established colloquial grammar rules and the usage of plain language (so that, in theory, the Constitution could be accessible to the average man) have certainly contributed to a complicated American legal culture (Llewellyn 1950, 1960).

DOI: 10.4324/9781003153771-16

Since the beginning of the 20th century, the judicial adjudication strategy in the American system was generally shaped according to the methods of the interpretation Constitution focused on understanding the meaning of constitutional concepts (Landis 1930; Posner 2010).

Chronologically, the first of this method of judicial interpretation referring to the concept of meaning is textualism. The second method of judicial interpretation that developed on textualism's basic concept of the proper interpretation is originalism, followed by the youngest method, or rather interpretative technique, which is judicial activism. It should be noted that these theories, though they may be nominally opposed, give much room for overlap in actual practice. Emerging theories of judicial behaviourism present opportunities to reconcile with these approaches, and the chapter concludes by attempting such a synthesis, demonstrating how it improves our understanding of the science of legal meaning and argumentation.

2 Approaches to interpretation

2.1 Textualism

Textualism is associated with the concept of the plain meaning of words. Describing textualism, Justice Oliver Wendell Holmes Jr argued that the proper meaning of the Constitution derives from the plain meaning concept of the language of the Constitution. The doctrine of the plain meaning of constitutional words assumes that the language of the Constitution is simple and natural (Holmes 2005; Cohen 1935, p. 822). Therefore phrases, and especially the meanings of terms used in the Constitution, should be understood as they were understood by the plain meaning at the time of the Constitution's creation.[1] Holmes specifically noted that

> we ask, not what this man meant, but what those words would mean in the mouth of a normal speaker of English, using them in the circumstances in which they were used.
>
> (Holmes 1899, pp. 417–418)

Correct determination of the plain meaning of words requires obtaining sources of understanding meaning from popular use in society (Manning 2005). Textualism as an approach to legal interpretation quite firmly distinguishes itself

1 Julie Pelegrin indicates the current understanding of the plain meaning doctrine as it is seen in the Colorado statute, section 2–4–101, C.R.S., supporting the Plain Meaning Rule. "Words and phrases shall be read in context and construed according to the rules of grammar and common usage. Words and phrases that have acquired a technical or particular meaning, whether by legislative definition or otherwise, shall be construed accordingly" (Peegrin 2013).

both from the intention behind why a statute was written and from its legislative history.

Lawrence Solum claims that in order to correctly understand textualism, we should ask what we mean when we say the "plain meaning" of the text. "The plain meaning of a legal text is the meaning that would be understood by regular folks who were competent speakers of the language and who knew that they were reading a statute (or court decision)" (Solum 2004).

The most prominent textualist US Supreme Court Justice was Antonin Scalia, who believed that a textualist judge should have no authority to pursue those broader purposes or write new laws (Scalia 1997, p. 23). A textualist interpretation should be construed reasonably to contain all that it fairly means (Scalia 1997). The most popular explanation of Scalia's textualism is:

> Most words are open and have multiple interpretations, are ambiguous, and cannot be interpreted strictly.
>
> (Scalia 1997, p. vii)

> Words do have limited range of meaning, and no interpretation that goes beyond that range is permissible.
>
> (Scalia 1997, p. 24)

Scalia claims that text should not be construed strictly, and it should not be construed leniently; it should be construed reasonably, to contain all that it fairly means (Scalia 1997, p. 23).[2] It is very difficult to explain what the fair meaning of the textualism is because many people consider textualism to be wooden, unimaginative or pedestrian (Scalia 1997, p. 23). Nothing could be more wrong, as textualism does not mean simply reading the text literally but tries to understand the law and its rules. It theoretically assumes that the interpretation should look for the meaning most like that used by the Founding Fathers in the Constitution, while the context of applying the law should be added to it. This context is the long-established and well-established principles of legal application (Scalia 1997, p. 27).[3]

2 In addition, Solum claims that the plain meaning is not a literal meaning or purposive meaning, and even the plain meaning of a text may not be the "reasonable" or "desirable" meaning (Solum 2015).

3 In literature there is also intentionalism, which seeks to reveal the intention of the Founding Fathers. Intentionalism is not a method of interpretation but rather by a conception of law, it can be most simply thought of as a complete rejection of textualism, or the idea that texts themselves convey meanings (Fish 2005). Rather, it is an assertion that legal texts and documents are written by authors for a specific purpose, just as much as novels or letters are. Their meaning can only come from what the author intended to write, such as a reaction to an event or to put forward a certain idea. As noted above, intentionalism stands opposed to textualism. Some originalists employed the term to describe the intentions of the Founding Fathers. Justice Scalia claims that when a judge finds intentionalism "we do not really look for subjective legislative intent. We look for a sort of 'objectified" intent – the intent that a reasonably person

2.2 *Originalism*

The word "originalism" was coined by Paul Brest in 1980 in a law review article titled *The Misconceived Quest for the Original Understanding*. Brest provides the following definition: "By 'originalism' I mean the familiar approach to constitutional adjudication that accords binding authority to the text of the Constitution or the intentions of its adopters" (Brest 1980, p. 204; Solum 2011, p. 2).

Originalism seeks to use an original meaning close to the meaning used in the documents written at the time when the Founding Fathers lived.

> Almost all originalists agree that the original meaning of the Constitution was fixed at the time each provision was framed and ratified. Most originalists agree that the original meaning of the Constitution should strongly constrain the content of constitutional doctrine.
>
> (Solum 2011, p. 41)

Robert H. Bork laid the foundation for originalism in a 1971 *Indiana Law Journal* article and then wrote a definitive defence of originalism in *The Tempting of America* (Bork 1991). The main idea presented in his book is that the role of judicial philosophy is to solve the Madisonian dilemma, which establishes judicial ground rules on when the majority and the minority ought to rule, respectively (Calabresi 2007). Originalists claim that this is only one of the judicial philosophies that seeks to satisfy the Madisonian dilemma because judges' interpretations follow the intention of the Framers. The only way of constraining judicial discretion is if the judges interpret the Constitution's words according to the intentions of the Framers (Powell 1985). Originalism is promoted by the Federalist Society as not only the proper way to interpret the law, but also as a correct way to politically interpret the will of the Framers of the Constitution. Its followers promote this method of interpretation as the proper way to interpret the Constitution (Sherry 1998, p. 795).

In his 1985 speech to the American Bar Association, Attorney General Edwin Meese said that Americans "pride ourselves on having produced the greatest political wonder of the world – a government of laws and not of men" (Calabresi 2007, p. 3). Meese went on to quote Thomas Paine as saying, "America has no monarch: Here the law is king" (Calabresi 2007, p. 3). Originalists believe that the written Constitution is fundamental to the American law (McGinnis and Rappaport 2007). Those who subscribe to originalism believe that justices who abandon the original meaning of the text try to replace it with their own political philosophies (Solum 2011, p. 1). Originalists say that Americans have to decide

would gather from the text of the law, placed alongside the remainder of the corpus juris" (Scalia 1997, p. 17). Justices Frankfurter and Jackson in their opinions agreed with Holmes, that "Only a day or two ago – when counsel talked of the intention of a legislature, I was indiscreet enough to say I don't care what their intention was. I only want to know what the words mean" (Scalia 1997, p. 22). But now, "We do not inquire what the legislature meant; we ask only what the statute means" (Scalia 1997, p. 23).

whether they want a government of laws or rule by the judges. The essence of this branch of originalism is the belief that judges must interpret the law, not rewrite the text of the Constitution. In a similar vein, Meese says in his speech "that the Constitution is a limitation on judicial power as well as executive and legislative" power (Calabresi 2007, p. 3).

Although originalism has been the predominant interpretive methodology for constitutional meaning (Danaher 2015, pp. 397–398), in American history, there still remains in American jurisprudence the problem of correct understanding the meaning originalism.[4]

Mark Greenberger and Harry Litman (1998, p. 573) suggest that there are two different notions of meaning. The first notion is

> the meaning of the term roughly what a dictionary definition attempts to convey – the semantic or linguistic understanding is necessary to use the term, as opposed to nonlinguistic facts about the object or activities to which the term applies. In contrast, according to the second, looser notion, the meaning of a term incorporates the objects or activities to which the terms is applied.
>
> (Greenberg and Litman 1998, p. 573)

In other words, the second meaning should be understood as something like original constitutional practice (Solum 2008).

Daniel Smyth says,

> the original public meaning – not the original understanding – of a constitutional word or provision, unless unrecoverable, to be the controlling meaning of that word or provision. The original public meaning is the meaning that a "reasonable speaker of English" during the founding era would have ascribed to the word or provision.
>
> (Smyth 2017, p. 306)

The original understanding and original public meaning of a constitutional word or provision are often identical, but a conflict is possible (Smyth 2017).

2.3 Judicial activism

The youngest method, or rather interpretative technique, is judicial activism (Holland 1991). While the idea of judicial activism (that judges can use extra-textual or extra-constitutional sources when making decisions) has existed much longer

4 Contemporary originalism is a family of constitutional theories, united by two core ideas, fixation and constraint because the original meaning ("communicative content") of the constitutional text is fixed at the time each provision is framed and ratified. The Constraint Principle claims that constitutional actors (e.g. judges, officials, citizens) ought to be constrained by the original meaning when they engage in constitutional practice (paradigmatically, deciding constitutional cases (McGinnis and Rappaport 2017).

than the term (Kmiec 2004, p. 1444), arguably even as far back as Marshall's Supreme Court against Jefferson's administration (Green 2009), as a coherent method and doctrine, it is quite new. Activism is a tool, a breakthrough, enabling a departure from the traditional interpretation in favour of a new one, which aims to meet society's expectations of the law. Activism is used by judges who confess their political preferences. Thanks to activism, they engage in a dialogue with society regarding the evolution of language and changing the meaning of existing concepts. Activism, to put it briefly, looks for the understanding of words that is most anticipated by the society.

In recent American jurisprudence, both textualism and originalism have ceased to be sufficient for the theoretical justification of judicial arguments. It was noted that each of these methods relates to the concept of the meaning of meaning (Solum 2011), but none of them explains exactly how to understand the meaning of meaning (Greenberg and Litman 1998).[5] These issues in American jurisprudence derive from the philosophy of understanding the world through the development of a philosophy of linguistic meaning (Solum 2011; Solum 2020).

According to this paradigm, though the classics of American legal theory formulated the most important postulates on how to properly understand the meaning of words, they took up a purely philosophical perspective, which is not sufficient in the work of a judge (Smith 2011). When looking for the correct meaning of words, the judge must refer not only to the philosophical conception of the meaning of meaning but must also combine this concept with the concrete facts of the case. Searching for the correct meaning of words, the judge adjusts the meaning of the words contained in the Constitution to the meaning of the facts of the case under examination (Dworkin 1978).

The modern conceptualising of judicial activism emerged from intentionalism, opposed to textualism and originalism (Green 2009). This doctrine is based on the concept of the "living Constitution", the opinion that words of the American Constitution are alive, always evolving and adapting to new circumstances (Balkin 2011; Jefferies 2001; Karkkainen 1994). This means that the Constitution is not a dead letter but is dynamic, and judges should interpret its words according to current social meaning and usage.[6]

Living Constitutionalists base their argument on the words of Thomas Jefferson:

> I am not an advocate for frequent changes in laws and constitutions, but laws and institutions must go hand in hand with the progress of the human mind. As that becomes more developed, more enlightened, as new discoveries are made, new truths discovered and manners and opinions change, with the

5 The language of the law is a central part of the learning lawyers in legal education. Some scholars claim that this is not all language, but the content of language, limiting it to word meanings and grammatical rules. See: McGinnis and Rappaport (2017).

6 The philosophy of living constitutionalism gives grounds for the creation of activist political movements supporting active judicial interpretation aimed at giving constitutional concepts new, evolving meanings.

change of circumstances, institutions must advance also to keep pace with the times. We might as well require a man to wear still the coat which fitted him when a boy as a civilized society to remain ever under the regimen of their barbarous ancestors.

(Jefferson 1819)[7]

3 Theory of judicial behaviourism

Critics of all these methods claim they have neither logical nor philosophical foundations. Further, they argue that focusing legal interpretation on how the Constitution justifies legal meaning, but then only emphasising linguistic or textualist or originalistic meaning, allows judges to manipulate its words. In other words, the constitutional text is considered an objective social fact, but the mechanisms to interpret it remain subjective and generally without firm epistemological justification.[8] To provide a more objective mechanism of interpretation, it has been recognised that a science is needed, which should focus on creating some rigid theoretical standards for judicial adjudication (Scalia and Garner 2008). As Richard Posner famously stated, if there does not exist "a body of objective norms (either 'positive law' or 'natural law') or a set of analytic methods ('legal reasoning') that can be used to ensure that judicial decision will be objective", then "judges [are] reduced to ruling by fiat made impressive by the hieratic stagecraft of judging – the raised bench, the robes, the oaths, the jargon and the rhetoric" (Posner 1993, p. 7).

Taking Posner's criticism to heart, some legal scholars are seeking more rigid standards to discover the meaning of words, which has given birth to a new discipline in American jurisprudence, namely judicial science (Cohen 1962). This new discipline focuses on finding the theoretical grounds for justifying judges' decisions, which are the purpose of judicial argumentation. So much of previous research into jurisprudence has considered legalistic aspects so deeply that they have forgotten that judges are not machines but human beings (Bever 1970). Any complete theory of jurisprudence requires not just legal theory but also legal practice. In other words, a complete judicial science must be complemented by a theory of *judicial behaviour*. The latter is examined by means of *adjudication standards*, which are created by the judge's behaviour. But what do we mean by behaviour, precisely? How is it applicable to judges? How are such standards created? The first understanding of the concept of behaviour was created in J.B. Watson's psychology (Watson 1913, 1925). As a result of various theoretical and

7 See www.let.rug.nl/usa/presidents/thomas-jefferson/letters-of-thomas-jefferson/jefl246.php

8 For example, there is no precise meaning for judicial activism, as it potentially includes understandings of any judge who does not accept the assumptions of textualism or originalism. Currently, judicial activism in American jurisprudence is perceived as a political phenomenon, a psychological attitude of a judge, but also a way of interpreting the Constitution. See Kmiec (2004).

terminological changes that took place in the metatheories of psychology, biology and sociology, the concept of "behavioral sciences" began to be used, which includes psychology, sociology, political science and economics.

Nancy N. Maveety suggests that the theoretical foundations for judicial behaviour should be sought in psychological and sociological sciences, not in legal sciences (2005). Glendon Schubert, one of the pioneers of behavioural science, contends that "behavioral judging theory" sets a new direction for all judgment science (Maveety 2005). He names this new branch *behavioural jurisprudence* (Schubert 1975; Pritchett 1968).[9]

3.1 The meaning of judicial behaviour

The turn of judicial studies to a more behavioural orientation brought new problems for the meaning of meaning words (Maveety 2005, p. 17). Nancy Maveety says, "The term – *behavioral science* – later corrupted to *behavioralism* – was originally coined by a group of quantitatively oriented 'rigorously' inclined social scientists at the University of Chicago" (Maveety 2005, p. 9).

Richard Posner gave nine different theories trying to analyse judicial behaviour (Posner 2010):[10] the attitudinal, the strategic, the sociological, the psychological, the economic, the organisational, the phenomenological, the pragmatic and the legalist (Posner 2010, p. 19). The attitudinal theory claims that a judge's decision is best explained by the political preferences which they bring to their cases (Posner 2010; Segal and Spaeth 2002). The strategic theory of judicial behaviour hypothesises that judges do not always vote as they would if they did not have to worry about the reaction to their votes of other judges, legislators and the public (Burbank 2009). The sociological theory of judicial behaviour focuses on small-group dynamics and hence on appellative judging. The psychological is part of the economic theory of judicial behaviour (Burbank 2009). The organisational theory claims that some judges are the faithful agents of Congress. The phenomenological theory of judicial behaviour is a bridge from the pragmatic theory to the legalist. The legalist theory hypothesises that judicial decisions

> are determined by the law, conceived of as body of preexisting rules found stated in canonical legal materials, such as constitutional and statutory text and previous decision of the same or a higher court, or deliverable from those materials by logical operation.
>
> (Posner 2010, p. 41)

9 The new human (i.e. behavioural) jurisprudence has had an important influence in redirecting research, publication and teaching in political science (Schubert 1975, pp. 41–42).

10 John B. Watson created the school of behaviourist methodology within psychology, and he published his views on this psychological theory in 1913. The article was titled "Psychology as the Behaviorist Views It", and it is commonly considered a manifesto on behaviourism.

There is also the "logical behaviorist" approach (Sawyer 2019). A philosophical discussion of awareness and behaviourism led to opinions that identification of mental states refers to the experience of consciously picking up language. In other words, an adequate interpretation of the meaning of the words of the Constitution is a correct response to a consciously read legal text. This highlights how learning a language, communicating, and reading are all conscious acts that can be connected in an overall science of behaviourism.[11]

Finally, there are approaches that attempt to create standards for judicial ethics more directly. Demonstrating that ethical judicial behaviourism is compatible with originalism, Strang contends that originalism only makes sense as a doctrine and method when informed by Aristotelian ethics and natural law. More precisely, Strang makes the case that a core principle of originalism is the idea of self-restraint by judges and that judicial discretion is best informed by developing practical wisdom and the virtues of temperance and fortitude (Strang 2012).

A more sophisticated approach is given by Lieber's vision of hermeneutics. To Lieber, since human beings cannot read each other's minds, all communication is inevitably dependent on outward signs, most notably words, especially in law and politics. *Interpretation* is the attempt to recover the original meaning of a text, or the *letter of the law*, whereas *construction* is expanding it to new situations and cases that the writers could not think of by way of analogy and is the *spirit of the law*. Though constitutions should be interpreted as narrowly as possible, as time passes we drift further and further away, and because of it construction is not only inevitable but necessary. Lieber referred that distinguishing between interpretation and construction, and what principles to use, is the juridical science of hermeneutics, which guided judges' behaviour. Neither interpretation nor construction was arbitrary, and while he used intentionalism, textualism and historical contextualism for the former, his construction was guided by ethical principles he thought were necessary to preserve democracy; in ambiguous situations, those with less political and economic power should be given the benefit of the doubt and mercy whenever possible. He believed that all laws were subject to a more fundamental law, that of human freedom and justice. To Lieber, constitutions did not make liberty, but the citizens did, and that the judge has this duty as citizen (Lieber 1839).

The correct interpretation of the Constitution means, therefore, the correct application of adjudication standards, which establish expectations for the good conduct of a judge, namely judicial behaviour. It seems that unlike the version from the alternative search for the answer to the question, "What is the correct

11 Logical behaviourism was developed in a time of strong mentalistic terminology, where circular reasoning towards behaviour was common, and human action was sometimes treated as indescribable, and the mind in some ways untouchable by science. To the logical behaviourist, the semantics, or language of what we study and talk about when we try to describe behaviour, even internal processes, must in some way be verifiable, or objective, to be useful in a scientific sense.
See also Foxall (2004).

meaning of the word of the Constitution?", the predictions generated by the theory of judicial behaviour are generally well supported by the data that provide an agenda for future research (Posner et al. 2010, p. 23).

4 Conclusion

The problems of the meaning of words in legal studies must take into account the relationship between the linguistic meaning of words and their constitutional provision. The meaning of meaning the words in the American Constitution is still a vital one.

Moreover, as the discussions of the main methods of interpreting the American Constitution show, American researchers are still unable to clearly define the understanding of the meaning of the textual or original meaning. The main problem arises from the fact that original meaning is associated with two or more concepts of meaning (Greenberg and Litman 1998, p. 573).[12]

How are these words to be interpreted correctly when there is no standard definition of the term "meaning" used in the above-mentioned methods of interpreting the Constitution (Berger 1970)? Clearly, a more precise understanding of meaning is necessary to develop the science about the concept of judicial behaviour (Maveety 2005).[13]

Although the concept of judicial behaviour seems impossible to standardise, the examples of its use as a criterion for correct interpretation seem to be more precise and specific than the concepts of the original, plain, or intentional meaning. Judicial behaviour is a holistic notion and thus it does not distinguish the act of interpretation into colloquial semantic meaning from legalistic meaning, and this opens the way to new research paradigms in American jurisprudence. This is due to the uniqueness of the American Constitution, which did not develop a specific legal language and terminology when it was written. Instead, the text was intended to be as comprehensible as possible and in conformity with everyday linguistic usage. To interpret the Constitution in the best possible way, judges must consider the meaning of each word. They can interpret the Constitution correctly only if the judges are versed with the methods and concepts related to the meaning of words and, more generally, the language. On a final note, we refer to Justice Antonin Scalia's well-known saying, that not every word is sacred but every word matters.

12 Some scholarship has suggested that the language of the law is essential to deciding who can hold the highest office in the land. Thus, Michael Ramsey argues that by treating a constitutional provision as written in the language of the law, the judge found its meaning in legal history. The language of the law is also at the heart of reevaluation of the meaning of the Necessary and Proper Clause (McGinnis and Rappaport 2017, p. 1411).

13 Thus, as originalist scholarship has grown more sophisticated and serious in the past decade, academics have turned to the language of the law to understand the Constitution's meaning. These interpretations cannot be derived from ordinary meaning. This legal turn provides more evidence that the Constitution is best understood as written in the language of the law, not ordinary language (McGinnis and Rappaport 2017, p. 1411).

References

Austin, J.L., 1993. *How to do things with words.* England: Clarendon Press.

Balkin, M.J., 2011. *Living originalism.* Cambridge, MA: Harvard University Press.

Balkin, M.J., 2016. The construction of original public meaning. *Constitutional Commentary*, 31, 71–98.

Baude, W., & Sachs, E.S., 2017. The law of interpretation. *Harvard Law Review*, 130, 1079–1147.

Berger, R., 1970. Impeachment of judges and good behavior tenure. *The Yale Law Journal*, 79(8), 1475–1532.

Bever, T.G., 1970. The cognitive basis for linguistic structures. *In:* John R. Hayes, ed., *Cognition and the development of language.* New York: John Wiley & Sons, 279–362.

Bork, R.H., 1991. *The tempting of America: The political seduction of law.* New York: Touchstone.

Brest, P., 1980. The misconceived quest for the original understanding. *Boston University Law Review*, 60(204), 204–238.

Burbank, S., 2009. On the study of judicial behaviors. *Faculty Scholarship at Penn Law*, 266(1). [online] Available from: http://scholarship.law.upenn.edu/cgi/viewcontent.cgi?article=1265&context=faculty_scholarship [Accessed October 28, 2020].

Calabresi, S.G., ed., 2007. *Originalism: A quarter-century of debate.* Washington, DC: Regnery.

Cohen, F.S., 1935. Transcendental nonsense and the functional approach. *Columbia Law Review*, 809–849.

Cohen, L.J., 1962. *The diversity of meaning.* London: Methuen.

Danaher, J., 2015. The normativity of linguistic originalism: A speech act analysis. *Law and Philosophy*, 34(4), 387–431.

Dilthey, W., 1883. *Introduction to the human sciences.* Princeton, NJ: Princeton University Press.

Dworkin, R., 1978. No right answer? *New York University Law Review*, 53(1), 1–32.

Fish, S., 2005. There is no textualism position. *San Diego Law Review*, 42, 1–22.

Foxall, G., 2004. What judges maximize: Toward and economic psychology of the judicial utility function. *Liverpool Law Review*, 25, 177–194.

Green, C., 2009. An intellectual history of judicial activism. *Emory Law Journal*, 58, 1195–1264.

Greenberg, M., & Litman, H., 1998. The meaning of original meaning. *The Georgetown Law Review*, 86, 569–618.

Hohfeld, W.N., 1923. *Fundamental conceptions.* New Haven, CT: Yale University Press.

Holland, K.M., ed., 1991. *Judicial activism in comparative perspective.* London: Macmillan.

Holmes, O.W., 1899. The theory of legal interpretation. *Harvard Law Review*, 12(25), 417–420.

Holmes, O.W., 2005. *The common law.* New York: Lawbook Exchange Clark.

Jefferies, K., 2001. Judicial activism and the necessity of auxiliary precautions. *South Texas Law Review*, 43, 101–119.

Jefferson, T., 1819. Quote by Thomas Jefferson: "I am not an advocate for frequent changes in la . . ." (goodreads.com) [Accessed April 23, 2021].

Karkkainen, B.C., 1994. "Plain meaning": Justice Scalia's jurisprudence of strict statutory construction. *Harvard Journal of Law & Public Pol'y*, 19, 401–477.
Kmiec, K.D., 2004. The origin and current meanings of "judicial activism". *California Law Review*, 92(5), 1441–1477.
Landis, J.L., 1930. A note on "statutory interpretation". *Harvard. Law Review*, 43, 886–893.
Lieber, F., 1839. *Legal and political hermeneutics, or principles of interpretation and construction in law and politics with remarks on precedents and authorities*. Boston: Little, Brown.
Llewellyn, K.N., 1950. Remarks on the theory of appellate decision and the rules or canons. *Vanderbilt Law Review*, 395–401.
Llewellyn, K.N., 1960. *The common law tradition*. Boston: Little Brown.
Manning, J.F., 2005. Textualism and legislative intent. *Virginia Law Review*, 91, 419–450.
Maveety, N., ed., 2005. *The pioneers of judicial behavior*. Ann Arbor: University of Michigan Press.
McGinnis, J.O., & Rappaport, M.B., 2007. Original interpretative principles as the core of orginalism. *In: Northwestern university school of law. Public law and legal theory research paper series. Constitutional commentary*. Original Interpretive Principles as the Core of Originalism, 371–382 [Accessed April 23, 2021].
McGinnis, J.O., & Rappaport, M.B., 2017. The constitution and the language of the law. *Legal Studies Research Paper Series*, 17(262), 1321–1411.
Peegrin, J., 2013. *Introduction to statutory construction – the plain meaning rule*. Introduction to Statutory Construction – The Plain Meaning Rule – Colorado LegiSource. [online] Available from: https://legisource.net/2013/09/12/introduction-to-statutory-construction-the-plain-meaning-rule
Posner, R.A., 1993. *The problem of jurisprudence*. Cambridge, MA: Harvard University Press.
Posner, R.A., 2010. *How judges think*. Cambridge, MA: Harvard University Press.
Posner, R.A., Landes, W.M., & Epstein, L., 2010. *Why (and when) judges dissent: A theoretical and empirical analysis*. Chicago: University of Chicago.
Powell, J.H., 1985. The original understating of original intent. *Harvard Law Review*, 98, 885–948.
Pritchett, C.H., 1968. Public law and judicial behavior. *Journal of Politics*, 30(2), 480–509.
Sawyer, C.H., 2019. *The philosophy of logical behaviorism*. The Philosophy of Logical Behaviorism | Behavioral Inquiry. [online] Available from: https://behavioralinquiry.com/2019/06/17/the-philosophy-of-logical-behaviorism/
Scalia, A., 1997. *A matter of interpretation. Federal courts and the law*. Princeton, NJ: Princeton University Press.
Scalia, A., & Garner, B.A., 2008. *Making your case. The art of persuading judges*. St. Paul, MN: Thomson West.
Schubert, G., 1975. *Human jurisprudence: Public law as political science*. Honolulu: University of Hawai'i Press.
Segal, J.A., & Spaeth, H., 2002. *The supreme court and the attitudinal model revisited*. New York: Cambridge University Press.
Sherry, S., 1998. Judicial independence: Playing politics with the constitution. *Georgia State University Law Review*, 14(4), 795–816.

Smith, P.J., 2011. How different are originalism and non-originalism? How different are originalism and non-originalism? *Hastings Law Journal*, 62, 707–737.

Smyth, D.J., 2017. The original public meaning of amendment in the origination clause versus the patient protection and affordable care act. *British Journal of American Legal Studies*, 6(2), 301–361.

Soeteman, A., 1989. *Logic in law*. The Netherlands: Kluwer Academic Publisher.

Solum, L.B., 2004. *Legal theory lexicon 030: Textualism.* [online] Available from: Legal Theory Lexicon 030: Textualism (typepad.com) [Accessed 23 April 2021].

Solum, L.B., 2008. Semantic originalism. *Illinois Public Law and Legal Theory Research Papers Series*, 7–24, 1–176. https://sreekumarenglishliterature.blogspot.com/2016/12/is-there-text-in-this-class-stanley-fish.html [Accessed October 28, 2020].

Solum, L.B., 2011. *What is originalism? The evolution of contemporary originalist theory. Georgetown University Law Center* (www.georgetown.edu), 1–41 [Accessed April 23, 2021].

Solum, L.B., 2015. The fixation thesis: The role of historical fact in original meaning. *Notre Dame Law Review*, 91(1), 1–78.

Solum, L.B., 2017. Originalist methodology. *University of Chicago Law Review*, 84(1), 269–295.

Solum, L.B., 2020. *Legal theory lexicon 089: Speaker's Meaning and Sentence Meaning*. [online] Available from: https://lsolum.typepad.com/legal_theory_lexicon/ [Accessed April 23, 2021].

Strang, L.J., 2012. Originalism and the Aristotelian tradition: Virtue's home in originalism. *Fordham Law Review*, 80(5), 1997–2040.

Watson, J.B., 1913. Psychology as the behaviorist views it. *Psychological Review*, 20, 158–177.

Watson, J.B., 1925. *Behaviorism*. New York: Norton.

Whittington, K.E., 1999. *Constitutional interpretation. Textual meaning, original intent, and judicial review*. Lawrence: University Press of Kansas.

14 How interdisciplinarity could improve the scientific value of legal studies of international judicial decisions

Marek Jan Wasiński

1 Introduction

This chapter discusses whether, to paraphrase Louis Henkin (1979, p. 47), what is done with decisions of international courts by most scholars of international law – in most academic institutions, most of the time – can be classified as *scientific* effort. Judicial decisions are at the heart of international adjudication as courts pass them to settle disputes, stabilise normative expectations, control public authorities and influence international lawmaking (Bogdandy and Venzke 2013, pp. 52–59). Essentially, all the functions of international adjudication seem reducible to one point, that is providing independent information on the law, which is critical in a decentralised international society (Guzman 2008, pp. 178–182). Every verdict, be it on procedural issues or on merits, is an output of a convoluted, multifarious decision-making practice. Inescapably, the core framework of the process is shaped with choices revolving around determination, interpretation and application of relevant facts and norms (Pound 1923, p. 947). Yet, the practice also entails biases and heuristics as well as a plethora of circumstantial decisions. The former are systematic patterns of deviation from rationality in judgment, making verdicts clearly incorrect when compared with outcomes of rational, unbiased decision. In other words, judgments are sometimes based on certain simplifying problem-solving patterns rather than on more formal and extensive algorithmic processing (Gilovich et al. 2002). An interesting example of international judges favouring parties in particular settings is given by Posner and de Figueiredo (2005). The circumstantial decisions include balancing interests of various actors (of parties, of a court, of a judge) with a recourse to the law's purposes, to internal values as well as to other extralegal factors. The extralegal factors can relate to political constraints and to effectiveness of adjudication, that is a function of success in achieving one or more objectives of a court (Helfer 2013).

Once the decision-making process has concluded and a judicial decision is published, the judgment becomes a subject of experts' reflection, engaging members

DOI: 10.4324/9781003153771-17

of the invisible college of international lawyers. Jennings (1997, p. 413) accurately notes:

> It is safe to say that there is probably no other system of law in which the individual workers and scholars enjoy such telling influence over the shaping of the content of the rules and even of the principles of law. Accordingly, international legal scholars have an influence probably unparalleled since the jurisconsults of classical Roman law.

Although professional commitments of judges, advisors, activists and academics are centred, to varying degrees, on application, promotion, teaching and research of the discipline of international law, the position of academics is significantly distinct inasmuch as it remains attached to the *scientific* paradigm (Koskenniemi 2017, p. 63). Even though, according to Orford (2014, p. 370), the paradigm has been neither static nor well defined, the concept is highly esteemed and its awareness percolates through foundational programmes of international legal research (Oppenheim 1908). In fact, through the contemporary systems of academic promotions, the number of *scientific* research papers often increases the chances of internal promotion more than didactic success (Dobele and Rundle-Theile 2015, p. 421). What is more, the concept seems deeply ingrained in the minds of individual scholars who claim to possess, and are widely considered as having, *une vocation scientifique* (Samuel 2009, p. 435). For example, I once shared my scepticism concerning the scientific value of normative research on international adjudication with a colleague and member of the law faculty. He reproached me with thinly disguised amusement: "Naturally, we [normative researchers] are scientists, as members of the Academia, and science is what we do!" Still, the crafty idea of the administrative act of admission to professorship serving as a rubber stamp that makes every single piece of professorial writing *scientific* stuff (in so far as methodologically accurate) is hardly convincing.

This chapter argues that *scientification* of the dominant normative approach to international law is feasible. The matter is explored by starting with a general overview of the normative jurisprudence that predominates in the research on international adjudication (Section 2). I follow with a presentation of the debate regarding the scientific paradigm in the discipline of international law, and the relevant charge of unscholarliness directed against the mainstream approach (Section 3). The next part briefly sketches key modern research agendas addressing international adjudication from obviously non-normative positions, and asking questions beyond the reach of the mainstream scholarship, thus fending off the charge of unscholarliness (Section 4). While these new trends were snubbed or rejected by orthodox followers of normativism, a part of the normative scholarship actually borrows from the non-mainstream toolbox. Finally, it is posited that expanding normative scholarship, to include interdisciplinary research agendas or methods, allows avoiding the accusation of subjectivism and unscientific practice, thus opening the mainstream approach for new discoveries (Section 5).

2 What is done most of the time?

The international legal scholarship is not epistemologically homogenous. Without pretending to present an exhaustive topology, this scholarship can be roughly split into three separate factions: normative, realist and critical. Each faction explores different research themes, asks different questions, and uses different methods. Generally, the normative approach finds, describes and interprets rules searching for their intelligibility and mutual supportiveness within the legal system (Simma and Paulus 1999). The realist scholarship examines a dynamic structure of international relations made of power and values in order to predict facts (Wiessner and Willard 1999). Critical legal studies explore international law understood as a flux of different interpretations and applications of rules, in this way revealing the impact of legal institutions on individuals and on various social groups (Koskenniemi 1999). This critique differs from the insight provided by mainstream scholars. In short, the former discloses a hidden impact of regulatory agenda on, for instance, low socio-economic status, race and gender, while the latter analytically approaches interpretation or application of a norm in a given way (Stappert 2018, p. 977). Although there are no exact figures, Schlag claims (2009, p. 821) that the normative "black letter" approach continues to flourish in the academic writing on law:

> We still need some treatise writers (say six or seven for each field) who can continue to shelve the cases into the corpus. It's a helpful thing to do. It's helpful to judges and lawyers. A responsible thing to do. I'm glad someone is doing it. But we probably don't need five hundred people in each field doing that.

While concurring with Peters (2017, p. 118), Roberts (2017, pp. 218–221), and Vranken (2012, p. 47), who view the approach as dominating in Europe, I would add that it has completely overtaken the Central European scholarship on international adjudication.

The mainstream normative faction adopts the perspective of an insider in the legal system, being preoccupied with mapping international law and pursuing coherence of various building blocks, that is principles, rules, and institutions (Peters 2017, p. 151). As a result, this approach advances interpretation and critique of judicial decisions, analysed in order to reveal statements on the relevant law – sometimes obviously missing both in the text and in the underlying reasoning. It also ensures its coherence and ascertains the validity of legal claims or accuracy of verdicts with respect to the law itself. According to Samuel (2009, p. 435):

> This approach views law uniquely from its interior, within which the aim is to analyse and to explain in a coherent and logical manner a legal text or court decision and, continuing in this same methodological mode, to guide

> the reader towards future outcomes with respect to the positive law under consideration. One studies law using analysis and synthesis in as strict a manner as the pharmaceutical chemist studies the body.

Therefore, the vast areas of normative research are engulfed in debates on positive law pertinent to issues decided, on its interpretation pursuant to secondary norms, and finally on appropriateness of its application by courts. For example, the European Court of Human Rights was harangued by scholars in the wake of the admissibility decision in *Banković and Others v. Belgium and Others* (Steinorth 2012)[1] for its allegedly too restrictive approach to the Convention's extraterritorial application (Steinorth 2012). Chronically, scholarly writing (especially on individual judgments) replicates, develops, complements, or rebukes arguments presented by parties in their written memorials or oral pleadings. Parts, sentences, or even single words are dissected, studied, and sometimes used out of context to support a preconceived argument (Bianchi 2016, p. 31). The scholarly comments may include recommendations on the law as it should be with resulting glosses advancing authors' views on decided issues – somewhat like the guidance of advice columnists. For instance, McCrudden (2006, p. 634) rightly observes that normative analysis takes the form in which an author argues that "this or that is the 'best' solution to a particular problem, 'best' meaning having the best fit with what already exists". Sporadically, comparative or historical intercalations embellish the insights. However, entire parts of the multifarious decision-making process are usually neglected as irrelevant. As a result, the output of the traditional normative effort oddly resembles argumentative practice before judicial bodies. Unquestionably, scholars are not judges as the former cannot pass binding judgments with their responsibilities limited to researching, teaching and advising (Hernández 2017). However, studies of professional trajectories of judges sitting in international courts reveal academic background of numerous adjudicators (Madsen 2018). Considering these trajectories and the fact that both normative scholars and judges ask virtually the same questions, take the positions of insiders in the system[2] and adopt similar methodologies to find answers, it comes as no surprise that the distinction between scholars and judges becomes blurred in practice. Stappert highlights (2018, p. 978) the scores of academic writings cited in judgments of international criminal courts being authored by current or former employees of these institutions, and warns that this practice leaves room for promoting only selected scholarly interpretations. Likewise, this situation can lead to odd academic discourses in the courtroom. For instance,

1 123 ILR 94.

2 This position was defined by the International Court of Justice as follows: "Law exists, it is said, to serve a social need; but precisely for that reason it can do so only through and within the limits of its own discipline. Otherwise, it is not a legal service that would be rendered", South West Africa Cases (1966), para 49, [1966] ICJ Report.

Lasser (2009, p. 125) presents an example of a scholastic polemic between scholars and the Court of Justice of the European Union asking if:

> [The Court's] entry into this interpretive controversy could have any effect other than to add another voice to the already cacophonous doctrinal chorus [thus blurring] the line between assorted judicial and non-judicial speakers, and thus to reduce judicial pronouncements to simply one more voice or perspective among many.

As a result, articles and edited chapters on decisions of international courts serve other academics, legal advisors, policymakers and judges[3] as databases of arguments and counterarguments handy for other judicial disputes, prompting polemics in law journals, and boosting citation indexes. In sum, the normative writing constitutes a reservoir of expertise potentially guiding future judicial decisions (Werner 2014, p. 62). At the same time, the bulk of the writing confirms Fred Rodell's blunt opinion that "it would be hard to guess, from most of the stuff that is published in the law reviews, that law and the lawyers had any other job on their hands than the slinging together of neat . . . legalistic arguments" (Rodell 1937, p. 42). The argumentative exercise focused on *how to do law* constitutes the linchpin of professional activities for judges or legal advisors, hence this practice inescapably and understandably attracts attention of academics. Yet, if members of the academia do their research emulating practitioners and entirely neglecting questions *about the law*, they face recurring accusation of disregarding the scientific paradigm.

3 Scientific paradigm in the discipline of international law

International law emerged as a separate academic discipline, essentially adopting the normative incarnation, in the second half of the 19th century[4] amid enduring ontological and methodological debates. International lawyers had to prove that the subject of their research constituted something more than positive morality endorsed by sovereign states, and not backed by any sanction. Scott (1905, p. 124) summarises the critique, and reports that international law

> has been variously denounced and praised as international morality or ethics; international courtesy or convention in the social sense of the word; comity as distinguished from the rule of law, or merely and finally as the foreign

3 The International Court of Justice has cited specific works of publicists on a point of law merely seven times in five cases, yet Helmersen (2019) proves that the influence of their work on opinions of individual judges is remarkable. The influence of legal scholarship on judges was discussed generally by Duxbury (2001).

4 According to Neff (2014, p. 304), Henry Wheaton was allegedly prevented by illness to accept an offer of the Harvard Law School to teach international law in the 1840s. The first professorships in the subject were established soon after at the Universities of Turin (1851), Wisconsin (1852), Montreal (1856), Oxford (1859) and Cambridge (1867).

policy, such as the "Monroe Doctrine" which at a particular time happens to catch the fancy of nations.

What is more, international lawyers were also compelled to demonstrate, thus making a common cause with all lawyers,[5] that the dominant normative jurisprudence was more scientific than harnessing draught horses. The charges against the scientific quality of this approach to law have varied to a significant degree throughout the years. However, the pervasive criticism boils down to three fundamental charges targeting the seemingly unscientific subject, research agenda and methods coupled with resulting outcomes.

First, from the Aristotelian perspective, positive law is a social fact, hence it does not belong to the realm of universal, necessary subject matters (Aristotle, Nicomachean Ethics 1139b). Therefore, jurisprudence focused on law, as applied by courts, is nothing more than knowledge of a human-created artefact akin to a sculpture, an engine or an idea. This strand of criticism has persisted through the ages. For example, in the 1840s German jurist and philosopher Julius Hermann von Kirchmann delivered a lecture uncompromisingly titled "The Worthlessness of Jurisprudence as a Science". He put forward three arguments to make a case for excluding jurisprudence from the realm of science: the matter of law is continually changing, the law lives also in feeling and the law rests on human enactment. It is worth emphasising that von Kirchmann stopped short of defining the fundamental notions of science or scientific paradigm, excusing himself by the shortness of time allocated for his lecture (Stammler 1923, pp. 778–779). Yet, the excusal appears far-fetched in so far as he seemingly never presented the missing definition in public. This omission, in turn, can be explained by the highly relative character of the notions of science and of the scientific paradigm. In particular, Becher and Trowler (2001, p. 33) convincingly argue that the paradigm constitutes a set of ideas and techniques, beliefs and values which serve to define a *disciplinary* culture. Similarly, Kuhn (2011) defines the scientific paradigm as a "disciplinary matrix", being the common possession of the practitioners of a professional *discipline*. Unsurprisingly, an embedded conventional paradigm determines inter alia a research agenda of a discipline, that is, questions asked and methodologies to be followed, all with profound consequences for the sociology of science. For example, the problem of international lawyers shaping their arguments and methodology in order to secure validation of their research outputs by the international law community is discussed by d'Aspremont (2016). Similarly, Vick (2004, p. 170) observes that researchers tend to choose between a broad highway for approval-seeking conformists and a definitely less well-worn path of "independent evangelists for truth". Regrettably, the bulk of PhD candidates,

5 Even Austin, the ardent advocate of the view that law of nations constitutes nothing more than a positive morality, maintained (Austin 2001, p. 112) that "the science of positive morality" is as feasible as "the science of positive law" if only "treated by writers in a scientific or systematic manner". Weber (2012) developed similar argument for social science.

who are typically advised by older colleagues to appease reviewers of their dissertations, follows the wide road of normative approach.

Turning to the second thread of the accusations against the scientific quality of the normative approach to law, one needs to refer to logical positivism of the so-called Vienna Circle, a milieu of philosophers and scientists formed in the 1920s in order to investigate scientific language and methodology (Sigmund 2017). They distinguished between empirical questions and questions of meaning, claiming that solely the former relate to scientific problems, as tautologies are the only possible answers to the latter. Therefore, if a research question is framed in a normative way – for example, in terms of "correctness" or "appropriateness" of a judicial determination, interpretation and application of a norm to established facts – then the normative jurisprudence on international adjudication boils down to a scientifically meaningless enterprise. Alf Ross, the most prominent scholar among the Scandinavian legal realists (Roucounas 2019, p. 163; Eliasz and Jakubiec 2016), theorised on international law based on a scientific approach explaining how the empirical method makes prediction of judicial decisions feasible:

> If . . . prediction is possible, it must be because the mental process by which the judge decides to base his decision on one rule rather than another is not a capricious and arbitrary matter, varying from one judge to another, but a process determined by attitudes and concepts, a common normative ideology, present and active in the minds of judges when they act in their capacity as judges. It is true that we cannot observe directly what takes place in the mind of the judge, but it is possible to construct hypotheses concerning it, and their value can be tested simply by observing whether predictions based on them have come true.
>
> (Ross 1959, p. 75)

Ross expressed *der Geist* of the Vienna Circle, which persevered and rejuvenated in the empirical turn in international legal research, brought up here briefly in Section 4.

Finally, it is said that science entails unbiased observations, systemic experimentation and falsifiable theories (Popper 2002, pp. 17–20). Therefore, a scientific method should produce intra-subjective knowledge with universal validity in order to secure uniformity of the output irrespective of who applies the method. This requirement of universality has particular importance for jurisprudence even if one assumes that international law can be reduced to argumentative practice, which exploits the intrinsic epistemological and ontological uncertainty of this legal system. The former boils down to inherent limits as to how one perceives law. This means that the perimeters of knowledge are delineated by questions which cannot be answered with absolute certainty. For example: How are the applicable rules identified? How can the content of said rules be determined in the process of interpretation? On the other hand, the ontological indeterminacy relates to ambiguity ensuing from the said epistemic limits, which constitute a major impediment in understanding what happens to international law when its norms are indeterminate (Kammerhofer 2010, pp. 3–4). Weil points out (1983, p. 414) that the system of international law contains more and more norms so vague and nebulous in substance that mutual rights and obligations "all but elude the mind". The system goes to extremes with Articles 31–32 of the Vienna Convention on the Law of Treaties (VCLT), adopted to facilitate interpretation of international agreements but which instead dissected in practice and gave rise to endless polemics about the meaning of a single word. This means there is no one correct answer to a problem regarding the interpretation of a norm but rather an assortment of results admissible under certain methodological presumptions adopted by the epistemic community, which is dominant within the invisible college of international lawyers. It is not uncommon that criminal lawyers, human rights lawyers, and international lawyers have different perceptions of the same issue (Clapham 2011). Students of international law would find it also puzzling that practice of the International Court of Justice regarding determination of customary international law not only falls short of canonical schemes taught during courses in their law schools, but also varies depending on the case decided. Against this backdrop, if normative researches take the form of argumentative practice (for example: "this court should have interpreted this norm as requiring X, not Y – because Article 31 VCLT should have been read as meaning A, not B"), normative scholars exploit the imminent uncertainty of the system *doing law* in the same way as do judges and legal advisors. Consequently, this part of normative scholarship neither describes nor explains reality, but instead contributes to the growth of ambiguity of a researched problem.

There are attempts to rebut the presented charges. First, it is argued that these are led from the positions or are inspired by the achievements of natural sciences, thus ignoring fundamentally different, specific objects and cognitive methods of social sciences (Creager et al. 2007, pp. 1–4). For instance, Koskenniemi maintains (2012, p. 19) that law in action is inherently nothing more than argumentative practice that must be perceived in specific contexts characterised by adversity. The key point of legal practice is to prevail over those holding an opposite view. As a result, the criticism overestimates alleged universality of the so-called scientific paradigm, which was forged initially for physics and astronomy. In particular, Jellinek rebuts the charge, asserting (1905, p. 20) that law has legal power and definite calculable effects, thus becoming a fully-fledged object of science. Finally, it is posited that the accusations entirely overlook the dialectic between episteme, doxa and techne, thus allowing strict juxtaposition of the concepts, which is not necessarily the case (Bianchi 2019, pp. 256–257).

Nevertheless, even if the charges are kept at bay by deconstructing and relativising the notion of scientific paradigm, there still persists a perplexing, overarching question which should be asked at the outset of every *scientific* endeavour: What is the justification for a *scientific* research, a paper, a chapter, or a symposium on international adjudication? That question was astutely answered by Wolfrum (2010, p. 225), who said that "the only justification . . . for doing research . . . is curiosity". Indeed, curiosity along with veracity and imagination are key virtues of every scientific enterprise, if only one accepts that cognition is the principal aim of science (Pennock 2019, p. 26). However, curiosity is present neither in the normative argumentative practice if it strives solely for persuasion, and obstinately seeks for reason; nor in the efforts aimed at finding coherence between judicial pronouncements within the normative framework. In this last regard, Schlag observes (2019, p. 732) that normative researchers have a tendency to serve as guardians of non-existent coherence and reasonableness of the legal system:

> Academics will too often reach for reason and presume that in law, reason rules. That is perhaps a bit more mysterious – because after all, legal academics are not judges. What is more, legal academics have the breadth of perspective to know better – to appreciate that law is not *simply* the unfolding of "singing reason".

Yet, there have been several attempts to indulge pure curiosity, and hence to strengthen the scientific core of the legal jurisprudence.

4 Towards curiosity

The history of various scholarly approaches to international law can be viewed neither as a history of revolution nor as displacement of passé by en vogue (d'Aspremont and Singh 2019, p. 19). It is also not a history of transformation or accumulation, as scholars are often unaware of or even despise paradigms alien to their epistemic community. Hence, this history should be seen as a sequence of localised turns with a potential to provoke new forms of reflection on international law.

There have been several major paradigm shifts in international law throughout the ages: secularisation of natural law (Le Fur 1927); a move from natural law to positivism (Ago 1957); a *chique* of studying law the Kelsenian way, that is more *geometrico* (Roucounas 2019, pp. 87–91); a shift towards political economy in international legal studies (Posner and Sykes 2013); and, more recently, an interest in behavioural (Broude 2015), psychological (van Aaken and Broude 2019), linguistic (Mowbray 2012), empirical (Shaffer and Ginsburg 2012; Holtermann and Madsen 2015) and even mathematical (McDermott and Aitken 2017) or anthropological (Fraser and Leyh 2020) approaches to research, to name only the most prominent trends. An orthodox normative scholar would be probably horrified and disgusted by the very idea of studying international law through the perspective of emotions (Popovski 2016). It seems plausible – as clear authority seems to be missing – that at least some of the new approaches were conceived out of curiosity spurred by dilemmas that could not be researched, described, diagnosed, or even conceptualised with the use of the normative method apparatus.

Considering the scope of the present volume, one needs to highlight the proliferation of contemporary scholarship exploring the impact of language on human expressions associated with international law, and mapped by Roucounas (2019, pp. 29–36). This strand of reflection is diverse and covers theoretical, critical, and genuinely interdisciplinary research. For instance, Allot (1971) takes up methodology discussing the relationship between the language of international law and methods applied to study the system. d'Aspremont (2012) touches upon the problem of normative scholarship by arguing that words are used as weapons in competition for "persuasiveness and semantic authority". Koskenniemi (2009) bridges a gap between international law and international relations by tracing the politics behind the vocabulary of transboundary governance. Tzouvala (2020, p. 167) combines law, economy and language, critically arguing that there are phrases and argumentative patterns in the vocabulary of international legal argumentation which are aimed at disciplining States "along the lines of capitalist modernity". Finally, de Carvalho (2011) and Bianchi (2013) deal with the impact of language on international adjudication. The former discusses decisions of the WTO Appellate Body applying semantics and semiotics. The latter analyses the rhetorical structure of the International Court of Justice's case law, positing that the Court adjusts rhetorically persuasive arguments in order to ensure influence on future practice of States.

The part of international legal scholarship receptive of interdisciplinary research techniques avoids the fundamental critique aimed at the allegedly unscientific subject, research agenda and methods of the discipline. It operates with the law perceived not only as a human artefact but also as a psychological, social, cultural and linguistic phenomenon. As the interdisciplinary turn coincided with the proliferation of international adjudication in the 20th century, it quite naturally set foot in the new territories of legal research. Therefore, the new agendas allow for causal explanation and prediction through the formulating of diverse theories regarding international adjudication. They explore problems concerning compliance with judicial decisions; effectiveness of international adjudication, independence, and political constraints faced by international courts; cross-pollination between domestic and international adjudicative bodies; language as an instrument of rhetoric; and judicial behaviour or why judges make their choices (Romano et al. 2013). Finally, the agendas advance an inductive treatment of international adjudication with a potential to produce synthetic theories amounting to new discoveries. When the propositions are no longer merely speculative, their underlying assumptions may allow falsification, adding to intra-subjective and universal knowledge.

5 On the want and the feasibility of the *scientific* normative jurisprudence

There is a hiatus separating the mainstream normative jurisprudence from the recent "law & (psychology, linguistic, etc.)" approaches (Klabbers 2018, p. 1068). At least three factors have added to the width of the chasm.

The most fundamental cause of the rupture rests on a belief,[6] adopted by the normative scholars, that there is nothing left for the academic research beyond the limits of the normative method (Koskenniemi 2012, p. 19). In this way, they are like Nietzschean spiders sitting within their net, catching nothing at all except that which allows itself to be caught precisely in the net. Further, even if the cognitive obstacle is removed, numerous academics (mainly from Central European institutions) permanently ignore the distinction between theoretical inquiry and legal practice, thus committing themselves to the recognition of normative scholarship as a supplementary source of law (Kahn 1999, p. 18). Their position is seemingly fortified by Article 38.1.d of the Statute of the International Court of Justice, which stipulates that the teachings of the most highly qualified publicists of the various nations constitute a subsidiary means for the determination of rules of law. In this way, the doctrine and the case law become conflated into a single source, providing seemingly independent information on the law. Consequently, if the principal aim of legal normative jurisprudence is cognition of law, there is no need to perceive and to understand international adjudication as a convoluted and multifarious decision-making practice. Such efforts are doomed to be belittled as unnecessary, à la mode holism, admixture, and willy-nilly (Kammerhofer 2013, p. 366). Vick observes (2004, p. 164) that many normative scholars regard interdisciplinary research as amateurish dabbling with theories and methods that the researchers do not fully understand. Besides, the aversion is reciprocal, as interdisciplinarians perceive normative scholars to be intellectually rigid and inflexible. Finally, there remains a barrier of opportunism, frequently disguised as utilitarianism. In particular, academic enterprises embracing the "law and" approach are being disparaged by normative scholars as unrealistic and for ignoring the needs of students and legal practitioners, who want to know how to do law (i.e. *what* the content of the norm is) and not about the law (*why* the norm is so interpreted, applied, etc.). However, some embarrassing reasons may be hidden behind the explanation. For example, limited knowledge of interdisciplinary research, the urge to stay within the limits of the intellectual comfort zone, and the need to appease gatekeepers of academic recognition, including peer-reviewers serving for "old, good" law journals (Becher and Trowler 2001, pp. 75–103). Consequently, the traditional, calcified argumentative normative approach to international adjudication remains entrenched.

Nonetheless, bridging the chasm between the normative stance and other approaches is still feasible, even if the former is doomed to be principally focused on providing independent information on law, and hence it must remain invariably centred on norms as determined, interpreted and applied by international courts. Holtermann and Madsen present a taxonomy consisting of ideal types of relationship between law and empirical studies, arguing, inter alia, that synthesis between

6 On the role of belief in the study, and in the practice of international law, see d'Aspremont (2017, p, 73). The impact of framing on knowledge production processes is discussed by van Aaken and Elm (forthcoming).

normative and empirical studies of law is possible and, in some instances, necessary to guarantee a comprehensive understanding of law. The synthesis stands for "mutual recognition of and simultaneous engagement in both doctrinal legal science and variations of empirical studies of law" (Holtermann and Madsen 2016, p. 1008) and materialises, for instance, in the work of Weiler and Koskenniemi, who address international law as expression of historical and political processes (Weiler 1997; Koskenniemi 2001). Moreover, a faction of normative researchers began to develop an awareness of the structural, rational and linguistic indeterminacy of international law (Miles 2019). In particular, the linguistic indeterminacy implies the perception of norms as, to borrow from quantum physics terminology, amplitudes of probability. It means that a norm should not be perceived as carrying a single possible disposition, fixed yet unseen, until finally detected and revealed by a lawyer equipped with the most subtle device for application of logical syllogism. To the contrary, when a decision of an international court determines, interprets and applies the norm, parameters of the norm's disposition are set in a given case only. Irrespective of the flaws (sometimes quite deep) in judicial reasoning, the parameters lay inexorably within the amplitude of probability, hence it is epistemologically meaningless to discuss whether the judgment was "correct" or "incorrect". Therefore, the normative research on international adjudication should explain causes and effects of determination, interpretation and application of a norm in a given case, or in the case law of a court. To illustrate the point: if the issue of damages before the European Court of Human Rights is examined, scientific normative research moves beyond affirmative or critical comments, instead amplifying topology of judgments and explaining why judges chose certain remedies (Fikfak 2019). To this end, a theory is needed to reduce the complexity of observations and to model relevant processes both preceding and succeeding the verdict of the Court (e.g. Yildiz 2020). In general, such theories explain how and why a norm "behaves" in a given way in the environment of a particular court: how and why it is so determined, interpreted, applied and used by all relevant stakeholders.

6 Conclusion

This chapter offers a critical consideration of the normative approach to analysing decisions of international courts and of the expansion of legal research to include diverse approaches and methodologies that can advance our current understanding of international adjudication. This chapter does not announce proscriptions on traditional critical comments regarding individual judicial decisions, or on efforts presenting rational and coherent systematisation of the case law, thus making the indigestible digestible. It would be unrealistic and unwise to ignore the needs of students and legal practitioners. Yet, reflection on international adjudication borrowing from the "law and" toolbox opens the legal normative research to the new and much-awaited scientific discoveries. Such an approach has the potential to facilitate successfully tackling some perplexing dilemmas as, for instance, how international courts interpret norms of customary international law although relevant secondary norms are lacking. Furthermore, it would positively influence didactic activities of academics, increasing the predilection of new generations of researchers of international law to find intellectual inspiration in concepts taken from outside of the normative field.

References

Aaken Van, A., & Broude, T., 2019. The psychology of international law: An introduction. *European Journal of International Law*, 30(4), 1225–1236.

Aaken Van, A., & Elm, J-P. forthcoming. Framing in and through international law. *In:* A. Bianchi & M. Hirsch, eds., *International law's invisible frames – Social cognition and knowledge production in international legal processes.* Oxford: Oxford University Press. [online] Available from: https://papers.ssrn.com/sol3/papers.cfm?abstract_id=3678551.

Ago, R., 1957. Droit positif et droit international. *Annuaire Français de Droit International*, 3, 14–62.

Allott, P., 1971. Language, method and the nature of international law. *British Yearbook of International Law*, 45, 79–135.

Aristotle. *Nicomachean ethics.* H. Rackham, trans. [online] Available from: www.perseus.tufts.edu/.

Austin, J., 2001. *The province of jurisprudence determined.* Cambridge: Cambridge University Press.

Becher, T., & Trowler, P.R., 2001. *Academic tribes and territories.* Buckingham: Society for Research into Higher Education and Open University Press.

Bianchi, A., 2013. Gazing at the crystal ball (again): State immunity and *jus cogens* beyond *Germany v. Italy. Journal of International Dispute Settlement*, 4(3), 457–475.

Bianchi, A., 2016. *International law theories: An inquiry into different ways of thinking.* Oxford: Oxford University Press.

Bianchi, A., 2019. Epistemic communities. *In:* J. d'Aspremont & S. Singh, eds., *Concepts for international law. Contributions to disciplinary thought.* Cheltenham: Elgar, 251–266.

Bogdandy Von, A. and Venzke, I., 2013. On the functions of international courts: An appraisal in light of their burgeoning public authority. *Leiden Journal of International Law*, 26(1), 49–72.

Broude, T., 2015. Behavioral international law. *University of Pennsylvania Law Review*, 163, 1099–1157.

Clapham, A., 2011. Concluding remarks – three tribes in the future of international criminal law. *Journal of International Criminal Justice*, 9(3), 689–695.

Creager, A.N.H., Lunbeck, E., & Wise, M.N., 2007. Introduction. *In:* A.N.H. Creager et al., eds., *Science without laws: Model systems, cases, exemplary narratives.* Durham, NC: Duke University Press, 1–22.

d'Aspremont, J., 2012. Wording in international law. *Leiden Journal of International Law*, 25(3), 575–602.

d'Aspremont, J., 2016. *Epistemic forces in international law. Foundational doctrines and techniques of international legal argumentation.* Cheltenham: Elgar.

d'Aspremont, J., 2017. *International law as a belief system.* Cambridge: Cambridge University Press.

d'Aspremont, J., & Singh, S., 2019. Introduction. The life of international law and its concepts. *In:* J. d'Aspremont & S. Singh, eds., *Concepts for international law. Contributions to disciplinary thought*. Cheltenham: Elgar, 1–24.
De Carvalho, E.M., 2011. *Semiotics of international law. Trade and translation*. Dordrecht: Springer.
De S.-O.-L'E. Lasser, M., 2009. *Judicial deliberations: A comparative analysis of transparency and legitimacy*. Oxford: Oxford University Press.
Dobele, A.R., & Rundle-Theile, S., 2015. Progression through academic ranks: A longitudinal examination of internal promotion drivers. *Higher Education Quarterly*, 69(4), 410–429.
Duxbury, N., 2001. *Jurists and judges. An essay on influence*. Oxford: Hart.
Eliasz, K., & Jakubiec, M., 2016. The Vienna circle and the Uppsala school as philosophical inspirations for the Scandinavian legal realism. *Semina Scientarum*, 15, 107–123.
Fikfak, V., 2019. Changing state behaviour: Damages before the European Court of Human Rights. *European Journal of International Law*, 29(4), 1091–1125.
Fraser, J., & Leyh, B., eds., 2020. *Intersections of law and culture at the international criminal court*. Cheltenham: Elgar.
Gilovich, T., Griffin, D., & Kahneman, D., eds., 2002. *Heuristics and biases. The psychology of intuitive judgment*. Cambridge: Cambridge University Press.
Guzman, A.T., 2008. International tribunals: A rational choice analysis. *University of Pennsylvania Law Review*, 157(1), 171–235.
Helfer, L.R., 2013. The effectiveness of international adjudicators, *In:* C.P. Romano et al., eds., *The Oxford handbook of international judication*, Oxford: Oxford University Press, 484–502.
Helmersen, S.T., 2019. Finding "the most highly qualified publicists": Lessons from the International Court of Justice. *European Journal of International Law*, 30(2), 509–535.
Henkin, L., 1979. *How nations behave: Law and foreign policy*. New York: Columbia University Press.
Hernández, G., 2017. The responsibility of the international legal academic. *In:* J. d'Aspremont et al., eds., *International law as a profession*. Cambridge: Cambridge University Press, 160–188.
Holtermann, J., & Madsen, M., 2015. European new legal realism and international law: How to make international law intelligible. *Leiden Journal of International Law*, 28(2), 211–230.
Holtermann, J., & Madsen, M., 2016. Toleration, synthesis or replacement? The "empirical turn" and its consequences for the science of international law. *Leiden Journal of International Law*, 29(4), 1001–1019.
Jellinek, G., 1905. *Allgemeine Staatslehre*. Berlin: Häring.
Jennings, R., 1997. International lawyers and the progressive development of international law. *In:* J. Makarczyk, ed., *Theory of international law at the threshold of the 21st century: Essays in honour of Krzysztof Skubiszewski*. Leiden: Martinus Nijhoff.
Kahn, P.W., 1999. *The cultural study of law. Reconstructing legal scholarship*. Chicago: University of Chicago Press.
Kammerhofer, J., 2010. *Uncertainty in international law. A Kelsenian perspective*. London: Routledge.
Kammerhofer, J., 2013. The pure theory of law and its "modern" positivism: International legal uses for scholarship. *Proceedings of the ASIL Annual Meeting*, 106, 365–367.

Klabbers, J., 2018. On epistemic universalism and the melancholy of international law. *European Journal of International Law*, 29(4), 1057–1069.

Koskenniemi, M., 1999. Letter to the editors of the symposium. *The American Journal of International Law*, 93(2), 351–361.

Koskenniemi, M., 2001. *The gentle civilizer of nations: The rise and fall of international law 1870–1960.* Cambridge: Cambridge University Press.

Koskenniemi, M., 2009. Miserable comforters: International relations as new natural law. *European Journal of International Relations*, 15(3), 395–442.

Koskenniemi, M., 2012. Law, teleology and international relations: An essay in counterdisciplinarity. *International Relations*, 26(1), 3–34.

Koskenniemi, M., 2017. Between commitment and cynicism: Outline for a theory of international law as practice. *In:* J. D'Aspremont, T. Gazzini, A. Nollkaemper, & W. Werner, eds., *International Law as a Profession*. Cambridge: Cambridge University Press, 38–66. doi:10.1017/9781316492802.004

Kuhn, T.S., 2011. *The essential tension. Selected studies in scientific tradition and change*. Chicago: University of Chicago Press.

Le Fur, L., 1927. La Théorie du droit naturel depuis le XVIIe siècle et la doctrine moderne. *Académie de droit international. Recueil des cours*, 18(III).

Madsen, M.R., 2018. Who rules the world? The educational capital of the international judiciary. *UC Irvine Journal of International, Transnational, and Comparative Law*, 3, 97–118.

Mc Crudden, M., 2006. Legal research and the social sciences. *Law Quarterly Review*, 1(22), 632–650.

Mc Dermott, Y., & Aitken, C., 2017. Analysis of evidence in international criminal trials using Bayesian belief networks. *Law, Probability & Risk*, 16(2–3), 111–129.

Miles, C., 2019. Indeterminacy. *In:* J. d'Aspremont & S. Singh, eds., *Concepts for international law. Contributions to disciplinary thought.* Cheltenham: Elgar, 447–458.

Mowbray, J., 2012. *Linguistic justice: International law and language policy*. Oxford: Oxford University Press.

Neff, S.C., 2014. *Justice among nations. A history of international law*. Cambridge, MA: Harvard University Press.

Oppenheim, L., 1908. The science of international law: Its task and method. *American Journal of International Law*, 2(2), 313–356.

Orford, A., 2014. Scientific reason and the discipline of international law. *European Journal of International Law*, 25(2), 369–385.

Pennock, R.T., 2019. *An instinct for truth. Curiosity and the moral character of science*. Cambridge, MA: The MIT Press.

Peters, A., 2017. International legal scholarship under challenge. *In:* J. D'Aspremont, T. Gazzini, A. Nollkaemper, & W. Werner, eds., *International Law as a Profession*. Cambridge: Cambridge University Press, 117–159. doi:10.1017/9781316492802.007

Popovski, V., 2016. Emotions and international law. *In:* Y. Ariffin et al., eds., *Emotions in international politics. Beyond mainstream international relations.* Cambridge: Cambridge University Press, 184–204.

Popper, K., 2002. *The logic of scientific discovery*. London: Routledge.

Posner, E.A. and De Figueiredo, M.F.P., 2005. Is the International Court of Justice biased? *Journal of Legal Studies*, 34(2), 599–630.

Posner, E.A. and Sykes, A.O., 2013. *Economic foundations of international law*. Cambridge, MA: Harvard University Press.

Pound, R., 1923. The theory of judicial decision. III. A theory of judicial decision for today. *Harvard Law Review*, 36(8), 940–959.
Roberts, A., 2017. *Is international law international?* Oxford: Oxford University Press.
Rodell, F., 1937. Goodbye to law reviews. *Virginia Law Review*, 23, 38–45.
Romano, C.P.R., et al. eds., 2013. *The Oxford handbook of international adjudication*. Oxford: Oxford University Press.
Ross, A., 1959. *On law and justice*. Berkeley: University of California Press.
Roucounas, E., 2019. *A landscape of contemporary theories of international law*. Leiden: Brill Nijhoff.
Samuel, G., 2009. Interdisciplinarity and the authority paradigm: Should law be taken seriously by scientists and social scientists? *Journal of Law and Society*, 36(4), 431–459.
Schlag, P.R., 2009. Spam jurisprudence, air law, and the rank anxiety of nothing happening (a report on the state of the art). *The Georgetown Law Journal*, 97, 803–835.
Schlag, P.R., 2019. Reason. *In:* J. d'Aspremont & S. Singh, eds., *Concepts for international law. Contributions to disciplinary thought*. Cheltenham: Elgar, 730–739.
Scott, J.B., 1905. The legal nature of international law. *Columbia Law Review*, 5(2), 124–152.
Shaffer, G., & Ginsburg, T., 2012. The empirical turn in international legal scholarship. *American Journal of International Law*, 106(1), 1–46.
Sigmund, K., 2017. *The exact thinking in demented times*. New York: Basic Books.
Simma, B., & Paulus, A.L., 1999. The responsibility of individuals for human rights abuses in internal conflicts: A positivist view. *American Journal of International Law*, 93(2), 302–316.
Stammler, R., 1923. Fundamental tendencies in modern jurisprudence (Continued). *Michigan Law Review*, 21(7), 765–785.
Stappert, N., 2018. A new influence of legal scholars? The use of academic writings at international criminal courts and tribunals. *Leiden Journal of International Law*, 31(4), 963–980.
Steinorth, C., 2012. Banković case. *In:* R. Wolfrum, ed., *Max Planck encyclopedia of public international law*. [online] Available from: https://opil.ouplaw.com/home/mpil.
Tzouvala, N., 2020. *Capitalism as civilisation: A history of international law*. Cambridge: Cambridge University Press.
Vick, D.W., 2004. Interdisciplinarity and the discipline of law. *Journal of Law and Society*, 31(2), 163–193.
Vranken, J., 2012. Exciting times for legal scholarship. *Recht en Methode in onderzoek en onderwijs*, 2(2), 42–62.
Weber, M., 2012. The "objectivity" of knowledge in social science and social policy. *In:* H.H. Bruun & S. Whimster, eds., *Max Weber. Collected methodological writings*. London: Taylor & Francis Group, 100–138.
Weil, P., 1983. Towards relative normativity in international law? *American Journal of International Law*, 77(3), 413–442.
Weiler, J., 1997. The reformation of European constitutionalism. *Journal of Common Market Studies*, 35(1), 97–131.
Werner, W.G., 2014. The politics of expertise: Applying paradoxes of scientific expertise to international law. *In:* M. Ambrus et al., eds., *The role of "experts" in international and European decision-making processes: Advisors, decision makers or irrelevant actors?* Cambridge: Cambridge University Press, 44–62.

Wiessner, S., & Willard, A.R., 1999. Policy-oriented jurisprudence and human rights abuses in internal conflict: Toward a world public order of human dignity. *American Journal of International Law*, 93(2), 316–334.
Wolfrum, R., 2010. Concluding remarks. *In:* R. Wolfrum & C. Kojima, eds., *Solidarity: A structural principle of international law*. Heidelberg: Springer, 225–228.
Yildiz, E., 2020. A court with many faces: Judicial characters and modes of norm development in the European Court of Human Rights. *European Journal of International Justice*, 31(1), 73–99.

Part IV

Clarity in judicial discourse

15 Conveying the right message

Principles and problems of multilingual communication at the European Court of Human Rights

James Brannan[1]

1 Introduction

The message conveyed by an international court such as the European Court of Human Rights (hereinafter the Court or ECtHR) in Strasbourg should be accessible to all citizens of the States within its jurisdiction. The accessibility and foreseeability of domestic case law is one of the principles that this Court itself requires of States, for the sake of legal certainty, yet its own judgments have sometimes been criticised for lacking those qualities. Since 1959 it has developed a body of case law securing rights under the European Convention on Human Rights (hereinafter the Convention) to citizens and residents of the 47 Member States of the Council of Europe. However, it delivers its judgments only in English and/or in French, whereas the number of national languages across those States can be estimated at nearly 40, thus hindering effective communication of that case law. In that sense it cannot be described as a truly "multilingual" institution (Weston 2005, p. 448), unlike the European Court of Justice (ECJ) in particular.

Before assessing whether the Court's message is nevertheless conveyed effectively, consideration should be given to the audience: who actually reads its case law? Gerards (2017, pp. 267–268) admits that "the audience of the Court's judgments is rather difficult to establish". She lists the following readers: the parties to a given case (both the applicant and the respondent Government); national authorities (including those of other States); and domestic courts. The judges who have to apply Convention law in their respective jurisdictions can certainly be regarded as primary addressees of the Court's case law. However, certain judgments may not always be easy to interpret or apply, on account not only of the language barrier but also of a style which is sometimes perceived as "foreign".[2] Those two aspects will be examined in turn, from both negative and

1 All opinions in this chapter are those of the author.

2 This point is made by Kjær (2011, p. 328), who comments that Scandinavian judges face the double challenge of "comprehending the foreign languages in which the judgments of the European Court of Human Rights are phrased, and understanding the alien line of thinking developing in the case law of the Court".

DOI: 10.4324/9781003153771-19

positive standpoints. As to whether the general message (not necessarily the legal intricacies of a judgment) is accessible more broadly to citizens, this is achieved through various media. While whole judgments (many of which are lengthy) will no doubt be read more by the lawyer than the layperson,[3] there are other formats through which the case law, or at least the key principles, can be conveyed. Thus this contribution will begin with an overview of the Court's "production", which may be monolingual, bilingual or multilingual.

2 Forms of case law dissemination

The adjudicatory texts of the ECtHR fall into a number of categories. A *judgment* is delivered by the Grand Chamber[4] (of 17 judges), a Chamber (of seven) or a Committee (of three), while a *decision* (mainly on admissibility) may emanate from a Chamber (more rarely from the Grand Chamber), a committee or a single judge.[5] Advisory opinions are dealt with by the Grand Chamber. Judgments and advisory opinions, but not decisions, may be accompanied by the separate opinion (dissenting or concurring) of one or more judges. All these texts, except for single-judge decisions and certain committee decisions, are available on line via the Court's HUDOC database.[6] This facility dates back to the late 1990s and has constantly been developed with the aim of becoming more user-friendly (one aspect being the search refiners or filters). The interface is now available in English, French, Georgian, Russian, Spanish, Turkish and Ukrainian. HUDOC has today become the primary means of disseminating the Court's case law.

Older case law can also be found in printed official reports, but these were discontinued with effect from January 2016; the Rules of Court have been amended accordingly.[7] In spite of their "prestige" value, it was not considered worthwhile to maintain this form of publication, which had become increasingly irrelevant to the public in the digital age. This development has had repercussions for the volume of compulsory translation, as there is no longer any strict obligation to translate Chamber judgments and decisions into the other official language post-delivery. Such translation is nevertheless completed where they are listed

3 Peruzzo (2019, p. 60) comments that in spite of certain strategies to facilitate the understanding of "alien" elements, "the resulting texts could hardly be considered comprehensible for the non-legally educated"; but this is a generalisation and arguably does not apply to all judgments (besides, the "facts" part should always be easier to follow).

4 Abbreviated "[GC]" in citations; the Grand Chamber hears cases referred to it by a party after a Chamber judgment or where jurisdiction is relinquished by a Chamber (because the case raises a serious question affecting the interpretation of the Convention or there is a risk of inconsistency with a previous judgment).

5 A useful simplified diagram can be found on the Court's website see https://echr.coe.int/Documents/Case_processing_Court_ENG.pdf (Accessed January 31, 2021); also reproduced in Peruzzo (2019, p. 24).

6 Now provided for specifically by Rule 104A, the HUDOC database is available free of charge through the Court's website (http://hudoc.echr.coe.int).

7 In particular, the former Rule 78 has been deleted.

as "key cases" (Rule 104B), and in a small number of other cases, time permitting. However, it is now an obligation to deliver Grand Chamber judgments and decisions (Rule 76) and Advisory Opinions (Rule 88 § 1B and Rule 94 § 7B) in both languages, whereas this practice had not previously been provided for in the Rules. Thus the category Key Case (no longer Case Reports) in HUDOC is now used to flag the most important judgments and decisions that are selected every quarter (after delivery) by the Court's Bureau upon the recommendation of the Jurisconsult.[8]

The Court produces a series of other documents with the aim of making its case law more accessible,[9] one being the bilingual Case-Law Information Note (CLIN), mainly aimed at lawyers: a monthly round-up of case law (legal summaries), news and publications. Cases of particular legal interest are flagged, by the Jurisconsult's department or drafting lawyers, as they are being finalised. The note focuses on the key legal issues, with a few lines on the facts, omitting aspects of the judgment that are less significant or where there is already established case law. The CLIN has the added advantage of being available (ultimately) in both official languages (i.e. even if the judgment itself is in only one). It is provided in various electronic formats, no longer being disseminated as a hard copy.

A broader range of cases are earmarked for inclusion in press releases.[10] The Court uses this medium to announce forthcoming judgments with summaries of the facts; then the more significant cases will give rise to separate press releases, incorporating a summary of the Court's reasoning, on the day of delivery. Even inadmissibility decisions may be worthy of selection, in part to dissuade would-be applicants from bringing unmeritorious cases. As press releases are intended for the public, more factual details are given than in the CLIN and the findings are presented in a more straightforward and simplified manner. The selection may depend on the media interest of a given case, unlike the strict criterion of legal interest for the CLIN. Thus a separate press release will be issued for a political or high-profile case, such as *Berlusconi v. Italy*[11] or *Von Hannover (no. 2) v. Germany*.[12] Of course the public interest will depend on the country concerned, and it is thus unfortunate that press releases are mostly confined to the two official languages.

8 The list of key cases is published on the Court's website with links (27 cases were so designated in 2019).
9 An overview of case law information and outreach is given in the Annual Report, of which the relevant extract is published under the title "Bringing the Convention home"; see https://echr.coe.int/Documents/Case_law_info_training_outreach_2019_ENG.pdf (Accessed January 31, 2021).
10 For an overview of the Court's Press Unit, see Titiun (2015).
11 Grand Chamber strike-out decision of 2018 with no particular legal interest.
12 Grand Chamber judgment of 2012 cited by Titiun (2015, p. 132) as an example of media interest (a German version of the press release was also exceptionally issued on this occasion).

Multilingual Factsheets and Case-law Guides (produced by the press unit and the research department, respectively) are aimed at lawyers and laypersons alike. The constantly updated guides, on each Convention Article, may be particularly useful for applicants and their legal representatives in preparing an application before the Court (see Villiger 2019, pp. 457, 461) and also for students of law. The Court uses Twitter to announce the delivery of judgments and decisions, usually coinciding with a separate press release. Webcasts of hearings ensure greater visibility. Its website also contains a large number of information documents with translations into various languages. By way of example, a simplified version of the Convention is available in 33 languages[13] and "The European Convention on Human Rights – A Living Instrument" was published to mark its 70th anniversary, while the "Applicants' pages" can be accessed in 36 languages.

3 The language barrier

English and French have remained the Court's sole official and working languages since 1959. In principle, Chambers and the Grand Chamber conduct bilingual deliberations on the basis of a draft which itself will only be in both languages before the latter (with a few rare exceptions of bilingual processing in a Chamber). Whereas the English version of judgments at the ECJ in Luxembourg will be a translation from the French, most Strasbourg judgments are now drafted in English. Prior to the merger in 1998 of the Court with the European Commission of Human Rights, all judgments were published in both of the official languages, but for the past 20 years or so the vast majority have been monolingual. As mentioned above, a change in policy has further reduced the volume of systematic translations from one official language to the other (except in "key cases"); Cohen (2016, p. 505) thus comments that "the ECtHR's crushing docket has led to rationing bilingualism".

The Court's publication policy has been criticised over the years for its linguistic limitations. In 1998 it was suggested that judgments should be translated into the language of the country concerned, or that Russian should be added as an official language, but no such changes came about (Brannan 2018b, p. 4), mainly for economic reasons. In a work dealing with the Danish perspective, Garre (1999, pp. 38–39) makes a comment that could still apply to the situation in most Member States:

> Thirty years of practice has resulted in a large number of decisions, judgments and statements all of which are relevant to Denmark and must be taken into account when considering and applying the Convention. Hardly any of these texts have been translated into Danish, but nevertheless they

13 https://echr.coe.int/Documents/Simplified_Conv_ENG.pdf (Accessed January 31, 2021).

do apply in Denmark and it therefore falls to government officials, judges, lawyers, etc. to read and understand the original English or French texts and make them accessible to other Danish citizens.

Chlebny (2014, pp. 248–249) identifies the same problem in Poland: with only a limited number of judgments available in Polish, he sees this as an obstacle to the application of ECtHR case law by domestic judges. He adds that "this situation is remedied to some degree only by the fact that a limited number of judgments or their summaries are available on websites established by NGOs or government agencies or [are] presented in legal periodicals", concluding that "the deficiency in the access to Strasbourg jurisprudence in the national language of the judge is not a problem that may be overlooked".

Over the past 10 years or so, efforts have certainly been made to promote translation of case law into non-official languages. The 2015 Brussels Declaration (point B § 2(f)) called upon States Parties to promote its accessibility by translating or summarising significant judgments, on the basis that improved knowledge of the Convention is key to ensuring that the principle of subsidiarity is fully effective.[14] The translation of judgments against a given State into its own language(s) should also be a priority. Sub-paragraph (g) called for the maintaining of financing to enable the Council of Europe to continue its commissioning of translations (made possible, for example, through the Human Rights Trust Fund from 2012), but many translations emanate from the States themselves, for example through the Ministry of Justice or of Foreign Affairs, or are provided by institutions and non-governmental organisations. All such translations, centralised in HUDOC, thus come from outside the Court and carry a disclaimer that the only authentic version of the text is that published on delivery in one or both of the official languages. Admittedly, there is a risk of error or misunderstanding to the extent that translators into non-official languages may not be familiar with the Court's use of the source language, and they will inevitably have to develop new terminology; but this risk will be reduced if only a summary is translated, as is often the case. The selection translated into any given non-official language nevertheless remains a small fraction of the entire body of case law, the focus rightly being placed on "key cases".

In spite of the above-mentioned efforts, the vast majority of judgments will still have to be read by Europeans in a language other than their mother tongue, unlike the judgments of the ECJ, which (with some exceptions today) are available in all EU languages (as emphasised by Sedley (2011, p. 572)). Lawyers, judges and students seeking an in-depth understanding of the case law will need to have a good grasp of French and/or English (see Kosař et al. 2020, p. 240 on judges).

14 www.echr.coe.int/Documents/Brussels_Declaration_ENG.pdf (Accessed January 31, 2021). The non-official-language translations programme dates back to the Brighton High-Level Conference in April 2012 (see Brighton Declaration, point 9); see also Brannan 2018a, pp. 173–174; Peruzzo 2019, pp. 38–40.

4 The style barrier

Relatively little has been written about the style adopted by the ECtHR (there is more literature on that of the ECJ, with which it is often confused). Merrills (1993, p. 29) praises the decision to abandon the early "single sentence form" (used for the Court's first four judgments) in favour of more conventional sentences, but goes on to question whether the style is nevertheless conducive to adequate reasoning. There have been varying comments, both negative and positive, on the language used, but the general structure of judgments does not appear to have been criticised. It typically consists of the "Facts", often followed by a section of summarised or quoted domestic and/or international law, then the "Law" part, containing the parties' arguments and the Court's assessment: the general principles and their application to the present case, leading to a conclusion as to whether or not there has been a violation of the Convention (see Brannan 2018a, p. 177; Peruzzo 2019, pp. 60–68). This structural approach has been described by former judge Villiger (2019, p. 462) as "syllogistic"; while logical and "easy to navigate" (White 2009, pp. 15, 17), such a method may also be seen in a negative light as mechanical or artificial.

The Court's judgments on the whole remain relatively lengthy, certainly longer than those of the ECJ, for reasons relating to style and structure[15] (in particular, they contain more detail on the facts and extensive reference to previous case law in the reasoning). The ECJ style was based from the outset on that of the French *Conseil d'état* and the succinct nature of its judgments has been criticised by various authors. Weiler (2001, p. 225), for example, describes them as having a "cryptic, Cartesian style", as commonly found in civil law jurisdictions. Cohen (2016, p. 513) finds Strasbourg judgments to be "longer and more discursive", while nevertheless following a "French-like format". Rietiker (2013, p. 44) rightly points out that the ECtHR adopts a hybrid style, combining civil law formalism with common law length and detail. Former judge Garlicki (2009, p. 391) describes its style as "disciplined but also quite elaborate", comparing its judgments to those of constitutional courts in terms of its methodological approach, "oriented . . . towards explaining and convincing [rather] than simply . . . issuing dry commands". Senden (2011, p. 21) confirms that this style is "born out of the wish to engage national courts and . . . authorities", this being "the key to successful implementation of the Convention". Strasbourg judgments are somewhat comparable to the style of the International Court of Justice (ICJ), which inspired its functioning at the outset and has the same working and official languages, maintaining a similar parallelism in its bilingual texts. The principle of allowing separate opinions was also "copied" from the ICJ (not being ECJ practice) and is more generally a feature of common law jurisdictions (see Rietiker 2013, p. 44). Judges freely express their personal views in separate opinions

15 Gerards (2017, p. 268), out of a sample of 40 leading cases, found an average length of 50 pages, of which about 20 pages consisted of reasoning.

(White and Boussiakou 2009, p. 60),[16] often helping the reader to understand the controversial issues and reflecting the points of disagreement during the deliberations. The style of opinions is usually much more idiomatic than that of the judgment itself, and they "generally make for interesting reading" (Gerards 2017, p. 269), although they may also be quite lengthy and academic. Senden (2011, p. 21) comments that the existence of separate opinions obliges the majority to express "solid reasoning" for the judgment's conclusions and avoids the sort of "vague and opaque reasoning" that might otherwise stem from the need to reach a consensus among the judges.

By way of example, certain opinions of Judge Pinto de Albuquerque in particular are comparable to academic articles (see, e.g., his 34-page opinion[17] in *Chiragov and Others v. Armenia* [GC] 16/06/2015). A more recent opinion of his has been commended for "handily setting out the main pros and cons of the judgment".[18] Some opinions are erudite, with abundant use of Latin; others are more entertaining, with quotations from Shakespeare (dissenting opinion of Judge Zupančič in *Khan v. Germany*, 23/04/2015) or from the lyrics of Bob Dylan (dissenting opinion of Judge Kūris in *Selahattin Demirtaş v. Turkey*, 23/06/2015). Dissenting opinions may herald a future change in case law[19] – indeed, "today's dissent might be tomorrow's majority" (White and Boussiakou 2009, p. 54) – and concurring opinions may also contribute to its development.[20] Many opinions will shed light on a controversial point of the reasoning; some even concern a subject that has not been dealt with at all in the judgment. Opinions may reflect considerable tension among judges.[21] Disagreement on a major point can be seen, for example, in the partly dissenting opinion of Judge Koskelo in *N.D. and N.T. v. Spain* ([GC] 13/02/2020); she begins, "I have regrettably been unable to agree with the majority's conclusion that Article 4 of Protocol No. 4 is applicable in the circumstances of the present case". In the judgment

16 The authors conclude their study of separate opinions by saying, "These personal voices are to be welcomed as an antidote to the increasingly formulaic style of judicial reasoning in the judgments of the Court".

17 Opinion commended in a blog as a "very strong dissent", illustrating an "allergic reaction" to this and a related case; see www.ejiltalk.org/the-nagorno-karabakh-cases/ (Accessed January 31, 2021).

18 https://strasbourgobservers.com/2019/07/30/volodina-article-3-and-russias-systemic-problem-regarding-domestic-violence/ (Accessed January 31, 2021).

19 The dissenting views expressed in the dissenting opinions in the Chamber case of Güzelyurtlu and Others v. Cyprus and Turkey were later endorsed by the majority in the Grand Chamber judgment ([GC] 29/01/2019).

20 A passage from the concurring opinion of Judge Zagrebelsky in Salduz v. Turkey ([GC] 27/11/2008) about "the whole range of services specifically associated with legal assistance" has since been incorporated into related case law (e.g. Beuze v. Belgium [GC] 09/11/2018, § 36).

21 In the blog EJIL Talk, Milanovic points out that there are as many as nine detailed separate opinions in Georgia v. Russia (no. 2), thus illustrating "the tensions between the majority and the minority"; www.ejiltalk.org/georgia-v-russia-no-2-the-european-courts-resurrection-of-bankovic-in-the-contexts-of-chaos/ (Accessed January 31, 2021).

itself there are as many as 37 paragraphs devoted to this issue of applicability, thus reflecting a need to justify the majority position. However, the majority do not always provide such detailed and clear reasoning; in one case, Judge Pinto de Albuquerque berates the "vagueness of the language" and laments that "where linguistic clarity and legal certainty were most needed the Court fails to deliver".[22]

The style of the original draft will depend to some extent on the novelty of the case (Grand Chamber judgments are thus particularly "elaborative"), but the cutting and pasting of passages from relevant case law ("authorities") is commonplace. Lengthy sections of judgments are basically "hidden quotes": the reproduction of previous findings (especially on general principles) without quotation marks but followed by numerous references (Cohen (2016, p. 515) sees this is as another example of French influence). This practice may arguably render the text less readable; the references could be relegated to footnotes, but this is not the Court's practice, except in some separate opinions. More generally, the resulting compilation of principles may appear awkward. Whether the text is copied from previous case law or drafted from scratch, it will be deliberated upon by a collegial panel of judges from diverse legal traditions. Key findings may be the result of a degree of compromise, sometimes resulting in convoluted language[23] and possibly nuancing, complementing or truncating previous wording (both features presenting difficulties for translators). The finalising of a draft often gives rise to discussion of language-related points, but however much a text could be fine-tuned linguistically, the judges clearly have the last word.

In the Court's case law, there are many examples of convoluted sentences as a result of juxtaposing segments of previous judgments to formulate a general principle; one illustration from *Morice v. France* is given by Brannan (2018a, p. 179). Here is a key finding which has been reproduced with slight variants in different cases (English translation):

> A court or tribunal is characterised in that substantive sense by its judicial function, that is to say determining matters within its competence on the basis of legal rules, *with full jurisdiction* and after proceedings conducted in a prescribed manner.
>
> (from *Mutu and Pechstein v. Switzerland*, 02/10/2018, § 139; emphasis added)

Referring to the two cases cited in the French source text, the English translator was careful to note that the words emphasised (*de pleine juridiction*) had been added; they appeared in three other cases drafted in French, but not in

22 See his partly concurring, partly dissenting opinion (§ 8) in Guðmundur Andri Ástráðsson v. Iceland ([GC] 1/12/20).

23 In her concurring opinion in Kurban v. Turkey (24/11/20), Judge Koskelo criticises a "convoluted formulation" in the reasoning.

the relevant sentence in cases drafted in English.[24] Moreover, the words "legal rules" had, in the earliest authority cited, read "rules of law", suggesting an attempt by a later drafter to avoid confusion with the notion of "rule of law". The reader may thus find the result of such restitution of previous findings, subject to adaptation, to be awkward and confusing. Even though a general principle is being conveyed here, the meaning of expressions such as "substantive sense" and "with full jurisdiction" will not be understood by all non-lawyer readers. An obvious change in the wording of the general principles under Article 6 "in its criminal aspect" can be seen in *Beuze v. Belgium* ([GC] 09/11/2018) at § 120, when compared to *Ibrahim and Others v. the United Kingdom* ([GC] 13/09/2016) at § 250: in the earlier case, the paragraph begins with "the right to a fair trial under Article 6 § 1 is an unqualified right", and this became "the fairness of a criminal trial must be guaranteed in all circumstances". In view of the importance of this passage, the change must reflect a deliberate attempt at clarification, perhaps because the term "unqualified right" was unsatisfactory. The variations in such findings make it difficult to establish a "standard" citation (one that is not case-specific) to be used in subsequent drafts; a project is underway to encourage drafting lawyers to insert such citations automatically, with the aim of ensuring greater consistency, but the definitive version first has to be identified (in both official languages).

The Court's style has been criticised for being stilted or unidiomatic for native speakers of English.[25] In the view of Merrills (1993, p. 30), "the tone of the Court's judgments is usually rather flat". He sees this, compared to common law judgments, as inevitable: "This, of course, is a reflection of the way they are produced which . . . is almost guaranteed to eliminate excitement or the telling phrase". Its earlier judgments have been described as "show[ing] all the signs of having been written by a civil servant according to a pre-determined formula".[26] Merrills (1993, p. 36) also refers to the "tendency of the Court to build its judgments around certain almost ritualistic formulae". Such criticisms of ECtHR judgments are rather stereotypical and not totally justified today. They will clearly not be as idiomatic as, say, those of the UK Supreme Court, where the majority opinion is presented by a judge in his or her own words. By contrast, former UK Justice of Appeal Sir Stephen Sedley (2011, p. 573) opines that Strasbourg judgments are no longer laconic (if they ever were) but "have come to resemble the British narrative judgment", and he commends them for being "self-sufficient

24 In a more recent Grand Chamber case, Ástráðsson, cited above (§ 219), these words have again been omitted from the variant of the sentence in question; but the notion of "full jurisdiction" appears in many other cases where the same finding is formulated differently and it is regarded as having an "autonomous definition" (see Ramos Nunes de Carvalho e Sá v. Portugal [GC] 06/11/2018, § 177).

25 Criticism of the original French texts appears more infrequent, but some inconsistency of terms and unnatural usage have also been identified in that official language.

26 Lord Hope of Craighead, "Writing Judgments", Judicial Studies Board Annual Lecture 2005 (p. 1).

and self-explanatory"; he nevertheless adds that "much of it is unnecessary to an understanding of exactly what the particular case has established".

Merrills (1993, pp. 30–32) identifies the "criteria of good judicial style" as successful communication of the point or points being made; whether the judgment is persuasive; and completeness, with every essential point being addressed fully. The Court cannot seriously be criticised for a lack of completeness, especially not in Grand Chamber judgments, whose aim is to consolidate, clarify and sometimes develop the existing case law (Peruzzo 2019, p. 67). For example, the recent judgment of *Muhammad and Muhammad v. Romania* ([GC] 15/10/2020) deals with each aspect of the applicants' right to procedural safeguards in expulsion proceedings, repeatedly reaching similar conclusions in a manner that may appear unnecessary to the reader. As Merrills rightly comments: "The persuasiveness of a judgment is also enhanced if a court can support its conclusion with cumulative reasons instead of resting the decision on a single point". This practice may perhaps render the style somewhat cumbersome or long-winded, but arguably for good reason.

Cohen has described the influence of French as the "French capture" in the ICJ, the ECJ and the ECtHR, although she admits that these courts' judgments "tend to be longer and more explanatory than the typical terse French opinion" (Cohen 2016, p. 513). Such influence will clearly be more prevalent in ECJ judgments, which are initially drafted in French. At the ECtHR, this will to some extent depend on the drafting language, but in the early days French was used more commonly, so it has heavily influenced the style of key case law and has given rise to certain Gallicisms. The fact of alternating between two drafting languages means that the translation process, and therefore back translation over many years; may perpetuate certain unclear wording or literal renderings; result in an infelicitous variation of terms for the same concept;[27] or worse still, risk producing diverging strands of case law in each language. Cohen (2016, pp. 501, 513) rightly identifies one feature of the "French style" as the use of "judicial mannerisms", by which she means connectors such as "consequently". This is certainly a common drafting technique, as a means of linking the reasoning in successive paragraphs or sentences, common to both Strasbourg and Luxembourg. In addition to appearing somewhat unnatural in English, it may on occasion be perceived as an overly casual mechanism, taking shortcuts in the reasoning; especially in Chamber judgments, the chain of reasoning may appear incomplete, passing from an intermediate conclusion to a final one without clear explanation. The use of "filler phrases" such as "the Court takes the view that" could also be seen as French style, not always being necessary in the English text.

In its assessment of the case the Court seeks to use culture-neutral words and expressions and this may reinforce the perception of unfamiliar language or

27 See the criticism by Judge Pinto de Albuquerque of the "uncertain, vague language" used to designate a single concept, the "essence" of a right, in his concurring opinion appended to Muhammad and Muhammad v. Romania ([GC] 15/10/2020), § 8.

jargon; the definition of the concepts thus designated may appear vague. Thus even where the judgment is drafted in English, or translated into English, it may seem "foreign" to a native speaker (particularly to a common law lawyer) in view of the inherent stylistic features mentioned above; this may well detract from the Court's capacity to convey its message effectively and persuasively.

5 Overcoming the barriers

Regardless of the form or language in which the Court's message is conveyed, it will never be immune from a degree of criticism, especially by those who disagree with its findings. The dismissal of its judgments as the work of "foreign judges" (Petrov 2020, pp. 497, 500) is surely more to do with content than with style. While there may be room for improvement, Gerards (2017, p. 267) is right to say that "the Court endeavours to frame its judgments in understandable and transparent language, making [them] readable even to non-lawyers". In terms of reasoning, she commends the "neutral, objective and logical fashion" in which it derives conclusions from earlier cases or from underlying principles (Gerards 2017, pp. 266–267). White (2009, p. 15) finds that the "formulaic structure" is actually conducive to better understanding. Some parts of the judgment, in particular the operative paragraphs, will be more formulaic than others. The repetition of key notions, while perhaps appearing stilted, undoubtedly helps to bridge paragraphs,[28] whereas by contrast, as shown above, variation in terminology may cause confusion.

For the public, there is always room for improvement in the communication of information, including via social media (to be used prudently by any court). To convey the Court's message to domestic courts, an effective solution is to maintain a degree of "dialogue between judges", a dialogue that has been conducted through certain judgments[29] and by means of a now well-established network of apex courts in the participating States (currently 92 courts from 40 States), known as the "Superior Courts Network". A core feature of the network is the exchange of information on case law, involving reports and regular meetings with representatives from these national courts (see Villiger 2019, p. 459).

While the use of supranational language and "autonomous" Convention terms (see Brannan 2013, pp. 911–913), or repeated "mantras", may seem unfamiliar and "foreign" to some readers, especially non-lawyers, this constraint can be circumvented by freer renderings in other material for the public, as presented above. Because such material carries a disclaimer, it does not have to reproduce the exact technical wording of a judgment. In any event, this feature of judgments can also

28 See, e.g., Vinter and Others v. The United Kingdom ([GC] 09/07/2013), §§ 114–18, with the repetition of "rehabilitation" and "rehabilitative".

29 An example often quoted is the "dialogue" with the UK Supreme Court in the case of Al-Khawaja and Tahery v. The United Kingdom ([GC] 15/12/2011) on hearsay evidence (see Gerards 2017, p. 268).

be seen in a positive light, as neutral language should be more readily understood by people across Europe than if terminology specific to a given State were to be used. As discussed by Brannan (2013, pp. 920–923), the Court, being faced with the diversity of legal systems, finds suitable generic terms to cover domestic realities. Weston (2005, p. 459) explains that the English translators are "continually carrying out a balancing exercise": on the one hand, their translations must be "readily intelligible and persuasive to lawyers in [common law] jurisdictions", but on the other hand, they have to remember that the majority of their readers, in other Member States, are unlikely to be familiar with highly idiomatic or culture-bound expressions in English.

Sedley (2011, p. 572) refers to the "relative poverty of the Strasbourg arrangements" on the linguistic front compared to those of the ECJ. But within its limited means, the Court makes every effort to produce high-quality texts. Its English and French language divisions include language checkers to ensure that drafts are accurate and grammatically correct when the drafting lawyer is not a native speaker of either official language. The language barrier can be overcome by continuing the above-mentioned drive to incorporate external non-official language translations in HUDOC, or to publish explanatory documents in various languages. One must not forget locally produced material such as textbooks and ECtHR commentaries in local languages, which are also crucial for spreading the knowledge of case law (see Kosař et al. 2020, p. 241). As White (2009, p. 16) observes, as regards disseminating case law in non-official languages, "standardisation of presentation and to some extent vocabulary must be of considerable assistance to translators", and the quality of the source text will be all the more important.

To improve the readability of judgments there have been various in-house proposals over the years but little actual change. In terms of style, drafters have been encouraged to use "plainer" English and to avoid Latin; while this may well have helped, certain judges, in particular, are still keen on using the latter! Efforts have been made to shorten judgments, especially in repetitive cases (mainly by referring back to previous cases for the facts and domestic/international law) and in cases with a large number of applicants complaining of similar facts. Some changes have recently been made to the format of Chamber judgments, based on the recommendations of a working group in 2018. The previously short preamble and longer "Procedure" part have now been merged into a single sentence beginning with "Having regard to", resembling the preamble to ECJ judgments. This is followed by a one-paragraph introduction identifying the main complaint(s), and then the "Facts" and the "Relevant Legal Framework and Practice" (the latter no longer being a subdivision of the former). Probably the most striking innovation is the introduction of a headnote with the key concepts (in both Chamber and Grand Chamber judgments). It must be said, however, that these modifications are relatively minor and rather cosmetic.

Finally, the role of press releases is essential in conveying the Court's message to the outside world, as relayed via journalists in the more high-profile cases. Their accessibility will depend to some extent on the complexity of the judgment itself. They must remain "as close to the judgment as possible", but without necessarily "copying and pasting" (Titiun 2015, p. 130). There is a balance to be struck between the need to simplify the message on the one hand, and the risk of conveying the wrong message on the other.[30] Simplification, which is not an easy task, also lies in the avoidance of certain more erudite legal terms (e.g. "discretion" may be preferred to "margin of appreciation").[31] Separate press releases serve to identify the most relevant points of a case, as emphasised in their heading and summary. The measure of their success is that they are often used, sometimes being reproduced word for word, in newspaper articles.[32]

6 Concluding remarks

The accessibility and quality of case law are crucial for the ECtHR's visibility, authority and long-term effectiveness. It endeavours to convey a clear and persuasive message, not only to the parties to a given case but also to national courts and authorities, and more generally to citizens. While some may criticise its repetitive or unidiomatic language, these features may also be seen in a positive light as being necessary to ensure the requisite consistency of the case law, with generic terminology that avoids obscurity and confusion. Its communication must reflect both the solemnity of a court of law and an openness to the outside world – a balance that is not always easy to strike. In spite of the inevitable barriers, its high caseload and relatively limited resources, the Court has found ways to compensate for its lack of official multilingualism and succeeds in conveying its message through judgments and other texts, especially in key cases, to secure the protection of human rights in 47 diverse States.

References

Brannan, J., 2013. Coming to terms with the supranational: Translating for the European Court of Human Rights. *International Journal for the Semiotics of Law*, 26(4), 909–925.

Brannan, J., 2018a. Specificities of translation at the European Court of Human Rights: Policy and practice. *In:* F. Prieto Ramos, ed., *Institutional translation for international governance*. Oxford: Bloomsbury, 170–180.

Brannan, J., 2018b. *Translation of judgments (European Court of Human Rights), Max Planck encyclopedia of international procedural law [MPEiPro]*. Oxford: Oxford University Press (last updated: May 2018).

30 Press releases carry the disclaimer that they are not binding on the Court.

31 An expression dating back to the 1960s that has been criticised as a Gallicism (Weston 2015, p. 456); while perhaps not readily understood by all readers, it has become one of the Court's key legal doctrines.

32 For example, the coverage in the British press (e.g. The Guardian) of the Knox v. Italy judgment (24/01/2019), and the Platini v. Switzerland inadmissibility decision (11/02/2020), while neither has been translated into English to date.

Chlebny, J., 2014. How a national judge implements judgments of the Strasbourg court. *In:* A. Seibert-Fohr & M. Villiger, eds., *Judgments of the European Court of Human Rights: Effects and implementation*. Nomos: Baden-Baden, 237–249.

Cohen, M., 2016. On the linguistic design of multinational courts: The French capture. *International Journal of Constitutional Law*, 14(2), 498–517.

Garlicki, L., 2009. Judicial deliberations: The Strasbourg perspective. *In:* N. Huls, M. Adams, & J. Bomhoff, eds., *The legitimacy of highest courts' rulings*. The Hague: T M C Asser Press, 389–397.

Garre, M., 1999. *Human rights in translation*. Copenhagen: Copenhagen Business School Press.

Gerards, J., 2017. The European Court of Human Rights. *In:* A. Jakab, A. Dyevre, & G. Itzcovich, eds., *Comparative constitutional reasoning*. Cambridge: Cambridge University Press, 237–276.

Kosař, D., et al., 2020. *Domestic judicial treatment of European Court of Human Rights case law*. London: Routledge.

Kjær, A., 2011. European legal concepts in Scandinavian law and language. *Nordic Journal of International Law*, 80, 321–349.

Merrills, J., 1993. *The Development of International Law by the European Court of Human Rights*. Manchester: Manchester University Press.

Peruzzo, K., 2019. *National law in supranational case-law: A linguistic analysis of European Court of Human Rights judgments in English*. Trieste: Edizioni Università di Trieste.

Petrov, J., 2020. The populist challenge to the European Court of Human Rights. *International Journal of Constitutional Law*, 18(2), 476–508.

Rietiker, D., 2013. The European Court of Human Rights from a comparative law viewpoint: A logical example of a "mixed jurisdiction" court. *Cyprus Human Rights Law Review*, 2(1), 36–52.

Sedley, S., 2011. Speaking in tongues: The dissemination of human rights judgments. *In:* P. Titiun, ed., *La conscience des droits: mélanges en l'honneur de Jean-Paul Costa*. Paris: Dalloz, 571–573.

Senden, H., 2011. *Interpretation of fundamental rights in a multilevel legal system, an analysis of the European Court of Human Rights and the Court of Justice of the European Union*, Antwerp: Intersentia.

Titiun, P., 2015. La création d'un service de presse de la Cour à Strasbourg: enjeux passés, présents et futurs. *In:* E. Lambert-Abdelgawad & P. Dourneau-Josette, eds., *La Cour européenne des droits de l'homme dans la presse*. Brussels: Nemesis, 129–136.

Villiger, M., 2019. The research division of the European Court of Human Rights and its relevance for the court's case-law. *In:* K. Lemmens, S. Parmentier, & L. Reyntjens, eds., *Human rights with a human touch: Liber Amicorum Paul Lemmens*. Cambridge, Antwerp and Chicago: Intersentia, 449–466.

Weiler, J., 2001. Epilogue: The judicial après Nice. *In:* G. de Búrca & J. Weiler, eds., *The European Court of Justice*. Oxford: Oxford University Press, 216–226.

Weston, M., 2005. Characteristics and constraints of producing bilingual judgments: The example of the European Court of Human Rights. *In:* J.C. Gémar & N. Kasirer, eds., *Jurilinguistics: Between law and language*. Brussels: Bruylant, 445–459.

White, R., 2009. *Judgments in the Strasbourg court: Some reflections*. Available from: http://doi.org/10.2139/ssrn.1435197 [Accessed January 31, 2021].

White, R., & Boussiakou, I., 2009. Separate opinions in the European Court of Human Rights. *Human Rights Law Review*, 9(1), 37–60.

16 Concision and clarity in Italian court proceedings

Antonio Mura and Jacqueline Visconti

1 Critical issues concerning language in court proceedings

Lengthy, obscure judicial texts hinder both the right to an efficient and fair trial and the right to understand the law. As Lord Neuberger once said in a speech on open justice, judges should avoid making judgments that are "readable by few, comprehensible by fewer still", as "a clearly reasoned judgment enables the public to understand the law and to see how justice is being dispensed".[1]

The quality of each judicial text can be considered (besides its legal basis) with reference to both its length and to the clarity of its content. These perspectives interact, with repercussions on the quality of the response provided to citizens by the judicial system.

Several European documents highlight how form and comprehensibility of judicial decisions impact on the quality of justice. According to Opinion 7(2005) of the Council of Europe Consultative Council of European Judges (CCJE) on "Justice and Society":

> the language used by the courts in their procedures and decisions is not only a powerful tool available to them to fulfil their educational role, but it is . . . the 'law in practice' for the specific litigants of the case. Accessibility, simplicity and clarity of the language of courts are therefore desirable.
>
> (§ 56)[2]

1 Cf. Neuberger 2012.

2 Cf. also, within the same perspective:

- the "Framework global action plan for judges in Europe", prepared in 2001 by the European Committee on legal co-operation (CDCJ) of the Council of Europe includes among its priorities "accessibility, simplification and clarity of the language used by the courts in proceedings and decisions" (§ V.d);
- the Recommendation Rec (2010) 12 of the Committee of Ministers of the Council of Europe on "Judges: independence, efficiency and responsibilities" states that "judges should give clear reasons for their judgments in language which is clear and comprehensible" (§ 63); the explanatory memorandum adds that "giving clear reasons in understandable

DOI: 10.4324/9781003153771-20

Similar principles are stated for public prosecution. The Rome Charter, approved in 2014 by the Consultative Council of European Prosecutors (CCPE) of the Council of Europe, containing "European Norms and Principles Concerning Prosecutors", reads as follows (§ 95): "Prosecutors should particularly be careful to express their decisions in an understandable manner to the parties concerned and when communicating with the public and media".[3]

In short, a well-written decision ought to be both clear and concise, while accounting for the logical processes underlying the decision: hence, the clear and concise exposition of the factual and legal background, evidential results, identification of the applicable principles and rules, and solution of the issues advanced with respect to the specific case.

Compliance with the duties of concision and clarity does not lie only with the judge – and with the public prosecutor in criminal proceedings – but also with the counsel, both in explaining the reasons in support of her/his client and in countering the arguments of the counterparty. A well-structured text or speech contributes to the logical progression of the reasoning and favours a constructive confrontation between the parties and with the judge; the judge, in turn, should conduct the trial orienting the parties to this effect.

The complexity of the law need not necessarily be expressed in an obscure language. On the contrary, an effort is needed to restore clarity in judicial prose and, therefore, the cultural foundations common to all legal science, which also concern language.[4] On a practical level, this effort can contribute to speeding up the proceedings and to making the judicial system more efficient. It goes without saying that clarity is not the only positive quality to be pursued: besides brevity, these include accuracy and the ability to persuade.

Clarity and concision have a bearing also in the realm of international judicial cooperation. Problems arise there with regard to the translation of proceedings, which makes it appropriate – in fact, necessary – to use a language that is as simple as possible.

---

language for their judgments is an obligation of judges. This is to ensure that the law is visibly applied and to enable the parties to decide whether or not to appeal" (reasons may be omitted for certain decisions, like those involving the management of the case or concerning minor procedural issues);

- the "Follow-up action by Member States" (2016), presented at the High-Level Conference of Ministers of Justice and representatives of the Judiciary, recognises that a clear reasoning of judgments is required in all legal systems, but States should ensure that appropriate actions are taken to improve the drafting of judgments "in a clear language, easily understood by the public";
- the "Magna Carta of European Judges", approved in 2010 by the CCJE, under the heading "Access to justice and transparency" (§ 16), reads as follows: "Court documents and judicial decisions shall be drafted in an accessible, simple and clear language".

3 The Opinion 11(2016) of the CCPE, under the heading "Clarity" (§ 53), emphasises that "any official acts given by prosecutors should be clearly understandable by those to whom they are addressed".

4 Our reflection does not include the drafting of legislation, notarial acts (in the legal systems where they are provided for) and contracts.

Clear/plain language has been the subject of extensive investigation both in common and civil law traditions,[5] although the debate has mainly concerned legislative drafting and judicial writing only to a lesser extent.[6] The question of concision, which touches upon both the linguistic and the logical-argumentative dimensions, has also been taken into consideration.[7]

Common law experts have elaborated on key aspects of legal writing: word choice, punctuation, grammar and syntax, rhetorical figures, exposition and argument, expressive tactics.[8] Yet the various judicial traditions – in line with diverse cultures – favour different styles of exposition.[9] As for the writings of judges, for example, the individualised, more immediate and colloquial style of the common law world (in some way marked by orality, sometimes with striking expressions) differs from the continental style (French, German, Italian), which is decidedly more solemn, formal, neutral, and impersonal.[10]

2 Italian judicial language

In Italy, no definitions of clarity and concision are given by procedural rules. Individual rules tend to promote the latter, because they are aimed at limiting the duration of the trial; on the other hand, there is no normative indication on clarity. As stated by the finest Italian doctrine already at the beginning of the

5 Cf. Williams (2018) and references therein for an updated discussion.

6 Cf. Kimble (2006) or Duckworth (1994) on "plain judicial language", and more recently, Williams (2020) on plain language developments in Canada and UK court judgments.

7 In the English Criminal Procedure Rules and Criminal Practice Directions (April 2018), thirty overall references to concision can be found, and even more references to clarity. These Rules present an incisive approach to the topic. CPD XII (General Application), D.23: "In R v James, R v Selby [2016] EWCA Crim 1639; [2017] Crim. L.R. 228 the Court of Appeal observed. . . 'Legal documents of unnecessary and too often of excessive length offer very little assistance to the court'. In Tombstone Ltd v Raja [2008] EWCA Civ 1441, [2009] 1 WLR 1143 Mummery LJ said: 'Practitioners are well advised to note the risk of the court's negative reaction to unnecessarily long written submissions. [. . .] An unintended and unfortunate side effect of the growth in written advocacy has been that too many practitioners, at increased cost to their clients and diminishing assistance to the court, burden their opponents and the court with written briefs. No area of law is exempt from the requirement to produce careful and concise documents': cf. Tchenquiz v Director of the Serious Fraud Office [2014] EWCA Civ 1333, [2015] 1 WLR 838, paragraph 10". The connection with the rule of law, outlined by Lord Bingham (2011), is also relevant; meaningful remarks are made by Lady Justice Arden (2012) on the "ever-growing length" of judgments (sometimes "longer than they need to be").

8 Cf. Ferreri (2019); Garner (2002); Williams (forthcoming).

9 An in-depth analysis would demonstrate the relevance of various aspects of legal traditions. For example, the provision of dissenting and/or concurring opinions enhances public scrutiny on the reasoning. This can positively stimulate each writer to be coherent and to use a more accessible language. Nevertheless, from another point of view, different opinions could raise "problems of length, prolixity and elaboration – leading to inaccessibility", as Lord Bingham (2011) remarked.

10 A deeper scrutiny would show significant differences also within each of these traditions in their actual developments in different countries.

20th century: "law is the art of drawing limits, and a limit does not exist unless it is clear".[11] Nevertheless, the issues of length and clarity of legal documents are particularly problematic in Italy, due to a long-standing tradition that encourages unduly verbose and convoluted arguments.

Justice, in its historical evolution, includes rituals that are not accessible to non-specialists and is often administered with almost esoteric formulas. The roots of this cant lie in ancient procedures which were surrounded by an aura of mystery and aimed to hinder rather than to foster understanding. Indeed, Italian court documents are often written in a difficult language, not so much because of the (inevitable) use of technical terminology, but rather because of long and intricate sentences and an excessive use of subordinate clauses; they are full of acronyms, archaic words, unnecessary Latinisms,[12] ambiguous terms, redundant paraphrases and bureaucratic expressions.[13] At the heart of this prolixity lies, perhaps, also the idea that a longer text is of greater value.

This contributes, moreover, to the present lack of efficiency of court proceedings in Italy, because both judges and counsels for the parties are strongly influenced by this culture. Therefore, contentions are more complicated, and decisions more time-consuming.[14] And yet, according to the modern conception, clearer, more transparent proceedings strengthen the legitimacy of an institution and make it more credible.

3 A project on concision and clarity in Italian justice proceedings

To tackle this complex question, a group of leading experts was appointed in February 2016 by the Italian Minister of Justice with the aim of improving clarity and concision in court proceedings.[15] The group, which was established in accordance with the multidisciplinary nature of the topic, included jurists as well as linguists. The overarching purpose of the project was to improve the efficiency of the Italian trial system through more concise and clearer court proceedings, thus allowing citizens to better understand the functioning of the legal system and thereby enhancing the democracy of justice. An innovative point of interest

11 Scialoja (1911, p. 942): "Il diritto è arte di tracciare limiti, e un limite non esiste se non in quanto sia chiaro" (our translation).

12 What is inappropriate is the abuse of "Latin gadgets" (supra, infra, contra, intuitu personae). On the contrary, some Latin terms can be appropriate when they define specific concepts, like stare decisis, res judicata and habeas corpus: such short locutions summarise complex concepts, with exactness. For a comparison between common law and civil law traditions in the use of Latin, see, e.g., Duparc-Portier and Masson (2006).

13 Suffice it to mention, Mortara Garavelli (2001) and references therein.

14 To give an idea of the extent of the problem in Italy, it should be remembered that – in some "maxi-trials" – there are decisions stretching to thousands of pages.

15 The working group was led by one of the authors of the present chapter, Antonio Mura, currently Prosecutor General in Rome, former judge and Head of the Department for Justice Affairs of the Italian Ministry of Justice.

in the proposal lies in the joint consideration of the language of judgments of the courts and of the arguments addressed to them.[16] Indeed, in any trial, each document produces effects on the subsequent phases, with consequences on the speed and effectiveness of the hearings as well as on the quality of arguments. Thus, a systematic structuring of the introductory proceedings (the summons in civil, the indictment in criminal proceedings) positively influences the development of the trial in its various phases: it favours a well-reasoned decision of first instance; in turn, a clearly reasoned decision usually carries clear appeals and subsequently clear appellate judgments.[17]

The study started from an in-depth analysis of the Italian Supreme Court (*Corte di cassazione*) proceedings, both in civil and criminal procedures. Two further mandates (in 2017 and 2018) extended the survey to include courts of appeal and, finally, first instance proceedings. The results were presented to the Italian Minister of Justice in February 2018. The report, accessible online,[18] opened with a general reflection on clarity and concision. First, concision should be viewed as an instrument, not as the ultimate purpose. It is aimed at the clarity and effectiveness of both judgments and defence pleadings. Clarity, in turn, does not tend exclusively to satisfy a need for speedy trials, but also to favour the quality of the judicial response.

Indeed, the principles of clarity and concision respond to several relevant needs: the need for citizens to understand decisions; compliance with the "principle of proportionality", that is, the aim of ensuring a proportionate use of judicial resources with respect to the purpose of the just definition of the case within a reasonable time lapse. The principles in question are thus consistent with the objective of reducing the duration of the trial. The same principles are also consistent with a guarantee function, as clearer proceedings allow the final decision to be reached on the basis of the essential issues. Long presentations, on the contrary, harm the efficiency of the justice system. In essence, excessively verbose proceedings violate the principles of a fair trial. In some cases, they can even border on the abuse of process, when excessiveness is the result of a voluntary choice and not of inexperience.

Concision is, indeed, a relational concept: it expresses the correct proportion between, on the one hand, the importance of the issues to be examined and, on the other hand, the size of the text that addresses them. As for judicial decisions, full understanding by the recipients (the parties and the community) is implied for at least two reasons. First, within the proceeding, the motivation offers the

16 A related project embracing this perspective is currently led by one of the authors of the present chapter, Jacqueline Visconti: Italian Ministero dell'Istruzione dell'Università e della Ricerca PRIN research project "Clarity in Court Proceedings (ClarAct): a new database for scholars and citizens", focusing on the written documents produced by counsels.

17 In this perspective, it is interesting to study indictments. Since they may affect the entire subsequent course of the trial, indictments should be based on synthesis, clarity, and precision.

18 www.federnotizie.it/wp-content/uploads/2018/10/CHIAREZZA_ATTI_PROCESSUALI.pdf

parties the possibility of understanding the rationale for the decision reached by the judge and constitutes the basis for its accountability, also in subsequent stages of the process; second, outside the proceeding, the motivation contributes to the predictability of future decisions (legal certainty), allowing citizens to understand the proper administration of justice and, ultimately, laying the foundations for a "democratic control" over it. The latter function, therefore, is not only legal but also social, in line with the value of "open justice" and with the rule of law. If it is true that democracy is based on a dialogue between rulers and governed, it must be highlighted that a dialogue is expressed through language. Therefore, if the language is not clear and understandable, democracy itself is impaired.[19]

Based on these considerations, the group proposed a twofold reform: on the one hand, a series of proposals aimed at spreading a culture of clarity and concision; on the other hand, a set of reforms in the legislation aimed at introducing the principles of concision and clarity in both civil and criminal codes of procedure.

3.1 Cultural proposals

Primarily, the group's proposals postulate a cultural perspective. Clarity of style is the cause and effect of clarity of thought; however (or perhaps precisely for this reason), it is also undisputed that clarity cannot be imposed by law. It is therefore necessary to aim, above all, at diffusing a genuine culture of clarity and concision, with a language that is a vehicle of ideas that are themselves clear and precise. Even before procedural rules (presented below), this presupposes a commitment in the training field, starting already at university level and further developed in professional training. The targets are the following:

- as for university training, the teaching of argumentation and legal language should be included in all university law courses; to date this has been entrusted mainly to the initiative of individual lecturers or universities;
- clarity and conciseness should become evaluation criteria in exams and public competitions for accessing judicial roles;
- language and argumentation should increasingly be the subject of theoretical and practical training programmes for judges, public prosecutors and counsels;
- concision and clarity should become relevant criteria within the professional evaluation of judges and public prosecutors.

As well as the cultural reform initiatives mentioned above, the working group has collected a series of indications for writing more effectively, without prescriptive value or ambitions of exhaustiveness. These indications refer to the planning and structure of the text, to its design, to both syntactic and lexical choices. This does

19 Cerexhe (2010, p. 888).

not entail the exclusion of specialist terminology, as technical expressions convey concepts more precisely than synonyms from everyday language.

These considerations resulted in a "Breviary for Good Writing", which incorporates cultural stimuli from the vast literature on the subject. Practical linguistic suggestions are offered, without imposing "cages" on the writers' creativity and personal style. For instance, it is desirable to use short sentences (20–25 words at most) to limit the number of subordinate clauses, passive forms, parenthetical clauses and capital letters. Double- or triple-negative propositions should be avoided, as should the display of erudition, both in general culture and in the legal sphere. The objective is to promote a cultural development for the legal professions without constraining the writer's individual sensibility and culture.

3.2 Developments in legislation

On the normative reform side, the main achievements of the Italian working group involved a critical overview of existing legislation relating to the length and clarity of court proceedings and a proposal for relevant modifications in the codes of procedure, aimed at introducing the principles of concision and clarity among the guiding principles of court proceedings.

The proposed amendments to the legislation concern both the civil and the criminal fields. They start from the introduction of a provision titled "Principle of Clarity and Concision of Proceedings", which reads as follows: "Court proceedings are written in a clear and concise manner; only necessary information and arguments are presented. The textual quotation of other judicial documents is inserted only to the extent that is actually necessary". It was then provided that complex texts are organised in numbered paragraphs, preceded by a general index, to facilitate their reading.

The rule on how to quote other earlier procedural documents constitutes a response to some bad practices that were favoured by modern word processing techniques. The ease of inserting long passages extracted from previous documents by copying and pasting removes the responsibility of the writer, as copying is easier than extracting the significant parts and summarising them. In practice, this often leads to the complete and uncritical transcription of minutes, cross-examinations, statements and so forth, or even previous decisions. As a result, texts are full of unnecessary details and do not indicate which passages play an important role in the argumentation. Instead, it is necessary to promote the inclusion of a reasoned summary of the cited documents, with textual reference (in quotation marks) limited to indispensable portions only.

Finally, the proposals include the establishment of an observatory on clarity and conciseness in court proceedings. This body should be set up on the initiative of the Minister of Justice, with the participation of representatives of all categories concerned. It is conceived as a cultural space for comparison and dialogue between judges, lawyers, judicial administration staff and other expressions of civil society. It would monitor the implementation of the principles of conciseness and clarity, and also create a database of good practices.

3.3 Follow-up

The group's report was presented by the Minister to both *Camera dei Deputati* and *Senato della Repubblica* on January 18, 2017; it was sent to the *Consiglio superiore della magistratura*, to the presidents of *Consiglio nazionale forense*, *Avvocatura generale dello Stato*, *Corte di cassazione*, *Consiglio di Stato*, and to the prosecutor general. As one of the targets is a reform of the university system in law faculties, the report was also sent to the *Conferenza dei Rettori delle Università italiane.*

On the cultural level, the impact was noteworthy. First, several training programmes for judges and public prosecutors, also open to counsels, were organised on this topic by the *Scuola superiore della magistratura*, in collaboration with the *Accademia della Crusca.*[20] Second, the principles of clarity and concision have been introduced as evaluating criteria in Italian bar exams. In Art. 3.2.d of the 2018 Rules for the training courses for bar exams,[21] drafting techniques of court proceedings according to the principle of concision are expressly indicated. As for the evaluation of judges, the group's report is among the documents provided to the Italian new Supreme Court justices in a dossier titled "Introduction to the *Corte di cassazione*".

On the normative level, the group's indications have been incorporated into parliamentary initiatives to amend the civil and criminal codes of procedure.[22] On January 15, 2021, the Council of Ministers adopted the "Proposal for a National Recovery and Resilience Plan", in which – among the reform measures for improving the efficiency of justice – it is specified that the principles of clarity and conciseness of court proceedings shall be introduced into the normative system. Notably, Art. 11.5 of the *decreto-legge* n. 44 (April 1, 2021) prescribes concision as a criterion to be met by candidates to the Italian national exam for becoming judges or public prosecutors.

4 An international overview

The supranational texts mentioned in Section 1 show that the problems under discussion here have a "transversal" scope across different cultures. This applies to both judgments and defence pleadings.

20 E.g., among many others, Laboratorio di scrittura giuridica: il linguaggio e gli stili delle sentenze e il principio di sinteticità degli atti, Scuola superiore della magistratura e Accademia della Crusca, Florence, 14–16 novembre 2018.

21 Decreto ministeriale 9/2/2018, n. 17, Regolamento dei corsi di formazione per l'accesso alla professione di avvocato.

22 For example, the draft law (disegno di legge) presented by the President of the Council of Ministers and by the Minister of Justice on January 9, 2020: article 12.1.d, Introduction of the principle of clarity and conciseness of Court proceedings.

4.1 Judgments

Opinion 7 (2005) of the Consultative Council of European Judges, on "Justice and Society", reads as follows:

- (§ 57) "In some European countries, judges believe that very short judgments reinforce the authority of the judgment; in some other countries, judges feel obliged, or are obliged by the law or practice, to explain extensively in writing all aspects of their decisions";
- (§ 58) "A simple and clear judicial language is beneficial as it makes the rule of law accessible and foreseeable by the citizens, if necessary with the assistance of a legal expert, as the case-law of the European Court of Human Rights suggests";
- (§ 59) "Judicial language should be concise and plain, avoiding – if unnecessary – Latin or other wordings that are difficult to understand for the public. Legal concepts and rules of law may be quite sufficiently explained by citing legislation or judicial precedents";
- (§ 60) "Clarity and concision, however, should not be an absolute goal, as it is also necessary for judges to preserve in their decisions precision and completeness of reasoning".

4.2 Defence pleadings

Stringent indications on the drafting of defence pleadings are given by both the European Court of Human Rights and the Court of Justice of the European Union.[23] Supranational courts, which share a considerable workload and critical issues connected to the different languages and legal systems involved in their activity, offer a significant field of application of the principles discussed above.

The European Court of Human Rights sets out the contents of individual applications (Rule 47);[24] and the EU Court of Justice focuses (in Art. 58 of the Rules of Procedure) on the "length of procedural documents". In short, the need for user-friendly documents is generally stated.

23 Obviously, the topic concerning drafting rules does not coincide with the cultural theme of concision. Nevertheless, mentioning the former completes the overview of the critical issues relating to the length of judicial writings.

24 Strict indications are given by the ECtHR not only to the parties but also to national Courts. In the guidelines on the implementation of the advisory-opinion procedure, introduced by Protocol No. 16 to the Convention, paragraphs 16–17 provide detailed prescriptions to the court or tribunal requesting an advisory-opinion on questions of principle relating to the interpretation or application of the rights and freedoms defined in the Convention and the Protocols thereto. Those detailed prescriptions refer to the length of the request (not exceeding 20 pages) submitted to the European Court, to format, fonts, line spacing, margins, page numbers and division of the text into numbered paragraphs. For the same purpose, also the EU Court of Justice has formal rules on how to draft judicial documents intended for it.

In the various national experiences too, there is a widespread need for an adequate downsizing of documents. For instance, the US Supreme Court, as well as other high courts of the United States, limits the admitted number of words in each brief on the merits.

The need for concision finds an interesting correlate – despite the peculiarity of the sector – also in the experience of British justice, which has seen the progressive expansion of "skeleton arguments". The skeleton argument is a document produced for the court. It is a written summary of the arguments that a party will put forward at a trial or other hearing. It should be user-friendly and should help counsel to present the case in a clear, concise and organised manner.[25] The court may require such a document to be served on the court and on the other party prior to a trial. The court may also give directions for the preparation of skeleton arguments, providing for the issues to be addressed and also for details like the number of pages (of specified size, fonts and line spacing) or the number of words. It must be emphasised that the skeleton argument is helpful for oral discussion but does not replace it; however, the goal of clarity concerns both the written and the spoken: being persuasive presupposes clarity.

5 Final remarks and future steps

It is well known that the international setting shows a variety of legal and procedural systems. Suffice it to mention that judicial decisions in continental law are reasoned in writing, even by constitutional prescription in various countries, whereas in the common law tradition the non-reasoned verdict on the merits of a case is applied in the jury trial, while other decisions (such as rulings by appellate courts) display ample written reasoning. The civil law tradition also ranges between succinct and extensive written reasoning, sometimes within the same legal system (e.g. in France, according to the type of court).

Despite the diversity of legal and procedural systems, the international overview outlined above and the outcomes of the reflection of the Italian Ministry of Justice working group converge on salient aspects.

25 As often indicated in instructions, a good skeleton argument must contain a numbered list of the points that the party wishes to make and be set out in numbered paragraphs. Each point should be stated as concisely as the nature of the case allows. See, e.g., CPD IX (Appeal), 39F.3: "Skeleton argument, if provided, should contain a numbered list of the points the advocate intends to argue . . . stated in no more than one or two sentences. It should be as succinct as possible". An introduction (including a statement of purpose), conclusions and requests are recommended. A summary of the relevant background to the case is appropriate, providing a clear framework in which to fit both the facts and the law. The document could include a chronology of events and a list of dramatis personae (Latin locution in CPD I – General matters, 3C.4). Precedents should be selected, with the strongest cases put at the highest level, identifying essential passages (as few as possible), with short extracts. Citations should be limited to truly key quotes. Using footnotes should be avoided; pages should be always numbered. Another characteristic of the skeleton argument is to be self-contained: it should not incorporate material from previous skeleton arguments.

All considerations and proposals focus on the objective of strengthening the essence of the judicial function: that of rendering justice by clearly ascertaining the facts and any responsibilities for those concerned, professionals and citizens. In this way, jurisdiction is freed from that bureaucratic drift, which inspires some habits and bad practices. Promoting concision in judgments and defence pleadings favours both promptness and clarity of presentation; a fair trial, the quality of the jurisdiction, its accessibility and its comprehensibility are enhanced through the clarity of the documents. The democratic control over judicial activities also benefits from this.

Economy of language and simplicity – in concept, language, style and presentation – work for better quality results. The overall result of this study is the perception that, in addition to (and more than) specific reforms in the legislation, what is necessary is the achievement of a global culture of clarity in judicial writing and speaking, one that would motivate both judges and counsels to distance themselves from stereotypical legalese habits.

In-depth studies are dedicated to the clarity and concision of legal language in the context of different cultures, but both the correlation between these concepts and their bearing on judicial texts could be more finely focused. Moreover, as pointed out by Arden (2012) and Andenas and Fairgrieve (2014, p. 362), style and form of judgments, traditionally overlooked in academic discourse, are presently subject to worldwide development.

Hence, some possible suggestions for further research concern, on the one hand, the relationship between concision and clarity of language, and also the impact of both values on a fair trial; and on the other hand, an enlargement of the scope of the investigation towards a comparison between different legal systems. This would allow for the highlighting of convergences, divergences and different interpretations of the principles of clarity and concision of language in the judicial sphere across different cultures and traditions. Such a comparison could prove particularly fruitful in so far as far as civil law and common law traditions are cross-checked.

Acknowledgement

We would like to thank Chris Williams and two anonymous referees for their insightful comments; needless to say, any remaining shortcomings are solely our responsibility.

References

Andenas, M., & Fairgrieve, D., 2014. Simply a matter of style? Comparing judicial decisions. *European Business Law Review*, 25(3), 361–387.

Arden, M., 2012. Judgment writing as literature? *Law Quarterly Review*, 128, 516.

Bingham, T., 2011. *The rule of law*. London: Penguin.

Cerexhe, E., 2010. Le langage juridique répond-t-il aux exigences d'un État de droit? *In: Liège, Strasbourg, Bruxelles: parcours des droits de l'homme*. Limal: Anthemis, 881–888.

Duckworth, M., 1994. Clarity and the rule of law: The role of plain judicial language. *Judicial Review: Selected Conference Papers: Journal of the Judicial Commission of New South Wales*, 2(1), 69–88.

Duparc-Portier, P., & Masson, A., 2006. De l'usage des adages latins en pays de common law et en pays de civil law. *Revue Lamy droit civil*, 30, 66.

Ferreri, S., 2019. *Falsi amici nelle corti. Leggere le sentenze di Common Law evitando le trappole linguistiche*. Turin: Giappichelli.

Garner, B.A., 2002. *The elements of legal style*. Oxford: Oxford University Press.

Kimble, J., 2006. *Lifting the fog of legalese. Essays on plain language*. Durham, NC: Carolina Academic Press.

Mortara Garavelli, B., 2001. *Le parole e la giustizia. Divagazioni grammaticali e retoriche su testi giuridici italiani*. Turin: Einaudi.

Neuberger, D., 2012. No judgment – no justice. *First Annual BAILII Lecture*, November 20, 2012.

Scialoja, V., 1911. Diritto pratico e diritto teorico. *Rivista del diritto commerciale*, I, 942.

Williams, C., 2018. Legal drafting. *In:* J. Visconti, ed., *Handbook of communication in the legal sphere*. Berlin: Mouton De Gruyter.

Williams, C., 2020. Court judgments and plain language: Some recent developments in Canada and the United Kingdom. *In:* S. Maci, M. Sala, & C. Spinzi, eds., *Communicating English in specialised domains: A festschrift for Maurizio Gotti*. Newcastle-upon-Tyne: Cambridge Scholars, 106–125.

Williams, C., 2018. *The impact of plain language on legal English in the United Kingdom*. London: Routledge.

Index

adjudication standards 191, 193
affect 127–128, 130–131, 136–137, 140–141
appraisal 126–128, 130–131, 137; theory 131
argumentation 6, 15, 20–21, 26, 30, 35–36, 99, 101–102, 104–105, 107; causal 112, 114, 115, 119, 121, 123–124; judicial 36, 83, 100, 112, 185, 213; legal 99–100, 109, 207; teleological-evaluative 98, 105, 109–110
argumentative patterns 10, 13, 15, 22–23, 113, 207
argumentative practice 201, 204–206
authorial presence 10, 14–15, 22–23

Baroness Hale 69, 75–76, 79–80
blasphemy 162; blasphemy laws 171; Polish blasphemy law 168–169

civil law 45–46, 128, 222, 233, 240–241
CJEU judgments 3–6, 10, 12, 14–17, 20–21, 23, 87; macrostructure of 7–9
clarity 40, 42, 62, 94, 177, 224, 231–241
collocations 58, 60–61, 63, 65–66, 71, 87
comments (digital) 75–76, 79–80; corpus analysis of 74
common law 7, 45–46, 126, 222, 228, 233; judgments 225; style 7; tradition 5, 240
community: epistemic 205–206; judicial 26; legal community 26, 99; LGBT/LGBTQ+ 98, 163, 170
consensus 51–53, 55; case law 51–52, 55–56; concept of 56–57; terms 60; tool 53
corpus-assisted discourse analysis 70, 80, 127
corpus-based discourse analysis (CBDA) 127
corpus linguistics 58, 85–86; corpus linguistics methodology 85, 87
Cour de Cassation 39, 40; decisions of 42–44
Court of Justice of the European Union (CJEU) 3, 87, 89, 93–94, 114, 202, 239
cultural keywords 174

defence pleadings 235, 238–239, 241
deontic modality 15
disciplinary culture 203
disciplinary values 26, 126

epistemicity 23, 36
epistemic modality 15, 22, 26; and evidentiality 27
epistemic stance 18
EUCLCORP 87–88, 94
EU English 5, 24
EU judgments 3, 6, 88
Eurolect(s) 3, 15, 17, 21; English Eurolect 5–6, 22, 24; judicial Eurolect 7, 23
European Convention on Human Rights (ECHR) 51, 121, 148, 162, 217, 220
European Court of Human Rights (ECtHR) 51, 55, 147, 156, 162–163, 201, 209, 217, 239; the consensus case law of 52–55
EU translation 85n1
evaluation 22–23, 99–100, 103; markers of 10, 18

evaluative language 98, 100–102, 105, 107–110, 126
evaluative lexicon 126
evaluative lexis 109
evidentiality 26–27, 33, 36

fair trial 225, 231, 235, 241
formula 16–17, 41–44, 65, 225, 234
framing 10, 21–23, 69–71, 80, 86, 155, 160; balanced 72; keyword analysis applied to 74; negative 72–73; overview of 71; positive 73; semantic keyness applied to 76
freedom of expression 140, 147–149, 152, 157, 160–164, 166–170

genre 3, 27, 88; genre features 10, 22; genre profile(ing) 3, 7; judicial genre 3

hate speech 140, 155, 157, 164–165
HUDOC database 58, 60, 218
hybridisation of judgments 3

immigration 127–129, 131–132, 137, 140
international adjudication 198–200, 204–205, 207–209
international law 3, 8, 45, 55, 65–66, 121, 123, 160–161, 198, 200, 202–207, 209–210, 222, 228; discipline of international law 199, 202
interpretation 4, 24, 53–55, 69, 86, 89–92, 94, 109, 113, 116, 128, 130, 149, 158, 166, 169, 170–171, 185, 188, 190, 193–194, 198, 200–201, 204–205, 209; adjudicative 92–93; cognitive 93; dynamic 104, 106; evolutive 51–52, 59, 67; judicial 145, 148, 150, 186; legal 86, 88, 186, 191; multilingual 85, 88; political 73; teleological method of 105–106; textualist 187
Italian judicial language 233

judicial activism 186, 189–191
judicial argumentation 36, 83, 100, 112, 185, 191
judicial behaviour 191–194, 207
judicial behaviourism 186, 191, 193
judicial discourse 23, 27, 36, 39–42, 100, 215
judicial opinion(s) 26–28, 33, 126
judicial reasoning 93, 114, 209, 223n16
judicial voice 26
jurisprudence 44, 55, 85, 88, 98, 112, 114, 116, 148, 162, 168, 175, 179–181, 206, 221; American 189–191, 194; behavioural 192; discourse of 185, 203–204, 206; normative 199, 203–204, 207–208
justification (of judicial decisions) 43, 98–102; language of 103, 107–110, 112–113, 190

key terms 10
keyword analysis 10, 70, 74, 76

language barrier 217, 220, 228
language of racism 173
language risk management 47, 49
Latinisms 5, 20–22, 234
legal language 40, 44–45, 48, 128, 173, 185, 194, 236, 241
legal reasoning 26, 51, 86, 88, 150, 191
legal writing 26, 233
lexical bundles 10, 115
logical positivism 204

margin of appreciation 52–55, 58, 63–64, 67, 147, 149, 151–152, 160, 164–168, 171, 229
media frames 70
media representation(s) 81
misogynist (discourse) 71, 81
modal verbs 15, 18
multilingual adjudication 85, 92–94
multilingualism 47

n-grams 10–11, 13, 87, 115nn1–7
normative scholarship 199, 205, 207–208

obscenity 149–152, 155
originalism 186, 188–190, 193

parallel corpora 86–88, 89, 92–94; multilingual parallel corpora of EU law 87
passive structures 26, 37; with reporting verbs 27; with say and tell 28–29, 36
passive voice 15, 27, 175
performative verbs 10, 15–16, 22
phraseology 114–115, 119, 123
plain language 185, 233
populism 67, 69, 77
pragma-dialectical theory of argumentation 101
pragmatic argumentation 110, 113
press releases 219, 228–229
prorogation of Parliament 69, 77
proximity and distance 10, 17; markers 17
public morality 166–167, 169–170

readability (of judgments) 43, 228
reasoning 5, 32, 37, 53, 63, 66–67, 73, 79, 85, 92, 119, 122–123, 163, 174–176, 193, 200, 219, 222–224, 226–227, 232–233, 239–240; judicial reasoning 89, 114–115, 209; legal reasoning 26, 51, 86, 88, 150, 191
reporting verbs 16, 26–28, 31, 35–37
rhetorical moves 7–9
rhetorical power 175, 179
rhetorical strength 176

scientific paradigm 199, 202–203, 205
SCOTUS corpus 28–29, 32–34, 36
semantic keyness 76
separate opinions 37, 176, 222–224
Sketch Engine 6, 12, 60–61, 63, 71, 74, 79, 87
stance 10, 12, 14, 18, 22, 26, 37, 71, 100, 105, 109–110, 123, 126–127, 157, 208
standard 39; in community procedural law 47; in positive law 45–47
standardisation 7, 39–40, 228; legal standardisation (standardisation at the legal level) 44–45, 47–50; linguistic standardisation (standardisation form the linguistic point of view) 40–41, 43–44
strategic manoeuvring 98–99, 101–102
style 40, 42–44, 54, 67, 218, 222–228, 233, 236–237, 241; drafting style 5, 7, 14; judicial style 3, 5, 24, 26, 226; style barrier 222
subjectivity 32, 43, 126
Supreme Court of Ireland 112
Supreme Court of the United States 26
systemic linguistics 127–128, 140

textualism 186–187, 190–191, 193
textual metadiscourse 10, 19, 22

UK (SC) judgments 3, 6–8, 10, 12–18, 20–23
Universal Declaration of Human Rights (UDHR) 160–163

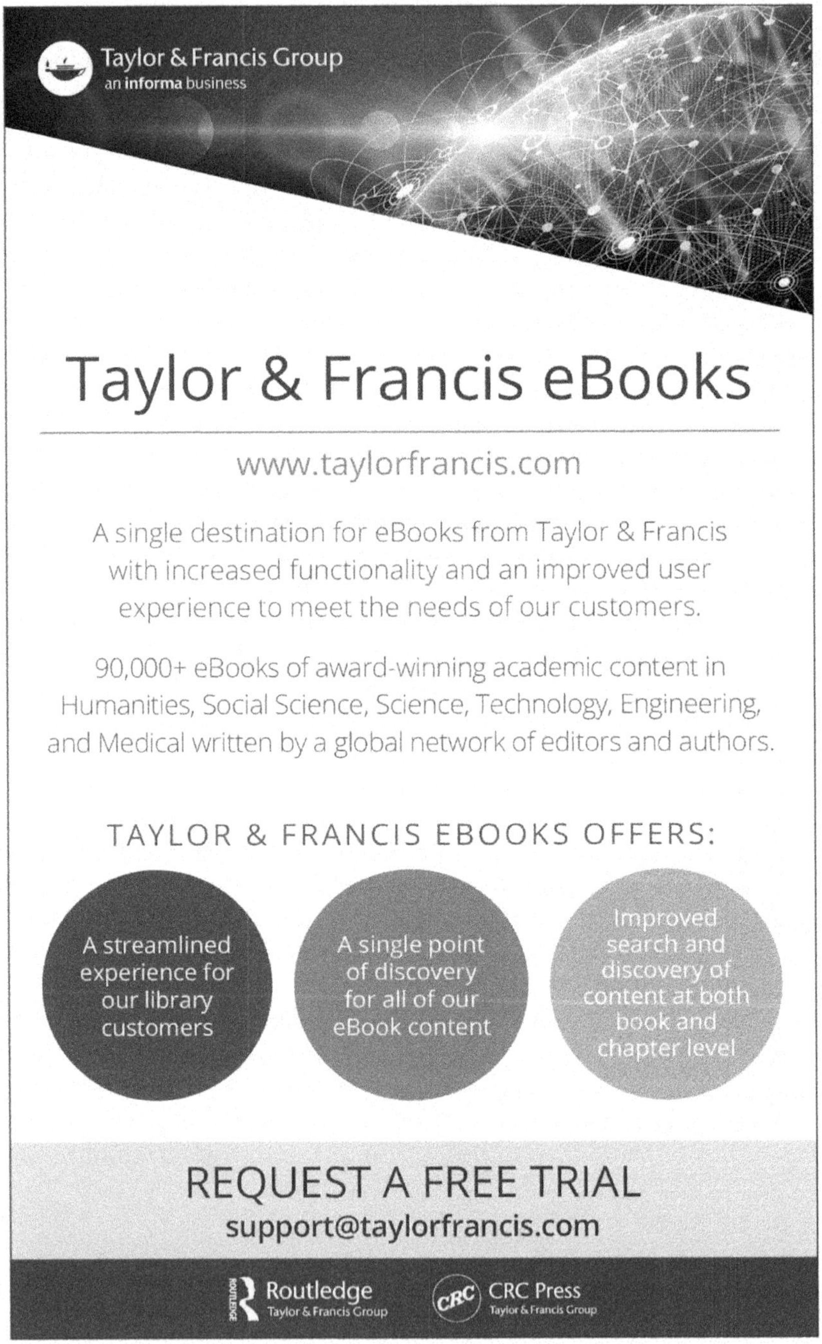

For Product Safety Concerns and Information please contact our EU
representative GPSR@taylorandfrancis.com
Taylor & Francis Verlag GmbH, Kaufingerstraße 24, 80331 München, Germany

www.ingramcontent.com/pod-product-compliance
Ingram Content Group UK Ltd.
Pitfield, Milton Keynes, MK11 3LW, UK
UKHW020012200926
475702UK00014B/1834
* 9 7 8 0 3 6 7 7 2 1 8 8 6 *